# using
# UNIX
# by example

---

# using
# UNIX
# by example

P.C. POOLE
N. POOLE
The University of Melbourne
Australia

ADDISON-WESLEY PUBLISHING COMPANY

Sydney · Wokingham, England · Reading, Massachusetts
Menlo Park, California · New York · Don Mills, Ontario · Amsterdam
Bonn · Singapore · Tokyo · Madrid · San Juan

The programs presented in this book have been included for their instructional value. They have been tested with care but are not guaranteed for any particular purpose. The publisher does not offer any warranties or representations, nor does it accept any liabilities with respect to the programs.

Cover design by 20/20 Graphics.
Set by the author using **ditroff,** the UNIX text-processing system, at the University of Melbourne, Victoria.
Printed in Finland by Werner Söderström Osakeyhtiö, member of Finnprint.
First printed 1986. Reprinted 1988 (twice).

**British Library Cataloguing in Publication Data**
Poole, P.C.
    Using UNIX by example.
    1. UNIX (Computer operating system)
    I. Title  II. Poole, N.
    001.64′25  QA76.76.063

    ISBN 0-201-18535-0

**Library of Congress Cataloging in Publication Data**
Poole, P.C.
    Using UNIX by example.

    Bibliography: p.
    Includes index.
    1. UNIX (Computer operating system)  I. Poole, N.
II. Title.
QA76.76.063P66  1986  005.4′46  85-15772
ISBN 0-201-18535-0

# PREFACE

Computing is about solving problems. UNIX is a system that enables you to tell a computer in a convenient and flexible manner what it is that you want it to do to obtain the results you require. This book has been written for those people who are about to start using UNIX in earnest for the first time. You may be an experienced user who is already familiar with other computer systems; alternatively, you may be a beginner who is starting to use computers for the first time. In both cases, we assume that you have access to a computer that supports UNIX. It may be one that can service a number of users simultaneously or it may be a personal computer that can only be used by one person at a time. The underlying philosophy of this book is "learning by doing", that is, it is not just for reading but rather, after you have studied and absorbed the material in a section, you should try out the examples presented in a real, live UNIX environment, experiment a little, see what happens, maybe make a few mistakes and reinforce through experience the concepts presented in the text.

For the real beginner, we have attempted to provide a comprehensive introduction to using a computer system as exemplified by UNIX. When new terms are introduced, they are defined in a glossary at the end of the book and we make very few assumptions about your background. However, in some sections, we have assumed that you are enrolled in a course about computing or have access to texts about aspects of computing not covered in this book. A bibliography of additional reading is included at the end of the book.

If you are already familiar with computers and are accustomed to using a particular operating system, you will probably be approaching your introduction to UNIX with some preconceived ideas. Some of your pet facilities may not be available and, at first, you might be inclined to be somewhat critical. But just persevere! Once you have grasped the underlying philosophy, you will come to appreciate the power and elegance of the system as well as its simplicity. This is not to say that UNIX is without faults. Like all computer systems, it has its bad points as well as its good ones. It is just that the good far outweigh the bad, making it superior to other comparable systems. Remember also that in making the transition to UNIX, you are freeing yourself of the chains that bind you to a particular manufacturer's hardware. Since UNIX is available on a wide range of machines from many different manufacturers, you can choose the computer which best suits your needs and pocket. Once you have mastered UNIX, a whole new world of computing will open up for you.

## *Using this Book*

Since this book has been written for beginners as well as experienced computer users, in Chapter 1, we introduce the concept of an operating system. We trace the evolution of operating systems and discuss what characteristics a good operating system should possess. If you are an experienced user already, the treatment of UNIX itself starts in Section 1.2. In Section 1.3, we describe briefly the various versions of UNIX currently available so you should find out which version of the system you will be using.

In Chapter 2, we introduce you to the basic facilities in UNIX – how to make contact with it, how to talk to the command language interpreter, how to issue commands, how to store and retrieve information. We hope that you will try out these facilities on your system. Having stored data in the computer, you will from time to time, want to change it. In Chapter 3, we show you how to do this using the text editors available in UNIX. Once you have mastered these tools, you can move on to Chapter 4 where we show you how to use UNIX to construct programs written in various high level languages. The emphasis is not so much on how to use a particular language but rather on how to compile and execute such programs, how to locate errors and how to integrate the programs you write into UNIX. The chapter also includes a section on creating your own commands using the basic commands in the system. This is a powerful feature of the command language interpreter which enables you to tailor your interface to UNIX to suit your own particular requirements. In Chapter 5, we show you how to manage various aspects of your use of UNIX – the information you store in it, the jobs that you will initiate and your communications both with other users and to other machines. Many examples are presented and again we strongly urge you to work through them on your system. Finally, we end the book by briefly tracing the history of the development of UNIX and taking a quick look at where it is likely to go in the future. By the time you reach this point, you will no longer be a UNIX beginner but someone ready to expand your horizons by delving deeper into what this system can do for you.

## *Acknowledgements*

We would like to thank the staff of the Department of Computer Science for their advice, comments and criticisms, particularly Robert Elz, Michael Flower, Rex Harris and Rodney Topor. Our special thanks also go to Prue Downie, Juliet Thorp and Sharon Vass for their assistance in typing and editing the manuscript. Mention must also be made of the many students who worked their way through the text and examples  pointing out errors and inconsistencies. We hope that there are not too many left. We are also grateful to Judy Kay and the Basser Department of Computer Science in the University of Sydney for permission to include some of their definitions in the glossary. Finally, our congratulations to the designers and implementors of UNIX without whose foresight and skill there would have been no need for this book at all

# CONTENTS

*Chapter 1*

# INTRODUCING

Welcome to the world of UNIX. We hope you are going to enjoy working in it. But what exactly is "UNIX"? Often it is called somewhat erroneously an "operating system". However, it is a lot more than just that. While indeed, at its heart, there is a powerful operating system, UNIX also includes a wide variety of *software tools* such as *command language interpreters, compilers, editors, symbolic debuggers* and *filters* as well as *subroutine libraries* and *communication subsystems*. In fact, it provides a superb environment for the development of *programs*. If these terms in *italics* don't mean much to you at this stage, don't worry — they will all become much more meaningful as you work through this book. Further, there is a very comprehensive glossary at the end of the book in which you can look up the meaning of a term if you are not too sure about it. But, first things first, let's start by taking a closer look at operating systems.

## 1.1 Operating Systems

In a modern *computer system*, there may be literally hundreds of software tools in addition to the ones already mentioned. Clearly, it could be very difficult for you to use such a wealth of facilities conveniently and effectively unless the *software* is organized in some coordinated manner. Further, dealing with the bare *hardware* directly each time you wanted to use the computer would be an arduous and time-consuming exercise. Hence the computer itself has to be *programmed* to help *users* access the facilities it provides. The *system software* which guides a computer in the performance of its tasks and assists users to achieve their goals by providing a variety of supporting functions is called an *operating system*.

Most modern computer systems come equipped with an operating system. Some are very simple ones indeed and provide a limited range of facilities for a single user on a *personal computer*; others are much more complex and are designed to support a community of users on a *minicomputer* or *mainframe*. These are often referred to as *general purpose* operating systems in contrast to those which offer *special purpose* facilities, for example, a *real time* operating system used to control a steel mill or support an air traffic control system. The UNIX operating system is classified as general purpose since it has been designed to satisfy the computing needs of a number of users and ensure that the resources of the computer are shared equitably amongst them.

Traditionally, operating systems were developed by the manufacturers of the hardware. Usually, they were written in *assembly language* and hence could only be used on the machines for which they were created. However, the UNIX operating system breaks with this tradition. About 95% of UNIX is written in a *high level programming language* called C. Hence, the cost of moving UNIX to a new machine is much, much less than that required to implement it again in assembly language. For this reason, the UNIX operating system is said to be *portable*. Consequently, it is available on a wide range of machines from different manufacturers, all the way from personal computers up to mainframes. The minimum configuration required to run a UNIX system is a 16-*bit CPU*, 256 *kilobytes* (Kb) of high speed *memory*, 10 *megabytes* (Mb) of *hard disk* and a *magnetic tape* or *floppy disk* drive. Depending on the speed of the CPU and disk drive, such a system could support from 1 to 3 *terminals*. Typically, a 32-bit minicomputer with 4 Mb of high speed memory, 500 Mb of hard disk and a magnetic tape unit could provide a UNIX service for perhaps 40 to 50 terminals.

## 1.1.1  Evolution

Let us now take a trip backwards in time to the beginning of the computer age to see how operating systems evolved. Fortunately, we will not have to travel too far — just 30 years or so to the early '50s. Let's imagine that you are one of the first programmers who is using an early electronic computer to solve a problem. When you enter the room which houses the computer, you would see a device vastly different from the computers we know today — rack after rack of valves and other electronic components interconnected with miles of wire. People were dwarfed by these massive machines which, by modern standards, were exceedingly slow, small in capacity, unreliable and extremely expensive. Nevertheless, they represented a major step forward in the development of devices capable of performing complex computations automatically at high speed.

To run your *job*, you would book the computer for some period of time and, when your turn came, bring your programs and data prepared on *punched cards* or *paper tape*. You might press some buttons to clear the memory of information left by the previous job and ready it to accept the next one. Then you would read in your program through the appropriate *input* device and eventually it would start to *execute*. If you were fortunate, it might run to completion and produce some results on an *output* device. If the program contained an error, the machine would stop, displaying some indication of why it did so on the console lights. You could examine its memory, make some changes if you wished and even restart the computation. Sometimes you could correct the *hard copy* of your program and read it in again. If the error was too difficult to correct on the spot, you could copy the contents of sections of the memory to an output device to take away and peruse at your leisure. Eventually, your time would be up. You would hand over the machine to someone else and leave the room with your *results* or, perhaps, reams of *diagnostic output* which, hopefully, might help you locate the error in your program. If you had a working program, it might run for many hours. Eventually someone else's program would take over the machine. A computer could only run one program at a time and, during the period between the end of one job and the start of the next one, would be idle.

As machines became faster but even more expensive, efforts were made by their designers to improve the efficiency of using them by collecting user jobs together in batches. These were submitted to the machine under the control of a supervisory program which read in each job, initiated it and "cleaned-up" after it had terminated in readiness for the next one. This approach was referred to as *batch processing*. Thus, the operating system was born — a program which was part of the computer system itself rather than one supplied by the user.

Although these prototype operating systems enabled computers to be used more efficiently, there were a number of problems, not the least of which was the possibility of long *turn-around times* on a heavily loaded system. After you had submitted a job for processing, you might have to wait many hours or even days before the output of your run was returned. This could be very irritating and frustrating, particularly when you discovered that your program had actually failed to execute because you had made some trivial error like leaving out a comma in the program text. Since you would not be in attendance when your job was processed, you could not make any "on-the-spot" fixes as were possible previously. Hence, increased efficiency in using the hardware was obtained at the expense of user convenience and satisfaction.

With further improvements in machine architecture and the development of faster and larger computer systems, it became possible to allow a number of jobs to be active simultaneously in what is known as a *multi-programming* environment. Obviously, this required a much more sophisticated operating system than had existed previously. When one job initiated an *input-output* operation, it would be *suspended* by the operating system and the *central processing unit* (CPU) allocated to another job that was ready to run again. Program execution and input-output transfers could then take place in parallel, thus making more efficient use of the CPU. When an I/O transfer terminated, the job could be restarted at the point where it was suspended and, when its turn came, be allocated the CPU. Jobs could be given a *priority* depending on the resources they required. Short high-priority jobs for program development could be completed before longer-running production jobs, even if they had been submitted later, thereby reducing turn-around time. However, a delay of even a few hours is still unacceptable to a user who has made some trivial error. You would still be rather cross if you found you had left out that proverbial comma. A further attempt to improve this situation led to the development of *interactive time sharing* systems.

The philosophy underlying the concept of time sharing is that, if the attention of the computer can be switched rapidly enough from one to another of a number of simultaneously connected terminals, then each user sitting at such a terminal could be made to feel that he is the only one using the machine. In a sense, the wheel had turned full circle back to the beginning of computing again. From a terminal, you could start up a job, terminate it and monitor its execution. If a job failed, the contents of memory could be examined or modified and the job restarted. Programming errors could be detected quickly and the program text changed using an interactive editor. This could improve productivity since you could concentrate on one task at a time rather than having to maintain a number in parallel to keep yourself occupied while waiting for the return of output from jobs run in a batch environment. The development of operating systems which supported time sharing was a major step forward and enabled computers to be accessed remotely from a distance, even over communications networks. Today, all modern operating systems on medium to large scale computers and even on some smaller *microcomputer* systems offer the capability of time sharing. The UNIX operating system is one such system.

## 1.1.2 Characteristics

To come to a deeper understanding of what an operating system does, let us examine the problems that could arise when a number of people want to share a computer system.

(i) *Security and Protection*:

If you plan to store data in a computer, you will want a guarantee that you will be able to retrieve that data at some later time and that nobody else has accessed or modified it in any way in the meantime without your permission. If you are running a job on the machine, you will want to have a high degree of confidence that no other program can interfere with your program in such a way as to cause it to fail or alter its behaviour in any way. You will also want to feel confident that no one can execute or inspect your programs without your approval. You will also want to know that it is extremely difficult, if not impossible, for someone to impersonate you, thereby gaining access to your programs and data and possibly consuming machine resources for which you might have to pay. If you are the manager of a computer system serving a community of users, you will want to be assured that no one can penetrate the system and steal resources or tamper with the system. Hence, an operating system has to provide a secure environment in which users can share data if they so desire but in which each authorized user is protected against interference, either inadvertent or malicious, by other users whether authorized or not.

(ii) *Resource Allocation and Scheduling*:

If you want to run a small job on a shared computer system, you would be rather annoyed to find that someone else was running a program that would execute for many hours using all of the available high speed memory. Similarly, it could be irritating to find that there is no disk space left just when you want to store some data in the system. *Response time* is another factor which has a considerable influence on your view of how useful a system is. It is defined as the time between when you issue a request to the system and when it responds with some output. You would probably find a response time of, say, 5 minutes for a simple request completely unacceptable. Hence, an operating system has to allocate resources to jobs and schedule their use of memory and CPU in such a way as to minimize response time and ensure that computer power is distributed equitably amongst the active users.

(iii) *User Interface*:

An important function of the operating system in any kind of computing environment is to provide an interface between the resources it controls and its users. This is usually referred to as a *command language*. It must be easy to learn and convenient to use, yet powerful enough to enable you to access all of the facilities in the system. If one of your jobs malfunctions, the system should inform you in a clear and unambiguous way about what went wrong and ensure that sufficient information is preserved to enable you to investigate the cause of the problem. In short, the system must be "friendly" and not put any impediments between you and the problem you want to solve.

(iv) *Usage Statistics*:

Since, in a time sharing environment, a group of users are sharing a common facility, it is necessary for the operating system to accumulate usage statistics for accounting purposes so that you know what proportion of the resources you are using and that you are not consuming more of the shared resource than you are entitled to do. This includes such factors at CPU utilization, memory occupancy, disk space and the elapsed time during which your terminal is connected to the system.

(v) *Reliability and Recoverability*:

If the hardware of a time sharing computer system malfunctions, a large number of users will be inconvenienced by a loss of service. Sometimes, nothing can be done to avoid this situation if the hardware error is a severe one. In other cases, the operating system can degrade gracefully so that some services are lost but not all. In both situations, it is important that the loss of work by individual users is minimized. The operating system must therefore contain mechanisms to be able to recover a previous state so that user inconvenience is kept as small as possible. It must also continually monitor the operation of the hardware to ensure that adequate diagnostic information is available to assist the engineers to repair the machine.

## 1.2  Overview of UNIX

The philosophy we have adopted in this book is that the best way to learn about the facilities in UNIX is to try them out. However, let us first set the scene by briefly describing the main features of the system so that, when you encounter each new facility, you will be able to see where it fits in the overall scheme of things.

### 1.2.1  File System

To store data in a computer system so that you can retrieve it at some time in the future, you place it in a *file* in the *file system* and give the file a *filename* so that you can reference it again later on. The process is very similar to the one you might use to store information in a folder in a filing cabinet. UNIX doesn't care what data you put in the file but it does guarantee that, when you want to use the data again, it will be there. Files are, in fact, stored on magnetic disk and hence continue to exist even if the computer is switched off. Further, in a properly managed system, copies of files are held on a *backup* medium such as magnetic tape or floppy disk so that even if some corruption of the file system occurs due to a hardware malfunction, your precious data can be recovered.

In addition to ensuring that data stored in the file system is preserved, UNIX also guarantees that no one can access it unless they have the appropriate authority to do so. If you place data in a file, you can feel confident that it will still be there in the future and that no other users will have accessed it in the meantime unless you have given them permission to do so. What is more, you can change your mind at any time and permit or deny access to anyone as you see fit.

UNIX distinguishes three types of files in its file system − *ordinary files, directory files* and *special files.* An ordinary file has no internal structure imposed on it by the system − it is simply a sequence of *characters.* How these are interpreted depends on what is done with the data in the file. For example, if each character represents a printable symbol, the file could be displayed on a terminal. A directory file stores names and information about other files and directories. This enables UNIX to organize its file system into a *hierarchy* of files and directories as we shall discuss in detail in Section 2.4. The special files are the input/output devices attached to a particular computer system. They are treated in much the same way as ordinary files which greatly simplifies I/O for the user.

### 1.2.2  Command Language

You direct UNIX to carry out tasks on your behalf by issuing *commands* through some input device such as a terminal. A command and any data associated with it are first processed by a special program called the *shell* which is often referred to as the *command language interpreter.* After you have made contact with UNIX and established your credentials to use the system, a shell will be initiated on your behalf. Thereafter, you will communicate your requests to the shell which will carry them out if it can and inform you of any errors if it cannot. You will stay in contact with the shell until such time as you terminate your UNIX *session*.

UNIX commands are stored in ordinary files and the name of the command is just the filename. You cannot print or display these files on a terminal since there may not be a visible representation for every character in the file. For this reason, they are called *binary* files in contrast to the *character* files which can be printed or displayed. However, what you can do is cause them to be executed, that is, obeyed by the computer to carry out specific tasks for you.

There are many commands available in UNIX which make it a rich programming environment. Some come with the system, some are written by other users and some you will write yourself. Since the shell can read commands from a file as well as from a terminal, you can store a sequence of commands in an ordinary file and then, just by specifying the name of that file to the shell, cause the commands to be executed. Such a command sequence is often called a *shell script*. By writing such scripts, you can easily create your own commands and tailor your interface to UNIX to one of your own choosing.

### 1.2.3 Jobs

When the shell initiates a command on your behalf, it first allocates some high speed memory, loads in the program and then arranges for the CPU to execute it. Such a program being executed is called a *process*. The shell itself is, in fact, a process which is created for you when you commence a UNIX session and only disappears when your session is finished. The sequence of events which takes place from the time you issue a command until the command terminates is called a *job*. It may involve just a single process or more than one process either executing in sequence or in parallel. Processes can communicate with each other either through the file system or via a *pipe* which is a link that enables the output of one process to become the input of the next one.

As we will see in Section 5.3, UNIX provides facilities that enable you to manage your jobs and processes. It also accumulates statistics on your use of machine resources so that you can be charged for them if necessary.

## 1.3 Versions of UNIX

UNIX comes in various flavours. Fortunately, they are all very similar which is why it is possible to a write book like this one which introduces you to UNIX irrespective of what version it is and on what machine it is running. Nevertheless, there are some differences between the various versions and it is therefore important to know just what exists and which one you are using.

UNIX was developed initially by AT&T Bell Laboratories in the USA. The first version distributed widely outside of the laboratory was Version 6 which appeared in the mid-seventies on PDP-11 computers. The first truly portable version of UNIX was Version 7 which has formed the basis of many of the commercial adaptations of the system.

When the 32-bit VAX minicomputer was developed by DEC, UNIX was transported to it and this version become known as 32V. Because UNIX had never been designed with virtual memory in mind, 32V did not make any use of the hardware facilities on the VAX to support paging of high speed memory. However, UNIX was modified extensively at the University of California (Berkeley) to incorporate virtual memory. Various versions of this system have been released, the most recent one being called 4.2 BSD.

Further developments of UNIX have also taken place at AT&T, building on Version 7 and 32V. The first of these is called System III and the most recent one, System V. Release 2 of System V, which we will often refer to in this book as "V.2", became available early in 1984. Again there have been many adaptations of these systems by machine manufacturers and software houses.

In this book, we will be treating primarily the facilities available in System V. However, where appropriate, we will also consider important features of 4.2 BSD. If you are using Version 7 or System III, you will still find that many of the examples can be carried out on your system. However, other examples are only meaningful in the latest versions of UNIX.

## Chapter 2

# STARTING

So you want to learn something about UNIX! In this chapter, we will introduce you to the system and show you how to use some of its facilities. We will do this mainly by example, that is, we will illustrate what happens when UNIX is asked to do various things. We hope that you will try these examples on your own system.

Whether you intend to use UNIX on a personal computer or in a multi-user environment, one of the first things you will need to do is choose a *username*, which is also called a *login identifier* or *login name*. It is the name by which you are known to UNIX (and to other users of the system). It may be your surname or your initials or a nickname or just some arbitrary name that you have selected. It is not a secret name but once you have chosen it (or it has been assigned to you), it may be difficult to change, particularly if other people have made use of it. There is no need to choose a long username − 3 or 4 letters are usually sufficient. The important thing is that it is unique so that there is no possibility that you can be confused with other users of the system. You can even have more than one username if you so desire and the rules of the installation permit it. Of course, if it's your personal computer, there is no argument − you can have as many as you like!

To simplify our discussion of the use of UNIX in this book, we are going to assume that your name is either "Yorick E. Whiffle" or "Yolanda E. Whiffle" and that your username is **yew**. Wherever you see this username in an example in which you are asked to try something, you should substitute your actual username, whatever that might be, for **yew**.

If you are about to use UNIX on a personal computer, you may be asking yourself why you have to choose a username to identify yourself to the system. After all, if the system can only support one user at a time, who cares! As you will see, the username plays an important role in the organization of the UNIX file system and will enable you to keep your files separate (and protected) from other users of your system, perhaps other members of your family. In the past, the only way to achieve this on a personal computer with floppy disk drives was for all users to have their own disks. Sometimes, people made mistakes, loaded the wrong disk and overwrote someone else's information, destroying it forever. UNIX allows a number of people to share disk space safely, providing each user has a unique username. However, you can still readily share information with other users if you wish.

Even if you know that you will be the only user ever on your UNIX system, it is still sensible to choose a username. The reason is that, when a UNIX system is first initialized, it comes up in what is known as *superuser* mode. All UNIX systems have a superuser with a username **root** who is all powerful and must therefore really know what he is doing. On a single user system, there may be some housekeeping chores that you have to carry out in superuser mode but, once these are done, you should give your username and switch into normal mode so that you can protect yourself against your own mistakes. Running in superuser mode all the time can be very dangerous and you are likely to regret it in the long run.

If you are planning to use UNIX in a multi-user environment, then, in the process of obtaining a username, you will also establish an account so that your use of system resources can be recorded and perhaps be charged for if that is the way it is done in your installation. In most instances, to obtain an account, you must complete a form specifying a proposed username and indicating how you will pay for your use of the system. This is submitted to the administration and ultimately, when the request has been approved, an account will be established for you. In some installations, this process is automated so that you can create an account from a terminal before using the system for the first time. Whatever the procedure, you will need that username before you can start talking to UNIX.

When you receive notification that your account is established, you may also be given a provisional *password*. We will have a lot more to say about passwords later. Suffice to say at this stage, it is something you must keep secret and, if one has been allocated, you will need it the first time you use the system. Armed with your username and (perhaps) provisional password, the next thing to do is find a terminal which can connect you to the UNIX system you have been authorized to use. Having located one, turn on the power — there may be a power switch on the terminal itself or it may be powered directly from the mains plug on the wall.

If you are not very familiar with terminals and keyboards, we suggest that you now read Appendix 1 entitled "Getting to Know Your Terminal". If you understand how to use a terminal and what the various keys mean, let us see if you can establish contact with UNIX. For a personal computer, follow the manufacturer's instructions for activating the system. For a terminal, first of all, ensure that it is in lower case mode if it is not an upper case only device. If UNIX sees an upper case username, it will assume that you are using an upper case only terminal and will respond with upper case characters which will be a bit of a waste if, in fact, your terminal supports both cases. Next, check to see that the terminal is in *full duplex* as opposed to *half duplex* mode. It may be that a key marked **FULL** must be depressed or a switch somewhere on the terminal must be set to a particular position. UNIX expects all terminals to operate in full duplex and the visual symptom of not being in the correct state is that, whenever you type something, the characters are duplicated on the screen.

Don't worry if you can't find the full/half duplex control. You'll soon find out if you are in the wrong mode and then you will have to ask someone. Now place the terminal in *remote* or *online* mode. This may be sufficient to cause UNIX to respond. Alternatively, you may have to *power-off* and *power-on* again. If this doesn't work, you will have to follow whatever the local procedure is to indicate to UNIX that you want to communicate with it. The result of this action will be a message from UNIX requesting you to *login*. Logging in (or logging on or signing on) is the procedure whereby you establish your credentials with UNIX indicating that you are authorized to use the system.

In the examples in this book, the conventions we have adopted are as follows:

(i)     What you type as input will be shown in **boldface** type, whereas what the system outputs will be shown in **normal** type. Comments included to help you understand the examples are shown in *italics*. They will not appear on your terminal nor should you try to type them.

(ii)    The **RETURN** required at the end of every input line will not be shown explicitly nor will we continually refer to it in the text. However, in a number of places where there is a possibility of misinterpreting the printed example, we have used Ⓡ for **RETURN**, Ⓢ for **SPACE**, Ⓣ for **TAB** and Ⓔ for **ESCAPE**. Remember that until you hit **RETURN**, the system is simply collecting the characters you have typed and will not act on them until the line is finished. In fact, **RETURN** generates a *newline* character which signals the end of the line. If the computer appears to be doing nothing after you have input a line, you have probably forgotten to press **RETURN**. If this is not the case and no output has appeared, the system is probably busy and you will have to wait.

(iii)   When a command is introduced for the first time, the command name and function are enclosed in a box. A single thin-lined box indicates those commands which exist in both the AT&T and Berkeley versions of UNIX. We have used a thick-lined box to indicate those commands which only exist in AT&T System V and a double box for those commands which only exist in the Berkeley system.

(iv)    We have attempted to mark clearly those sections of the text which only apply to the Berkeley system by introducing each such section with a double line of dashes and terminating it with a single dashed line. If you are using System V or one of the earlier versions of the AT&T system, you can skip over these sections without affecting your understanding of the material. Any facility which only exists in System V Release 2 will be indicated as such. We will often use shorthand notation "V.2" to refer to this system and "4.2" for the most recent release of the Berkeley system.

(v)     The shell prompt character will be represented by **$** unless some feature only available in the Berkeley system is being illustrated, in which case **%** will be used. The prompt character will appear before the characters you are expected to type and will be shown again, if appropriate, at the end of the response from UNIX.

(vi)    We have used a stippled rectangle ▓ in the examples to represent the position of the *cursor*, a cue on the screen of a *visual display unit* (VDU) indicating that the system is waiting for input and showing where the first input character will be displayed.

## 2.1  Logging In

Once you have made contact with UNIX, it will respond with a message giving a heading which is often the version number of the system in use and a login query, sometimes preceded by the name of the computer. The prompt:

        login: ▓

indicates that the computer is waiting for you to identify yourself as an authorized user of its system. You respond by typing your username terminated by **RETURN**. As you type, the system will echo the characters on the screen. Once the **RETURN** key has been pressed, the system will ask you for your secret password if it is expecting you to supply one:

        login: **yew**          *Type your username terminated by* **RETURN**
        Password: ▓        *Type your password terminated by* **RETURN**

Now you must reply by typing in your password followed by **RETURN** and, if the terminal permits it, the characters will not be displayed on the screen for obvious reasons. If this is the first time you have used the system, it may be that no password is required and no password prompt appears. Alternatively, you will have been given a password by the system administration. If your username and password do not correspond to those already stored in the system, then:

        Login incorrect         *You've botched it!*
        login: ▓            *Try again and type your username*

will appear on the screen and you are prompted again for your username. If you make a mistake while typing, just press on regardless since there is no penalty for a login failure and the prompt will be repeated. If, after a number of tries, you are still unable to login even though you believe you are supplying your correct username and password, you should consult the *system administrator* who perhaps may have been a little slow in establishing your authorization to use the system.

Once you have logged in successfully, various messages may appear:

```
login: yew                  Your username
Password:                   Your password
        TGIF today at 4.30 pm in the common room.
You have mail.
$                           Congratulations, you've made it!
```

The first message is called the *message of the day* and is altered from time to time by **root** at the request of the system administrator. Next, if there is *electronic mail* waiting for you, you will be advised of this fact. We will explain later how to deal with it. Finally, the system outputs a *prompt* character indicating that it is ready for you to type in something. In the above example, the prompt is a **$** sign. At this point, you are now communicating with the *shell*, the UNIX command language interpreter. Whenever the system returns to *command mode* and is ready to perform another action for you, the shell will output this character. The prompt varies from one UNIX system to another and may in fact be changed by the user. A **$** usually means that you are connected to Version 7, System III or System V UNIX running the standard shell, (sometimes called the *Bourne shell*); a **%**, on the other hand, indicates that your system is probably the one developed at Berkeley and you will be communicating with *C-shell*. Remember, don't take these as hard and fast rules. Prompt characters can be set at the whim of the system administration or the machine vendor.

On a subsequent login, the first output line will look something like:

```
Last login: Fri Apr 6 08:10:04 on ttyj
```

This indicates when you last logged in and on which terminal (**tty** is an abbreviation for **tele**type, a very common terminal in the early days of computing). If the date and time do not correspond to your memory of the event, either you are becoming very forgetful or someone has succeeded in impersonating you, in which case, you had better inform the administration.

## 2.2  Passwords

Your password is "precious" and should be safeguarded at all times. Remember that the machine can't sense who you are and, since your username is not secret, it is only your password that enables you to identify yourself to UNIX. If other people obtain your password, they can impersonate you and read information you have stored in the system or, even worse, change or destroy it. They can also consume machine resources for which you may be charged.

The designers of UNIX have gone to a great deal of trouble to safeguard your password in the system and ensure that even the system administrator cannot determine what it is. The character string you type is not stored in the system as such. Instead, it is scrambled so that, even if one knows the final form of the password, it is virtually impossible to reconstruct the original string.

You must exercise great care in choosing a password. It should be at least 6 characters long, or better still 8, and preferably contain upper and lower case letters, digits and punctuation marks. (In System V.2, a password must have at least 6 characters of which at least 2 must be alphabetic and at least 1, numeric or a special character.) Don't choose your middle name or your surname spelt backwards. These are all too easy to guess and some people take a great delight in trying to discover other people's passwords to play tricks on them. Similarly, if the password is too short, it is rather easy to find simply by writing a computer program to try all combinations until the right one is found. You should make every effort to keep your password secret − don't write it on a piece of paper or on the back of your hand; also check to see that no one is looking over your shoulder when you login. A word of warning − when you come to a terminal and see the **login:** prompt displayed, don't immediately assume that UNIX is awaiting your command. It may, in fact, be a trap left by the last person logged in at that terminal to capture your password. Once he has it, he can pretend to be you. You should always execute the standard connection procedure to produce the login query. Then and only then can you be sure that you are really communicating with UNIX.

---

| **passwd** - change login password |
| --- |

---

If this is the first time you have logged in, there will either be no password or else one will have been supplied by the system administrator (and hence be known to someone else). Your first task is therefore to give a password which is known only to yourself. To do this, you must issue the **passwd** command in response to the UNIX prompt:

    **$ passwd**                     *You want to change your password*

If a password already exists, UNIX will respond with the prompt:

    **Changing password for yew**
    **Old password:**                  *Type your current password*

If your response to this query is incorrect, UNIX will respond with **sorry** and return to command mode (UNIX may be terse at times, but it is always polite). A correct response, on the other hand, will produce the prompt:

    **New password:**                   *Then type your new password*

and you may then type in the character string you have chosen. For both prompts, of course, no echoing occurs. Just to make sure that you have not made a typing mistake, the prompt:

    **Retype new password:**            *And type it again*

is output and you must respond again in exactly the same manner as you did to the previous prompt. Failure to do this will produce a message something like:

      `mismatch — password unchanged`     *You'll have to try again*

Assuming both inputs are identical, then this becomes your new password until you change it at some future time. We strongly recommend that, indeed, you do change your password from time to time. Accidents do happen, someone might learn your current password and it is better to be safe than sorry.

Whilst on the subject of security, it is perhaps worth mentioning at this point that, even if you keep your password absolutely secret, the superusers can still impersonate you at will. Normally, they never do, except to help you or rectify some problem you or the system have created. But they are human too and, on rare occasions, a little inquisitive. Therefore, if you want to leave information in the system which you really want to keep private, you should encode it yourself using the **crypt** command which is described later in Chapter 5.

## 2.3 Commands and Arguments

Now that you have protected your future activities, let us try out a few simple commands to get a feel for the system.

                        | **date** - print the date and time |

Perhaps the simplest command in UNIX is one which produces today's date and the current time (just in case you don't have a watch or calendar readily available). If you type the command:

      `$ date`                        *You want the current date and time*

in response to the command prompt, UNIX will respond with output on your terminal which looks something like:

      `Fri Apr 6 8:40:30 EST 1984`       *You've got it!*
      `$`

(the letters EST stand for Eastern Standard Time in Australia; these may vary from place to place i.e. EDT on the east coast of the USA denotes Eastern Daylight Time). The output appears on your terminal because, at least initially, it is connected to UNIX as the *standard output* device and the **date** command has been designed to write its results to standard output. Note that spaces are not allowed between the letters (nor for that matter are any other characters). The command:

      `$ d a t e`                *A non-existent command*

is likely to produce the error message on your terminal:

      `d: not found`
      `$`

It certainly won't produce the date and time. The message appears on your terminal because it is also connected initially as the *standard error output* device.

| **cal** - print calendar |
|---|

If you want a little more information about dates, there is a command called **cal** which will print a calendar for any particular year between 1 and 9999 or for any month between 1 and 12 in any of those years. Now clearly you would never want a calendar for the whole of the 9999 years, so you must tell **cal** which year if you want a calendar for the whole year or which month and year if that is all that is required. The command:

```
$ cal 1984                    You want a calendar for 1984
```

will produce a calendar for all the months in 1984 while:

```
$ cal 12 1984                 You want a calendar for December, 1984
   December 1984
  S  M Tu  W Th  F  S
                    1
  2  3  4  5  6  7  8
  9 10 11 12 13 14 15
 16 17 18 19 20 21 22
 23 24 25 26 27 28 29
 30 31
$
```

outputs a calendar for just December in that year. The month and year are called the *arguments* to the command and control what output is produced. Notice how they are separated by *white space* (blank or tab). The order is important and must be correct:

```
$ cal 1984 12                 You won't get a calendar
Bad argument
$
```

The command expects an argument in the range 1–12 for the month. The response is a little cryptic since it does not tell you which argument is incorrect (**cal 13 1984** or **cal 6 0** would produce exactly the same response) or why. This illustrates the terseness of UNIX for which it has often been criticized, but you will soon get used to it.

If you are wide awake at this stage, you may be asking yourself why **cal 1984** was accepted whereas **cal 13 1984** was not since the first argument in the former command is outside the range 1–12. This illustrates a very convenient feature of UNIX, namely, the *default argument*. UNIX commands can determine how many arguments have been supplied as well as whether particular arguments are valid or not. If **cal** is given one argument, it assumes it is the year and that you want a 12-month calendar; if you supply 2 arguments, the first is taken to be the month and the second, the year. If more arguments are supplied than required, excess ones are ignored.

Suppose you have forgotten in which order arguments are to be supplied to **cal**. Then, just type the command name without any arguments and you might get a response that will help you (Note that, in V.2, **cal** on its own will produce a calendar for the current month):

```
$ cal                   What arguments does cal require?
usage: cal [month] year
$
```

The square brackets around `month` indicate that it is an *optional argument*, while the absence of such brackets around `year` indicates that it is mandatory. If you omit this argument, you get a message reminding you how to use the command.

## help - ask for help

Omitting arguments is not always the best way of finding out how a command works. Instead, in System V, you can use the **help** command to explain the use of a command. Let's try it for **help** itself:

```
$ help                      Ask for help
msg number or cmd name? help    About help
help:
              help [args]

(When all else fails execute "help stuck".)
$
```

The output indicates that **help** takes one or more optional arguments. If no arguments are supplied, it prompts for one. The command can also be used to explain messages produced by commands.

## who - who is on the system

Sometimes it is useful to know who else is logged into the system. You may simply be inquisitive or perhaps you want to send someone a message. Just type:

```
$ who                   You're inquisitive or talkative or both!
```

without any argument and you should get a response which looks something like:

```
rwt     tty9    Apr  6 09:42
gsp     ttya    Apr  6 08:30
yew     ttyj    Apr  6 08:10         Entry for yew
toh     ttyh    Apr  6 08:47
$
```

The first column gives the username of those users currently logged in and the second, their terminal name (it may be numeric or alphabetic). The remaining columns give the date and time when that user logged onto the system. Your own username should be in this list.

There is a variation in the use of **who** which is sometimes useful to users who have more than one username on one or more machines. You can remind yourself who you are logged in as by typing:

```
$ who am i                      You're a little forgetful
yew        ttyj    Apr  6 08:10
$
```

===============================================

In 4.2, the arguments **are  you** will also produce the same response as will, in fact, any 2 arguments. **who** doesn't care what arguments are supplied, just as long as there are two of them. (**who** with one argument is usually only available to superusers and is likely to produce a failure message if you try it.)

```
┌─────────────────────────────────────┐
│ whoami - print current username     │
└─────────────────────────────────────┘
```

There is even a command **whoami** in 4.2 that will behave in a somewhat similar manner to **who** and remind you what username you used to login:

```
% whoami                        You're both forgetful and lazy
yew
%
```

Surprisingly, it is quite easy to forget at times what login name you used at the beginning of a session, particularly when you can access a number of UNIX systems from the one terminal.

-------------------------------------------------------------------

```
┌─────────────────────────────────────┐
│ id - print user and group id        │
└─────────────────────────────────────┘
```

Another way in System V of finding out who you are is to use the **id** command:

```
$ id                            Print user id and group id
uid=8(yew) gid=1(admin)
$
```

Once again, you see that you are **yew** but you get some other information as well. The *user identifier* (UID) is a unique integer associated with each username in the system. Similarly, the *group identifier* (GID) is an integer attached to each *groupname*, in this case, **admin**. When your account is established, you will be assigned to some group of users or even to more than one group. We will have more to say about groups later.

To this point, although we have only asked you to type a few characters, nevertheless, we have assumed that you always typed the information correctly.

Of course, this will not always be so. Like the rest of us, you will, from time to time, make mistakes. Fortunately, UNIX provides facilities for correcting such errors. It allows you to *erase* preceding characters in the current input line or *kill* the line completely throwing away all characters typed so far.

| **stty** - set or inspect terminal options |
| --- |

The kill and erase characters differ from one terminal to another. To find out which characters are used on your terminal, type:

**$ stty**                           *What are the settings for my terminal?*

The command **stty** (set **t**eletype) enables you to set the operating characteristics of your terminal if you wish. In the absence of arguments, it lists out the current settings. We will ignore most of this output for the moment but look for the word **erase**. It will be associated with the names of one or more keys. (If you don't find it, you may have to execute **stty all** in 4.2 or **stty −a** in V.2 to obtain a more extensive listing.) For most terminals, you will see **#** or **ˆH** defined as the erase character. The notation **ˆH** stands for **control−H** and the character is generated by simultaneously depressing the keys marked **CTRL** (or **CONTROL**) and **H**. It not only erases the previous character in the current input line, but also moves the cursor to that position in the line. As **control−H** is generated by **BACKSPACE** on most terminals, repeated use of **BACKSPACE** will successively delete each of the preceding characters, back to the start of the line. Type in some garbage characters and experiment with erasing. The kill character is also defined in the output of **stty**. Find the word **kill** and note the character associated with it (usually **@** or **ˆX** or **ˆU**). Whenever this character is typed, the current input line will be deleted and the cursor returned to the start of a line.

Those of you who are thinking ahead may have already begun to wonder what would happen if you needed to input **@** as an item of data to a command and it was already defined as the kill character. No problem — you simply precede it with the backslash character, **\**. This is an escape mechanism which prevents **@** being interpreted as the kill character, i.e. **\@** is equivalent to the character **@** itself.

There is one more special character you will need to learn at this stage. Sometimes, you might initiate a command, it is sitting there waiting for data and then you change your mind; sometimes, a command might loop and not return control to the terminal; sometimes, you might decide that you have seen enough output and you want to stop the command. In each case, you need to *interrupt* the activity. To do this, simply hit the interrupt key, which on many terminals is called **BREAK**. There is also another interrupt key defined by **stty**. Look through the **stty** output again until you find the string **intr**. The key associated with this string will also interrupt a command. Usually, it is the **DELETE** key (which on some terminals is called **RUBOUT**). Try interrupting a command and note how the terminal returns to the command state:

```
$ cal 1984
```
                                        *Output calendar for 1984*

```
                           1984

            Jan                 Feb                 Mar
  S  M Tu  W Th  F  S    S  M Tu  W Th  F  S    S  M Tu  W Th  F  S
  1  2  3  4  5  6  7             1  2  3  4             1  2  3
  8  9 10 11 12 13 14    5  6  7  8 (I)$
```

In the above output,  (I)  indicates that the interrupt key was struck at this position (but nothing, of course, will appear on the screen).  Control returns to the shell which outputs its normal prompt character.

Suppose now that you want to change your erase or kill character.  Again, you use **stty**:

```
$ stty erase \^H kill \^X        Set the erase and kill characters
$
```

Now, your erase character is **^H** and your kill character is **^X**. The 2-character sequence  ^  followed by a letter is interpreted as the corresponding control character.  However, it must be preceded by a backslash to prevent  ^  from being given a special meaning by the Bourne shell.

=============================================

┌─────────────────────────────────────┐
│  **tset** - set terminal modes  │
└─────────────────────────────────────┘

In the Berkeley system, there is another command called **tset** which enables you to set the characteristics of your terminal:

```
% tset -e^H -k^X        Set the erase and kill characters
Erase is set to Ctrl-H
Kill is set to Ctrl-X
%
```

In the above command line, the name of the control character has been typed rather than the control character itself, i.e. two characters  ^  and H have been input following the **e** argument.  If the names of characters are omitted, the erase and kill characters are  set to whatever default values apply for the terminal you are using on your system.  You can suppress the output messages by including an argument −**Q**.

----------------------------------------------------------------------

$\boxed{\textbf{write} \text{ - write to another user}}$

From the previous output of the **who** command, you know who else is logged into the system at the moment. Suppose you decide that you want to send a message to one of these people. All you need to do is issue the **write** command with the username as an argument. Providing the other user is willing to accept the message, a header which looks something like:

```
Message from yew (ttyj) [Fri Apr 6 8:55:36] ...
```

will appear on that user's terminal. The remainder of the message will then follow.

Let us try sending a message. However, rather than annoying someone else, how about sending a message to yourself. Just type:

```
$ write yew              You want to send a message to yourself
                         Now type the message
```

and a header similar to the one above will appear on your terminal if you have correctly substituted your actual username for **yew**. You will notice that the cursor has returned to the left-hand margin, but no command prompt has appeared, i.e. the system is no longer in command mode, but is in *data mode*. The **write** command is waiting for you to input your message from the terminal which is connected to the system as the *standard input* device. This command has been designed to read from standard input as have most of the other commands in UNIX. As you type each line and end it with **RETURN**, that line will appear again on your screen since you are writing to yourself.

If you were writing to another user, you could hold a 2-way conversation since that user could write back to you. The convention used to synchronize the exchange is to end a section of input with **(o)** meaning "over to you".

As you go on typing lines, you may start to wonder "How do I end this message?" That's easy − just type ^**D**. The message <EOT> (end-of-transmission) will be sent to the other user's terminal (in our example, it will appear on your terminal) and a return to command mode will occur with the command prompt displayed. **Control–D** generates an end-of-file signal to terminate the transmission.

$\boxed{\textbf{man} \text{ - print out manual entries}}$

By this time, you may be getting a little confused and asking yourself "How am I going to remember all of this information?" Fortunately, UNIX comes to the rescue by providing documentation online, via the **man** command. Try:

```
$ man write              How does write work?
```

and you should see on your screen the first section of the manual entry for the **write** command which is shown in Figure 2.1. Because the entry is too large to fit on most screens, the first section may be terminated by the message:

    -- More --

Alternatively in V.2, you will see the message:

    Screen 1 (space to continue, q to quit)

If you want to see the next section, hit the space bar once. Continue this process until you have seen the whole of the entry and the terminal has returned to the command state.

In some versions of **man**, the output will not stop after the first section and it may flash past before you have had a chance to read it. Fortunately, there are two more general purpose control keys which will allow you to control output, **control–S** and **control–Q**. ^S will stop the output and ^Q will cause it to resume. If your **man** command behaves like this, try it again, this time using ^S and ^Q to control output.

---

**WRITE (1)**                                                          **WRITE (1)**

**NAME**

    write – write to another user

**SYNOPSIS**

    **write** user [ line ]

**DESCRIPTION**

    **Write** copies lines from your terminal to that of another user. When first called, it sends the message:

        **Message from** *yourname* **(tty?)** [ *date* ]...

    to the person you want to talk to. When it has successfully completed the connection, it also sends two bells to your own terminal to indicate that what you are typing is being sent.

    The recipient of the message should write back at this point. Communication continues until an end of file is read from the terminal, an interrupt is sent or the recipient has executed "mesg n". At that point **write** writes 'EOT' on the other terminal and exits.

    If you want to write to a user who is logged in more than once, the *line* argument may be used to indicate which line or terminal to send to (e.g. **tty00**);

*Figure 2.1*

---

There are many, many commands available to a UNIX user. Some come with the system, some are written by programmers at your installation, others you will write yourself. It is very important that there is adequate supporting documentation which follows the standard format shown in Figure 2.1. The first line gives the name of the command **WRITE (1)**. The number in parentheses refers to the section of the UNIX manual (in this case, 1 indicates that **write** is a command available to users). This is followed by a number of sections of which the first three are obligatory:

NAME:            the name of the command and a short description of what it does.

SYNOPSIS:        how the command is to be used, i.e. what arguments it requires. Optional arguments are enclosed in square brackets [ ], indicating that they may be omitted. A number of full stops (called an *ellipsis*) following an argument indicates possible repetition.

DESCRIPTION:     a short account of what the command does and how the arguments are to be interpreted.

FILES:           a list of the names of files used by the command.

SEE ALSO:        a list of related commands.

DIAGNOSTICS:     a description of any error messages the command might produce and how they are to be interpreted.

BUGS:            a list of known programming and design errors in the command.

Most UNIX installations have printed versions of the manuals available, but remember, they are much harder to keep up-to-date than documentation online. When in doubt, consult the online documentation via **man**.

```
mesg - permit or deny messages
```

In the documentation for **write**, you will see a reference to the **mesg** command which enables you to control whether other users can write to you or not. It may be that you just don't want to be interrupted or that you wish to ensure that the information currently displayed on your screen is not corrupted in any way. The command takes **y** or **n** as an argument depending on whether you are prepared to accept messages or not. Without an argument, it outputs the current setting of the write permission:

```
$ mesg n                          Turn off write permission
$ mesg                            Output current setting
is n
$ write yew                       Write to yourself again
You have write permission turned off.
$ mesg y                          Turn permission back on again
$
```

Normally, one leaves the write permission enabled since it is convenient to be able to send messages to other users who are logged in and receive replies from them.

> **learn** - computer-aided instruction

In addition to providing documentation online, most UNIX systems also include a command to help you learn about its facilities and reinforce the concepts you are acquiring. It is called **learn** and it is an example of *computer-aided instruction* (CAI for short). It presents lessons on various aspects of the UNIX system by asking you questions and then checking your response. If you get the answer right, you will proceed automatically to the next lesson; if not, the computer will tell you so and let you have another try. If you still get the answer wrong, you can try again or skip to the next lesson. So try **learn** on your system to see what lessons are available. Most of them will be on subjects we have yet to cover in this book, so there is no need to try them now. But remember the command and use it from time to time as you work through the material we present. You may find it very useful. One final point — to get out of the **learn** command you need to reply **bye** to one of its prompts.

So now you are making progress. You know how to login, how to change your password, how to issue commands with and without arguments, how to find and interpret UNIX documentation, how to correct typing errors and how to interrupt a command. One last thing — how do you *logout* and stop communicating with UNIX? One method is simply is to type ^**D** whilst in the command state, that is, send EOF to the shell; others (which may not always work) are to turn off the power to the terminal or switch into local mode. The system will enter a wind-up sequence so that everything is in order for you when you next login.

===========================================

> **logout** - terminate session

Another way of logging out, only available in the C-shell, is to type:

```
% logout                          Goodbye UNIX
```

------------------------------------------------

## 2.4  Files and Directories

Computing is all about the manipulation of information. You want to be able to store data representing information in the computer system and retrieve it to do something with it. You may simply want to look at it on a VDU screen or cause it to be output on a hard copy device such as a printer or plotter; you may wish to transform it in some way i.e. supply it as input to a program that will produce some other data as output; if the data can be "understood" directly by the computer, you may wish to tell the machine to obey the sequence of instructions comprising the data i.e. execute the program. Whatever it is that you want to do with the data, you need some way of referring to it and you must therefore give it a name. One way to do this is to store the data in a *file* in the computer system and then reference it by a *filename*. A file can be thought of as a container of information. Once information is stored in a file, it will remain there until it is changed or the file is removed from the system.

When a file is created, it is initially empty. As data is stored in it, the file grows in size and takes up space on the storage medium; conversely, if data is deleted from a file, its size contracts. There are lots of facilities in UNIX for doing things to files − copying, merging, sorting, compacting, comparing and archiving. We will discuss all of these in later sections. You may also want to protect the data stored in a file in various ways. Perhaps you would like to ensure that only the person who created the file can read it or alter it in any way; alternatively, you might be quite happy to have anybody else read it but only certain people authorized to change it. Again, the facilities available in UNIX for protecting files will be dealt with later.

### 2.4.1  Choosing Filenames

A filename in UNIX is simply a *string* of characters. In AT&T versions of the system, the number of characters is limited to 14; in the Berkeley system, there is virtually no limit. There are also no restrictions on what characters may be included in the string (with the exception of **/**). Of course, it would be rather foolish to use certain characters, for example, non-printing ones since you might forget where they occur in the string. Space and tab could also cause problems since you have already seen that arguments to commands are separated by white space. Some of the punctuation characters and mathematical symbols have special significance to the system and hence should be avoided. In practice, it is wise to restrict yourself (at least initially) to upper and lower case letters (which are considered to be different), digits, full stops (periods) and underscores. The following are all valid filenames:

```
abc        1234      my_prog    SECTION.1
A9.x       Report    a.b.c.1    prog.c
```

It would also be eminently sensible to choose filenames that have some mnemonic significance. Do not be lazy and use names with only one or two characters unless

the files are temporary ones that will soon be discarded.  A filename should help
you remember what information you have stored in the file.  If you are writing a
set of notes that can be divided into a number of sections, you might store the
text in a number of files called:

```
sect1        sect2        sect3        ...          etc.
```

Further, if each section can be broken up into subsections, you might use the
following filenames:

```
sect1.1      sect1.2      sect1.3
sect2.1      sect2.2
sect3.1      sect3.2      sect3.3      sect3.4
               .
               .
               .
```

and so on.  As you will see, there are many advantages to be gained from storing
a large amount of information in a number of files and naming those files in a
systematic way.  Conversely, there are virtually no disadvantages for adopting
this approach.  The more files there are (within reason), the easier it is to manage
them.

In addition to choosing filenames with mnemonic significance, it is also
sometimes useful if you use part of the filename to indicate something about the
type of information stored in the file.  The convention adopted in UNIX is that, if
the filename ends in a period followed by one or more letters, then special
significance can be attached to this extension which is often called a *suffix*.  For
example, a suffix of *.c* implies that the file contains a program written in the C
programming language; likewise, *.f* and *.p* are used for FORTRAN and Pascal
source files respectively.  If the filename ends in *.o*, it contains object code
produced by a compiler which may be loaded into memory to produce an
executable program.  A *.h* suffix indicates that the file contains headers that may
be included in a C program.  There are other conventions that we will not concern
ourselves with here but remember, they are only conventions.  UNIX does not
enforce them although it is certainly true that the compilers will not accept a file
for input unless it has the correct suffix.

Now, it does not require too much thought to realize that filenames must be
unique.  While you can change the information stored in a file (providing you
have the authority to do so), you cannot have two files with exactly the same
name since, apart from the fact that you might forget what was stored in each
one, UNIX would not know which one to use when you instructed it to carry out
some operation on that file.  Since an active user of the system might have
hundreds of files, it could be quite a headache choosing a new (and unique)
filename.  Worse than that, it could be quite disastrous, since you might instruct
the system to write information into what you thought was a new file but,
instead, the information in an existing file of that name would be overwritten and
perhaps lost forever.  In some of the older operating systems, this was exactly the

situation that existed but fortunately UNIX provides a solution to the problem. It uses a hierarchical naming structure based on directories.

## 2.4.2 Directories

A *directory* is simply a file that contains the names of other files and information about how to locate them. The name of a directory is chosen and constructed in exactly the same way as filenames of ordinary files. The name of a file is then the filename preceded by a slash (/) and the name of the directory in which it exists. If a file **beta** exists in a directory named **alpha**, its name is **alpha/beta**. If there were another file **beta** in a directory named **gamma**, its name would be **gamma/beta**. Since the names are unique, they refer to completely different files and the system will never get confused.

Since a directory is just a file containing the names of other files, there is no reason why one of these filenames could not be the name of another directory that contains the name of another directory that ... and so on. If file **f** exists in directory **dc** which exists in directory **db** which exists in directory **da**, the full name of this file is **da/db/dc/f**. A directory that exists in another directory is called a *sub-directory*. There is no limit imposed by UNIX on the number of levels of sub-directories that may be created by a user.

### 2.4.2.1 *Home Directory*

By this time, you may be asking yourself "Well, I know how to create unique filenames for my own files, but how do I ensure their uniqueness with respect to filenames chosen by other users of the system?" Don't worry, you don't have to ask all the other users what names they have chosen before choosing one yourself. Whenever a new account is established on the system, a directory is created for that user which has a unique name. This directory is called the *home directory* and its name is just the username you supply in response to the login query. If your username is **yew**, the name of your home directory is also **yew**. When you login successfully, UNIX makes your home directory the *current directory* and you are then ready to begin your session. You can create, modify and delete files; you can also make and remove sub-directories.

### 2.4.2.2 *Looking at Directories*

As you may eventually have many files and directories, it would clearly be very difficult to remember all their names and how they are organized. UNIX therefore provides a command that allows you to discover what files are in a directory.

---
**ls** - list contents of directory
---

The **ls** command is a request "to list a directory". You supply, as an argument, the name of the directory whose contents you want to see; if no directory name is specified, **ls** assumes, as the default, the directory in which you are currently working.

Let us assume that you have just logged in for the very first time and issue the **ls** command. You will be in your home directory and your screen may look like this:

```
$ ls                            List current directory
$
```

indicating that your home directory apparently contains no files or directories at all. Since there is nothing to list, UNIX says nothing and returns to command mode. This is in keeping with the UNIX philosophy that unnecessary messages should be kept to a minimum. It could have output something like:

```
FAILURE 6027 : DIRECTORY IS EMPTY
```

as is done in some other systems. Some people prefer this approach and criticize UNIX for being too terse. However, you will soon get used to it being so taciturn and appreciate its lack of verbosity.

It is hardly surprising that there are no files or directories in your home directory since we have assumed that this is the first time you have logged in and you have not as yet created any. However, there are in fact at least two entries in this directory that were put there by the system when the directory was created. **ls** used in the above manner simply ignored them. To display these entries, you can use **ls** again, selecting one of its many options that will list all entries in a directory:

```
$ ls -a                         List all entries in current directory
.
..
$
```

(If you are using the Berkeley version of **ls**, the output will occur on one line since an attempt is made in this command to maximize the amount of information that appears on the screen.) Depending on the conventions adopted by the organization operating the system you are using, there may be other filenames starting with a period. These are also ignored by **ls** used in its default mode. The "list-all" option must be used to output these names on the terminal. The minus sign in front of the **a** indicates to the **ls** command that one or more of its options are to be selected depending on what letters follow. This is a standard UNIX convention for supplying an argument to modify the default behaviour of a command. Let us explore this concept a little further.

Another option is one that produces a long listing with additional information associated with each filename. If you ask for a long listing for all files by using the command:

$ **ls -al**        *List all entries in current directory in long format*

you might obtain something similar to the following:

```
total 2
drwxr-xr-x 2  yew        512 May  8  00:22 .
drwxr-xr-x 24 root      1024 Sep 10  21:02 ..
$
```

This illustrates that there are two directories in your home directory as indicated by the letter **d** in the first column with names, as shown in the last column, of **.** (pronounced "dot") and **..** (pronounced "dot dot"). Don't worry about the remainder of the information in each line at this stage except for the third field which specifies the name of the owner of the directory. (In System V, there will be an additional field which we will also ignore for the moment.) The total given in the first line of the output is a count of the number of blocks of storage occupied, but more of this later.

The interpretation of "dot" in the above example is that it is shorthand for the name of the current directory. Since it is the home directory for **yew**, then, as you might expect, the name of the owner of that directory is **yew**. On the other hand, "dot dot" is shorthand for the name of the parent directory, i.e. a directory of which the current directory is a sub-directory. Observe that this directory is not owned by **yew** but by **root**. "Curiouser and curiouser" — there must be some directory structure above your home directory. Let us see if you can find out what it looks like.

### 2.4.2.3 *Directory Hierarchy*

To explore the structure of the file system, you will need to use some new commands that enable you to change from one directory to another and find out where you are at any time.

> **pwd** - print working directory name

The **pwd** command prints the name of the **working** directory which is simply the directory in which you are positioned at the moment. Since you have just logged in, you will be in your home directory and if you give the **pwd** command, you will see something like:

```
$ pwd                      Print working directory
/usr/staff/yew
$
```

on your terminal. **pwd** is a useful little command since, as you move around the file system from directory to directory, it is quite easy to forget where you are.

**pwd** simply reminds you.

The above response is the name of the home directory belonging to **yew** − to be more precise, it is the *full pathname* to this directory and is a complete specification of where that file is in relation to the rest of the file system. In the example, *yew* is a sub-directory of the directory *staff* that, in turn, is a sub-directory of the directory *usr*. Let us change from the current directory to its parent i.e. from *yew* to *staff*.

> ### cd - change working directory

The command required to change your working directory is **cd**. To move to the parent directory of your current directory, just type:

```
$ cd ..                        Change to the parent directory
$
```

Where are you now? To find out, try **pwd** and, in our case, the response would be:

```
/usr/staff
```

(You should execute the same command on your system, remembering that names of files and directories may differ from one system to another.) Let us have a look at what is in the directory *staff*. Try typing **ls −al** and you should see something that looks like this:

```
total 19
drwxr-xr-x 24 root          1024 Sep 10 21:02 .
drwxr-xr-x 32 root           524 Aug 10 03:00 ..
drwxr-xr-x  2 adj            512 Jul 17 15:33 adj
drwxr-xr-x  7 bec            512 Sep  5 09:20 bec
                  |
                  |
drwxr-xr-x 14 sl             512 Sep  7 15:52 sl
drwxr-xr-x  2 yew            512 May  8 00:22 yew
$
```

(To conserve space, we have abbreviated the above output as indicated by the vertical bars in the middle of the listing. Your output may be a lot longer than this one.) Our old friends **.** and **..** are there once again, both now owned by **root**, but this time they refer to the directory *staff* and its parent *usr*. Then there is a whole host of directories each owned by a user with the same name as the directory. These are just the home directories of the authorized users of the system in the category *staff*. (You should see your own username somewhere in the list.) Notice that the output has been sorted alphabetically by filename. This is the default ordering which you could reverse if you wish by using the **−r** flag. To help keep track of where you are, let us construct a diagram as shown in Figure 2.2. This illustrates that the directories *adj, bec, ... yew* are in the directory *staff*.

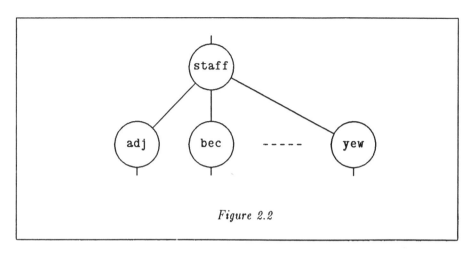

*Figure 2.2*

Okay, so let's go up again — **cd ..** and **pwd**. This time, you should see something like:

    /usr

since in our example *usr* is the parent directory of *staff*. **ls –al** will produce something like this:

```
total 38
drwxr-xr-x 32 root           524 Aug 10 03:00 .
drwxr-xr-x 19 root          1024 Sep  9 21:17 ..
drwxr-xr-x  3 root           512 Aug  4 04:00 adm
drwxr-xr-x  2 root          1536 Jul 27 20:53 bin
                   |
                   |
drwxr-xr-x 24 root          1024 Sep 10 21:02 staff
drwxr-xr-x 52 root          2048 Aug 13 01:40 studes
$
```

Again you see lots of directories owned by **root**. (There may be other owners in your output since this can vary from system to system.) One of these is *staff* and our diagram now looks like that shown in Figure 2.3. Ready to go again. "How many more times?" you might ask. Patience, you are nearly there. What is going to happen this time when you execute **cd ..** and **pwd**? Looking at the previous example, you will note that each time you moved to a parent directory, you lost the slash and the name of the current directory. So you might guess that, this time, you will obtain no output at all. Alas, you would be wrong! Try it and you will see just **/** (assuming of course that the full pathname of your original home directory had 3 components. If it had more, you will have to execute a few more **cd** commands; if less, you may already be there). The single slash output in response to **pwd** indicates that your current directory is a special directory called *root*. List the contents and you will see something like:

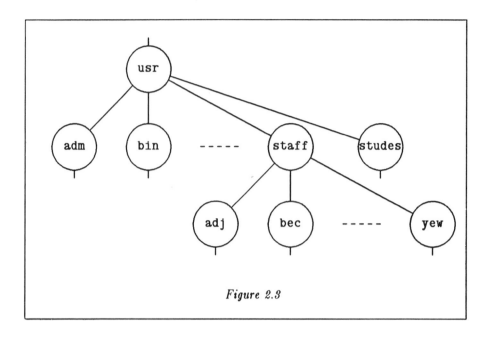

*Figure 2.3*

```
total 1787
drwxr-xr-x 19 root        1024 Sep  9 21:17 .
drwxr-xr-x 19 root        1024 Sep  9 21:17 ..
drwxr-xr-x  2 root        1536 Aug  5 16:46 bin
drwxr-xr-x  1 root          12 May  6 22:44 crp
                     |
                     |
-rwxr-xr-x  2 root      288161 Aug  2 14:15 unix
drwxr-xr-x 32 root         524 Aug 10 03:00 usr
$
```

Again, you will see a number of directories owned by **root** and maybe even a file (as indicated by the − instead of **d** as the first character in the line.) Let us update our diagram again as shown in Figure 2.4. Where to now? It would appear from the output that even **root** has a parent directory since it contains a **..** entry. So try **cd ..** and **pwd** again. Hey presto − you get **/** again. The parent of the root directory is itself and you have reached the end of the line i.e. the root of the file system. There is nowhere else to go. The first slash of a full pathname is special − it is the name of the root directory. Any further slashes just separate a directory from its parent (and ultimately the name of a file from the directory in which it was created).

The diagram shown in Figure 2.4 is called a *tree*. (In Computer Science, we tend to draw trees upside down with the root at the top.) A file is simply a leaf of the tree whereas a directory is a node from which emanate one or more branches. The full pathname of a file contains just the directories you must traverse

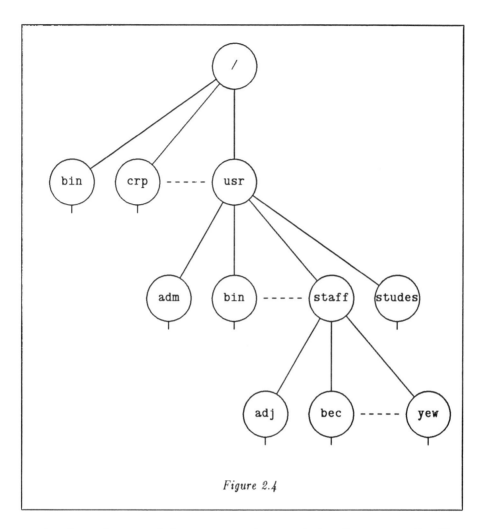

*Figure 2.4*

starting from the root of the tree to reach a particular directory or file. Your current working directory is **root** and you got there by climbing up through various directories to the root of the tree (sounds a little odd, doesn't it!). You could have got there much more rapidly by typing:

    **$ cd /**                         *Change to the root directory*
    **$**

i.e. by supplying, as an argument to **cd**, the name of the directory you wish to make your current working directory. How could you get back to your home directory? Just use **cd** again but, this time, specify the full pathname:

```
$ cd /usr/staff/yew          Go home
$
```

In fact, the command:

```
$ cd  usr/staff/yew          Another way of going home
$
```

would have taken you back home as well. This illustrates the concept of a *relative pathname*. If a filename starts with a /, UNIX takes this to be the full pathname and, starting from the root directory, traverses the various directories in the pathname until it locates the file or directory specified by the last name. If, on the other hand, the filename does not commence with /, UNIX starts its search from the current working directory. Since your current working directory is **root**, the initial / is not required.

Wandering around in a complex file system can become a little confusing at times and it is always nice to be able to go home. You can always find out where you are with **pwd** and **cd** with the full pathname of your home directory will always get you back to where you started. In fact, there is a much easier way of doing this — just type **cd** without an argument. It does not matter where you are in the file system or what your current working directory is, **cd** on its own will always take you home. For **yew** in our example, each of the following sequences of commands will also return to the home directory if the current working directory is **root** :

| $ cd | $ cd /usr/staff/yew | $ cd usr/staff/yew | $ cd usr |
|------|---------------------|--------------------|----------|
|      |                     |                    | $ cd staff |
|      |                     |                    | $ cd yew |

Try switching between your home directory and the root directory by various means, using **pwd** to check each time that your current working directory is the one you think it should be.

## 2.4.3  Some Files and Directories of Interest

Now that you know how to move around the file system and scuttle back home if you get lost, let us have a look at some of the files and directories in the system and, in the process, learn to use some of the commands for manipulating them.

First of all, change directory to **root** (if you are not there already) and execute **ls**. The names of files and directories in **root** will be listed on the screen. Amongst these, you should find the name *etc*. You don't know at this stage whether this is a file or a directory, so let us find out. To do this, use the **−d** option of **ls** which, for a directory, will list only its name and not its contents along with any other information requested:

```
$ ls -ld etc                    List directory details
drwxr-xr-x  3 root           2560 Aug  5 16:46 etc
$
```

Since it is a directory, execute:

```
$ ls etc                        List the directory etc
```

and another list of names will appear on the screen (which also indicates that *etc* is a directory). Amongst these, you will find **passwd**. Now execute:

```
$ cd etc                        Change working directory
$ ls -l passwd                  Long format listing of passwd
```

Output similar to the following will appear:

```
-rw-r--r-- 1 root          14884 Feb 24 16:19 passwd
$
```

**passwd** is a file and not a directory since the first character on the output line is a minus sign. **ls** when given the name of a file rather than a directory name as an argument echoes that name along with any other information that has been requested. This file contains a list of the authorized users of the system, their passwords and associated information. Let us now examine this directory entry in more detail.

The first 10 characters are called the *mode*. Following on from the first character which indicates whether the file is a directory or not are a further 9 characters organized as 3 groups of 3. These are the *read, write* and *execute permissions* for the following three classes of users:

Owner:  The user who created the file or directory.

Group:  Several users combined together so that they can share access to each other's files.

Others:  The remainder of the authorized users of the system — you can think of them as the general public.

Every file or directory in a UNIX file system has three types of permissions (or protections) that define whether certain actions can be carried out (or not). These permissions are:

*read* (**r**)    a user who has *read* permission to a file may look at its contents. For a directory, *read* permission enables a user to find out what files are in that directory.

*write* (**w**)   a user who has *write* permission to a file can alter the contents of that file. For a directory, the user can create and delete files in that directory.

*execute* (**x**)   a user who has *execute* permission for a file can cause the
contents of that file to be executed (providing, of course, that
it is executable). For a directory, *execute* permission allows a
user to change directory to that directory or search the
directory for a specified file.

If a particular permission is set, the appropriate letter appears in the
corresponding position, otherwise, a minus sign indicates that the permission is
not set. If all permissions for all classes of users are set, then:

    **rwxrwxrwx**                    *Read, write and execute for everybody*

would appear in the output from **ls**. If the owner of a file wishes to prevent
anybody else from accessing it in any manner, the setting might be:

    **rwx------**                    *Read, write and execute for the owner*

If a file is to be read and executed by everybody but overwritten by nobody, the
permissions would be:

    **r-xr-xr-x**                    *Read and execute for everybody*

Remember that the first three letters refer to the owner's permissions, the second
three, the group's and the last three define how the public may access the file. As
you will see later, the owner of a file may change the permission via the **chmod**
command. Having a file that is write protected against its owner is therefore not
as daft as its looks − it is a safeguard against accidental overwriting of the file by
the owner himself. A lesson you will soon learn, if you haven't learnt it already,
is that it's a very good idea to protect yourself against your own stupidity
whenever possible. We all make mistakes, some of us more frequently than
others.

The second field in the output from **ls** (1 in the above example) is the
number of *links* to the file. In most cases, this is just 1 but it is possible in UNIX
to have a number of directory entries all pointing to the one file i.e. a file can be
known by a number of different names in different directories, even ones belonging
to users other than the owner of the file. A file will only be removed "physically"
from the system when the value of the link count is 0. The third field, as we have
already mentioned, is the name of the owner of the file. If you are using V.2, the
next field will be the groupname which specifies group ownership of the file. The
−**o** option suppresses the inclusion of this field in the long output of **ls** whereas,
for 4.2 and most other systems, −**g** must be specified to cause the groupname to
be included in the output. The next field is the size of the file in characters which
is followed by the date and time at which the file was last modified. The final
field is just the name of the file. The interpretation of the various fields is
illustrated diagrammatically in Figure 2.5.

The *modification time* which is the default output for the −**l** option is the last
time when anything was written to the file. Other times recorded by the system

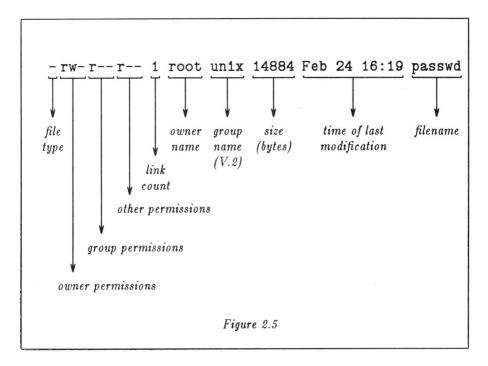

*Figure 2.5*

are the *access time* (the last time the file was read) and the *change time* (the last time the *index node* of the file was altered). The index node is a special block of data, often referred to as the *i-node*, associated with each file which is used to record such information as file creation time, permissions, number of links, size, owner, group and where the file is physically located in the file system. In fact, much of the information output by **ls –l** is extracted from the i-node of a file. It is changed whenever any information stored in it is updated.

Returning now to the **ls** output for *passwd*, you see that it contains 14884 characters of data, was last altered at 16:19 on 24th February, is owned by **root** and has only one link. When you look at the permissions, you see that only **root** can alter it but anybody else can read it. So let's have a look at it. "But wait", you say, "What sort of a dumb operating system is this that will let you inspect the password file. Haven't they ever heard of security? I'm not too keen on using a system where anybody can look up my password and then pretend to be me." Not to worry, it's quite safe. The password you supply using the **passwd** command is never held in its original form in the system. It is encrypted, before it is stored, in such a way that it is virtually impossible, even if you know the encrypted form and the encryption algorithm, to work out what the original password was. Whenever you supply your password as part of the login procedure, the same encryption algorithm is applied before the password file is consulted to see if you are an authorized user of the system. So even if people read the encrypted form of your password, they can never impersonate you.

Some system administrators do, in fact, turn off read permission on the password file as an added but somewhat unnecessary security measure. (If this is the case at your installation, you will not be able to carry out some of the following exercises. So just read the text and follow the examples in the book.)

| **cat** - concatenate files |

Well, since there is no danger in looking at the password file, let's do it by using the **cat** command. (**cat** is short for con**cat**enate and, in fact, can be used for joining a number of files together into a single file on standard output, but more of that later.) Just type:

**$ cat passwd**              *Output password file on your terminal*

and the password file will be listed on your terminal. If it is a large file in your system and you have a fast terminal, it may flash by too quickly for you to read it, apart from the tail of the file. Don't worry — we are not going to study it in detail. You could of course have controlled the output using ˆ**S** and ˆ**Q**.

=================================================

| **more** - file perusal filter for crt viewing |

If you are using the Berkeley system, there is a command called **more** that stops conveniently at the end of each screenful of information and only continues when you hit the space bar. A newline, on the other hand, will cause one more line to be displayed. If you have this command available, try it as it is much "more" convenient than **cat**. However, a word of warning — neither **cat** nor **more** will work correctly on directories since they contain non-printable characters. Use **ls** instead.

-------------------------------------------------

| **pg** - file perusal filter for soft copy terminals |

In System V.2, there is a command called **pg** which allows you to examine a file, one screenful at a time. At the end of each page, **pg** outputs a : as a prompt and waits for you to respond. A newline will cause the next page to be output on the screen. You should try this command on the password file if you have it available.

Did you see your entry in the password file? It should look something like the entry shown in Figure 2.6 which shows the various fields and their interpretation. The fields are separated by colons (:). The first is the username, the second is the encrypted form of that user's password, the third and fourth are the user

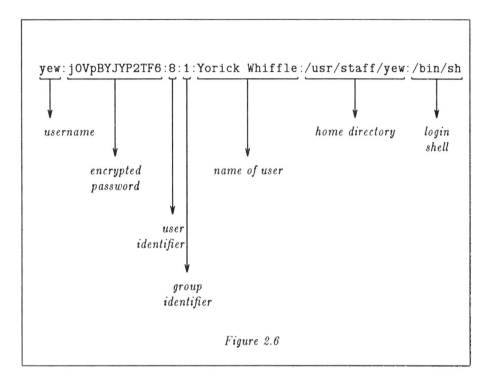

yew:jOVpBYJYP2TF6:8:1:Yorick Whiffle:/usr/staff/yew:/bin/sh

*username*

*encrypted password*

*name of user*

*home directory*

*login shell*

*user identifier*

*group identifier*

*Figure 2.6*

identifier and group identifier respectively, the fifth is the user's full name and the sixth is the user's home directory. The last field is the default login shell. Check that your details are correct and that the encrypted form of your password looks nothing like the original. If it does, logout immediately and complain loudly to your system administrator − your system probably isn't UNIX.

Another file you could look at while in this directory is *motd* which, in most systems, has the pathname */etc/motd*. This contains the message of the day that is output on the terminal immediately after a successful login. If at any time, you forget what the message was and want to refresh your memory, just list */etc/motd* using **cat**.

Let us now examine the contents of another sub-directory of *root* called *bin*. Currently you are in *etc* and can transfer to *bin* by:

    **$ cd /bin**                *Change to* **bin** *directory*
    **$**

(**cd ../bin** would have produced the same result. Why?) Now execute:

    **$ ls −l**                *And list it*

and you will see that this directory contains many files owned by **root** which are executable by everyone in the system. Look at the file names − *cat*, *date*, *ls*, *passwd*, *stty*, *who*, and *write*. Haven't you seen these names somewhere before? Indeed, you have − they are just some of the UNIX commands we have discussed so far. The directory **/bin** holds the most frequently used system commands that are available to all users. Fortunately, you did not have to supply the full pathname when you wanted to execute one of them. Whenever a command is issued, the shell looks in various directories for a file with that name to execute. As you will see later, you can actually define the *search path* if you so desire rather than take the default one used by the system. But what would happen if you did supply the full pathname? Try it and you will see that:

```
$ /bin/date                    Execute date command
Fri Apr 6 8:50:30 EST 1984
$
```

produces the same result as:

```
$ date                         And execute it again
Fri Apr 6 8:51:03 EST 1984
$
```

Thus, if the correct permissions are set, all you need to do to cause a program to be executed is supply its filename.

Having convinced yourself that the files in **/bin** are executable, what would happen if you tried to read them. You can try it if you like but be careful — all sorts of unintelligible rubbish will be sent to your terminal since these are *binary* files designed to be executed but not listed as are the *character* files you have been inspecting. Probably no harm will be done, but if your terminal locks up, you may have to switch off and on again or even disconnect and login again.

Another sub-directory of **root** that is worth a peek is **usr**; so change to that one and execute **ls –l**. You will see that it contains many sub-directories that look quite interesting, **games** for example. If you list the contents, you will see names like **adventure, chess, fortune, hangman, rogue, worms** and **zork**. Many of these are described in Section 6 of the UNIX manual. No, we won't play any of them at the moment but we will return to **rogue** again in the next chapter. You will also see a directory **bin**. What again? Yes, this holds the less frequently used system commands and hence helps to keep **/bin** down to a convenient size. Have a look at what it contains via **ls bin**. There are many commands including some of the others we have discussed already e.g. **man** and **mesg**. (For those using the Berkeley system, **ls ucb** will show additional or alternative commands developed at that institution.) The contents of these directories show that UNIX is very rich in system commands. Later on, you will see that you can add to these by constructing your own.

Now change to **/usr/pub** and use **ls –l** to list it. You will observe that it contains mainly files rather than directories. One in particular that is worth remembering is **ascii**. This contains tables for the *ASCII* character set showing the equivalence between characters and the internal codes used by the computer. The latter values are expressed in the *octal* number system in the first table and the *hexadecimal* number system in the second table.

## tail - print the last part of a file

You could inspect *ascii* using **cat**, **pg** or **more**. Alternatively, if you only wanted to see the last 4 lines, you could do so as follows:

```
$ tail -4 ascii              Output last 4 lines of ascii
| 60 ` | 61  a | 62  b | 63  c | 64  d | 65  e | 66  f | 67  g |
| 68  h | 69  i | 6a  j | 6b  k | 6c  l | 6d  m | 6e  n | 6f  o |
| 70  p | 71  q | 72  r | 73  s | 74  t | 75  u | 76  v | 77  w |
| 78  x | 79  y | 7a  z | 7b  { | 7c  | | 7d  } | 7e  ~ | 7f del|
$ 
```

The **tail** command writes the last few lines of a file on standard output. The actual number is defined by the argument. The default value is 10. The above output illustrates that the value of the character **a** is 61 hexadecimal which is equivalent to 97 in the decimal system. If, at any time, you need to determine the value of a character, you can do so by consulting this file online.

================================================

If the number of lines to be printed is followed by **r** in the Berkeley version of **tail**, the lines are output in reverse order:

```
% tail -2r ascii             Output last 2 lines of ascii in reverse order
| 78  x | 79  y | 7a  z | 7b  { | 7c  | | 7d  } | 7e  ~ | 7f del|
| 70  p | 71  q | 72  r | 73  s | 74  t | 75  u | 76  v | 77  w |
% 
```

## head - print the first few lines of a file

In the Berkeley system, there is a complementary command to **tail** called **head**. Again, the number of lines written to standard output is supplied as an argument with 10 as the default value:

```
% head -2 ascii              Output first 2 lines of ascii
|000 nul|001 soh|002 stx|003 etx|004 eot|005 enq|006 ack|007 bel|
|010 bs |011 ht |012 nl |013 vt |014 np |015 cr |016 so |017 si |
% 
```

The two- and three-letter names in the above output are those of control characters which do not have a printable representation. Thus **bel** generates an audible signal if sent to a terminal with a bell or equivalent. The above values are expressed in octal.

-------------------------------------------------------------

A rather odd directory in *root* is *dev* which, as its name implies, is where details of peripheral **dev**ices attached to the computer are stored. Use **ls –l** to list this directory on your system. You will see it is somewhat different from those you have examined before. The first character in each line is **b** or **c** and there is no file size in characters. Instead, there is a pair of small integers that enables UNIX to select the particular device when an input-output transfer is required. The fact that UNIX treats such devices as files greatly simplifies its internal structure and provides a very convenient way for programmers to access them using just the standard commands. But more of that later. All we want you to do for the moment is observe that even the terminal you are using is in **/dev** and, currently, is a file owned by **yew**. You may have seen it when you listed the directory.

```
tty - get terminal name
```

If you have forgotten what your teletype number is from the previous output of **who**, you can find out using **tty** and then examine the entry in the directory:

```
$ tty                       Output number of your terminal
/dev/ttyj
$ ls -l /dev/ttyj           List device details
crw--w--w-  1 yew        0,  19 Aug  5 08:48 /dev/ttyj
$
```

The first letter in the entry indicates that it is a **character** rather than a **block** device i.e. it processes a stream of characters rather than a block of them, as would be the case for a disk or magnetic tape unit. The read permission is only set on for the owner, but the write permission is public which is why any other user can write to your terminal, unless you use the **mesg** command to turn that permission off:

```
$ mesg n                    Turn off write permission
$ ls -l /dev/ttyj           And check permissions on your terminal
crw-------  1 yew        0,  19 Aug  5 09:43 /dev/ttyj
$ mesg y                    Turn on write permission again
$
```

You can use the name of the device in those places where previously you used a filename:

```
$ cat /dev/ttyj             Read from your terminal
abcd                        Type an input line
^D                          Terminate input
abcd
$
```

Input is read from the file up to end-of-file and then written to standard output. Later, you will see that the device can also be used as an output file.

Another useful file in **/dev** is **/dev/null**. This is a null device that can be used as an sink for output and an immediate end-of-file for input:

```
$ cat /dev/null             Read from null device
$
```

The command terminates immediately on reading EOF and produces no output.

You can look at some of the other directories in *usr* or *root* if you wish —
their function will become clearer later. But a word of advice — you may **cd** to a
directory and get a failure message such as:

```
no such file or directory
```

in which case you have probably spelled the filename incorrectly or:

```
Permission denied
```

which means that the directory is protected against you. Have fun and remember
when lost, **pwd** and, if very lost, **cd** all on its own to take you home.

## 2.4.4  Creating and Deleting Files

Find your way back home and let us see how you can make some files of
your own.

| **cp** - copy files |

The easiest way to create a file is to copy one belonging to someone else
(providing you have permission to do so i.e. read permission). You could use
*/etc/passwd* but that is usually quite large; so instead let's try */etc/motd*. To
make a copy, use the copy command **cp**:

```
$ cp /etc/motd   mess            Copy motd to mess
$
```

Now check with **ls −l** that a file called *mess* has appeared in your directory and
use **cat** to examine its contents. You will find that the settings for the
permissions on the copy are just those that existed on the original file (if you are
very secretive and don't like these, it is possible to alter them so that even read
permission is denied to everyone else). If the contents of your home directory
were just . and .. before the copy command executed, **ls −l** will produce
something like:

```
-rw-r--r-- 1 yew          81 Feb 26 08:39 mess
```

So now you have a file that is all your own. Normally, **cp** takes just two
arguments; the first is the source file and the second, the destination file. If the
last argument is, however, a directory, there can be one or more filenames as
arguments preceding it and those files will be copied into the specified directory
with the same filenames. For example, if you had used:

```
$ cp /etc/motd /etc/passwd  .    Copy 2 files to current directory
$
```

two files, *motd* and *passwd*, would have been created in your home directory
(remember that . is shorthand for the current working directory). If at any time
you forget how to use **cp**, just issue the command without arguments and it will
respond:

```
$ cp                        How do I use cp?
usage: cp: f1 f2, or cp f1 ... fn d2
$ ▓
```

So try:

```
$ cp /etc/motd  .           Copy motd to current directory
$ ▓
```

and **ls** to check that a second file has been created. So now you have two files,
*mess* and *motd.*

What happens if you specify a file that does not exist. Try:

```
$ cp abc  pqr               Try to copy non-existent file
```

and you will get a failure message something like:

```
cp: abc: No such file or directory
```

Suppose now, through error, you attempt to copy one of your files to a system file
owned by **root**. In all probability, unless you are a superuser, you won't be able
to do so since it will be write-protected against you. First of all, check that
*/etc/motd* has public write permission turned off and then try:

```
$ cp motd  /etc/motd        Try to overwrite the message file
```

You should see a failure message something like:

```
cp: /etc/motd: Permission denied
```

since you do not have write permission for this file. Suppose now you try:

```
$ cp motd  motd             Try to overwrite a file with itself
```

Again, the command will fail with a message something like:

```
cp: Cannot copy a file to itself
```

So **cp** is well protected against erroneous, foolish and even malicious use.

| chmod - change mode |

Now that you have some files to play with, let us experiment with changing
permissions using the **chmod** command (**ch**ange **mod**e). For the purpose of the
exercise, let us assume that the permissions set for *mess* are just those shown
above i.e. *read* for everybody, *write* for the owner and *execute* by no one. The
arguments supplied to **chmod** are a symbolic specification of the changes required
followed by· one or more filenames. The specification consists of whose
permissions are to be changed (**u** for user, **g** for group, **o** for others or some
combination thereof. **a** stands for **ugo**), how they are to be changed (+ adds a
permission, − removes a permission and = sets the specified permissions,
removing the other ones) and which ones (**r** for read, **w** for write and **x** for
execute). Let us first remove all permissions from *mess* :

```
$ chmod a-rwx mess        Remove read, write and execute from all
$ ls -l mess              And check permissions
---------- 1 yew          81 Feb 26 08:39 mess
$
```

(You could also have used **a=** to achieve the same effect.) Now turn on all read and write permissions:

```
$ chmod ugo+rw mess       Add read and write to user, group, other
$ ls -l mess              And check permissions
-rw-rw-rw- 1 yew          81 Feb 26 08:39 mess
$
```

Now remove write permission for groups and others:

```
$ chmod go-w mess         Remove write from group and others
$ ls -l mess              And check permissions
-rw-r--r-- 1 yew          81 Feb 26 08:39 mess
$
```

and you should be back to where you started. Finally, set the permissions to just read for everybody:

```
$ chmod u=r mess          Set user to read only
$ ls -l mess              And check permissions
-r--r--r-- 1 yew          81 Feb 26 08:39 mess
$
```

Now the file is classified as read only; it cannot be written to or executed by anyone including yourself.

**chmod** will also accept a permission setting expressed as a 3-digit octal number. To determine this, you first of all write a 1 if the permission is to be set and a 0 otherwise. This produces a binary number which can be converted into octal by grouping the digits in threes and replacing each group by the corresponding octal digit according to the following table:

| Binary | Octal |
|--------|-------|
| 000    | 0     |
| 001    | 1     |
| 010    | 2     |
| 011    | 3     |
| 100    | 4     |
| 101    | 5     |
| 110    | 6     |
| 111    | 7     |

Thus, if the required setting is rw-r--r--, the corresponding binary number is 110100100 which is equivalent to 644 in octal. For example:

```
$ chmod 644 mess          Equivalent to u=rw, go=r
$ ls -l mess              Check permissions
-rw-r--r-- 1 yew          81 Feb 26 08:39 mess
$
```

illustrates that the permissions for **mess** have been reset to their original values.
To change the permissions back to read only, you can execute **chmod** as follows:

```
$ chmod 444 mess          Equivalent to ugo=r
$ ls -l mess              Check permissions
-r--r--r-- 1 yew          81 Feb 26 08:39 mess
$
```

---

| **umask** - set file creation mask |
| --- |

By this time, you will have realized that when a file is created for you by the
system, it will be given an initial set of permissions. These will vary from
installation to installation and exactly what they are is controlled by the system
administrator.

If you don't like the default permissions, you can change them using **chmod**
as we have seen. However, it may be that you would rather have a different
default. You can choose your own by using the **umask** command which sets the
file creation mask.

First of all, issue the command without an argument to cause the current
setting to be output:

```
$ umask               Output current setting of file creation mask
0022
$
```

This is an octal number of which only the last 3 digits have any significance. If
you convert these digits to binary, you will obtain a bit pattern of 1s and 0s. A 1
indicates that the corresponding permission is to be turned off, a 0, that it is to be
turned on. Hence, the mask output above is 000010010 and produces a
permission setting of **rwxr-xr-x** i.e. write permission is turned off for group and
others.

Suppose you decide that the default setting you prefer is **rwxr-x---**. This
corresponds to the bit pattern 000010111 and the required mask is 027:

```
$ umask 27            Set new file creation mask
$
```

Now, whenever you create a new file, the permissions turned off will be at least
the ones you have selected.

> **rm** - remove files

Having created some files and examined them, you may at some future time want to remove them. Let us try that now. The **rm** command deletes or removes files from a directory:

```
$ rm motd            Delete motd
$
```

will remove the file *motd* from your current directory. Try it and check with **ls** to see that it has gone. Since you are the owner of the directory in which the file is located and have write permission to that directory, **rm** removes the file without question. This is not always a good idea since you may remove a file in error and it is better to be safe than sorry. If you supply **−i** as an argument to **rm**, it will query you for each file and you must reply **y** or **n** depending on whether you want the file removed or not. Create two files *aa* and *bb* by copying *mess* and then issue the **rm** command:

```
$ cp mess aa            Create file aa
$ cp mess bb            Create file bb
$ rm -i aa mess bb      Delete files interactively
```

(Notice that you can ask for more than one file to be removed in the one command.) If the following dialogue were to take place:

```
aa: ? y
mess: ? n
bb: ? y
$
```

then *aa* and *bb* will be deleted but *mess* will remain. Until you are fairly confident that you know what you are doing, it's a good idea to use **rm** only in this interactive mode.

So far, you have only tried to remove files to which you as the owner have write permission. However, *mess* is a read only file. So try to remove this file:

```
$ rm mess               Delete a read only file
mess: 444 mode ?
```

If you reply **y** (or any word starting with **y**), the file will be removed, otherwise it will be left untouched. The meaning of **444** in the above message is that the permissions are set to r--r--r--.

As with **cp**, **rm** will also tell you if you have specified a non-existent file. UNIX is not all that cryptic!

┌─────────────────────────────────┐
│ **mv** -  move or rename files  │
└─────────────────────────────────┘

Sometimes, after creating a file, you may decide that you have chosen the wrong name and wish to alter it. Clearly, you could simply copy the original file to a new one with a different name and then remove the first one. There is, however, a command called **mv** that will produce the desired effect in one operation. **mv** moves a file, in the process, creating a new one and removing the old one. Let us try it by changing the name of the file *mess* to *motd* :

```
$ mv mess   motd               Rename mess as motd
$ ls -l                        And check the effect
-rw-r--r-- 1 yew        81 Feb 26 08:39 motd
$
```

You see from the output of **ls** that the effect of executing **mv** has been to rename *mess* as *motd*. If *motd* had already existed, the effect would have been the same (except that the old *motd* would have been removed first).  As with **cp**, if you try to move a file to one that is write protected, **mv** will query whether the protection is to be overridden and the move will only take place if the user responds **y**, otherwise nothing is changed. If the file being moved cannot be deleted, **mv** will complain. So, providing you are not a superuser, try:

```
$ mv /etc/motd  motd       Try to rename the message file
mv: /etc/motd: rename: Permission denied
$
```

If an attempt is made to move a non-existent file, a failure will occur:

```
$ mv xxx motd              Try to move a non-existent file
mv: cannot access xxx
$
```

Now, the synopsis of **mv** is:

```
$ mv                       How do I use mv?
usage: mv [-if] f1 f2 or mv [-if] f1 ... fn d1
(`fn´ is a file or directory)
$
```

Hence, you can move one or more files to a directory and even move directories. The −**i** flag causes the system to query the move if an existing file will be overwritten; the −**f** flag forces the move irrespective of any mode restrictions.

## 2.4.5  Creating and Deleting Directories

Let us extend ourselves a little and make our part of the tree grow (downwards, of course) by creating a few directories.

| mkdir - make a directory |

This command **makes directories**. Try executing the following commands after removing any files in your home directory:

```
$ ls -l                         Check that your home directory is empty
$ mkdir letters memos           Create two new sub-directories
$ ls -l                         And list your home directory
total 2
drwxr-xr-x 2 yew        32 Mar  2 07:53 letters
drwxr-xr-x 2 yew        32 Mar  2 07:53 memos
$
```

You see from the output of the second **ls** that you have created two directories *letters* and *memos*. Change directory to *letters* and create two more directories, *personal* and *business*, so that you can easily keep your private and professional correspondence separate:

```
$ cd letters                    Change directory
$ mkdir personal business       Create two more sub-directories
$ ls -l                         Inspect your current directory
total 2
drwxr-xr-x 2 yew        32 Mar  2 08:20 business
drwxr-xr-x 2 yew        32 Mar  2 08:20 personal
$
```

Suppose you also wanted to divide your memos into internal and external ones. Then:

```
$ cd ../memos                   Change to a sub-directory of the parent directory
$ mkdir int ext                 And create two new sub-directories
$
```

will do the trick since .. refers to the parent directory of both *letters* and *memos*. Your directory hierarchy should now look like that shown in Figure 2.7. Now return to your home directory and inspect its sub-directories:

```
$ cd                            Return to your home directory
$ ls -l letters memos           And inspect its sub-directories

letters:
total 2
drwxr-xr-x 2 yew        32 Mar  2 08:20 business
drwxr-xr-x 2 yew        32 Mar  2 08:20 personal

memos:
total 2
drwxr-xr-x 2 yew        32 Mar  2 08:21 ext
drwxr-xr-x 2 yew        32 Mar  2 08:21 int
$
```

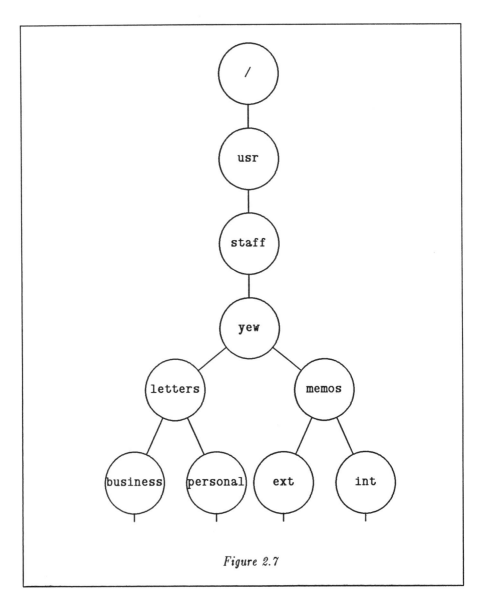

*Figure 2.7*

When more than one filename are supplied as arguments to **ls**, each section of the output is preceded by the name of the directory.

Suppose now that you decide that you are going to keep the previous week's messages of the day as external memos in a sub-directory *motd*. To create this directory, you could **cd** to its parent but there is no need to do this. Simply execute:

```
$ mkdir memos/ext/motd          Make a sub-sub-sub-directory
$
```

If today is **monday**, you could store the current message via:

```
$ cp /etc/motd  memos/ext/motd/mon     And copy a file to it
$
```

in a file called **mon**. If you had omitted **/mon** from the last command, **/etc/motd** would have been copied to a file whose relative pathname is **memos/ext/motd/motd** i.e. **motd** would be both the name of a file and the directory in which it exists. This is not a recommended practice since you could easily get confused. However, UNIX has no problems with the situation. Try this command and list the directory **motd** to check its effect:

```
$ cp /etc/motd  memos/ext/motd   Copy another file to the directory
$ ls memos/ext/motd              And list its contents
mon
motd
$
```

Suppose now that the message of the day stored in **motd** should in fact be in the file **tue**. Then, this can be accomplished by:

```
$ cd memos/ext/motd              Change directory
$ mv motd   tue                  And rename file
$ ls -l
total 2
-rw-r--r-- 1 yew         81 Mar  2 17:23 mon
-rw-r--r-- 1 yew         81 Mar  2 17:24 tue
$
```

Your file system relative to the home directory now has the structure shown in Figure 2.8 in which boxes represent files and circles represent directories. Suppose now you decide that **motd** is not an appropriate directory name and that you would like to change it to **messotd**. Then again you can use **mv** but you must be in the directory **ext** since you can only move a directory within its parent. The commands required (assuming your current working directory is **motd** ) are:

```
$ cd ..                          Change to parent directory
$ ls -l                          And inspect contents
drwxr-xr-x 2 yew        80 Mar  2 17:29 motd
$ mv motd   messotd              Rename directory
$ ls -l                          And list parent directory
drwxr-xr-x 2 yew        80 Mar  2 17:29 messotd
$
```

Execute these commands and check that the desired effect has been achieved.

Now let us see how you could move some files around within your own file system. Suppose, for some reason, you wanted copies of files **mon** and **tue** made in the directory **business**. There are a number of different ways that this could

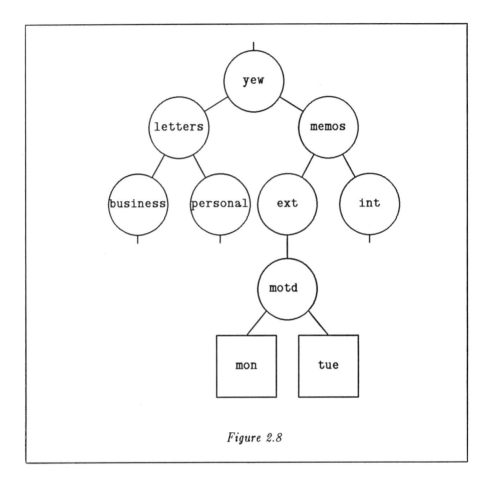

*Figure 2.8*

be achieved depending on your current working directory:

```
$ cd messotd                              Change directory
$ cp mon tue  ../../../letters/business   Copy 2 files
$
```

This will give the desired result although it is quite a mouthful. You are making use of the **..** notation to move from a directory to its parent until you reach the home directory. Note that **cp** is being used to copy a number of files into a directory, retaining their current names in the new directory. You could also use the full pathname of the home directory, in this case, */usr/staff/yew* as a prefix to *letters/business*.

================================================

If you are on the Berkeley system, you can always use the tilde character (˜) as shorthand for the path to your home directory. The command:

    **% cp mon tue ˜/letters/business**          *Another way in the C-shell*
    **%**

would also perform the required operation.

------------------------------------------------------------------

| **du** - summarize disk usage |
| :---: |

Already your file system is becoming a little complicated and a bit hard to visualize. Unfortunately, there are no utilities readily available that will produce a graphical representation in the form of a tree. However, there is a command **du** (**d**isk **u**sage) which, starting from a directory given as an argument or from the current directory if no argument is specified, works its way through the file structure listing the names of files and directories together with how much disk space they occupy. The unit of measurement is the block (1024 characters in System V and 4.2 BSD, 512 characters in other versions of UNIX). Return to your home directory using **cd** and execute **du** as follows:

```
$ du -a      Output numbers of blocks occupied by files and directories
1        ./letters/personal
1        ./letters/business/mon
1        ./letters/business/tue
3        ./letters/business
5        ./letters
1        ./memos/int
1        ./memos/ext/messotd/mon
1        ./memos/ext/messotd/tue
2        ./memos/ext/messotd
3        ./memos/ext
6        ./memos
12       .
$
```

The −a argument causes all filenames to be output; if no such argument is supplied, only directory names are listed. Observe from the output that **du** "walks" around the tree, starting at the leftmost path. After listing the files in a directory, it outputs the directory name and the total number of blocks occupied by the directory together with its files and sub-directories. The directory *personal*, which contains no files, occupies one block. The directory *business*, on the other hand, which contains the files *mon* and *tue*, each of size 1 block, is shown as occupying 3 blocks. Their parent directory *letters* has a size of 5 (1 for itself, 1 for *personal* and 3 for *business*).

The last line output by **du** gives the total number of blocks currently being used by **yew** since you changed to your home directory before issuing the **du** command. If all you are interested in is the total number of blocks occupied rather than a detailed breakdown, the −s option will cause only the last line of the previous output to appear on your screen:

```
$ du -s                    Output grand total of blocks occupied
12        .
$
```

Although the output from **du** is a one-dimensional rather than a two-dimensional representation of the file structure, it is a useful command to remember if you are feeling a little confused about the relationships of your directories and files.

| **rmdir** - remove directory |
| :---: |

Having created a number of directories and files, let us now get rid of them. **rm** and **rmdir** (for **rem**ove **dir**ectory) are the commands you need. Make *memos/ext* your current working directory and try removing *messotd*:

```
$ cd memos/ext             Change directory
$ rmdir messotd            Try to remove directory
```

You will hopefully get a failure message something like:

```
rmdir: messotd: Directory not empty
```

i.e. **rmdir** will only remove a directory if it does not contain any files or sub-directories. You could delete the files in this directory using **rm** and try again with **rmdir**. However, if you know for certain that you want to remove *messotd* and any files it contains, use the **-r** option:

```
$ ls                       List current directory
messotd
$ ls messotd               And its sub-directory
mon
tue
$ rm -r messotd            Remove files and directories recursively
$ ls
$
```

which will delete *mon*, *tue* and *messotd* for you. The *ext* directory is now empty as is *int*, so change directory to *memos* and remove them:

```
$ cd ..; ls                Change to parent and list current directory
ext
int
$ rmdir ext int            Remove sub-directories
$ ls                       And inspect current directory again
$
```

Now move up a level and remove *memos*:

```
$ cd ..; rmdir memos       Change to parent and remove directory
$
```

To get rid of *letters*, you will have to use **rm -r** as **rmdir** will fail on *letters* which is not empty. The command:

```
$ rm -r letters          Remove files and directories recursively
$
```

will work its way down the directory structure, removing the files **mon** and **tue**, then the directories **personal**, **business** and finally their parent directory **letters**. Your file system should now be empty and back to where it started.

## 2.5  Command Language Interpreter

After the login procedure has been completed successfully, a program called the *shell* is activated on behalf of the user. It is in fact a command language interpreter that processes the command lines supplied by the user in response to the command prompt. In its simplest form, a command line is just a sequence of words separated by spaces or tabs. The first word is the name of the file that contains the command to be executed. The shell searches through a number of directories in a certain order (the *default search path*) and, when it finds the file, loads the command into memory and causes it to be executed. The remaining words on the command line become the arguments to the command. Thereafter, the user is in communication with the command until such time as it terminates whereupon control is returned to the shell and the prompt for a command is displayed once again. If the shell cannot find a file with the name supplied by the user, it outputs a failure message:

```
$ zzz                    An illegal command
zzz: not found
$
```

### 2.5.1  Input-Output Redirection

There are a number of special characters that may occur in the command line which the shell detects and which cause it to alter its normal mode of behaviour. The first of these is the character > which is used to redirect standard output  away from the terminal to a file. The command:

```
$ cat alpha > beta       Redirect standard output
```

will cause the contents of **alpha** to be copied to the file **beta** instead of the terminal. If the file **beta** did not exist, it would be created by the shell. The redirection symbol (>) and the following filename are interpreted by the shell and are not passed on to the command as arguments. The overall effect is simply to redirect standard output for the duration of the command. Notice that this mechanism provides a simple way of creating a file containing some information. Try the following command:

```
$ cat > lines              Create lines by output redirection
line 1
^D
$
```

This creates a file *lines* that contains the line read from the standard input device:

```
$ cat lines                Copy lines to standard output
line 1
$
```

Not all output produced by a command will be redirected in this manner, in particular, error output will still be sent to the terminal. Any information already in the file will be replaced by the new information. If, on the other hand, the user required the new information to be appended to the old, then :

```
$ cat >> lines             Append standard output to lines
line 2
^D
$
```

would do the trick, i.e. >> not only redirects output but also appends it to the existing contents of the file. Once again, if the file does not exist, it is created before the information is appended. Let's inspect *lines* again, this time by copying it to the terminal which in the example given below is *ttyj* (you should substitute your own terminal number that you obtained from the output of **who** or **tty** for *ttyj*):

```
$ cp lines /dev/ttyj       Copy lines to terminal
line 1
line 2
$
```

Suppose now you wanted to create a record in a file *reclog* of the users logged in at a particular time. The required sequence would be:

```
$ date  > reclog           Redirect standard output to reclog
$ who  >> reclog           And append standard output to it
$
```

Issue these commands and then **cat reclog** to inspect the output. It works but, on reflection, the sequence of commands is a little clumsy. Surely there is a better way and indeed there is! More than one command can be placed on a command line if each command is terminated by a semicolon. The last command of the line may be so terminated but it is not necessary since Ⓡ also signals the end of a command. So try:

```
$ date; who > reclog       Execute 2 commands in sequence
Wed Apr  4 08:38:02 EST 1984   Output from 1st command
$
```

Unfortunately, that's not what you wanted — only the output from **who** has gone to the file; the output from **date** still appears on the terminal. What you need to do is group these commands using parentheses:

```
$ (date; who) > reclog          Two commands in sequence
$                               with output redirection for both
```

An inspection of **reclog** will show that this has worked correctly. The output of **date** and **who** have been concatenated and the sequence of commands inside the parentheses can be thought of as behaving as a single command.

The > character will only cause redirection of standard output. Suppose that you wanted to redirect standard error output rather than standard output. To do this, you need to know that internally there is a number called a *file descriptor* associated with each file. The default values assigned by the shell to standard input/output are:

```
0       for standard input
1       for standard output
2       for standard error output
```

In the Bourne shell, the output redirection symbol may be preceded by an integer that causes output destined for that file to be diverted. The command:

```
$ cat lines xxxx 2> error        Redirect standard error output
line 1
line 2
$
```

would cause messages written to standard error output to be sent to the file **error** whilst standard output would appear on the terminal:

```
$ cat error                      List the file error
cat: cannot open xxxx
$
```

If standard output is to be redirected as well, then:

```
$ cat lines xxxx > out    2> error     Redirect output
$                                      and error output
```

would have the required effect, as would:

```
$ cat lines xxxx  1> out    2> error   An alternative
$
```

If both standard output and standard error output are to be merged and redirected to the same file, the required notation is:

```
$ cat lines xxxx > out    2>&1         Redirect output and
$                                      error output merged
```

The **&1** causes file descriptor 1 to be duplicated and the preceding digit **2** then causes standard output to be directed to the file associated with file descriptor 1, in this case, *out*. The net effect is to merge the two output streams onto *out*:

```
$ cat out                          List the file out
line 1
line 2
cat: cannot open xxxx
$
```

==================================================

The notation in the Berkeley C-Shell is slightly different to that described above. The redirection symbol > may not be preceded by an integer but the notation >& instructs the shell to send both standard output and standard error output to the same file. The same effect illustrated by the previous example could be achieved by:

```
% cat lines xxxx >& out           Redirect output and
%                                  error output merged
```

Notice that although the notation is simpler for the most commonly used effect, at first sight, it appears not to be possible in the C-shell to redirect standard output and standard error output to different files. However, there is a way:

```
% (cat xxxx lines > out) >& error    Redirect output to out
%                                     and error output to error
```

Now inspect *out* and *error*. The former will contain the two lines, the latter, the failure message. Why is this so? The reason is that, since any sequence of commands inside parentheses can be treated as a single command, both standard output and standard error output will be redirected to *error*. However, the parenthesized commands produce no standard output since that emanating from **cat** has already been redirected to *out*. All that is left in *error* is the standard error output of **cat**.

-----------------------------------------------------------------

Input redirection is produced by the character < which causes input to be read from a file instead of from the terminal. The command:

```
$ write njp < mess1        Read standard input from mess1
$
```

would cause the contents of the file *mess1* to be sent to the user **njp** as a message. Let's try it:

```
$ write yew < lines        Read standard input from lines

Message from yew (ttyj) [Fri Apr 6 10:10:54]...
line 1
line 2
EOF
$
```

Any command that reads from standard input can have its input redirected in this manner. This is a convenient facility if you intend to input a large amount of data to a command since you can first prepare it in a file and validate it prior to execution.

## 2.5.2  Pipes

Another special character detected by the shell is | which causes the standard output of the command on its left to become the standard input of the command on its right. This is called the *pipe* operator. (For historical compatibility, System V also treats ^ as equivalent to | for the pipe symbol.) The two commands connected by a pipe are called a *pipeline* which is illustrated by:

```
$ who | wc -l          Pipe output of who into wc
     12
$
```

The output of **who** is piped into **wc**, the **w**ord **c**ount command, which, because of the –l argument, outputs only a line count. The final output is therefore the number of users currently logged in. (We will discuss **wc** in more detail later in Chapter 5.)

Another example of a pipeline is:

```
$ ls -l | pg           Inspect large directory listing
```

This would enable you to look conveniently at the contents of a large directory. If the **ls** command were used on its own, once the screen was full, output would continue until the command stopped and you would not be able to examine the early entries unless you stopped the output in time with ^S. By piping the output of **ls** into **pg**, output will stop at the end of the first page and you can continue when you are ready.

The pipe is an extremely powerful and convenient feature in UNIX and one that you will use frequently. It enables data to flow from one command to another with the synchronization being organised by the operating system. In the first example given above, when **wc** has nothing to read, it is halted; conversely, when the pipe is full and can hold no more output, **who** is halted. The same effect, of course, could be achieved with the commands:

```
$ who > tempfile       Redirect output to tempfile
$ wc -l tempfile       Count lines in this file
     12
$ rm tempfile          Delete file
$
```

However, this is probably less efficient since it requires the information to be written to the temporary file before it is read. Subsequently, **tempfile** has to be removed.

Pipelines are not restricted to just two commands. The command line:

**$ who | sort | pg**          *Inspect sorted list of users logged in*

will output, under the control of **pg**, a list of users currently logged in, sorted in
alphabetical order. (**sort** will be described in detail in Chapter 5.) Naturally,
input redirection can be specified for the first command in the pipeline and output
redirection for the last one. In the Berkeley system, you would use **more** instead
of **pg** to peruse the output.

> **lp** - line printer spooler

Pipes provide a very convenient way of obtaining a hardcopy listing of the
output of any command that writes to standard output. The command:

**$ cat filea fileb 2>&1 | lp**    *Spool output for printing*
**$**

will produce a line printer listing of standard output merged with standard error
output. The command **lp** causes files named in its argument list to be queued for
printing. If no filenames are supplied, it reads from standard input. Such a
command is required in a multi-user environment to access a shared device,
otherwise, output from a number of users would become mixed up if they all tried
to write to the device simultaneously. This process of queuing output is often
referred to as *spooling*.

===============================================

> **lpr** - off line print

The Berkeley equivalent of **lp** is **lpr**. In this system, you can merge standard
output and standard error output through a pipe as follows:

**% cat filea fileb  |& lpr**    *Spool output for printing*
**%**

----------------------------------------------------------------

> **pr** - print file

Another example of the use of pipes involves the **pr** command which can be
used to organize the contents of a file into a particular format for printing. If no
files are specified in the argument list, the command reads from standard input.
Hence, rather than include a complicated output routine in every UNIX
command, a programmer can keep the output simple since it could be piped into
**pr** if a fancy output format is required.

To illustrate the use of **pr**, suppose you want to print the contents of a file
which contains some numbers, one per line, and that you need the output

arranged in 4 columns. Create a file *numbs* containing the numbers 1—13 each on a separate line and then execute the following command:

```
$ cat numbs | pr -4 -l1 -t        Output numbs in 4 columns
1                2                3                4
5                6                7                8
9                10               11               12
13
$
```

The desired output in columns has been produced. The options of **pr** used here are −**4** to specify four columns, −**l1** to specify that each page is to contain only one line and −**t** to suppress the output of header and trailer information normally produced for each page. We refer you to the glossary for a more complete description of the command and the various options. However, the simple example shows how easy it is to obtain output in columns for any command using a pipe.

Pipes can be used to avoid one consequence of output redirection that can sometimes be irritating, namely, you can't see what output is being produced until after the command has finished, at which time you would have to inspect the output file. Suppose, for example, you wanted to preserve in a file *users* a record of who is currently logged in. Then, to look at this information as well, the commands required would be:

```
$ who > users               Create file of current users
$ cat users                 And list it
jas       ttyh      Aug  5    11:53
yew       ttyj      Aug  5    10:56
$
```

```
tee - pipe fitting
```

By using the command **tee** in a pipe, you can arrange to send a copy of standard output to one or more files:

```
$ who | tee users          Create file of and list current users
jas       ttyh      Aug  5    11:53
yew       ttyj      Aug  5    10:56
$
```

**tee** is a useful little command for manipulating pipes since all it does is copy its input to one or more named files as well as to standard output. Of course, it can appear anywhere in a pipeline:

```
$ who | tee users | wc -l       Create file and output
        2                       count of current users
$
```

The file *users* will now contain the required record of the 2 users currently logged in.

### 2.5.3  Filename Substitution

Once you begin to use the system in earnest, you will soon find that the number of files you own will increase quite rapidly. While each filename must be unique, there will often be groups of files that have similar names, for example, the same suffix. Let us first create a number of files using **tee**:

```
$ tee a.c a.o b.c b.o c.c c.o    Create 6 files
^D
$
```

Now suppose you wanted to remove all the *.o* files. You could do so by typing:

```
$ rm a.o b.o c.o                 Remove 3 .o files
$
```

but if there were 26 such files, it would be a little tedious to have to type all those filenames. Fortunately, the shell provides a facility that enables you to avoid having to do this. You can simply type:

```
$ rm *.o                         As above but more conveniently
$
```

Try it and then check with **ls** that the files have disappeared. The character **\*** is a pattern that will match any character string (including the null string) in filenames in the current directory. You can think of it as being like a "wild card" in poker − it will match anything at all.

The character **\*** does not have to be placed at the beginning of a filename. It can occur anywhere. Thus:

```
$ cat chap*                      List all files whose names start with chap
```

will list all files in the current directory whose name starts with the letters **chap**. It can even be used on its own. The command:

```
$ rm *                           Remove all files in current directory
```

will remove all files in the current directory with the exception of those that start with a period. This is the one exception to the general rules for pattern matching. A **.** at the beginning of a filename must be matched explicitly. **ls** does not output these names unless specifically asked to do so. Hence, one can easily forget that they exist and the exception to the rule is required to ensure that no inadvertent matching takes place.

You should exercise extreme caution when using **rm \***, since you can quite easily delete files that you did not intend to remove. To be on the safe side, you might select the option of **rm** that allows you to delete each file interactively:

```
$ rm −i *                        Remove each file interactively
```

This will ask, for each file, whether you want to remove it or not. In fact, any use of a pattern containing **\*** with **rm** can be risky.

| echo - echo arguments |

A good idea is first to check just what filenames are generated by **\***. To do this, you can use the **echo** command that does nothing more than write its arguments separated by spaces and terminated by newline on standard output:

```
$ echo *.c                    List all filenames ending in .c
a.c b.c c.c
$
```

lists all the filenames generated and then, if you are satisfied, the **rm** command could be used.

There are other characters besides **\*** that cause filename expansion to take place. The character **?** matches any single character. For example:

```
$ tee prog.1 prog.2 prog.12 prog.16    Create 4 files
^D
$ ls prog.?          List 6-character filenames starting with prog.
prog.1 prog.2
$
```

All the files in the current directory commencing with the string **prog.** which have a single character suffix are listed.

Sometimes it would be convenient to be able to specify alternative characters explicitly. This is done by enclosing them in the square brackets [ and ]:

```
$ tee prog.a prog.b prog.c prog.f prog.p    Create 5 files
^D
$ ls prog.[pfc]              List entries for prog.p prog.f prog.c
prog.c prog.f prog.p
$
```

Only those files with a single character suffix *p*, *f* or *c* are listed. If a range of consecutive letters or digits is to be specified, it can be abbreviated by giving the first and last characters separated by a minus sign. The command:

```
$ ls prog.[a-c]              List entries for prog.a to prog.c
prog.a   prog.b   prog.c
$
```

will list the filenames which consist of *prog.* followed by one of the  suffixes *a*, *b* or *c*.

Well, let us see if you understand filename substitution by asking you what is output by the command:

```
$ ls [A-Z]*temp*[,.]??
```

Your answer should be "filenames in the current directory that commence with a capital letter, contain the character string **temp** and are terminated by two characters preceded by  . or  *,* ":

```
$ echo > Progtemp.1a          Create file
$ ls [A-Z]*temp*[,.]??        List directory entry
Progtemp.1a
$
```

Congratulations, if you got it right! If you did not, go back and read this section again.

## 2.5.4  Escaping and Quoting

So far you have learnt that the following characters have a special meaning to the shell:

    <  >  *  ?  [  ]  |  ^

They are called *metacharacters* to distinguish them from ordinary characters. The shell searches through a command line and when it encounters any one of these characters, it takes some special action. But let's suppose you wanted to input one of these characters as an argument to a command, i.e. you want to prevent the shell from carrying out that special action. Fortunately, the designers of the shell foresaw this possibility and provided an escape character. If any of the metacharacters is preceded by a backslash (\), it is treated as an ordinary character and no special action takes place:

```
$ echo \*                     Output asterisk
*
$
```

The command outputs * to the terminal rather than all the filenames in the current directory. Obviously, the escape character is also special and hence, if you wish to input the escape character as an ordinary character, you must use it to escape itself:

```
$ echo \\                     Output backslash
\
$
```

The command simply echoes backslash. But let's say you typed:

```
$ echo \                      An incomplete command line
>                             Shell is waiting for further input
```

terminating the command line as usual with **RETURN**. Try it and you will see that the terminal waits for you to do something more as indicated by the secondary shell prompt >. The **RETURN** is no longer treated as a signal that the command line is finished. In fact, it has been *escaped* and is ignored by the shell. You must continue, ultimately terminating the line with a **RETURN** that has not been escaped.

```
> hello                     Your input
hello                       echo responds
$
```

This is a particularly useful feature for inputting command lines that contain many arguments. On the screen, they may appear as separate lines providing each **RETURN**, except the last one, is preceded by a backslash.

There is a slight problem with using the backslash character to escape metacharacters, namely, for every character escaped, you have to type two characters. This would become a little tedious if you wanted to input a long string of metacharacters. The shell therefore provides another mechanism called *quoting* that enables such a string of metacharacters to be input easily.

If a string is enclosed in a matched pair of quotation marks, the metacharacters including blanks and tabs are not treated as special. Within a pair of quotes, a newline, preceded by \ is preserved as a newline. To illustrate these points, suppose the current directory contains the files *inv22*, *stage2* and *t4*, and that there are no other filenames that end in a digit:

```
$ rm *[0-9]                 Remove filenames ending in a digit
$ tee inv22 stage2 t4       Create 3 files
^D
$ echo *[0-9]               List filenames ending in a digit
inv22 stage2 t4
$
```

The command echoes the expected filenames whereas the command:

```
$ echo '*[0-9]'             Output *[0-9]
*[0-9]
$
```

does not — it just echoes the characters themselves. Further:

```
$ echo abc\                 An incomplete command line
> def                       You continue
abcdef                      echo responds
$
```

illustrates that **RETURN** has been ignored whereas:

```
$ echo 'abc\                An incomplete quoted string
> def'                      You complete quoted string
abc\                        String is echoed as input
def
$
```

shows that **RETURN** has been preserved by quoting, as has the backslash.

========================================================

The behaviour of the C-shell is slightly different to that described above for the standard shell. An escaped newline is treated as a blank while, within quotes, it remains as a newline:

```
% echo abc\            An incomplete command line
def                    You continue
abc def                Newline replaced by space
% echo 'abc\           An incomplete quoted string
def'                   You complete quoted string
abc                    Quoted newline is preserved
def
%
```

Notice that there is no secondary prompt in C-shell.

-------------------------------------------------------------------

There is another form of quoting provided by the shell using double quotes, but discussion of this will be put aside until later.

## 2.5.5  Shell Variables

The shell provides a facility whereby a name may be associated with a value which is simply a string of characters. Such a named object to which values may be assigned is called a *variable*. The name of a variable must start with a letter and be composed of only letters, digits and underscores. To assign a value to a variable, you use the = operator. If you execute:

```
$ me=yew                Assign yew to me
$
```

the string **yew** will be assigned to the variable **me**. Note that spaces are not permitted around the = operator.

### 2.5.5.1  *Variable Substitution*

To access the value of a shell variable, you use the variable name or identifier preceded by a $ sign. This is known as *variable substitution*. Let us try it by writing a message to yourself once again:

```
$ write $me             Argument is value of me

Message from yew (ttyj) [Mon Feb 27 10:22:14]...
^D
EOF
$
```

The shell detects the metacharacter $ and replaces it and the following identifier by the value of the variable.

As you will see later, shell variables are particularly useful in writing *shell scripts* or sequences of shell commands that are read from a file and obeyed by the shell. However, there are some simple uses that we can illustrate at this point. Suppose, for example, you wish to carry out a number of operations on files in a particular directory owned by someone else but it is not convenient to **cd** to it.

Then, you can assign the pathname to a variable and hence provide yourself with a shorthand notation for referencing that directory. If you execute:

```
$ p=/usr/staff/another/alpha        Assign pathname to p
$
```

a file *f1* in this directory can now be referenced as *$p/f1*. You have to be a little careful using this facility since you must ensure that the shell can determine what the variable name is. For example, if you had added an extra / to the value assigned to p and then referenced the file as *$pf1,* you would not have obtained the result you expected. The shell would have taken **pf1** as the variable name which has the null string as a value, that is, a string that contains no characters since the variable has never been initialized. To handle such a situation, it is necessary to enclose the variable name in curly brackets i.e. *${p}f1* is the appropriate notation.

To illustrate the use of this facility, suppose you create a variable h that contains the pathname of your home directory:

```
$ h=/usr/staff/yew        Assign home directory pathname to h
$
```

Then, irrespective of where you are in your own directory hierarchy, you can easily access any file or sub-directory. Try:

```
$ ls $h                   List your home directory
```

just to prove that it will list the files in your home directory.

========================================

| **set** - assign new values to shell variables |

The C-shell also provides variables but the syntax for assigning a value is slightly different. The **set** command is used as illustrated below:

```
% set h=/usr/staff/yew        Assign home directory pathname to h
%
```

Accessing the value of a variable is similar to that described above for the standard shell.

--------------------------------------------------------------------

For both shells, if no value is provided after =, the null string is assigned to the variable. In both 4.2 and V.2, a variable may be removed by using the **unset** command. (Note that this command is not available in earlier versions of the standard shell.)

### 2.5.5.2 *Command Substitution*

Another way of giving a value to a shell variable in either shell is to follow =
by a command enclosed in graves (`` ` ``).  The effect is to cause the command to be
executed and to assign its output to the variable:

```
$ dt=`date`                      Assign output of date to dt
$ echo $dt                       And echo value of dt
Mon Feb 27   09:06:23 EST 1984.
$
```

If the output of the command contains trailing  newlines, these are removed
before the string is assigned to the variable. The command may take arguments:

```
$ cf=`cat lines`                 Assign output of cat to cf
$ echo $cf                       And echo value of cf
line 1 line 2
$
```

The string line 1Ⓡline 2 has been assigned to the variable **cf**. The newline
has been replaced by a space in the output of **echo**.

The above process is called *command substitution* since, in fact, the command
and its arguments together with the enclosing graves are replaced in the input line
by the output of the command itself.  If `` ` `` or **$** occurs in a string enclosed
between single quotes, then they lose their special meaning and command
substitution or variable substitution do not take place.  However, if double quotes
(**"**) are used instead, these substitutions are performed but all other shell
metacharacters including single quotes are considered to have been escaped:

```
$ echo "$me ´* `cat lines`"
yew ´* line1 line2
$
```

### 2.5.5.3 *Special Shell Variables*

In addition to user-defined variables, there are a number of special variables
in the standard shell whose values may be predefined.  Some of these are read
only; others can be altered by the user.

**set** - list shell variables

At any time, you can see what shell variables have been set and what their
values are by using the **set** command without any arguments.  This works for
both shells.  Try this command on your system and, for the standard shell
assuming you have defined the variables given in the examples, you should see
something like the following:

```
$ set                              Output shell variables
HOME=/usr/staff/yew                Home directory name
IFS=                               Internal field separators

PATH=:./bin:/usr/staff/yew/bin:/bin:/usr/bin   Search path
PS1=$                              Primary prompt
PS2=>                              Secondary prompt
SHELL=/bin/sh                      Shell pathname
TERM=vc404                         Type of terminal
USER=yew                           Username
cf=line 1
line 2
dt=Mon Feb 27 09:06:23 EST 1984
h=/usr/staff/yew
me=yew
$
```

What you actually see will depend upon the way your system has been set up. By convention, shell variables with special significance have their identifiers spelt with capital letters. If you want to look at the value of just one or two variables, use the **echo** command:

```
$ echo $HOME $PS2   Output home directory and secondary prompt
/usr/staff/yew >
$
```

The shell variables of interest to us at the moment are:

HOME    which is set to the pathname of the user's home directory i.e. it is the default argument of the **cd** command. **cd** without an argument is equivalent to **cd $HOME**. So you see that you did not actually need to go to the trouble of defining the variable h as you did above − HOME is already provided for you.

IFS     which defines the *internal field separator* characters. These are the characters used by the shell to break a command line up into its component words. In the above example, the characters are space, tab and newline. You could assign these characters to IFS as follows:

```
$ IFS='  Ⓣ Ⓡ         Assign space, tab and newline to IFS
>  '
$
```

Notice the use of the quotes to protect the characters from immediate interpretation.

PATH    which defines the sequence of directories that are searched when a user issues a command. The directory names are separated by colons (:). The setting:

```
$ PATH=.:./bin:$HOME/bin:/bin:/usr/bin
$
```

specifies the following search path:

| | |
|---|---|
| . | current directory |
| ./bin | *bin* sub-directory of the current directory |
| $HOME/bin | *bin* sub-directory of the user's home directory |
| /bin | *bin* sub-directory of the root directory |
| /usr/bin | *bin* sub-directory of the *usr* sub-directory of the root directory |

The logic of this particular setting is that the shell first searches your current directory followed by its *bin* sub-directory. If it does not find the file where you are currently working, it then searches the *bin* sub-directory of your home directory where you would normally store commands that you have developed yourself. If it still has no luck, the shell searches for one of the system commands that are kept in */bin* and */usr/bin*. If this is not what you want, then change it. The path set by the command:

```
$ PATH=/bin:/usr/bin:$HOME/bin:./bin:.
$
```

would give preference to system commands over those that you have developed yourself. With the previous setting, you might have to exercise some care that you do not replicate the name of a system command. Note that a null value is interpreted as the current directory. Hence, the value of PATH output by the **set** command above is equivalent to the first example.

MAIL     which defines the file where your mail is accumulated. From time to time, the shell inspects this file and, if the file has been modified since the last time it looked, issues a message **You have mail**.

A typical setting for **yew** might be:

```
$ MAIL=/usr/mail/yew        Define your mail file
$
```

but you will have to check the conventions in operation on your system.

PS1     which defines the prompt string output by the shell. The default value is $. If you wanted to change this to something else such as **What now?**, you would have to reset the variable:

```
$ PS1='What now? '          Define primary prompt string
What now?
```

PS2     which defines the prompt string used by the shell when it expects more input after the initial line has been terminated. This variable has a default value of >.

TERM   which defines the type of terminal you are using. If you use the same
       terminal each time you login, it can be useful to set this variable so that
       various programs that format their own output can make effective use of
       the facilities available in the hardware. For example, if the command:

    **$ TERM=vc404**                *Define type of terminal*
    **$**

has been executed, the system knows that you are using a Volker-Craig
404 terminal and can act accordingly.

The initial values of these special variables are obtained from the
environment by the shell when it is invoked. The environment contains a list of
the variable names, each associated with a value. These are installation-
dependent and vary from one system to another. If you change the value of any
of these variables, the new value will only apply within the current invocation of
the shell. If you start up a new shell, the value of any special variable will revert
to the predefined one. Similarly, any variable that you define is local to the shell
in which it was created and initialized.

To illustrate these points, suppose you decide you want to change the prompt
character from **$** to **#** and define a variable **abc** to have a value **xyz**:

    **$ PS1='# '**                  *Define a new prompt character*
    **# abc=xyz**                *Assign value to* **abc**
    **# echo $abc**             *And output this value*
    **xyz**
    **#**

The change to the prompt character takes place immediately and the output of
the **echo** command illustrates that the variable has been set correctly. Now
invoke a new shell with the **sh** command and look at **abc** again:

    **# sh**                      *Invoke a sub-shell*
    **$ echo $abc**             *Output value of* **abc**
                                     *It has no value!*
    **$**

The new shell reverts to the default value for the prompt and the value of **abc** is
null.

---

        | **export** - mark variables for export |

---

It is not always convenient to obtain the default value of a shell variable
when a new shell is invoked. For example, having redefined the prompt character
to something that suits you, you may wish to stick with it for any further
invocation of the shell. Fortunately, the shell provides an **export** command that
enables you to define which variables are to be exported from the login shell to
any subsequent ones. To experiment with this facility, issue **^D** to exit from the

current shell back to the login shell and then indicate that PS1 and **abc** are variables to be exported:

```
$ ^D                    Return to the login shell
# export PS1 abc        And mark 2 variables for export
#
```

Now when you invoke a new shell, the values of these variables will be retained:

```
# sh                    Invoke a sub-shell
# echo $abc             And output value of abc
xyz                     Previous value has been retained
# ^D                    Return to login shell
# PS1='$ '              Redefine default prompt string
$
```

Obviously, the values of any redefined variables will be lost when you logout.

==================================================

| | |
|---|---|
| **setenv** | - change values of environment variables |
| **printenv** | - print values of environment variables |
| **unsetenv** | - remove variables from environment |

In the C-shell, environment variables may only be set via the **setenv** command. The **printenv** command outputs the current settings and the **unsetenv** command is used to remove variables:

```
% setenv TEST 67        Assign value to new environment variable
% printenv TEST         And print it
67
% unsetenv TEST         Assign null value to environment variable
% printenv TEST         And check its value
%
```

The **printenv** command in the absence of any arguments will output a list of the environment variables and their values while the **set** command performs the same function for ordinary shell variables. If you are using C-shell, try both of these commands. You will see in these lists variables that we have not discussed as yet as well as some that we have. Observe that the C-shell prompt is controlled by an ordinary variable called **prompt** rather than PS1 as it was for the standard shell. Notice also that there is a correspondence between some of the environment variables and some of the shell variables. The environment variables USER, TERM and PATH are set automatically from the shell variables **user**, **term** and **path** and hence one does not need to use **setenv** to define them.

## 2.5.6  C-shell History List

By default, the C-shell keeps a copy of the last command line input by a user. You can actually re-run the previous command by responding **! !** to the shell prompt. Suppose you wanted, for some reason or other, two copies of a file *lines* in another file *line2*. Then, assuming *line2* does not exist or is empty:

```
% cat lines >> line2        Append lines to line2
% !!                        And repeat previous command
cat lines >> line2
%
```

would produce the desired result. Notice that the shell echoes the previous command line before re-running it. Even better than merely executing the command line again, you can actually change it before it is re-run. Try the following sequence:

```
% cp /etc/mtd   .           Try to copy non-existent file
cp: /etc/mtd: No such file or directory
% ^mt^mot                   Correct previous command and execute it again
cp /etc/motd   .
%
```

The name of *motd* has been misspelt, **cp** cannot find a file called */etc/mtd* and says so. On the next line, the carets (ˆ) act as delimiters to two strings. The first is the string you want changed and the second is what you want it to be. The shell echoes the changed line and obeys it, this time successfully. Clearly, this can be a very useful facility since simple errors can be corrected easily and the whole line does not have to be retyped.

Sometimes, of course, you may want to re-run a command that was issued prior to the previous one, perhaps also with alterations. The C-shell enables you to do this since you can set it up to remember more than just the last command. To do this, you assign an integer value to a shell variable called **history** e.g.:

```
% set history=10           Define size of the history list
%
```

Now, the shell will retain the last 10 command lines.

```
┌─────────────────────────────────┐
│ history - print history list    │
└─────────────────────────────────┘
```

You can inspect the contents of the history list at any time by issuing the **history** command:

```
% history                  Inspect contents of history list
   5 set history=10
   6 history
%
```

Each command line is numbered and the numbers you see will depend on how many  commands you have already obeyed in this session. Also, in some systems, the **history** variable is set automatically immediately after login has taken place. You may see more commands in the list than we have shown when you issue the **history** command. Since it is possible to look at what you have already done during a session, the history mechanism removes some of the disadvantages of using a VDU as a "glass" teletype compared with a hardcopy terminal.

To re-run a previous command, you make use of **!** as a metacharacter. Suppose that you have the following history list:

```
21 ls
22 write adj
23 who
24 pwd
```

The current event is therefore 25 and, to re-run event 22, you can use any one of the following:

```
!22     !-3     !wr     !?it?
```

The first gives an absolute event number, the second, a relative one, the third, the character string that starts the command line and the fourth, a character string (enclosed in question marks) that occurs somewhere within a command line. In the last two instances, the shell searches backwards through the history file so that **!w** would have re-run **who** rather than **write**. To help you remember what the current event is without having to consult the history list all the time, it is possible to produce the event number as part of the shell prompt by including it in the prompt string:

```
% set prompt='-\!- '                Define new prompt string
-26-
```

Notice that you had to quote the **!** with a **\** to prevent its immediate interpretation in the current command line. To re-run a previous command with corrections, it is first necessary to select the event and then specify some change. The command:

```
-26- !22:s/dj/mce/         Replace dj by mce in event 22 and re-run
write amce
```

would select event 22 from the history list, substitute **mce** for **dj** and then re-run the command. The string enclosed between the first pair of slashes is the one to be replaced, that between the second and third slash is the replacement string. Clearly, the facility is only useful if the amount of typing required in making the change is less than that required to retype the whole command line again.

Parts of a previous command may be extracted and incorporated into the current control line using the history substitution mechanism. For example, **!$** is replaced by the last argument of the previous command while **!*** is replaced by all of its arguments. To illustrate the use of this facility, suppose you have a number of files that you think are empty but you want to make sure before you remove them. Then:

```
% cat alpha beta gamma          Inspect 3 files
% rm !*                         Then remove them
rm alpha beta gamma
%
```

would produce the desired result. If, on the other hand, some other command were interposed between **cat** and **rm**, then **rm !-2:\*** would have been required to remove the files. The  : separates the event specifier from the designator that indicates which parts of the previous line are to be re-used.

There are many more facilities in the history substitution mechanism than are discussed here and the interested reader is referred to the documentation on the C-shell.

----------------------------------------------------------------------------

## SUMMARY

(Facilities only available in the Berkeley system and C-shell are marked with □)

- To access UNIX, supply your username to the **login** prompt, then your password if requested.

- Use the **passwd** command to change your password from time to time.

- The command language interpreter by default prompts for command lines with **$** if the Bourne shell or **%** if the C-shell.

- A command line consisting of the name of a command perhaps followed by one or more arguments separated by white space must be terminated by typing **RETURN**.

- The default behaviour of many commands may be modified by supplying an argument consisting of one or more characters preceded by a minus sign.

- Commands which require arguments will sometimes output usage details if no arguments are supplied.

- Typing errors may be corrected by hitting the erase key (usually ^**H** or **BACKSPACE**) to delete the previous character or the kill key (usually **@** or ^**X**) to throw away the current line.

- Terminal output is halted by hitting ^**S** and restarted with ^**Q**.

- A command may be aborted by hitting the interrupt key (usually **DELETE** or **RUBOUT**).

- The end-of-file signal is usually ^**D** which will terminate input to a command or log you out if supplied to the login shell.

- To determine the characteristics of your terminal and reset them if you wish, use **stty**.

- To find out in detail how a command works, use **man**.

- Use **who** to discover who is currently using the system and **write** to send messages to other users.

- The file system is a collection of ordinary files (binary or character information), special files (the input-output devices connected to the system) and directories which contain the filenames of other files.

- The structure of the file system is that of a tree with the base directory called *root*.

- The directory in which a user is placed after login is called the home directory and is therefore the initial current working directory.

- The pathname of a file relative to a particular directory is formed by concatenating with slash separators the directory entries that must be traversed to locate the file.

- The full pathname of a file is a slash followed by its pathname relative to the root directory.

- Associated with each file is a set of permissions which determine whether the owner or group of users or all users may read, write or execute the file.

- To list the contents of a directory, use **ls**, the most commonly used options of which are **l** for a long format, **a** for all files and **d** for directory details.

- The shorthand name of the current directory is **.** while **..** is the name of its parent directory.

- Use **pwd** to print the name of your current working directory.

- Use **cd** to change to the directory whose name is given as the argument; if no argument is supplied, **cd** will return you to your home directory.

- To examine the contents of a character file use **cat**, **more** (4.2) or **pg** (V.2).

- To examine the beginning or end of a character file, use **head** (4.2) or **tail**.

- Use **tty** to output the pathname of your terminal.

- The null device is called */dev/null* and acts as a sink for output.

- Use **cp** to copy existing files to create new ones and **rm** to remove files.

- To change permissions on a file or directory, use **chmod** which accepts either symbolic or absolute values for the new mode.

- The default file creation mask may be examined or reset using **umask**.

- A file may be renamed using **mv**.

- Use **mkdir** to create a directory and **rmdir** to remove an empty directory.

- To remove directories and files recursively, use **rm −r**.

- A file may have more than one directory entry and these are referred to as links.

- A file is only physically removed from the file system when its link count becomes 0.

- Use **du** to determine how much disk space you are using and give you some idea of the structure of your file system.

- Standard output may be redirected to a file using the > metacharacter.

- If >> is used instead of >, standard output will be appended to the file.

- To redirect standard input, use the shell metacharacter <.

- Use ; to separate commands on the same command line and enclose them in parentheses if you want them to behave as a single command.

- The file descriptors for standard input, standard output and standard error output are 0, 1 and 2 respectively.

- Use **2>** to redirect standard error output and **2>&1** to merge in standard output in the Bourne shell.

□ In the C-shell, the notation **>&** causes standard output and standard error output to be merged and redirected.

- In a pipe, the standard output of the command on the left of the metacharacter | becomes standard input to the command on the right.

- There may be more than one pipe in a command line.

- Use **lp** or **lpr** (4.2) to spool output for printing on a line printer.

- **pr** is a useful command for formatting output into columns.

- The pipe fitting command **tee** writes its output to one or more files as well as to standard output.

- To reference one or more files conveniently in a command line, use the shell metacharacter * which matches 0 or more characters, ? which matches a single character and [ ] which groups alternative characters and ranges of the form **a−z**.

- Use \ to escape a metacharacter and turn it into an ordinary character.

- Any string of characters including white space and metacharacters which is enclosed in single quotes (´*string*´) is not processed by the shell in any way and is simply passed on to the command as an argument.

- Shell variables may be created and values assigned using the = operator in the standard shell or **set** in the C-shell.

- A shell variable may be accessed from a command line by preceding its name with the metacharacter $ which causes $*name* to be replaced by the value of the variable in a process known as variable substitution.

- If a command with its arguments is enclosed between graves in a command line (` *command args* `), it will be executed by the shell and the output of the command used to replace the graves and the enclosed string in a process known as command substitution.

- Any string of characters enclosed in double quotes (*"string"*) is not processed by the shell except for variable substitution (**$**) and command substitution (` ` `).

- To output a list of shell variables and their values, use **set** without any arguments.

- The environment is a list of variables that is passed to a program to be executed in much the same way as arguments.

- To add variables to the environment of the standard shell, mark them as such using **export**.

- To remove variables from the standard shell, use **unset**.

□ In the C-shell, use **setenv** to assign a value to a new or existing environment variable, **printenv** to output the value of an environment variable and **unsetenv** to remove an environment variable.

□ To activate the C-shell history list, assign an integer value to the variable `history`.

□ Use **history** to inspect the history list.

□ Use `!!` to re-run the previous command and `!n` to re-run event *n*.

□ To alter and then re-run the previous command, use `^str1^str2` to change *str1* to *str2* in the command line.

*Chapter 3*

# EDITING

Now that you are familiar with the file system in UNIX and have created some of your own files using **cat**, you will want to find a more convenient way of doing this. UNIX provides a direct and easy method of creating files. You may type your own program, essay or letter straight into a file, using what is called an *editor*. While the UNIX editor is similar to its human counterpart, in that it can be used to change already established text, it can also be used to create text.

In this section we will be teaching you how to use two popular editors, **ed** and **vi**. It is important that you work through all the exercises and do some of your own experimenting. Rome wasn't built in a day and the only way to get the most out of your editor is to put in a lot of time and practice at the terminal. After you have learnt the basics, you should start giving your editor some real work straight away. Don't be afraid to tackle something complicated and long; that's the best way to come to grips with the more sophisticated commands which can speed up mundane corrections immensely. Editing can be quite fun in itself, especially with **vi**, where the possibilities are almost limitless. Even after you've been using **vi** for a long time, you'll still be discovering new and wonderful things to do with it. Sounds like a game doesn't it — actually, this is a surprisingly good analogy for editing in UNIX.

Before we start the games, it is probably a good idea to understand some of the theory behind the UNIX editors since it might save you some heartbreak in the future. To begin with, we will create some new files. However, after you have been working with UNIX for a while, you will probably have a well established collection of files and directories — it is amazing how they pile up after you realize how useful they are for storing programs, games and whatever else happens to be your particular interest. When you access a file you already own for an editing session, the original file is left untouched. This is one of the useful precautionary measures taken by UNIX to ensure that it isn't too easy for you to lose or destroy a file. When you are editing a file with **ed** or **vi**, UNIX creates a copy of the original which it keeps in a temporary workspace called a *buffer*. All the changes you make to the file during the editing session will be made to the copy in the buffer. Before you terminate the editing session, you must issue a specific command to copy the contents of the buffer back to the file, thereby overwriting it. If, on the other hand, you decide at any time that you don't want to preserve the changes you have made to the buffer, then it is possible to exit from the editor without overwriting the previous contents of the file. All this may sound a little confusing at this stage but it will become clearer as you gain familiarity with the editors and appreciate the advantages of using a file buffer.

Well, that's your major theory lesson for this section, although there will be more later on the workings of the individual editors. We will start by learning how to use **ed**, which is the most widely available of the UNIX editors. Also, once you have learnt how to handle **ed**, you will find **vi** a lot easier and quicker to master since it contains another editor **ex** which has commands and facilities very similar to those of **ed**. Once you are familiar with **ed**, you can easily convert to **ex**. However, if you are really itching to tackle **vi** and feel you are up to it, we would still advise you to read through the section on **ed** first, without doing the exercises, as references will be made later to some of its similarities with **vi**.

## 3.1  A Line-Oriented Editor

> **ed** - text editor

In **ed**, there are two major modes of editing. These are called *command mode* and *text input mode*. When you first enter **ed**, you will be placed in command mode. You can then issue one of a number of commands. Most of these will return you to command mode when they have completed their task. However, there are three commands which will switch you into text input mode and allow you to type in new text from the keyboard until you indicate that you have finished text input and wish to return to command mode.

The main feature of **ed** which distinguishes it from **vi** is that it is a line-oriented editor. Sometimes it can be frustrating not to be able to work with a large block of text as you can with a page from an essay. However, some people feel it simplifies things to work with only one line at a time. Furthermore, **ed** does have facilities which allow you to obtain an overview of the file and it is possible to use *global* commands which operate on the whole file or large sections of it. The best advice we can give you here is "know your editor well" so that you can use it to maximum potential.

### 3.1.1 Entering ed

Well, let's start by creating some text so that you have something with which to experiment. You should be sitting in front of a terminal connected to UNIX, logged in and ready to go. Make a directory *edex* in your home directory and change to it:

```
$ mkdir edex; cd edex      Make directory and change to it
$
```

Now type:

```
$ ed rogue                 Initiate the editor
```

to invoke the editor, which will respond with something like:

```
?rogue
```

The `?rogue` means that there is no file called *rogue* in your current directory, but **ed** is prepared to create one for you as soon as you tell it to do so.

The editor is now ready to accept commands. Notice that it does not output a prompt automatically. However, you can make it prompt with ∗ in System V by issuing the **P** command:

```
P                          Turn on prompt
*
```

If you get tired of the prompt at any time, you can also turn it off by using **P** again. In this book, we will use ∗ as the prompt character so that you can see clearly what you are expected to type.

If you don't like ∗ as a prompt and want to choose another character, you can do so in the V.2 version of **ed** by using the −p option:

```
$ ed -p \> rogue           Initiate ed with > as a prompt
?rogue
>
```

Here, we have chosen > as the prompt but notice that it had to be escaped in the command line since it is a shell metacharacter. Some versions of **ed** actually generate > automatically as a prompt; other versions contain no prompting facilities at all.

As a note of explanation, *rogue* is a game which is available on UNIX and may well be around on your system. This game has been the downfall of many a person coming into contact with UNIX and is well known for its addictive qualities. Some of the text you will be typing into this file will give you an idea of what the game involves and will probably whet your appetite to try it out. If you have ever played Dungeons and Dragons, you will realize that **rogue** is based on the same principles, only in this case, the computer acts as the dungeon master.

### 3.1.2  Creating a File

To change the editor from command to text input mode, you can give it one of three commands to append, change or insert text. We will use **a** to begin a new file, as it *appends* lines. The cursor should be positioned next to the prompt character, waiting for your fingers to bring it to life in the creation of some new text. Remember, if you make a mistake, just backspace over it and start again. When you reach the end of the line, hit **RETURN** to begin a new line. If you discover too late that you have made some drastic mistakes, don't be too upset as you should soon be proficient enough with **ed** to fix them for yourself. In any case, the following text contains some deliberate mistakes and total nonsense which we will be correcting later. We would like you to type it exactly as it appears in this book. First type **a** next to the prompt (which we will show in our examples but you should ignore just as you did the **$** shell prompt) and hit **RETURN**:

```
*a                          Enter append mode
                            ed is waiting for new text
```

The cursor should be at the beginning of a new line. The editor is now in text input mode. You can type in lines of text, as many or as few as you like. When you have finished, you type a single dot (.) at the beginning of a line. When you hit **RETURN**, the editor will go back to command mode. This is the way of telling **ed** that you have finished typing in the text. Enough explanations, let's give those itching fingers of yours something to work with. Remember to hit **RETURN** when you wish to start a new line (i.e. when we have started a new line in the example):

```
Yew have just started a game of rogue.
Yewr goal is to grab as much food as yew can,
find the Amulet of Yendor,
and get out of the Dungeons of Danger dead.
On the screen, a map of where yew have been
and what yew have been
on the sultana dungeon level is kept.
As yew explode more of the level,
it appears on the screen behind of yew.
.                          Terminate text input mode
*                          And return to command mode
```

The editor should return to command mode now with its prompt displayed. That should be enough text for a start.

### 3.1.3  Leaving ed

If you run out of time while doing these examples and wish to come back to them later, it is important to know how to write out a file with the **w** command and quit from the editor using the **q** command. Now let's try typing:

```
   *w                              Write edit buffer to file
```
The editor should respond with:
```
   335                             No. of characters in file
   *
```
which means that you have just created a new file on the disk containing 335 characters. If the output from your editor doesn't agree with ours, don't worry — you've probably made a few of your own mistakes and that is something that will happen from time to time! Anyway, the response should be a number fairly close to 335.

Before you go any further, we had better explain that **ed** has its own little way of complaining if you give it a command which it does not recognize or understand. For example, if you were to type:
```
   *y                              An illegal command
```
which has no meaning to **ed**, it will respond with a question mark:
```
   ?                               ed's cryptic response
   *
```
Perhaps one of **ed**'s infamous faults is its terseness for it will give no indication of exactly what it is that you have done wrong. However, in System V, you can type **h** to get an explanation of the most recent query diagnostic or **H** to enter help mode in which explanations are generated automatically. If you have this facility available, let's turn it on so that you will get error messages subsequently:
```
   *H                              Enter help mode
   unknown command                Explanation of previous ?
   *
```
Most versions of **ed** will respond with a **?** if you try to quit without writing out the file. Thus, the session may appear as follows:
```
   *q                              Try to quit
   ?                               ed queries your command
   warning: expecting `w´
   *w                              Write edit buffer to file
   335                             Number of characters in file
   *q                              Quit
   $                               You are back in the shell
```
**q** stands for *quit* and will take you back to the UNIX shell which will output its prompt. If you have already written out the file, **ed** will make no complaints if you try to quit and one **q** will be sufficient to end the editing session. If you have not written out the file and have no desire to (perhaps it contains too many mistakes and you've decided to retype it or else you may have made some changes to an old file and decided not to keep them after all), **ed** is not too stubborn and can be coerced into quitting. Thus:

```
*q                           Try to quit
?                            But you really mean it
warning: expecting `w´
*q                           Quit
$
```

will get the message through. Alternatively, you can pre-empt **ed**'s questioning by typing:

```
*Q                           Quit without any argument
$
```

which is a strong way of saying you want to quit regardless. **ed** won't argue at all. On the other hand, it is also a rather dangerous way of ending an editing session and we would not recommend that you make a habit of it. Try to be patient with **ed**'s quibbling and, more often than not, you'll be glad of it. It is surprisingly easy to make horrible mistakes when editing files. The other problem with making typing mistakes and not noticing them before you hit **RETURN** is that you may inadvertently choose a character or sequence of characters which *do* mean something to **ed**, but not what you intended them to mean. Hopefully you won't make this mistake until you are better acquainted with **ed**, and usually it should be fairly easy to correct your error. Until you are more familiar with the other **ed** commands, do be careful to watch what you are typing. On the other hand, you may be lucky enough to have somebody nearby who can answer your questions and help you if you make any mistakes. But let's see if we can get by alone.

You should have written your file by now and discovered how many characters it contains. You may have even tried quitting from the editor already. If you have not, then do so. You will then be back in the shell where you can have a look at what you have typed using **cat**, **more** or **pg**. As you can see, there are lots of mistakes that require your immediate attention. Notice also that the line containing the single dot which terminated your input does not appear in the file.

### 3.1.4 Moving Around the Text

If you want to correct those mistakes, you will have to bring the editor to life again and locate the lines containing the errors. You invoke **ed** just as you did the first time:

```
$ ed rogue                   Initiate the editor again
335
P                            You turn on prompting
*H                           Enter help mode
*
```

only this time the editor should respond with the number of characters in the file *rogue*, since this file already exists. Remember that any changes you make during this editing session are being made to a copy of the original file in the buffer. These changes will not be made to the original copy until and unless you write the file again using **w**. If you quit without writing, the changes will be discarded. In fact, you might consider discarding the corrections the first time round so that you can go through the exercises a second time to practise them. However, that is only a suggestion for the enthusiastic who wish to master **ed** as quickly as possible. If you haven't the patience to repeat the exercises we give you, it's no great loss as practice will come with time of its own accord.

Another thing you might do is make a copy of *rogue* as it stands at the moment. If you want to repeat the exercises or get hopelessly lost when you come to modify the file, you won't have to type the text in again. To make a copy, just use **w** supplying a filename as an argument:

```
*w roguecopy              Make a copy of rogue
335
*
```

This command won't change the name of the file you're editing which you can check on at any time by using the **f** command:

```
*f                        Print current filename
rogue
*
```

We will start by having another look at the file using **ed**'s printing facilities:

```
*1,$p                     Print all lines in the file
```

**ed** should now respond by printing the first through to the last line on the screen. Now let's take a look at what you did. **ed** commands have a general format which may contain from one to three parts:

   i)    *address(es)*
   ii)   *command*
   iii)  *parameter(s)*

The *address* references the line(s) you wish to modify or examine. In the above example, you addressed lines **1** through to **$** which is another way of saying "the last line in the file" and is one of several characters in **ed** which have a special meaning. A single character *command* could be a request to **ed** to print or delete the aforesaid lines. There are many different commands in **ed** other than the ones we have just mentioned. A list of the more frequently used commands is shown in Table 3.1. In the above example, you used the print command **p** to display the text in the file. The *parameter* contains additional information for the command such as the details of a substitution of some characters for others. However, you will not be using any parameters just yet and the substitute command comes a little later in the section. For the moment, you will learn how to move around in the file.

| Table 3.1 | | | |
|---|---|---|---|
| **Command** | **Function** | **Command** | **Function** |
| **a** | *append* | **l** | *list* |
| **c** | *change* | **m** | *move* |
| **d** | *delete* | **n** | *number* |
| **e** | *enter* | **p** | *print* |
| **f** | *file* | **q** | *quit* |
| **g** | *global* | **r** | *read* |
| **h** | *help* | **s** | *substitute* |
| **i** | *insert* | **t** | *transcribe* |
| **j** | *join* | **u** | *undo* |
| **k** | *mark* | **w** | *write* |

### 3.1.4.1  *Location by Line Numbers*

Just as the first and the last lines of the file have addresses (1 and $), so too do the rest of the lines in the file. If you look at the file, you will be able to count the number of lines in it. Alternatively, in some versions of **ed**, you could list the file again with the **n** command which outputs a line number on the left for each line. Let's suppose you want to print out the line which contains the word **Amulet**, that's the third line:

    **\*3**                  *Print line 3*

**ed** will respond by typing out a single line of text:

    `find the Amulet of Yendor,`
    `*`

Now let's have a look at the first line:

    **\*1**                  *Print line 1*
    `Yew have just started a game of rogue.`
    `*`

and the last line:

    **\*$**                *Print the last line*
    `it appears on the screen behind of yew.`
    `*`

and back to the third line:

    **\*3**                  *Print line 3*
    `find the Amulet of Yendor,`
    `*`

Before we go any further, we will have to introduce you to a new concept — the *current line*.

As we explained before, **ed** is a line-oriented editor which means that normally you can only work on one line at a time, although there are ways around this. The line you choose becomes the *current line* and may subsequently be referenced by the address **.** ("dot"). To determine the line number of the current line, you can use the = command. Thus:

     **\*.=**                    *Print line number of current line*
     **3**
     **\***

tells us that 3 is the current line number. You can always find out where the editor has focussed its attention by typing this simple command. If you type:

     **\*1,\$p**                 *Print all lines in file*

the last line of the file will become the current one and the value of **.** will be 9:

     **\*.=**                    *Print line number of current line*
     **9**
     **\***

If you give the editor a command without an address, it will assume the current line is the one you are addressing. Thus:

     **\*p**                    *Print the current line*
     **it appears on the screen behind of yew.**
     **\***

will now print out the last line of the file since this is the current line.

Now type:

     **\*1**                    *Make line 1 the current line and print it*
     **Yew have just started a game of rogue.**
     **\***

to return to the first line of the file which is now the current line. Then type:

     **\*.+1p**               *Make the next line the current line and print it*
     **Yewr goal is to grab as much food as yew can,**
     **\***

that is, print out the next line after **.**, and make that the current line. Next type:

     **\*.+1**               *A shorter version of the previous command*
     **find the Amulet of Yendor,**
     **\***

and you will find that the **p** command is not needed to cause the current line to be printed. In fact, you could type:

     **\*+1**                *An even shorter one*
     **and get out of the Dungeons of Danger dead.**
     **\***

leaving out the **.** and you will see the same effect again. Okay, so you really want to be lazy, then try:

```
*+                          It's getting smaller all the time
On the screen, a map of where yew have been
*
```

As you can see, **ed** is very easy to get on with when it comes to abbreviating these more mundane commands for moving through a file. If you return to the first line now:

```
*1                          Go back to line 1 and print it
Yew have just started a game of rogue.
*
```

and try hitting **RETURN** repeatedly, you will be able to move through the file, line by line, until you reach the last of them. If you get bored doing this, throw in a few of the equivalent commands. If you hit **RETURN** after the last line, **ed** will complain with a ? in the usual way with a diagnostic message 'line out of range'. When you reach the last line, try typing:

```
*$-1p                       Print penultimate line in file
As yew explode more of the level,
*
```

Can you guess what follows? Yes, you can move backwards too and be just as lazy with your minuses as you were with your pluses. Try some of the abbreviations yourself and see if − behaves the same way as +:

```
*-2                         Back 2 lines
and what yew have been
*-                          And another 1
On the screen, a map of where yew have been
*.-3                        And another 3
Yewr goal is to grab as much food as yew can,
*
```

If you want to get a bit more sophisticated with your line numbers, try the following commands:

```
*+3                         3rd line after current line
On the screen, a map of where yew have been
*$-2                        3rd last line
on the sultana dungeon level is kept.
*++                         2nd line after current line
it appears on the screen behind of yew.
*2,4p                       lines 2,3 and 4
Yewr goal is to grab as much food as yew can,
find the Amulet of Yendor,
and get out of the Dungeons of Danger dead.
*--                         2nd line before current line
Yewr goal is to grab as much food as yew can,
```

```
*-,+p                            Print from previous to next line
Yew have just started a game of rogue.
Yewr goal is to grab as much food as yew can,
find the Amulet of Yendor,
*                                Next line
and get out of the Dungeons of Danger dead.
*
```

The combinations are virtually unlimited, but become a little tiresome after a while, so let's move on to other methods of finding your way around a file.

### 3.1.4.2  *Location by Marks*

If you find it tedious to remember line numbers, **ed** will allow you to mark a line with **k***x* where *x* is any single lower case letter.  The address ´*x* may then be used to reference the line subsequently. Thus:

```
*2                               Locate line 2
Yewr goal is to grab as much food as yew can,
*ka                              And mark it as line a
*$                               Make last line the current line
it appears on the screen behind of yew.
*´a                              And return to line marked a
Yewr goal is to grab as much food as yew can,
*$                               Make last line the current line
it appears on the screen behind of yew.
*´a-                             Line before line marked a
Yew have just started a game of rogue.
*´a+3                            3rd line after line marked a
On the screen, a map of where yew have been
*
```

### 3.1.4.3  *Location by Context*

So far you have only been working with a very small file and have not had any difficulty in counting the number of lines in the file.  However, you will soon find yourself editing much larger files where it would be ridiculously time consuming to have to know the line number of each line in the file.  Even the marking facility won't help you very much.  It is for this reason that *context searching* is perhaps the most useful facility in **ed**.

Let us suppose that you wanted to find again the line containing the word Amulet.  You could list your file and see that it is the third line, as you did previously; but with this new facility at your finger tips, all you need to know is that the line contains the word for which you are searching.  So try typing:

```
*/Amulet/                        Locate line containing Amulet and print
find the Amulet of Yendor,
*
```

**ed** responds in exactly the same way as when you typed:

```
*3                              3 is the current line
find the Amulet of Yendor,
*▒
```

Now let's have a look at what you have done. You have in fact used another valid form of an address in just the same way as you did previously with integers. The most commonly used form of address for context searching is a pair of slashes enclosing a string of characters which is referred to as a *pattern* or *search string*. The pattern matches a sequence of characters in a line and hence addresses the line. The pattern could be a word, a number, several words or some combination of characters. You will learn later that there are a certain characters with special meanings to **ed** which can be very useful in context searching. For now, try typing:

```
*/xx/                    Try locating non-existent pattern
?
search string not found
*▒
```

**ed** will respond with its usual question mark (and failure message if the help facility is available). This means that it has searched for the pattern **xx** in the text, but has not found it. You should be worried if it does find something as you know your file does not contain such a string. Since line 3 was the current line when you asked **ed** to search for something that did not exist, it will return to that line after the unsuccessful search. Check this by typing:

```
*.=                      Print current line number
3
*▒
```

You are probably wondering what happens if there is more than one occurrence of the pattern you are searching for in the file. Well let's see:

```
*/yew/                   Locate line containing yew and print
```

This command will search forwards through the file from the current line for the first occurrence of **yew**. In this case:

```
On the screen, a map of where yew have been
```

since your current line was the one containing **Amulet** when you issued this command. If this is not the line you wanted, there is a way of repeating the search without having to type it out in full again. Try typing:

```
*//                      Locate next line containing pattern and print
and what yew have been
*▒
```

This is the next line containing **yew**. Hence, a null pattern is interpreted as the last one used. Now keep repeating your search until you come full circle to:

```
On the screen, a map of where yew have been
```

As you see, the search loops back to the beginning of the file when it reaches the last line in the file and can go no further. In System V, it is possible to abbreviate `//` to `/` when repeating a search. However, in other versions, if you leave off the last slash, **ed** will not understand you at all. Always check that you have formulated your commands correctly before you start tearing your hair out in the belief that **ed** has lost some of your file.

Sometimes it is quicker to search backwards through the file for a pattern, especially if you know it is only a few lines back but you can't remember exactly how many. This is done by replacing the slashes with question marks:

```
*?yew?              Search backwards for line containing yew
Yewr goal is to grab as much food as yew can,
*
```

This is, in fact, the first occurrence of **yew** in your file. If you repeat the backward search:

```
*??                 Search backwards for next line containing yew
it appears on the screen behind of yew.
*
```

**ed** will respond by printing the last occurrence in the file. So you see that `//` and `??` work in exactly the same manner, except in opposite directions through the file. `??` may even be abbreviated to `?` on some systems. The other useful and interesting thing about these two commands is that they are interchangeable. Try typing:

```
*?level?            Search backwards for line containing level
As yew explode more of the level,
*
```

This command will search backwards for **level**. Repeat the search in the same direction:

```
*??                 Repeat previous search backwards
on the sultana dungeon level is kept.
*
```

Now repeat the same search forwards:

```
*//                 Repeat previous search forwards
As yew explode more of the level,
*
```

and you are back where you started.

Before you can start to use **ed** with any great proficiency, you will have to learn that there are a few characters that have very special meanings to the editor and cannot be used without great care. Before you get too worried about what new monsters we are springing on you now, think back to the metacharacters of the UNIX shell. In fact, many of the characters are the same as those which have special meanings in the shell. However, they do not necessarily have the same meanings as their counterparts. It is possible to see similarities but, on the whole, it is probably a good idea to keep them quite separate in your mind. You will be able to see the differences for yourself as you work through the examples.

The characters which have a special meaning to **ed** when used in a pattern are listed in Table 3.2 with their names and effects.

| Table 3.2 | | |
|---|---|---|
| **C** | **Name** | **Function** |
| ^ | caret | *Match beginning of line* |
| $ | dollar | *Match end of line* |
| . | dot | *Match any single character* |
| * | star | *Repetition of previous match* |
| [ | left square bracket | *Open alternatives* |
| ] | right square bracket | *Close alternatives* |
| \ | backslash | *Escape* |

The caret, dollar, dot, star and square brackets are all used in pattern matching. The backslash is used to escape the special meaning of all these characters, including itself.

Now, let us have a look in more detail at what effect each of these metacharacters has. ^ matches the non-existent 0th character in a line. For example, if you were to type:

    **\*?^an?**                    *Search backward for* **an** *at start of line*
    **and what yew have been**
    **\***

**ed** will search backwards for the first occurrence of **an** at the beginning of a line. If you had not included ^ at the beginning of the pattern, **ed** would have found the line:

    **on the sultana dungeon level is kept.**

instead.

Similarly, **$** will match the character after the last character in a line. It is the end of line character, the opposite of ^. Now type:

    **\*/en$/**                     *Search forward for* **en** *at end of line*
    **On the screen, a map of where yew have been**
    **\***

You see that the pattern that you are searching for is in the end position. If you had not included **$** in the pattern, the search would have located the line:

    **it appears on the screen behind of yew.**

instead of the one you wanted.

Now that you are equipped with both `^` and `$`, you can try typing:

```
*/^$/
?
search string not found
*
```

Can you guess what you have just searched for? The beginning of the line followed immediately by an end of line character constitutes a blank or null line. As you know, this file contains no blank lines and, hence, **ed** responds with a query since it cannot find what you have specified.

The metacharacter `.` can be very useful since it  will match exactly one character, which can be any character. For example:

```
*/^.$/                      Locate line consisting of a single character
```

will match the next line containing a single character and nothing else. It could be a line containing a number or a letter or even a special character such as  . itself. Now type:

```
*/f..d/                     Locate f, any 2 characters, d
Yewr goal is to grab as much food as yew can,
*//
find the Amulet of Yendor,
*
```

to locate the occurrences of `food` and `find` in the file.

`*` is very different from `.` in that it can be used to define a pattern that will match a sequence of characters including the null string.  `*` is always preceded by another character when used in pattern matching. So try:

```
*/A.*m/                     Locate A, zero or more chars, m
As yew explode more of the level,
*//
find the Amulet of Yendor,
*
```

which will locate lines containing **A** followed by zero or more characters, then **m**.

`[` and `]` are somewhat similar to their counterparts in the shell. For example, `[123]` will match either **1** or **2** or **3**. Now try typing:

```
*/[Dd]un/                   Locate Dun or dun
and get out of the Dungeons of Danger dead.
*//
on the sultana dungeon level is kept.
*
```

which will find the next occurrence of **Dun** or **dun**. This facility can be very useful when searching for words which occur at the beginning of sentences as well as in the middle.

A range of characters may be specified between [ and ] by separating two characters by a minus sign. The first of these must precede the second in the ASCII character set. Thus [1-5] abbreviates [12345] while [w-z] stands for [wxyz]. If - is to be included as an alternative, it must be the first or last character in the string. The character ] loses its special significance if it is the first character in the string. Thus, []-] will match either ] or -. If the first character immediately following [ is ^, then the characters matched are those *not* in the remainder of the string. Thus, [^1-3] will match any character except 1, 2 or 3. The characters *, ., $, and \ lose their special meaning when used in the string as does ^ if it is not the first character.

To illustrate the use of these pattern matching facilities, consider the problem of locating a line which does not contain any punctuation. You could search for a line composed of letters, digits and spaces:

```
*/^[a-zA-Z0-9 ]*$/          Find line of letters, digits and spaces
and what yew have been
*
```

Alternatively, your search could be for a line composed of characters which are not punctuation marks:

```
*/^[^,.]*$/                 Find line without punctuation
and what yew have been
*
```

Finally, \ preceding a character just matches the character itself even if it is one with a special meaning. Thus:

```
*/yew./                     Find yew followed by one character
As yew explode more of the level,
*
```

locates a line containing yew followed by any character whereas:

```
*/yew\./                    Find yew followed by .
it appears on the screen behind of yew.
*
```

locates yew followed by a full stop.

While there may not seem much point in searching randomly through the file at the moment, we will soon see how indispensable this facility is when changing the text. You will probably find it is the one that you use most of all in **ed**.

In discussing how to construct patterns, we have, in fact, been giving an informal description of something called a *regular expression*. This is a rule or formula for generating a set of character strings. The regular expression is said to match any member of the set that it generates. A more complete treatment of regular expressions is given in Section 5.2.4. What you have learnt so far will give you sufficient mastery of the concept to enable you to use it effectively in **ed** and **vi**.

## 3.1.5  Modifying the Text

By now, you must be thoroughly sick of shifting about through this nonsensical file which tells you almost nothing about what is involved in the exciting game of *rogue*. However, now that you have mastered moving around in the file, you should be well equipped to be able to modify the text.

Having located a line containing an error, the next thing you will want to do is correct it. You could delete the line and then insert a new one. However, in many instances, this would require unnecessary typing since, in fact, there may only be a few characters that need to be changed. Hence, **ed** enables you to substitute one string in a line with another.

### 3.1.5.1  *Substituting Strings*

The substitute command **s** is very similar to context searching in format. The best way for you to understand how it works is to try it out. We will begin by substituting You for Yew in the first line of the file. Knowing this, you could either type **1** or **/Yew/** to get to the right line. **ed** should have responded with:

```
Yew have just started a game of rogue.
*
```

You can see this is the line you wish to change, so you type:

```
*s/ew/ou/p                      Substitute ou for ew and print
You have just started a game of rogue.
*
```

If you break this command up into its elements, you can see that **s** stands for *substitute*, /ew/ searches for the pattern **ew** in the current line, and /ou/ defines the replacement string. However, note that there is only one **/** between **ew** and **ou** in the actual command. The **p** command you learnt earlier and this merely prints out the current line showing the result of your substitution. If you did not place a **p** on the end of the command line, the substitution would occur anyway, but silently. You could have typed:

```
*s/ew/ou/                       Substitute ou for ew
*p
You have just started a game of rogue.
*
```

with the same result. It is sometimes the case in **ed** that more than one command can be executed on one line. In fact, **p**, **l** and **n** can be appended to most other commands. Familiarity with **ed** will help you learn which commands can be combined and which can't.

Earlier in this section, we explained that **ed** commands are made up of three parts — an address, the actual command and a parameter. Now try:

```
*/Yewr/s/food/treasure/          Substitute treasure for food
*▓                                in line containing Yewr
```

In this example, /Yewr/ is the address telling **ed** to search for the line that contains Yewr, s is the actual command and /food/treasure/ is the parameter, in this case, details of the substitution you wish to make. Now type:

```
*p                               Print current line
Yewr goal is to grab as much treasure as yew can,
*▓
```

The same change could have been achieved with less typing by:

```
/food/s//treasure/
```

which substitutes **treasure** for **food** in the line containing **food**. // uses the previous search pattern, in this case, **food**. But we will try another example, since this mistake has already been corrected.

If you are not too sure what is in the file, it is usually safer to search for the right line first and then make the substitution. Otherwise, if there is more than one occurrence of a word, you may find yourself substituting the word in the wrong place. Let's suppose you wanted to change **dead** into **alive** in the fourth line of the file (which you do). First you will search for **dead** to make sure the first occurrence of this word is the one you wish to change:

```
*/dead/                          Locate line containing dead and print
and get out of the Dungeons of Danger dead.
*▓
```

Yes, this is the line you want, so now you can type:

```
*s//alive/p                      Replace dead by alive and print
and get out of the Dungeons of Danger alive.
*▓
```

which will substitute **alive** for the last pattern you located, in this case, **dead**. Well, this game **rogue** is certainly making a lot more sense now that one of the goals is *not* to "get out of the Dungeons of Danger dead". While you are correcting this line, you notice you have typed **Danger** instead of **Doom**, so you correct it thus:

```
*s/anger/oom/p                   Replace anger by oom and print
and get out of the Dungeons of Doom alive.
*▓
```

The address of a substitution command need not be a pattern. You will remember how earlier in this chapter you tried out many different ways of addressing particular lines or groups of them. These earlier addresses involved combinations of ., +, -, $ and integers. Thus, if you wished to change **yew** to **you** in the fifth and sixth lines, you would type:

```
*5,6s/yew/you/          Replace yew by you in lines 5 and 6
*
```

A range of addresses has been specified rather than a single address. The substitute command will be obeyed for each line in the range. Not all of the lines need to match the pattern but it is considered an error if none of them does. If you print your current line, it will be 6, since this is the last line that you changed. If you wish to see that both lines have been changed correctly, try:

```
*-,.p                   Print previous and current lines
On the screen, a map of where you have been
and what you have been
*
```

A command like this is useful if you wish to operate on a few lines at once. However, it is usually a lot easier to use context searching when trying to position yourself in a file.

Now that you have actually started changing the text, it is important to understand how easy it is to make drastic mistakes. For this reason, you should always check that the changes you have made are actually the changes you wanted to make. **ed** does have a provision for correcting a mistake in a substitution, but it is rather limited. If you have just made a substitution and realize it is wrong, it is possible to reverse it, but only if you wake up to it before you have made any other changes to the text. The command to *undo* your last substitution is **u**. Let's suppose you typed:

```
*/Amulet/               Locate line containing Amulet and print
find the Amulet of Yendor,
*s/of/in/p              Replace of by in and print
find the Amulet in Yendor,
*
```

then realized this was wrong. You could then type:

```
*u                      Undo last change
*p                      And print current line
find the Amulet of Yendor,
*
```

It is possible to combine the **u** and **p** commands into one command **up**. Of course, you could have just made the opposite substitution, but it is a lot simpler just to type **u**, especially if it was a particularly lengthy or complicated substitution. And substitutions can become very complicated if you start using metacharacters to construct patterns.

Before you go any further, it would be a good idea to get some practice at substituting one string for another by doing the exercises in Figure 3.1 to correct some of the other mistakes in your file. Now, the whole thing is beginning to make a lot more sense although there are still some errors which we will correct later.

```
*/sultana/s//current/p
on the current dungeon level is kept.
*1s/started/begun/p
You have just begun a game of rogue.
*/lode/s/d/r/p
As yew explore more of the level,
*+s/behind/in front/p
it appears on the screen in front of yew.
*?been$?s/b/s/p
and what you have seen
*1,$p
You have just begun a game of rogue.
Yewr goal is to grab as much treasure as yew can,
find the Amulet of Yendor,
and get out of the Dungeons of Doom alive.
On the screen, a map of where you have been
and what you have seen
on the current dungeon level is kept.
As yew explore more of the level,
it appears on the screen in front of yew.
*▓
```

*Figure 3.1*

There is another special character **&** which is not in quite the same category as the other metacharacters. In a pattern, it is just an ordinary character. However, in the replacement part of a substitution command, it is used to mean the string that has just been matched. Try typing:

```
*s/screen/large &/p          Insert large before screen
it appears on the large screen in front of yew.
*up
it appears on the screen in front of yew.
*▓
```

This example shows you how **&** may be used, but in this case we undid the substitution since it is not one of the corrections we wish to make to our file. You might have typed:

```
*s/screen/large screen/p          Same as before
```

with the same result. While **&** may be very useful when you wish to modify a particularly long string matched by a complicated pattern, it is easy to forget its special meaning when making substitutions. The point to remember about **&** is that it is only special in the replacement string. It loses this special meaning if preceded by **\**.

Another useful thing about \ is that it can be used to escape a newline character. Try typing:

```
*1s/gun /gun\              Replace space by newline
/p
a game of rogue.
*-,.p                      Print previous and current lines
You have just begun
a game of rogue.
*▦
```

This is a useful feature as it makes it very easy for you to break up a file into smaller but more numerous lines.

Up to this point, we have only considered examples in which you replaced a single string in a line. But suppose there were multiple occurrences of the same string that had to be changed. It would be a bit of a pain if you had to issue a substitute command for each such occurrence. Fortunately, there is a more convenient way. All you have to do is append **g** as a parameter and all occurrences of the matching string will be replaced, not just the first one. To try out this facility, first of all locate line 3:

```
*3                         Make 3 the current line and print
Yewr goal is to grab as much treasure as yew can
*▦
```

You will note that there are 2 occurrences of **ew** that need to be changed to **ou**:

```
*s/ew/ou/gp               Replace all occurrences of ew by ou
Your goal is to grab as much treasure as you can
*▦
```

So now, you have made all the necessary corrections. In V.2, if an integer $n$ is specified instead of **g**, then only the $n$th occurrence of the string is replaced.

### 3.1.5.2 *Adding Lines*

It's probably about time we paid some more attention to the file *rogue* by adding some more text to it. You have already learnt how to use the **a** command which will append the following text after the addressed line. Once again reproduce the errors exactly when typing the text into your file:

```
*$a                        Append some more lines at end of file

Rogue differs from most computer fantasy games
in that it is screen oriented.
Comands are all one or two keystrokes
are displayed graphically on the screen
rather than being explained in words.
Some rubbish or other
.
*▦
```

We will go back to fix the spelling mistake and get rid of the rubbish later.

The **i** command is very similar to **a**, except that it inserts text before the current line.  In the above paragraph, a line has been left out:

```
*/displa/                    Locate line containing displa
are displayed graphically on the screen
*i                           And insert a line before it
and the results of your comands
.                            Terminate insert
*-,+p                        List previous, current and next line
Comands are all one or two keystrokes
and the results of your comands
are displayed graphically on the screen
*
```

Your file now makes a lot more sense than it did before.  Are you getting the idea now?  But wait, there is more to come.

### 3.1.5.3  *Removing Lines*

The **d** command is used for deleting lines and if issued without an address will delete the current line.  Thus, repeated typing of **d** deletes one line after another.  If **p** is appended to **d**, the new current line is printed so that you can see whether you really want to delete the next one or not.

You may now delete the final line of your file which contains rubbish anyway:

```
*$d                          Delete last line of file
*
```

If you try typing:

```
*$                           Print last line
rather than being explained in words.
*
```

you will see that you still have a last line but it is now the one before the previous last line.  In System V, the effect of a **d** command can be undone with the **u** command.  However, only the last **d** command can be nullified, so it is important to be very careful when you use it.  It is possible to delete multiple lines at once by preceding **d** with a pair of addresses separated by a comma.  This **1,$d** would delete the whole file, so beware now and avoid heartbreak later!  Otherwise, **d** is a very simple command and one that you will probably find yourself using constantly.

### 3.1.5.4  *Changing Lines*

The **c** or *change* command has the same effect as **d** followed by **i** (or **a** if there is only one line to start with), that is, it deletes the current line or a range of lines and inserts the following lines of text terminated in the normal way by a

single period. It is merely a short cut for replacing incorrect lines of text. For
example:

```
    *1i                          Insert line at beginning of file
    Instructions on using ed:
    .                            Terminate input of new lines
    *c                           Change current line
    Guide to the Dungeons of Doom
                                 Blank line
    .                            Terminate input
    *1,3p                        Print first 3 lines
    Guide to the Dungeons of Doom

    You have just begun
    *
```

You will probably find that the need to change parts of lines occurs more
frequently than the need to change whole lines. However, it is a good idea to
prepare yourself for those times when the rarely used commands can make a
complicated correction far less time consuming.

Finally, just as you may wish to separate one long line into several shorter
ones, so you may wish to join a number of short lines together, that is, replace
one or more lines with a single line. **j** will join the current line with the next line.
Alternatively, you may also give the command an address as in:

```
    m,nj p                       Join lines m to n and print them
```

which will join a range of lines from $m$ through to $n$ together and print them. In
your file, try:

```
    *jp                          Join current line and the next one
    You have just beguna game of rogue.
    *s/na/n a/p                  Insert space between n and a
    You have just begun a game of rogue.
    *
```

As you see, **j** is another command that can be combined with **p**.

### 3.1.5.5  *Moving Lines*

Sometimes your file will contain lines of text which are repeated over and
over again. **ed** provides facilities for copying and moving lines. The **t** command
will *transcribe* or copy and the **m** command will *move* specified lines to after a
given address. Both commands are unusual in that they contain addresses before
and after the command character — the addresses of the original lines and the
address after which they are to be placed. Let's suppose you wanted to copy the
first line so that it was repeated after the last line:

```
    *1t$                         Make copy of line 1 the last line in file
    *
```

Now check the first and last lines to see that the copy has taken place:

```
*p                              Print current line
Guide to the Dungeons of Doom
*.=                             Print current line number
19
*1                              Print line 1
Guide to the Dungeons of Doom
```

There are now 19 lines in the file since the last one added is a copy of the first one.

Now suppose you wish to move the new last line back to the beginning of the file:

```
*$m2                            Move last line to after line 2
*1,3p                           And list first 3 lines of the file
Guide to the Dungeons of Doom

Guide to the Dungeons of Doom
*
```

so that it is the third line of the file. Notice that line 3 is now a different one to what it was before. Hence all subsequent lines have had their line numbers increased by 1. Since you probably don't really want two identical lines in your file, you can delete the second occurrence:

```
*dp                     Delete line 3 and print new line 3
You have just begun a game of rogue.
*
```

and once again you are back where you started. It is possible to use more complicated addresses such as patterns for these commands, but it may confuse matters unnecessarily. It is so easy to find the lines you wish to manipulate just by typing:

```
*.=                             Output current line number
3
*
```

and then use their exact line numbers as addresses so that no mistakes are made. The only problem with this method is that, if you are changing the ordering of lines in the file, the line number of a line may change just as it might any time you insert or delete lines. Hence, the best way to copy or move lines is to use marks since these are not affected by changing line numbers.

And that is about as much as you can do with **ed** on a line by line basis. The next step up is ...

### 3.1.5.6 Global Editing

Sometimes you realize you have made exactly the same mistake over and over again and it is tedious to have to go through correcting each such error, one by one. At such times, the global command **g** is indispensable. It allows you to operate on a whole file with one or more commands.  The command format is:

    **g**/*pattern*/*command-list*

The first action is to scan the file and mark every line that matches the pattern.
Then, *command-list* is executed for each such line.  Thus, the command:

```
*g/yew/p                  Print all occurrences of yew
As yew explore more of the level,
it appears on the screen in front of yew.
*
```

prints  every line that contains the string **yew**. By executing:

```
*g//s//you/p              Replace all yew by you
As you explore more of the level,
it appears on the screen in front of you.
*
```

you can replace all occurrences of **yew** with **you** and print each changed line.
Also, you can now correct your other spelling mistakes globally:

```
*g/[Cc]omand/s/oman/omman/gp       Change all oman to omman
Commands are all one or two keystrokes
and the results of your commands
*
```

**g** has been appended as a parameter just in case there is more then one
occurrence of the string to be changed in any line.

In the previous example, if you had known that your mistakes were
contained between, say, lines 14 and 18, you could have used the command
**14,18g** instead of just **g** which causes all the lines in the file to be searched i.e.
the default addresses for this command are **1,$**.

Getting more complicated yet; let us suppose you wished to start every line
of text with a space and end it with a star.  Then you would type:

```
*1,$s/^.*$/ &*/p           Insert space at start and * at end of lines
 rather than being explained in words.*
*
```

that is, replace the whole line (^.*$) with a space followed by the whole line,
followed by a star, and then print the last changed line.  Now try typing:

```
*g/^/p                    List all lines in file
Guide to the Dungeons of Doom*
*
You have just begun a game of rogue.*
Your goal is to grab as much treasure as you can,*
find the Amulet of Yendor,*
and get out of the Dungeons of Doom alive.*
On the screen, a map of where you have been*
and what you have seen*
on the current dungeon level is kept.*
```

```
As you explore more of the level,*
it appears on the screen in front of you.*
*
Rogue differs from most computer fantasy games*
in that it is screen oriented.*
Commands are all one or two keystrokes*
and the results of your commands*
are displayed graphically on the screen*
rather than being explained in words.*
   *
```

and you will find that it has the same output as **1,$p**. In System V, these commands may be abbreviated to **g/^** and **,p** respectively. The latter is possible since **,** stands for the range **1,$**.

Furthermore, it is possible with the **g** command to execute several commands at once and even commands which switch to text input mode. Let us suppose that you wanted to replace all the lines that were originally blank and now contain a star, with a null line followed by another line containing the words This is a null line followed by another blank line. Then type:

| | |
|---|---|
| **\*g/^ \\\*$/c\\** | *Change each line consisting of* * *only* |
| **\\** | *Replace by null line* |
| **This is a null line\\** | *Append comment line* |
| **\\** | *Append another null line* |
| **.** | *Terminate input* |
| **\*** | |

In the above example, newlines have been escaped with **\\** to postpone execution of the command. Such a command applied globally can often save a great deal of time. You should list the file now to see that the changes you requested have indeed taken place. In fact, if you don't have the **n** command available and want to have the lines printed and numbered, you can try the following:

| | |
|---|---|
| **\*g/^/.=\\** | *Print line number for each line* |
| **p** | *Print line* |

This time, there are 2 commands applied globally to the file. The first prints the line number and the second, the line itself.

Other interesting examples of the **g** command are **g/^/j** and **g/^/t$**. Don't try these immediately on your current file as you may not like the results. You can use them later on a small test file if you wish. The first command marks every line and then joins the current line with the next one. Now, you might think that, after joining lines 1 and 2, the next lines to be joined are 2 and 3 but since 2 has already been joined to 1, line 3 will be joined to the combined line so that ultimately the file is just one long line. However, **ed** is not as silly as that! In fact, after the first two lines have been joined, the old line 3 becomes the new line 2 and that is what is joined to the next line. Hence, the net effect is to join together each pair of lines in the file. If there are an even number of lines in the file, the command will be executed silently; for a file with an odd number of lines,

**ed** will complain since there won't be a mate for the last line. However, all the preceding pairs of lines will have been joined.

The other command **g/^/t$** is more straightforward. It simply copies the current line to after the last line to give a new last line. The overall effect therefore is to append to a file a copy of itself.

Less often used than the **g** command is its counterpart **v** which will find all lines that don't match a pattern. If you wished to delete all those lines which did not start with a space, you could type:

  **\*v/^ /d**        *Delete lines not starting with a space*
  **\***

## 3.1.6  Accessing Files

It's time now to close off your editing session:

  **\*w**          *Write edit buffer to file*
  **628**
  **\*q**          *And exit from* **ed**
  **$**

If the terminal hangs up while a file is being edited, it will be saved in your current directory under the filename **ed.hup**. If this happens you should compare the original file and **ed.hup** before you decide which version you wish to keep.

Sometimes, when editing, you may wish to copy the contents of another file, to which you have read access, into the file you are currently editing. We will try to do this now, but first you must create another file:

```
$ ed smallfile            Invoke the editor
?smallfile
P
*a                        Append new lines
This is another file
which might contain
some extra information
about the game of rogue.
.                         Terminate input
*w                        Write edit buffer to file
89
*q                        Exit
$
```

Now let's reopen the file **rogue**:

```
$ ed rogue                Invoke the editor
628
P
*r smallfile              Append smallfile to rogue
89
*
```

The command **r** will read in (or copy) the contents of another file. If no address precedes **r**, the default is the last line in the file. In this case, you have copied the contents of *small file* after the last line of *rogue*.

Now write the combined file and return to editing *small file*:

```
*w                              Preserve changes
717
*q                              And quit
$ ed smallfile                  Invoke editor again
89
P
*e rogue                        Read rogue into edit buffer
717
*f                              Print current filename
rogue
*
```

The edit command, **e**, will delete the entire contents of the buffer and then read in the named file, in this case, *rogue*. The current line is set to the last line of the buffer. Consequently, you are now editing the file *rogue* again as indicated by the output of the **f** command. If you had made any changes to *small file* before executing the **e** command, **ed** would have objected and you would have had to save them before **e** would be obeyed. However, if you use **E** instead of **e**, the contents of the buffer will be replaced without any questions being asked. **e** is very useful if you wish to edit a selection of files without having to return to the shell in between each editing session.

You can now remove the contents of *small file* from the end of *rogue* as follows:

```
*$-3,$d                         Delete last 4 lines
*w                              Preserve rogue
628
*
```

Perhaps now you would like to have a look at what files you have in your current directory. **ed** allows you to execute shell commands without quitting the editing session. This is done by preceding the command with a **!**. So you might type:

```
*!ls                            Escape to list working directory
rogue roguecopy smallfile
!
*q                              Then quit
$
```

to obtain a list of your files before quitting.

Well, so much for **ed** — all in all, a very useful little program. For a summary of its commands and facilities, we refer you to Appendix 4. Now, let us turn our attention to **vi**.

## 3.2  A Screen-Oriented Editor

Well, it's time for the games again — but like most worthwhile and interesting games, the rules are complicated and it will take you some time to get the hang of them. The name of this game is **vi** (pronounced "vee-eye") and, in many ways, it is quite different from **ed**. Don't be put off by the seemingly complicated and numerous commands available in **vi**. It won't be long before the most useful ones are second nature to you. You'll hardly have to stop and think what you are doing. The text will just be transformed upon the screen before your eyes.

> **vi** - a screen-oriented display editor

Unlike **ed**, **vi** is a *screen editor*, and it is therefore *display-* (rather than *line-*) oriented. The screen acts as a *window* to the edit buffer and may display up to 23 lines at a time on most terminals. The cursor may be compared to a pointer which can move from line to line, word to word or even letter to letter. This allows for very precise positioning and editing.

**vi** has three major modes of editing. The first two are equivalent to those of **ed** — the *command mode* and the *text input mode*. The other mode is really a separate editor called **ex** to which you have access. It is a line-oriented editor and many of its commands are exactly the same as those in **ed**. For this reason, we won't be spending a great deal of time describing **ex**. If you have mastered **ed**, **ex** will also be your obedient slave. There are some differences but the main point is that **ex** is a more advanced version of **ed**, so you can do more with it.

In **vi**, the text input mode is initiated by a large number of commands which we will describe in later sections. The command mode is the default in **vi**. It may be dressed up with **ed**-type commands by using **ex** which is invoked by preceding the command with a  : which will appear at the bottom of the screen along with the cursor. **ex** commands are executed by hitting **RETURN**. You are then returned to command mode automatically. Most of the commands in **vi** which don't involve text input will be executed immediately though there are a few which require you to hit **RETURN**. **DELETE** or **RUBOUT** will interrupt your last command and return **vi** to its original state with the cursor at its previous position, assuming the damage hasn't been done already. If you type an illegal character or an inappropriate command, **vi** will "beep" at you (on most terminals) as a warning that you are trying to do something silly. Most **vi** commands may be remembered by simple mnemonics, just as in **ed**.

It is not easy to represent the effects of **vi** commands in a book since you will be making changes to a screenful of text. It would be very wasteful of space to show you the whole screen each time a command is executed. Instead, what we will do in most instances is give you the command you are to try on the left of the page and show you, on the right, the current line containing the cursor after the command has been executed. We will represent the position of the cursor by over-printing the particular character in the text with a stippled rectangle. If the cursor is positioned on a space, we will just show the rectangle. Further, in the character sequences you are to type within **vi**, we will represent certain special characters according to the following conventions:

&#9415;  **RETURN**
&#9409;  **ESCAPE**
&#9417;  **TAB**
&#9406;  **BACKSPACE**
&#9416;  **SPACE**

The representation for a space will only be used if there is a possibility of misinterpretation of the text. To represent control characters in the examples, we will enclose the corresponding upper case letter in a rectangular box. Thus:

&#9410;  means  **control–V**

However, within the accompanying text, we will still use the same convention that we have used elsewhere in this book, namely, **^V** for **control–V**.

Before you can use **vi** effectively, you will need to ensure that the terminal type is set correctly in the shell. Otherwise, **vi** may not be able to exploit the full potential of your terminal. So first, output the terminal type:

    `$ echo $TERM`                      *Output terminal type*

and check that it has been set correctly. If it has not, then what you will have to do depends on which shell you are using. For instance, if you are using an **esprit** terminal and **sh**, you would type:

    `$ TERM=esprit`                     *Define terminal type*
    `$ export TERM`                     *And mark variable for export*
    `$`

========================================

If, on the other hand you are using the C-shell, the required command is:

    `% set TERM=esprit`                 *Define terminal type*
    `%`

-----------------------------------------

Find out what type of terminal you are using and the name which will identify it to the shell. Then substitute this name for `esprit` in the appropriate command given above. When using **vi**, the speed of the terminal should preferably be **9600** baud. However, **vi** is still worthwhile at 1200 baud. Below 1200 baud, **vi** is still usable but somewhat inefficient and **ed** is the better choice if you need an editor.

Enough theory for now, let's invoke **vi** and see what it has to offer. While our coverage of **vi** will not be exhaustive, we will discuss all those commands which you are most likely to need or find useful. Note that **vi** commands are often placed on separate lines for clarity and this does not mean that you should hit the **RETURN** character after each one.

## 3.2.1 Entering vi

Rather than creating a whole new file for the exercises in this section, you will be changing and extending your file *rogue* which you created in the section on **ed**. If you have skipped **ed** and don't have a file *rogue* in a directory *edex*, go back now to Section 3.1.2 on "Creating a File" and use the basic principles described there to create a file containing the text shown in Figure 3.2. Don't forget to write the file before you quit. Note that the ⁻'s and the bottom line in the figure are provided automatically by **vi** and you do not need to type them into the file.

Create a directory *viex* in your home directory, change to it and copy *rogue* across from *edex*:

```
$ mkdir viex; cd viex        Make directory and change to it
$ cp ../edex/rogue .         Obtain a copy of rogue
$ 
```

**vi** is invoked just as **ed** was by typing:

```
$ vi rogue                   Invoke vi on rogue
```

(If you are using System V, you could also invoke **vedit** which is a version of **vi** intended for beginners.) The effect of the command is to locate the file and, providing you have read permission, to copy it into an edit buffer in much the same way as occurred for **ed**. On the screen before you, you should see something looking like the output shown in Figure 3.2. Notice that the whole file is less than one screenful since it only contains 16 lines. The sequence of ⁻'s underneath the text indicate non-existent lines and are used as a filler for the rest of the screen. You may see a different number of these fillers from what we show in the figure depending on the characteristics of your terminal. In fact, you may not see the last line of the file if your terminal is operating at 1200 baud since the default window size at this speed is usually set at 16 lines.

The bottom line in the above output tells you the name of the file you are editing and the number of lines and characters it contains. Once you begin editing, this information will disappear as the bottom line is either filled with more text, a message from **vi** or used to echo certain commands. Also, it will disappear if you move the window. Notice that the cursor is positioned on the first non-blank character of the first line. This defines the current position in the text.

There is a special version of **vi** which allows you to edit a file without making any changes to the original file by accident. This has the same effect as quitting from **ed** without writing the contents of the edited buffer to the file. This version is invoked by:

```
Guide to the Dungeons of Doom*
You have just begun a game of rogue.*
Your goal is to grab as much treasure as you can,*
find the Amulet of Yendor,*
and get out of the Dungeons of Doom alive.*
On the screen, a map of where you have been*
and what you have seen*
on the current dungeon level is kept.*
As you explore more of the level,*
it appears on the screen in front of you.*
Rogue differs from most computer fantasy games*
in that it is screen oriented.*
Commands are all one or two keystrokes*
and the results of your commands*
are displayed graphically on the screen*
rather than being explained in words.*
~
~
~
~
~
~
~
"rogue" 16 lines, 628 characters
```

*Figure 3.2*

$ view rogue                    *Invoke read only* **vi** *on rogue*

**view** will not allow you to overwrite the original file although you may make changes to the buffer contents and then write these to a new file. This provides a very useful way of examining a file with all the advantages that **vi** gives you over commands like **more** and **cat**. You may jump backwards and forwards through the file as you wish.

### 3.2.2 Leaving vi

As with **ed**, there are quite a few methods of closing off the editing session. If you wish to save your changes in the original file, just type:

ZZ                              *Exit from* **vi**
$

which will write the buffer back to the file if there have been any changes and quit or:

:w®                             *Write buffer back to file*

followed by:

    :q⊙                  *And quit*
    $

The last two are examples of **ex** commands. Remember that all **ex** commands (those preceded by : ) can only be executed by hitting **RETURN**. Alternatively, you can combine these commands:

    :wq⊙                   *Write buffer back to file and quit*
    $

If there have been any changes, **vi** will respond to a command to write the edit buffer with something like:

    **"rogue" 16 lines, 628 characters**

telling you its name and the number of lines and characters it contains, once again. When you quit the editing session, **vi** will return you to the shell. If you wish to preserve the original file and write the changes you have made to a new file, you could type something like:

    :**w newrogue**⊙          *Write buffer to **newrogue***
    :q⊙
    $

If you wish to discard all changes, then:

    :**q!**⊙                   *Quit without saving buffer*
    $

will do the job without raising any objections from **vi**.

If you are using the read only option (i.e. **view**), you can return to the shell by typing:

    :q⊙                  *Quit from **view***
    $

You can of course write the changed version to another file before quitting.

If the system crashes or the terminal hangs up during an editing session, a copy of the editor buffer will be saved in a file. Usually you will find some mail, when you login again, which will tell you how to retrieve your file. **vi** has a recover option, so all you have to do is type:

    $ **vi −r** *filename*         *Invoke **vi** on file preserved after crash*

which will call up the saved buffer and allow you to continue the editing session in **vi** or write it and quit, as you wish. Even so, it is a good idea to save any text you've typed in or changes you have made every fifteen to twenty minutes by typing:

    :**w**⊙                   *Write buffer to file*

Sometimes disasters do occur and the buffer can be lost which may mean a lot of wasted time and effort.

## 3.2.3  Moving around the Text

To edit a file of text, you must first locate a particular position in the text and then make some change. Whereas, in **ed**, you moved around the file by locating a specific line, in **vi** it is possible to move the window to another part of the file, to locate lines, words and even individual characters. Moving the window is done by *scrolling* or *paging*. If the file is scrolled, lines disappear from the top or bottom of the screen and new lines are introduced at the opposite end. The cursor is returned to the start of the current line and maintained, if possible, at that position in the window as the text scrolls past. Paging, on the other hand, involves redrawing the screen to display another section of the file. The cursor is repositioned at the start of the first line in the window for a forward page or the last line for a backward page. Locating a line, a word or a character causes the cursor to move to a new position in the file. If that position already exists on the screen, no movement of the window takes place. Otherwise, scrolling or paging will occur. The method used to move the window will depend on the distance the cursor has to travel.

### 3.2.3.1  *Scrolling and Paging*

The scrolling and paging commands give you window control. This is particularly useful in a larger file which cannot be contained within a single window, as your present file *rogue* can be. For this reason, you will be trying out these commands later when your file has expanded. But so that these commands are seen in context, we will list them and describe their effect now.

The scrolling commands are:

    ^D      *scroll Down half a screenful*
    ^U      *scroll Up half a screenful*

whereas the paging commands are:

    ^F      *page Forward a screenful*
    ^B      *page Backward a screenful*

You can see the mnemonic significance in all four commands in the description of what they do. Scrolling is usually preferable to paging since it is a much smoother movement and leaves more context from the previous screen. It allows you to continue reading whereas the paging commands draw a fresh screen and only leave two lines of context from the previous one.

Two more useful commands for window control are:

    ^E      *Expose one more line at the bottom of the screen*
    ^Y      *Yank another line onto the top of the screen*

Also ^L can be used to redraw the screen if it has been messed up by incoming messages, for example, from another user.

We will return to these commands later in the chapter.

## 3.2.3.2  *Locating Lines*

Okay, it's time to get your fingers into gear and start moving that cursor around. First of all, initiate **vi** again as you did before:

    **$ vi rogue**                    *Invoke* **vi** *on* ***rogue***

and the cursor will be positioned on the first non-blank character of the first line in ***rogue***. The simplest way to locate a new line is to type **RETURN** or +:

    Ⓡ    **You have just begun a game of rogue.***

which moves the cursor to the first non-blank character in the next line. As with many of the commands in **vi**, it may be preceded by an integer count:

    2Ⓡ    **find the Amulet of Yendor,***

Reverse motion is produced by the − command:

    −    **Your goal is to grab as much treasure as you can,***

The next commands to try are those which locate special lines on the screen:

    **M**    *locate* **M***iddle line*
    **L**    *locate* **L***ast line*
    **H**    *locate* **H***ome (first) line*

So try these commands, one after the other, and you should see the cursor jumping from its initial position in the window to the line about halfway through the text, to the last line of your file and then back to the first line on the screen:

    **M**    **on the current dungeon level is kept.***

    **L**    **rather than being explained in words.***

    **H**    **Guide to the Dungeons of Doom***

These are all commands for locating lines within the current window. Normally, the effect of **L** would be to move you to the last line on the screen, but since your file is shorter than the length of the screen, it moves the cursor to the last line displayed instead.

  **H** and **L** can also be prefixed by a count to give you a greater range of labelled lines. For **H**, the count refers to a subsequent line, for **L**, to a preceding one. If the specified line is not on the screen, scrolling or paging will occur:

    **3H**    **Your goal is to grab as much treasure as you can,***

    **2L**    **are displayed graphically on the screen***

    **7H**    **and what you have seen***

    **15L**    **You have just begun a game of rogue.***

    **2M**    **on the current dungeon level is kept.***

In each case, the cursor has been positioned at the first non-blank character in the line. Notice that a count with the **M** command is meaningless and has the same effect as **M** by itself.

Each line in a file has a number or address which you can use for moving about the file. If you type ^G, you will be told the current line number and the name of the file to which it belongs. For example:

> H        Guide to the Dungeons of Doom*

> ⌐G⌐       "rogue" line 1 of 16 --6%--

G by itself will tell the cursor to go to the last line in the file and *n*G will move the cursor to the *n*th line of the file. It is just like giving a line number in **ed**, except that it must be followed by a **G**. However, if you were to type:

> 10Ⓡ       Rogue differs from most computer fantasy games*

the effect would be the same as hitting **RETURN** ten times, so don't make the mistake of thinking this is the 10th line in the file. Now try:

> 1G        Guide to the Dungeons of Doom*

> 16G       rather then being explained in words.*

> 7G        and what you have seen*

It is possible to *mark* lines in **vi** by giving them single character names. This command is similar to **k** in **ed**, but easier to remember because it is mnemonic. Thus **ma** will mark the current line **a** and remember its position. Why don't you try this new command:

> H        Guide to the Dungeons of Doom*

> ma       Guide to the Dungeons of Doom*

Okay, so you've labelled this line that you want **vi** to remember, now how do you get back to it? Well, first we'll get away from it:

> L        rather than being explained in words*

> 'a       Guide to the Dungeons of Doom*

You should now be back on the home line of your window, since this is the line marked **a**, i.e. the name of the line preceded by a prime is a command which will locate the named line. While this command may not seem particularly useful at the moment, you will see later how it can be used in commands which change the text − for instance, to delete from the current line to a marked line. However, there is one variant which is immediately useful. The command ' ' will return you to the previous line on which the cursor was positioned:

> rather than being explained in words*

Perhaps you would like to experiment a little more with these commands before going on to the next section. Because there is so much to cover in **vi**, it isn't possible to give you a lot of practice exercises for each new set of commands the way that we did with **ed**. If you want to master **vi**, you will have to be a little inventive and try out lots of variations on the examples that we do give you.

### 3.2.3.3 *Locating Words*

Okay, now get the cursor back to the first line in the file:

    H        Guide to the Dungeons of Doom*

The cursor will be positioned on the first non-blank character in the line, **G** in this case, for the following exercises. Now type:

    w        Guide to the Dungeons of Doom*

**w** will move the cursor to the beginning of the next word defined as a sequence of alphanumeric characters including optional underlines or a sequence of non-alphanumeric characters excluding underline, space, tab and newline. Now try typing **w** repeatedly or preceding it with the appropriate integer count until you reach the second word of the next line:

    7w      You have just begun a game of rogue.*

Now try typing:

    b        You have just begun a game of rogue.*

**b** will take the cursor back to the beginning of the previous word. Now type **b** repeatedly or use a preceding count until you are back at the first word in the file:

    7b      Guide to the Dungeons of Doom*

Then type:

    e        Guide to the Dungeons of Doom*

**e** will move the cursor to the end of the current word or, if it is already there, to the end of the next word. Once again, repeat this command till you reach the end of the 3rd word in the second line of the file:

    9e      You have just begun a game of rogue.*

You should note that all these commands ignore newlines — actually you could get from the first word in the file to the last, just by typing **w** or **e** over and over again.

All three commands may be capitalized as **W**, **B** and **E**. In these cases, a word is defined as a sequence of non-blank characters. Position the cursor as shown below:

    5w      You have just begun a game of rogue.*

and then use **w** once again:

**w**        You have just begun a game of rogue.*

The cursor stops on the full stop as the start of the next word. If the command is used again, the first character in the next line will be selected:

**w**        Your goal is to grab as much treasure as you can,*

If now **B** is used, the cursor will return to the start of the last non-blank word in the second line:

**B**        You have just begun a game of rogue.*

You can think of the capitalized commands as operating on "BIG" words. This can speed things up a lot when moving through a file if it contains a lot of punctuation and special characters.

### 3.2.3.4  *Locating Characters*

Position the cursor at the beginning of the 3rd line on the screen by typing **3H** or using the **w** command. Then type:

**$**        Your goal is to grab as much treasure as you can,*

This command positions the cursor on the last character in the line. Now try:

**0**        Your goal is to grab as much treasure as you can,*

**0** (the digit) will return the cursor to the first position in the current line. The ^ command, on the other hand, will position the cursor on the first non-white character in the line. Neither of these commands has any further effect if you try to repeat them.

Your terminal may have arrow keys with which to move the cursor up or down, line by line, and sideways, character by character. If not, the commands **h**, **j**, **k** and **l** have the same effect. Furthermore, these letters are far more accessible on the keyboard since they are positioned under your right hand fingertips and therefore more conducive to speed. The direction in which the cursor is moved by each key is as follows:

| h | j | k | l |
|---|---|---|---|
| ← left | ↓ down | ↑ up | → right |

These commands are obviously not mnemonic, but it is easy to remember what they do because of their respective positions on the keyboard. There is no real way of distinguishing between **j** and **k** except by memory and you'll find that you learn quickly enough with a little practice. Any of these commands may be preceded by a count to speed up the movement of the cursor.

Try hitting **h** and **l** now to see how they work. You can also use **SPACE** instead of **l** and **BACKSPACE** instead of **h**. See for yourself what happens when the cursor comes to a blank which is just treated as another character. Notice, however, that if you type **h** at the first character in the current line or **l** at the last, **vi** will beep at you by way of complaint.

Now try out the **j** and **k** commands. The position of the cursor in the adjoining line will be exactly the same as the previous one unless the position of the last character in that line is less than the previous position. In this case, the cursor is positioned on the last character. However, the original position is remembered so that subsequent movements will cause the cursor to be returned to that position if possible. **vi** will complain if you type **j** when the cursor is positioned somewhere on the last line of the file; similarly, **k** will produce a complaint if the cursor is anywhere in the first line of the file.

One very useful command for locating a character is **f** which is the *find* command. **f**c will search for the next occurrence of c within a line where c is any character whether punctuation, alphanumeric or white space. **F**c will execute a search for the character c backwards in the line.  ; will repeat the most recently executed **f** or **F** command in the same direction and  , will repeat it in the opposite direction.

Position the cursor on any line of text that contains more than one or two words and try to find a common character such as a vowel or a comma. Repeat the **f** command using  ; until **vi** beeps at you to tell you there are no more occurrences in this line. However, if you hit **RETURN**, **vi** will remember the character of your last find command and you will be able to continue searching on the next line.

If you use **t** instead of **f**, the character located is the one *before* the character specified. Similarly **T** searches backwards in the line and places the cursor one position to the right of the specified character. Again  ; and  , can be used to repeat the search.

In the examples shown in Figure 3.3, we have used the string **(BEEP!)** to indicate the response from **vi** to a command which it cannot carry out. Try these commands along with some of your own concoctions.

### 3.2.3.5  *Locating High Level Objects*

A line, a word or a character is an example of what is called in **vi** an *object*. To move the cursor around the file, you simply specify some object and **vi** will locate it for you. **H**, **M** and **L** are also examples of objects. More complex objects than the ones we have discussed so far are called *high level objects*, for example, a *sentence* or a *paragraph*. The former ends with a **.** **!** or **?** followed by newline or two spaces while the latter is defined as beginning and ending with a blank line.

The commands to locate high level objects are as follows:

| | |
|---|---|
| ) | *move cursor to end of current sentence* |
| ( | *move cursor to start of current sentence* |
| } | *move cursor to end of current paragraph* |
| { | *move cursor to start of current paragraph* |

| | |
|---|---|
| 11H | Rogue differs from most computer fantasy games* |
| 5l | Rogue differs from most computer fantasy games* |
| 3⑧ | Rogue differs from most computer fantasy games* |
| $ | Rogue differs from most computer fantasy games* |
| 1 | (BEEP!) |
| j | in that it is screen oriented.* |
| 3k | As you explore more of the level,* |
| - | on the current dungeon level is kept.* |
| j | As you explore more of the level* |
| H | Guide to the Dungeons of Doom* |
| k | (BEEP!) |
| L | rather than being explained in words.* |
| j | (BEEP!) |
| fb | rather than being explained in words.* |
| tx | rather than being explained in words.* |
| Fh | rather than being explained in words.* |
| ; | rather than being explained in words.* |

*Figure 3.3*

You can try these out if you wish but, at this stage, the file only contains one sentence and one paragraph so all they will do is move the cursor from the first position in the file to the last one and back again.

### 3.2.3.6  *Location by Context*

As in **ed**, it is possible to search for a particular word or string of text by specifying a pattern. This is done by first typing:

  /

Notice that the cursor jumps to the bottom of the screen where this character is printed just as with the  :  in **ex** commands.  Now type in what it is you are looking for, in this case, `alive` followed by /Ⓡ and the appropriate line will be located with the cursor correctly positioned:

`/alive/`Ⓡ      `and get out of the Dungeons of Doom alive.*`

The terminating / may be omitted if nothing else follows. Thus, you could have typed:

`/alive`Ⓡ      `and get out of the Dungeons of Doom alive.*`

to achieve the same effect.

After you hit **RETURN**, the cursor will return to the first / and remain there until **vi** has found the pattern you are looking for so that it can reposition the cursor appropriately on the first character of the string. If it cannot find the pattern, a failure message like:

`Pattern not found`     or     `Fail`

will be displayed on the bottom line of the screen and the cursor will be set back to its previous position. The rules for constructing patterns are basically just those you have already learnt for **ed**.

It is also possible to search backwards for a pattern e.g. you could locate the word `Amulet` by typing:

`?Amulet`Ⓡ      `find the Amulet of Yendor,*`

**vi** makes it very easy for you to repeat your context searches.  The command **n** will repeat your previous search in the same direction. **N** will repeat it in the opposite direction. Try:

`?Doom`Ⓡ      `Guide to the Dungeons of Doom*`

`N`            `and get out of the Dungeons of Doom alive.*`

You should practise interchanging these commands before moving on.

A line displacement of the form ±$n$ may be appended after the terminating / of a pattern. This will leave the cursor positioned on the first non-blank character in a line $n$ lines before or after the line containing the pattern:

`/begun/+3`Ⓡ   `and get out of the Dungeons of Doom alive.*`

Notice that in this instance the terminating / must be supplied.

## 3.2.4  Modifying the Text

Having located a specific position in the file, the next thing you may want to do is modify the text. You can *add* new text by *appending* or *inserting* it before or after the current cursor position or the current line; you can *remove* text by *deleting* all or part of an object; you can *replace* text which is equivalent to removing some and then adding some more; finally, you can *move* text by copying or deleting an object or part thereof and then adding it to the file somewhere else.

### 3.2.4.1 *Adding Text*

The simplest way of adding text to a file with **vi** is to use one of the following commands:

| | |
|---|---|
| **a** | *append after the current character* |
| **i** | *insert before the current character* |
| **o** | *open file to append lines after the current line* |

After giving any of these commands, you simply continue typing in the text that you want to add. The text input mode is terminated by **ESCAPE**. This is rather like typing **.** when using **ed** to create new text except that Ⓔ does not have to be at the beginning of a line.

These three commands, **a**, **i**, and **o** may be capitalized to give them slightly different meanings:

| | |
|---|---|
| **A** | *Append at the end of the current line* |
| **I** | *Insert at the beginning of the current line* |
| **O** | *Open file to insert lines before the current line* |

Before you add any more text to the file, you should note the function of certain commands which you can use while in text input mode:

| | |
|---|---|
| **RETURN** | *begins a new line* |
| **^X** | *erases the current input line* |
| **^W** | *erases the current input word* |
| **BACKSPACE** | *erases the current input character* |
| **ESCAPE** | *returns* **vi** *to command mode* |

The above assumes that **BACKSPACE** is your erase character and **^X** is your kill character. Now you know everything you need to expand your file *rogue*. We would like you to do the exercises shown in Figure 3.4, ignoring once again the obvious mistakes which you will learn how to correct later. However, a word of warning — if the lines you are adding are indented one position to the right and line up with the existing text, then your version of **vi** has its auto-indentation option turned on. You can either live with it or execute the command:

　　　**:set noai**Ⓡ

We will have more to say about **vi** options later. Remember to hit Ⓡ at the end of each line and Ⓔ when you have finished typing the new text. Some more exercises to practise the other text input commands are given in Figure 3.5. There is no need to hit **RETURN** unless specified. Notice that the very last line is terminated by Ⓔ and not by Ⓡ. The only time you follow Ⓡ by Ⓔ is when you want the last line of the file to be blank.

You could go on indefinitely adding more and more monsters to the list — whether it be at the end of the list or at the beginning or indeed anywhere within it. Just remember that **o** and **O** are used for adding new lines of text whereas **a**,

```
G        rather than being explained in words*
o
Letters (both) represent the variousⓇ
inhabitants of the DungeonsⓇ
Watch out, they can be nasty and.Ⓡ
Many of them are inclined to physicallyⓇ
tear yew to pieces, but others attackⓇ
in more subtle weighs.Ⓡ
Here are some of the exotic creatures yewⓇ
find in the dungeons:Ⓡ
Ⓡ
Ⓡ
ⓉcentaurⓇ
Ⓣfloating eyeⓇ
ⓉhobgoblinⓇ
ⓉimpⓇ
ⓉquaggothⓇ
ⓉunicornⓇ
ⓉdragonⓇ
ⓉzombiⓇ
Ⓣshadow demonⓇ
Ⓣpurple wormⒺ
```

*Figure 3.4*

**i**, **A** and **I** are used for adding text to lines which are already there.

Well, your file is now a lot longer and it's time to illustrate the window control commands. First of all, issue the command **1G** to reset the cursor to the first line. Your screen should now look like what is shown in Figure 3.6 with 23 lines displayed. If you now page forward using **^F** , the screen will change to that illustrated in Figure 3.7.

The first two lines in Figure 3.7 are the last two lines from Figure 3.6 which have been retained as context to help you relate the new page to the previous one. Notice that the last two lines in Figure 3.7 are displayed as ‾, the standard **vi** filler character. If you now page backwards using **^B**, the screen will change back to Figure 3.6, again retaining the first two lines of Figure 3.7 as context. Notice that the cursor is positioned on the last line and not the first line of the screen. Now reset the cursor to the first line and try **^D** to scroll downwards. The cursor will be positioned as illustrated below:

D        It appears on the screen in front of you.*

**^U** to scroll up simply reverses the above movement. Also try **^E** and **^Y** to expose one more line at the bottom and top of the screen respectively. Experiment a little with all of these commands until you get a feel for them.

| /Lett(R) | Letters (both) represent the various |
|---|---|
| eee | Letters (both) represent the various |
| a cases(E) | Letters (both cases) represent the various |
| (R) | inhabitants of the Dungeons |
| A of Doom.(E) | inhabitants of the Dungeons of Doom |
| ji vicious(E) | Watch out, they can be nasty and vicious. |
| 5(R) | find in the dungeons: |
| iwill (E) | will find in the dungeons: |
| (R)(R)o | |
| (T)dwarf(E) | dwarf |
| /imp(R) | imp |
| 0(T)jackal(E) | jackal |
| G | purple worm |
| o(T)zlaad(E) | zlaad |
| 0(T)vampire(E) | vampire |
| 1G | Guide to the Dungeons of Doom* |
| o(E) | |
| /explore(R) | As you explore more of the level,* |
| 0(E) | |

*Figure 3.5*

They provide a convenient and efficient method of scanning backwards and forwards through a large file.

Well, the next step is changing the file that you have created.

---

```
Guide to the Dungeons of Doom*


You have just begun a game of rogue.*
Your goal is to grab as much treasure as you can,*
find the Amulet of Yendor,*
and get out of the Dungeons of Doom alive.*
On the screen, a map of where you have been*
and what you have seen*
on the current dungeon level is kept.*

As you explore more of the level*
it appears on the screen in front of you.*
Rogue differs from most computer fantasy games*
in that it is screen oriented.*
Commands are all one or two keystrokes*
and the results of your commands*
are displayed graphically on the screen*
rather than being explained in words.*
Letters (both cases) represent the various
inhabitants of the Dungeons of Doom.
Watch out, they can be nasty and vicious.
Many of them are inclined to physically
tear yew to pieces, but others attack
```

*Figure 3.6*

---

### 3.2.4.2  *Removing Text*

Before we go any further, we had better stop for a moment and look at the structure of **vi** commands. You were told how **ed** commands can contain up to three parts — an address, a command and a parameter. Similarly, most **vi** commands contain between one and three parts:

    i)     a count
    ii)    an operator
    iii)   an object

The count corresponds roughly to the address except that it specifies a repetition factor as opposed to the address of a line (with the exception of the **G**, **H** and **L** commands). The operator corresponds to the command which is usually a single mnemonic letter such as **d** for *delete*. The object describes what it is that the command is to operate on. An exception is made in the case of lines where the operator is simply doubled; thus **dd** deletes the current line. All this may sound a bit confusing but will soon become clear when you put it into practice.

You already know some of the objects that can be used in **vi** commands:

```
Many of them are inclined to physically
tear yew to pieces, but others attack
in more subtle weighs.
Here are some of the exotic creatures yew
will find in the dungeons:


        dwarf
        centaur
        floating eye
        hobgoblin
        jackal
        imp
        quaggoth
        unicorn
        dragon
        zombi
        shadow demon
        purple worm
        vampire
        zlaad
    -
    -
```

*Figure 3.7*

**b        e        w        B        E        W**

You encountered these first as commands. Thus **w** on its own advances the cursor to the start of the next word. If, however, it is used as an object with the **d** operator, the effect of the command **dw** is to delete characters up to, but not including, the first character of the next word. Similarly, **de** deletes the remaining characters in a word and **db** deletes the previous word. Each of these commands may be preceded by a count e.g. **4dw** deletes the next 4 words.

In a similar fashion, some of the other commands you have met already can be used as objects:

| | |
|---|---|
| d$ | *delete from current cursor position to end of line* |
| d0 | *delete from position on left of cursor to 0th position in line* |
| dl | *delete current character* |
| dh | *delete character to left of current cursor position* |
| dL | *delete from current line to end of screen* |
| dH | *delete from current line to top of screen* |
| d) | *delete to end of current sentence* |
| d( | *delete to start of current sentence* |
| d{ | *delete to start of current paragraph* |
| d} | *delete to end of current paragraph* |

You can get a feel for how the command works by imagining that **d** sets a flag telling **vi** to discard characters and lines as the cursor moves to its new position instead of leaving them unchanged.

The **f** or **F** command can also be used as an object of the **d** command. For example, **df***x* will delete up to and including the next occurrence of the character *x*:

/hobg(R)                     hobgoblin

dfb                          goblin

**t** may be substituted for **f** in the command if you wish to delete up to but not including the character *x*. Thus, in the above example, you could have typed **dtg** instead of **dfb**. **t** can also be capitalized to search backwards, for example, **dT***x*.

Because some commands are used much more frequently than others, **vi** provides synonyms. For example, **x** deletes the current character under the cursor and is a synonym for **dl**:

x                            oblin

Now try using this command with a count to delete a group of characters:

2x                           lin

.                            n

In the final line of the above example, we have used the **.** command which repeats the last command that changed the buffer, in this case, **2x**. This command is very useful when deleting characters, words or lines. Having deleted an object with **x** or **dw** or **dd**, you can delete more of the same objects by using the **.** command. You may precede the **.** command with a repetition count if you wish.

Before you have deleted all the characters, add some more and try typing **X**, a synonym for **dh**, which will delete the previous character. Continue deleting characters until the whole line is emptied:

ahob(E)                      nhob

X                            nhb

.                            nb

x                            n

.

Suppose now you decided that you didn't mean to remove all the characters from this line. You could use the **u** command to *undo* the last change:

u                            n

So if you delete something from a line or even a number of lines or even the whole

file and then change your mind, you can recover the previous situation by typing
**u**. But be careful — don't type it a second time, otherwise, you will simply get
back into the situation that you didn't want, i.e. **u** undoes the effect of the last
command and a second **u** just reverses the result of the previous one. However, if
you have really made a mess of editing the current line after a number of
commands, you can recover the line in its original state by using the **U** command:

    U              `hobgoblin`

Now we'll get you to try out the exercises given in Figure 3.8 and show you
the results that should be achieved.

### 3.2.4.3  *Replacing Text*

The replacement of text is essentially *removal* followed by *addition*. The
commands provided by **vi** to enable you to change text in a file are there mainly
for convenience and efficiency of use.

The simplest of the replacement commands is **r** which takes a character as
an object and uses it to replace the current character under the cursor:

    rI            `In more subtle weighs.`

This command is very useful if you wish to break a single line into two lines:

    -tb          `tear you to pieces, but others attack`

    r&#9415;          `but others attack`

In other words, you simply replace the space where you want to make the break
with a newline character.

If **R** is used instead of **r**, **vi** enters a text input mode. Each character you
type replaces the current one and moves the cursor one position to the right until
**ESCAPE** is hit.

Another useful command is **J** which will join the current line with the next
one leaving a space in between. The combined line replaces the current one. It
could therefore be used to reverse the effect of the previous **r** command:

    -              `tear yew to pieces,`

    J            `tear yew to pieces, but others attack`

If the first line is the end of a sentence, **J** will actually leave two spaces between
the joined lines. The **J** command can be preceded by a count which specifies the
number of lines to be joined together:

    /centa&#9415;      `centaur`

    3J         `centaur`       `floating eye hobgoblin`

    u            `centaur`

| | |
|---|---|
| /wei®     | in more subtle ░eighs. |
| dw        | in more subtle ░ |
| u         | in more subtle ░eighs. |
| b         | in more ░ubtle weighs. |
| de        | in more ░weighs. |
| u2e       | in more subtle weigh░. |
| db        | in more subtle ░. |
| 2b        | in ░ore subtle s. |
| d)        | in░ |
| U         | ░n more subtle weighs. |
| dd        | ░ere are some of the exotic creatures yew |
| u         | ░n more subtle weighs. |
| x         | ░ more subtle weighs. |
| X         | (BEEP!) |
| w         | n ░ore subtle weighs. |
| X         | n░ore subtle weighs. |
| U         | ░n more subtle weighs. |

*Figure 3.8*

If you want to change the case of a character, there is a special command to do this. Once again, position the cursor over the incorrect character and hit ~. This command will change upper to lower case and vice versa:

| | |
|---|---|
| ?In®     | ░n more subtle weighs. |
| ~        | i░ more subtle weighs. |

After you have tried out this command a few times, go back over the same words with ~ and change them back to lower case.

Another operator used frequently is **c** which enables you to change an existing object into a new one. When you use a **c** operator, **vi** will identify the letter up to which the text will be changed by replacing it with a **$** sign. Depending on the type of terminal you are using, you may notice that, as you type in the replacement text, you appear to be overtyping text which you did not wish to change. You'll find that once you hit **ESCAPE**, this text will reappear as **vi** redraws the screen to incorporate the new text. Remember that **c** followed by an object is one of the text input commands and must be terminated by **ESCAPE**.

One of the most useful versions of the **c** command is **cw** — *change word*:

| | |
|---|---|
| /wei(R) | in more subtle ▒eighs. |
| cw | in more subtle ▒eigh$. |
| ways | in more subtle ways▒$. |
| (E) | in more subtle ways▒. |

Another variation of the **c** command is **C** which will change the rest of the line.

The command **s**, which is a synonym for **cl**, will substitute a string of characters for the cursor character. After you have finished typing in the replacement string, you must hit **ESCAPE** so that **vi** knows you are finished:

| | |
|---|---|
| /zom(R) | ▒ombi |
| e | zomb▒ |
| s | zomb▒ |
| ette(E) | zombett▒ |

If you use **S** instead of **s**, you can substitute one or more lines with new input.

Why don't you try out all the different combinations you can think of with **d** and **c**, not forgetting to undo the changes that you make. You may even wish to create a file of your own and make a few modifications to it yourself.

Before you go on, don't forget to correct the two occurrences of **yew**:

| | |
|---|---|
| /ew(R) | Here are some of the exotic creatures y▒w |
| cw | Here are some of the exotic creatures y▒$ |
| ou(E) | Here are some of the exotic creatures yo▒ |
| n | tear y▒w to pieces, but others attack |
| . | tear yo▒ to pieces, but others attack |

In the final line of the above example, we have again used the **.** command which repeats the last command that changed the buffer, in this case, **cwou**(E).

### 3.2.4.4 *Moving Text*

To move text, you must first preserve the text to be moved in a buffer, then locate a new position in the file and place a copy of the buffer at that position. In the process of storing the text, you may simply take a copy or actually delete it from the file. Such operations are often referred to as "cut and paste".

To illustrate moving a line, suppose that you decide you want to reposition one of the monsters in the list. Just locate the required line, delete it and move the cursor to another line in the file. You can now *put* a copy of the deleted line either before or after the current one by using the **P** or **p** command respectively:

| | |
|---|---|
| /dwa(R) | dwarf |
| dd | centaur |
| 3(R) | jackal |
| p | dwarf |
| -P | dwarf |
| dd | jackal |

The delete command actually saves the deleted text in a buffer and you can take as many copies of it as you like.

The operator **y** standing for *yank* will make a copy of the object you specify in the internal buffer:

| | |
|---|---|
| **yy** | *Yanks a whole line* |
| **yw** | *Yanks the current word* |

You can yank any of the objects we have encountered before including paragraphs and sentences. Note that **Y** is a synonym for **yy**.

As an example of using the yank command, suppose you decided to add some more worms of different types to the list of monsters. You could proceed by locating the line **purple worm**, making a copy using **yy** and then replicating the line any number of times using **p**:

| | |
|---|---|
| /purp(R) | purple worm |
| yy | purple worm |
| p | purple worm |
| p | purple worm |
| p | purple worm |
| p | purple worm |

You could now go through the four extra occurrences of `purple worm` changing the word `purple` to another adjective using the **cw** command:

| | |
|---|---|
| **cwcrimson**Ⓔ | c̈rimson worm |
| – | p̈urple worm |
| **cwkhaki**Ⓔ | k̈haki worm |
| – | p̈urple worm |
| **cwdemon**Ⓔ | d̈emon worm |
| – | p̈urple worm |
| **Rorange**Ⓔ | örange worm |
| – | p̈urple worm |

Notice in the above example, that **p** put back a line since a whole line had been yanked. If you yank part of a line, **p** or **P** will insert that object into the current line:

| | |
|---|---|
| **?imp**Ⓡ | ïmp |
| **yw** | ïmp |
| P | imp̈imp |
| **a** Ⓔ | imp imp |
| **I1**Ⓔ | l̈imp imp |

A `limp imp` may not sound very fearsome, but at least you are getting an idea about how the **y** and **p** commands work.

**vi** preserves the last text object deleted, changed or yanked in a hidden buffer which you cannot reference directly. However, there are also two sets of *named buffers*. The first of these with names **1–9** is used to store the last 9 deleted blocks of text where a block is one or more lines. When a new block is deleted, it is stored in buffer 1 after the contents of each existing buffer is moved to the next highest numbered buffer. Any text previously stored in buffer 9 is discarded. The second set of buffers with names **a–z** can be referenced directly in a delete or yank command.

As an example of the way the unnamed buffer is used, consider the following commands:

| | |
|---|---|
| **xp** | *exchanges the cursor character with the next* |
| **ddp** | *exchanges the current line with the next* |

Try the first command on your current line:

| | |
|---|---|
| `dw` | `imp` |
| `xp` | `mip` |
| `xhP` | `imp` |

Now, try rearranging the position of one of the monsters using **ddp** repeatedly:

| | |
|---|---|
| `?cent`®  | `centaur` |
| `ddp` | `centaur` |
| `ddp` | `centaur` |

The word `centaur` should gradually move down the list.

Let's suppose now that you deleted some text:

| | |
|---|---|
| `/purp` | `purple worm` |
| `dd` | `orange worm` |
| `.` | `demon worm` |
| `.` | `khaki worm` |
| `.` | `crimson worm` |

and then change your mind. You can check back through the delete buffers and recover it by typing:

| | |
|---|---|
| `"1P` | `khaki worm` |
| `"2P` | `demon worm` |
| `"3P` | `orange worm` |
| `"4P` | `purple worm` |

The `"` notifies **vi** that you are about to quote the name of a buffer and **P** places its contents before the current line. When searching through these buffers looking for a particular section of deleted text, be careful to use **u** rather than just redeleting the unwanted text, as that will then be put in a new buffer and you may lose the previous deletion you were looking for. Alternatively, you can retrieve all nine buffers by typing:

`"1P . . . . . . . .`

and sort through the deleted text at your leisure. When used in this way, the `.` command automatically increments the buffer number. Why don't you go to the end of your file and try this now, then redelete all the unwanted lines (**9dd**).

There are also 26 alphabetic buffers over which you have far more control. You can decide on their contents which will remain unchanged until you either

replace them or close off the editing session. You may either delete or yank text
into the buffers depending on whether you wish to move the text or make a copy
of it. For example, **"a5dd** deletes 5 lines into buffer **a** and **"z2yy** yanks 2 lines
into buffer **z**:

| | |
|---|---|
| **?uni**Ⓡ | unicorn |
| **"b3dd** | shadow demon |
| **}** | zlaad |
| **"bp** | unicorn |
| Ⓡ | dragon |
| Ⓡ | zombette |

If you wish to append text to these buffers without destroying their current
contents, you can do so almost indefinitely using the same command format but
capitalizing the alphabetic name of the buffer **A** through to **Z**.

## 3.2.5  Miscellaneous Commands

The following commands are rather less useful than the ones already
discussed but there may well be times when they could make your life a lot easier.
For these reasons, we will cover them, but only very briefly. We won't be giving
any examples for you to try out on **rogue** for all of them, but feel free to concoct
some of your own. It's a good idea to know what they all do, even if you never
use them again.

**>>** indents the current line by a number of spaces (default = 8) and **<<**
removes the indent:

```
<<          zombette
>>                  zombette
```

**z.** redraws the screen with the current line at the centre while **z**Ⓡ redraws
the screen placing the current line at the top. **^L** can be used to redraw the
screen if it becomes garbled and **^R** reformats the screen to remove logical lines.
These are represented by **@** signs and are generated to save the time required to
redraw the screen at that particular instant.

**!***x***cmd** filters the object *x* to the specified shell command **cmd**, the output of
which replaces the object. *x* may be **!** for a line or one of the symbols
representing a high level object. *x* and **cmd** are read from the last line of the
screen. For example, **!!who** will replace the current line with the output of the
**who** command. However, if you really want an exciting example to try out,
position the cursor at the beginning of the list of monsters in your file **rogue**, then
type:

     **!}sort | pr -2 -11 -t**Ⓡ                *Sort and print in 2 columns*

These commands will sort the current paragraph, in this case the list of monsters, into alphabetical order and replace the unsorted paragraph with the sorted list arranged in two columns. So next time you have a list of words you want to sort alphabetically, remember this command.

### 3.2.5.1 *Using ex*

**ex** is very similar to **ed** and is available within **vi**. You have already met some of the most common **ex** commands such as **:w**, **:q** and **:q!**.

There are times when **ex**- or **ed**-type commands are more efficient than **vi** commands, for instance, in a global search or substitution. In such cases, look up the section on **ed** regarding command format and the use of special characters. Then follow the same rules, always preceding your commands with  : as for all **ex** commands.

If you wish to stay in **ex** for a while, the **Q** command will give you a  : prompt until you type **vi** to return to the visual editor.

Some of the more useful **ex** commands, again in brief are:

| | |
|---|---|
| **:.=** | print the current line number, although ˆ**G** is faster to type. |
| **:s** | substitute one string for another. **&** will repeat the last **:s** command. |
| **:g** | globally search for a string. |
| **:r** | read in a file. |
| **:e** | edit a new file. |
| **:u** | undo last change made to the buffer. |
| **:!** *cmd* | execute a shell command *cmd* then return to **vi**. |
| **:sh** | execute a shell which you must terminate with ˆ**D** to return to **vi**. |

You can now use **ex** to adjust the left hand margin so that each line in the text commences with a space:

     **:/ˆLett/,/ˆwill/s/ˆ/ /p**Ⓡ           *Insert space at start of lines*

     **will find in the dungeons:**

     **[Hit return to continue]**

     Ⓡ          **will find in the dungeons:**

The last line affected is printed and you are then asked whether you want to issue another **ex** command by typing  : or return to **vi**. If you choose the latter, the cursor will be repositioned in the text at the current line.

### 3.2.5.2  *Setting Options*

There are quite a few options which may be set in **vi** by using the **ex** command **set**. Some have a value; others are either on or off. They may either be set temporarily for the duration of the editing session or more permanently in a shell variable. If you type:

    :**set** **all**Ⓡ           *List settings of all options*

your editor will list those options which are set currently.

Certain options are set initially by default but can be changed to suit your purpose. An option value can be altered with a command of the form:

    :**set** *option-name=value*Ⓡ     *Assign value to option*

Other options may be turned on or off by commands of the form:

    :**set** *option-name*Ⓡ         *Turn option on*
    :**set** **no***option-name*Ⓡ     *Turn option off*

For a partial list of the options available along with their default values, we refer you to Appendix 5.

These options may also be set in the shell variable **EXINIT**. Suppose you want to give the **wrapmargin** a value of 10 and set the **autowrite** option on so that the buffer will be written automatically whenever a **:n** or **!** command is issued. How you do this depends on the shell you are using.

===============================================

If you are using **csh**, you could execute the following command:

    **% set EXINIT=´set aw wm=10´**   *Assign value to environment variable*
    **%**

-------------------------------------------------------------------

If you are using the standard shell, the following two commands would produce the required effect:

    **$ EXINIT=´set aw wm=10´**     *Assign value to shell variable*
    **$ export EXINIT**              *And mark it for export*
    **$**

Of course, the above options are only a few examples amongst the many which you may set. The wrap margin option is extremely useful if you are typing bulk text into a file. For instance:

    :**set** **wm=10**Ⓡ           *Assign* 10 *to* **wrapmargin**

will set the right margin 10 spaces from the edge of the screen. When you are typing in text and reach the 70th column, the cursor will begin at a new line. But better than that, if you are in the middle of a word, **vi** will move the whole word to the next line. Why don't you try setting this option now and adding some more text to the end of your file.   We will use a value of 20 rather than 10 to ensure that the lines fit on the printed page:

```
:set wm=20Ⓡ                    Assign 20 to wrapmargin
G              ẓlaad           zombette
o
Ⓡ
Well that is all we are going to tell you in this book about
the game rogue.  We hope that we have inspired you to find
out more about it and perhaps even set out to find the
fabulous amulet yourself.Ⓔ
```

It is a good idea to set this option automatically in the shell variable.  If you ever want to use all 80 columns, you can always reset the wrap margin by typing:

```
    :set wm=0Ⓡ                 Assign 0 to wrapmargin
```

### 3.2.5.3  Macro Commands

One more special feature of **vi** which makes it such a fun editor to use is its capacity to map a common sequence of commands to an unused character on the keyboard.  For example:

```
    :map K eas⟦V⟧ⓔⓇ            Define K command
```

defines **K** to be equivalent to **eas**, followed by **ESCAPE** where the **control–V** escapes the **ESCAPE** character when typing in the above mapping.  In other words, if the cursor is at the beginning of a word and you type **K**, the word will have an **s** added to it.

Another example is:

```
    :map = :.=⟦V⟧ⓇⓇ           Define = command
```

which defines = to be equivalent to  :.= followed by **RETURN** where the **control–V** is again the escape character.  Whenever you type =, you will be told the current line number which can be quite useful at times.

The following characters have no associated meaning in **vi** and can therefore be used as macro commands:

```
    K     V     g     q     v     _     *
```

Macro commands can also be set in the shell variable **EXINIT** along with the options:

```
    $ EXINIT='set aw wm=10|map = :.= ⟦V⟧Ⓡ|map K eas⟦V⟧ⓔ'
    $ ▒
```

Notice how the various commands have been separated with a  |.

Now that you have the macro commands at your fingertips, it's time to get rid of all those unnecessary **\***s in your file.  Set up the following macro:

```
    :map V $x⟦V⟧ⓇⓇ            Define V command
```

Once you have done this, go to the first line in the file and, for every line that ends with *, type **V**. Skip those that don't by hitting **RETURN**. Imagine that **V** stands for Vacuum and this command is a * vacuum. Of course, you could have achieved the same effect by using an **ex** command but this will give you some practice using **vi** macro commands. Also, you will need to insert a space at the beginning of each of the last 4 lines to keep the left hand margin straight. Again, we will use a macro but, this time, another type in which the macro body is stored in a buffer register. First of all, add the following line to your file:

> :i V(E)                                    *Define macro command*

Then, use **"zdd** to delete the line and place it in buffer **z**. This macro will insert a space and then locate the next line since the line you created is terminated by a newline character. Next, locate the line you wish to change and execute the macro command **@z**. You can repeat the macro by typing **@@** until all lines have been shifted right by one space. Once you have cleaned up your file, it should look something like that shown in Figure 3.9.

You can now exit from **vi** in readiness for the next exercise:

> ZZ                                         *Write file and exit*
> $ ▓

## 3.2.6  Editing Multiple Files

In **vi**, it is possible to edit a number of files one after the other. Thus, you begin:

> $ vi *file1 file2* ...                     *Invoke* **vi** *on multiple files*

When you have finished editing the first file, you type:

> :w(R)                                      *Write the current file*
> :n(R)                                      *Read in the next file*

**:n** reads the next file into the buffer but will not do so until you have written any changes made to the current file. However, if you have set the automatic write option, **:n** will write the file automatically.

Now try:

> $ cp ../edex/smallfile .                   *Make copy of* **smallfile**
> $ vi smallfile rogue                       *Invoke* **vi** *on 2 files*

and issue as the first command:

> :n(R)                                      *Read in next file*

You should then be back in **rogue** again. If you try to type **:q** or **ZZ** before all the files listed have been edited, **vi** will refuse to exit unless you try again in which case it will be persuaded that you are quite serious.

Guide to the Dungeons of Doom

You have just begun a game of rogue.
Your goal is to grab as much treasure as you can,
find the Amulet of Yendor,
and get out of the Dungeons of Doom alive.
On the screen, a map of where you have been
and what you have seen
on the current dungeon level is kept.

As you explore more of the level,
it appears on the screen in front of you.
Rogue differs from most computer fantasy games
in that it is screen oriented.
Commands are all one or two keystrokes
and the results of your commands
are displayed graphically on the screen
rather than being explained in words.
Letters (both cases) represent the various
inhabitants of the Dungeons of Doom.
Watch out, they can be nasty and vicious.
Many of them are inclined to physically
tear you to pieces, but others attack
in more subtle ways.
Here are some of the exotic creatures you
will find in the dungeons:


         centaur              crimson worm
         demon worm           dragon
         dwarf                floating eye
         hobgoblin            imp
         jackal               khaki worm
         orange worm          purple worm
         quaggoth             shadow demon
         unicorn              vampire
         zlaad                zombette

Well that is all we are going to tell you in this book about
the game rogue.  We hope that we have inspired you to find
out more about it and perhaps even set out to find the
fabulous amulet yourself.

*Figure 3.9*

**:e** *filename* will allow you to edit any file in the list, regardless of its order, or indeed any file to which you have access.  Compare this to the **e** command in **ed**.

The contents of the alphabetic buffers will be remembered throughout the editing session so long as you don't quit **vi** altogether.  Consequently, it is possible to move and copy text between files.  This may not be necessary very often but, when it is, you will find this facility invaluable for speed and efficiency.  We will give you an example so you can see how it works:

```
:e smallfileⓇ              Read smallfile into buffer
G              about the game of rogue.

"ayy           about the game of rogue.

1G             This is another file

"Ayy           This is another file

:e rogueⓇ                 Read rogue into buffer
G              fabulous amulet yourself.

"ap            about the game of rogue.
```

The last two lines of your **rogue** file should now be:

```
about the game rogue.
This is another file
```

As there's no need to keep them, you may as well undo that last **p** command.

### 3.2.7  Some Final Comments

**vi** is such a large and sophisticated editor that it is virtually impossible to cover all of the commands available in any great depth.  For this reason, we have skimmed over the intricacies of some commands, particularly the **ex** commands and options, and have left out other less frequently used commands altogether.

Some of the features we haven't covered are: adjusting the size of the screen, adjusting the size of the indentation tabs, using abbreviations to simplify typing a repetitive text entry and some of the more esoteric **ex** commands.  However, if you are really keen, you can always look up the documentation on **vi** and fill in for yourself all the gaps that we have left.  An appropriate reference is "An Introduction to Display Editing with Vi" by William Joy published by the University of California (Berkeley) and included also in the *UNIX System Documentation Workbench*.  Further, there is a convenient summary of **vi** and **ex** commands given in Appendix 5.

Although the effort to master **vi** is considerably more than that required for **ed**, you will find it very worthwhile in the long run.  Experience shows that you can edit documents much more rapidly with **vi** than you can with **ed**. And since you can always slip into **ex** for those global changes, you've really got the best of both worlds at your fingertips. So good luck in your future as a competent **vi**-user and may the games never stop!

## *SUMMARY*

- An editor is used to create and change text in a file.
- The two most widely available UNIX editors are **ed**, a line editor, and **vi**, a screen editor.
- Both editors copy the file to be edited into a buffer and only make changes to the text in the buffer.
- To preserve changes, you must issue a command to write the buffer back to the file.
- **ed** operates in either command mode or text input mode.
- To edit a file, supply the name of the file to **ed** as an argument and, if the file exists, it will report how many characters the file contains and place you in command mode ready to start editing.
- If the file specified as an argument does not exist, **ed** prints a *?filename* and places you in command mode ready to create a new file.
- An **ed** command consists of a single command character optionally preceded by one or two addresses and optionally followed by parameters.
- A line is referenced by specifying its address which may be an unsigned integer, a special character, a pattern, a mark or a signed integer.
- An unsigned integer *n* specifies the absolute line number *n* in the file.
- The special characters **.** and **$** represent respectively the current line and the last line of the file.
- The patterns */re/* and **?***re***?** specify respectively the next or previous line containing a string which matches the regular expression *re*.
- A regular expression defining a pattern consists of ordinary characters which match themselves and special characters which are treated differently.
- The special characters used by **ed** in pattern matching are **.** [ ] * \ ^ and **$**.
- **.** matches any single character.
- [*s*] matches any character in string *s* unless the first such character is ^ in which case it matches any character other than the remaining ones in *s*.
- \ causes the following special character to become an ordinary character.

- **\*** causes the preceding ordinary character, **.** or **[s]** to match the longest sequence of matching characters including none.
- **^** matches the beginning of a line.
- **$** matches the end of a line.
- A mark takes the form **'x** where $x$ is a single lower case letter specifying a buffer into which the line number has been placed.
- A signed integer **±n** may be attached to any of the preceding addresses to specify a line $n$ lines after or before the addressed line. (If $n$ is omitted, 1 is assumed; if the address is omitted, **.** is assumed.)
- If a command requires two addresses, these are separated by a comma.
- To locate a line and make it the current line, specify its address terminated by **RETURN**.
- Use **p** to print the current line, a specified line or a range of specified lines.
- **l** does the same thing as **p** except that the output is unambiguous.
- **n** behaves in the same way as **p** except that each line is preceded by a line number.
- Use **=** to output the line number of the addressed line.
- To remove one or more lines, use **d** which deletes the addressed lines.
- To add new text read from standard input up to but not including a line containing a single period, use **i** to insert the text before and **a** to append it after the current line.
- To change existing lines of text, use **c**.
- Use **m** or **t** to move or copy the addressed lines to after the address supplied as a parameter.
- Use **j** to join the addressed lines.
- To change parts of addressed lines, use **s** to substitute a string for a pattern (if **g** or an integer $n$ is specified as a parameter, every occurrence or the $n$th occurrence of the pattern in the line is replaced).
- Use **g** or **v** to execute commands supplied as a parameter for every line within the addressed lines which respectively matches or does not match a regular expression.
- Use **e** to replace the contents of the buffer with that of a file providing the buffer has not been changed since the last time it was saved; if you don't care about any changes, use **E** instead.
- Use **r** to read in lines from a specified file and append these after the addressed line.
- If you have made a mess of things, use **u** to undo the last change to the buffer.

- If you are really lost, use **h** (if it exists) to get an explanation for the most recent **?** diagnostic, or **H** (also if it exists) to enter a help mode in which error messages are more informative.

- To print the name of the current file, use **f** which can also be used to change the current filename.

- Use **w** to write addressed lines to the current file or a specified file.

- To exit from **ed** if no changes have been made to the buffer since the last write, use **q**; otherwise, a **Q** produces an exit with no questions asked.

- To escape from **ed** to the shell, type **!** followed by the shell commands you want executed.

- For a summary of **ed** commands, see Appendix 4.

- **vi** operates in command mode, text input mode or last line mode which is in fact another line editor **ex** with facilities very similar to those of **ed**.

- To edit one or more files, supply the filenames as arguments to **vi** and, if the first file exists, you will be placed in command mode with the first page of text displayed on the screen, the cursor set to the first non-blank character in the first line and non-existent lines indicated by a tilde (~) or an **@** sign.

- If the first file does not exist, you will be placed in command mode with the screen showing a number of non-existent lines.

- A **vi** command is a single character optionally preceded by an integer and optionally followed by parameters.

- To move the viewing window a number of lines or pages, you can scroll up (**^U**) or down (**^D**), page forward (**^F**) or backward (**^B**), expose a line at the bottom (**^E**) or a line at the top (**^Y**).

- To locate a new line still keeping the cursor positioned on the first non-blank character, you can move up (−) or down (+ or ⓡ) some number of lines.

- You can also specify the middle line (**M**) on the screen and lines relative to the first line (**H**) or the last line (**L**).

- Use **G** to locate a specific line whose number you know (default is the last line) and **^G** to output the current filename and line number.

- To mark a line use **m** and **´** or **`** to locate that line subsequently (**´´** locates the line defined by the previous context with the cursor on the first non-blank character, whereas **``** locates the same line with the cursor positioned wherever it was previously in that line).

- You can locate the cursor at the beginning (**w**) or end (**e**) of the next word or the beginning of the previous word (**b**) where word is sequence of alphanumeric characters including underlines or a sequence of special characters excluding underline, space, tab and newline (you can do the same things for strings using **W**, **E** and **B** where a string is a non-empty non-blank sequence of characters).

- You can move the cursor left (**h** or ⒝), right (**l** or ⒮), up (**h**) or down (**j**), to the first (**0**), last (**$**), first non-blank (**^**) or a specified position (**|**) in the line.

- You can locate the cursor on, before or after a specific character in the current line by searching forwards (**f** or **t**) or backwards (**F** or **T**) and cause this search to be repeated in the same direction (**;**) or the reverse direction (**,**).

- You can search forward (**)**) or backwards (**(**) for a sentence, also forward (**}**) or backwards (**{**) for a paragraph.

- To locate a string which matches a regular expression, search forwards (**/**) or backwards (**?**). You can repeat the previous search in the same direction (**n**) or the reverse direction (**N**).

- New text terminated by ⒠ can be appended after (**a**) or inserted before (**i**) the current cursor position, also appended after the end (**A**) or inserted before the start (**I**) of the current line.

- New lines of text terminated by ⒠ can be placed below (**o**) or above (**O**) the current line.

- Use **x** to delete the next character and **X** to delete the previous one.

- Use **dd** to delete lines, **D** to delete the rest of the current line and **d** followed by an object to delete characters from the current position of the cursor up to but not including the start of the specified object, e.g. **dw** deletes the current word.

- To change text, use **c** and **C** instead of **d** and **D**, with the replacement text terminated by ⒠, e.g. **cc** changes the current line.

- To yank (copy) text, use **y** instead of **d**, e.g. **yy** yanks the current line but note that so does **Y**.

- The **c**, **d** and **y** commands place the changed, deleted or yanked text into an unnamed buffer.

- The **c**, **d** and **y** commands can also place the affected text in a named buffer **a–z** by preceding the command with **"** and the buffer name, e.g. **"adw** places the deleted word in buffer **a**.

- The **c** and **d** commands automatically place affected lines of text in one of a set of named buffers **1–9** which are used in a first-in, last-out manner so that the most recently stored lines are in buffer **1**.

- Text can be recovered from the unnamed buffer and placed after (**p**) or before (**P**) the current cursor position or below (**p**) or above (**P**) the current line.

- If **p** or **P** is preceded by **"** and a buffer name **1–9** or **a–z**, text is recovered from that buffer rather than from the unnamed one.

- Use **r** to replace a single character and **R** to replace a string of characters with new text terminated by Ⓔ.

- To change the case of an alphabetic character, use ~.

- You can substitute a string of characters (**s**) or a number of lines (**S**) with new text terminated by Ⓔ.

- Use **J** to join two or more contiguous lines.

- Use **.** to repeat the last command that changed the buffer.

- If you want to change your mind about the alterations you have made, use **u** to reverse the last change and **U** to undo all changes made to the current line.

- You can redraw (**^L**) the screen if it becomes garbled or reformat (**^R**) it to remove non-existent line indicators.

- Use **z** to reposition the window with respect to the current line.

- The **!** command will read an object together with a UNIX command from the last line on the screen and replace the object by the output of the command applied to the object as input.

- Use **:** to read and execute an **ex** command from the last line on the screen or **Q** to switch into **ex** from **vi**.

- Use **ZZ** to exit from **vi** back to the shell, rewriting the buffer if necessary.

- For a summary of **vi** and **ex** commands, see Appendix 5.

*Chapter 4*

# PROGRAMMING

UNIX contains such a wealth of system commands that it is possible to do many, many things without ever actually having to write a program yourself. For some people, the commands supplied with the system are enough. However, there are others who will want to write programs in one language or another and therefore we will give some consideration as to how user-constructed programs can be compiled and executed under UNIX. Further, the shell itself provides a type of programming language which enables a user to tailor the interface to the system to his own particular needs and requirements. Even if you don't want to write programs in one of the common programming languages, you may still wish to develop shell scripts or procedures which will facilitate your use of the system.

Now it is not our intention in this book to teach you how to program in a particular language. There are many books available which will help you do just that and we refer you to those listed in the bibliography if you are so inclined. Instead, what we will do is show you how to run, under UNIX, programs written in three languages – Pascal, FORTRAN 77 and C. Further, we will also show you how to use shell commands as a programming language.

========================================

## 4.1  Using Pascal

Pascal is a general purpose programming language ideally suited for *structured programmming*. It is widely used throughout the world in introductory programming courses and is also finding application as a language for the development of systems software. It is a far superior language to BASIC for the writing of well-structured programs i.e. programs whose structure makes them readily understandable by people and which are much more likely to be *correct* in that they do not contain residual errors that are hard to detect. However, unlike BASIC, it is not an interactive language which can be compiled line by line as it is input from the terminal. A Pascal program must be created in a file before being compiled and executed. If the program is found to contain errors, these must be corrected using an editor before compiling the program again.

### 4.1.1  A Simple Pascal Program

Let us create in a directory **pex** a simple program in Pascal and then try compiling it:

```
% cd; mkdir pex; cd pex          Create directory and change to it
% ed greet.p                     Create Pascal program
?greet.p
a
program greet(output);
{output a greeting}

begin
    writeln('Hello there')       Output greeting
end.
.
w
82
q
%
```

Notice that we have named the file **greet.p** with a suffix **.p** indicating that it contains source code written in Pascal. Most Pascal compilers under UNIX require source files to be so named. The program will output the message **Hello there** on your terminal after it has been compiled and executed.

There are a number of different Pascal compilers available under UNIX. However, the ones we will use for our examples in this chapter are those which form part of the Berkeley system. Even if your version of UNIX is not the one from Berkeley, it is possible that these compilers may be available since they are very portable and can easily be moved to other versions of UNIX.

| **pi** - Pascal interpreter code translator |
| --- |

The first one we will try is **pi**, an interpretive Pascal compiler. An interpretive compiler is one which converts a program in the source language into an intermediate language which is then *interpreted* by another program. This is to be contrasted with an ordinary compiler which converts the source language program into machine code to be executed directly by the hardware. The advantages of an interpretive system are that compilation is fast, it is easy to detect errors and produce informative error messages; the disadvantage is that execution is slow. Execute the command:

```
% pi greet.p                    Compile Pascal program
%
```

and providing your file contains no *syntactic errors*, you will get no output on
your terminal. If you see error messages, check the contents of **greet.p** and correct
it so that it contains exactly what you meant to put into it.  Try **pi** again until no
error messages are produced.  Now check via **ls** that a file *obj* exists in your
current working directory.  This is the name always used by **pi** for the
intermediate language version of the Pascal program:

```
% ls                            Inspect current directory
greet.p  obj
%
```

```
┌─────────────────────────────┐
│ px - Pascal interpreter     │
└─────────────────────────────┘
```

To cause the program **greet** to be executed, issue the command **px**:

```
% px                            Execute Pascal program
Hello there

1 statements executed in 0.00 seconds cpu time.

%
```

The expected greeting is produced followed by some system information
indicating the number of statements obeyed and the amount of central processing
time consumed.  In this case, it is small and rounds off to zero.  If you want to
remove the execution statistics, recompile the program using the **−p** option:

```
% pi −p greet.p                 Compile Pascal program again
% px                            And execute it
Hello there
%
```

If you want to produce a listing of your program in which the lines are numbered,
use the **−l** option available for this purpose:

```
% pi −l greet.p                 Compile and list Pascal program
Berkeley Pascal PI -- Version 2.0 (Wed Aug 19 10:00:15 1981)

Thu Jan 26 10:56 1984  greet.p

    1   program greet(output);
    2   {output a greeting}
    3
    4   begin
    5       writeln('Hello there')
    6   end.
%
```

Since **pi** always generates a file *obj*, the next time you use another Pascal program, the existing intermediate file will be overwritten. Let us rename it by:

```
% mv obj grp          Rename obj as grp
%
```

Then, any time you want UNIX to greet you, just say:

```
% px grp              Execute grp
Hello there
%
```

i.e. supply the name of the file to be interpreted as the first argument. If you give **px** a file which is not the output of **pi**, it will complain:

```
% px greet.p          Try to execute a text file
greet.p is not a Pascal interpreter file
%
```

An alternative to the above procedure is simply to give the name of the object file. Providing no other file of the same name is found in the search path before your current working directory, it will be executed. **grp** and **px grp** have exactly the same effect.

---

**pix** - Pascal interpreter and executor

---

Now try the command **pix**:

```
% pix greet.p          Compile and execute Pascal program
Execution begins...
Hello there
Execution terminated.

1 statements executed in 0.04 seconds cpu time.
%
```

**pix** is a combination of **pi** and **px** and is often called the "load and go" compiler i.e. if the program compiles successfully, it is executed immediately. No object file is produced or retained. If you wish to keep a Pascal program in its source form rather than as intermediate code, you can since the one command **pix** will compile and execute it. The various options and redirections available for **pi** are also available for **pix**:

```
% pix -l greet.p > results     Compile with listing and execute
%
```

will send both a listing and output to the file *results*. The −**p** option is also available to suppress output of the execution statistics.

| **pc** - Pascal compiler |
| --- |

There is another Pascal compiler available under UNIX called **pc** which produces directly executable rather than interpreted code. Hence, it is more efficient at run time. Try:

```
% pc greet.p        Compile Pascal program to produce a.out
%
```

and then **ls**. You will find a file called **a.out** in your current directory which is the output of **pc**. Unless otherwise directed, all compilers produce an **a.out** object file by default. It is an executable file and hence:

```
% a.out             Execute object file a.out
Hello there
%
```

demonstrates that it will produce the desired output. The various options available for **pi** are also available for **pc** (where meaningful). There are a number of additional options for the latter compiler, for example, the **–o** option can be used to name the output file:

```
% pc -o gr greet.p      Compile Pascal program to produce gr
%
```

produces an output file **gr** instead of the default **a.out**. It is also executable:

```
% gr                Execute object file gr
Hello there
%
```

## 4.1.2  Compile Time Errors

Now let us see how clever **pi** is at detecting errors. Using an editor, modify *greet.p* by removing the right parenthesis from the **writeln** statement. Now execute **pi** on the modified file *greet.p* containing a syntax error:

```
% pi greet.p                Compile illegal Pascal program
Wed Jan 11 15:52 1984  greet.p:
     6  end.
e ------^--- Inserted ')'
%
```

The error indicates the line number of the offending line (in this case, 6) and the position in the line where the compiler detected the error (in this case, the first letter of **end**). But you say "I removed a right parenthesis from the end of line 5, so how come?" Well, the syntax of Pascal does not care about lines so the compiler just processes the program as a string of characters until it detects some illegal construct. In this instance, it found a reserved word **end** while it was still processing what it thought were arguments for **writeln**. It can only indicate the position in the text where it first detected a syntax error which is not necessarily the exact position at which it occurred. To determine why a failure message has been generated, it might be necessary to look back through the text for the actual error itself. Sometimes, this is not all that easy to find. But as you will undoubtedly be making plenty of errors, you will get lots of practice.

We note from the above output of **pi** that it not only detected an error but also attempted to correct it and continue. This is illustrated by the fact that the line which gives the position where **pi** became aware of the error starts with **e** indicating that it is a non-fatal error and that **pi** will continue to produce object code. In our example, it tells us that it has inserted a ) before continuing and the program will therefore be executed correctly by **px**. Neat, isn't it? But beware, **pi** cannot always recover so completely and its attempts to correct your program may produce something different from what you intended. Further, if you make a real mess, **pi** will generate an error message commencing with E and not produce any object file at all. Let us modify *greet.p* again, putting back the missing parenthesis, but, this time, removing **begin**. Now try compiling *greet.p* again:

```
% pi greet.p              Compile illegal Pascal program
Wed Jan 11 15:55 1984  greet.p:
      4        writeln('Hello there')
E ----------^--- Malformed declaration
      5  end.
E ------^--- Malformed declaration
E ------^--- Unrecoverable syntax error - QUIT
%
```

A fatal error is signalled when the compiler encounters **writeln** in line 4 since an optional section of a Pascal program before the first **begin** is one in which variables are declared. Since there are no variables in this program, the section is not required but as the compiler never sees the **begin** introducing the executable section, it believes there is a syntax error in the variable declarations and hence produces the error message **Malformed declaration**. It then attempts to recover and continue so that other syntactic errors will be uncovered. Eventually, it reads the reserved word **end** which causes the same error message to be generated. Finally, it outputs the failure message **Unrecoverable syntax error** and gives up in disgust.

The lesson to be learned from the previous examples is that an error early in the text of a program can generate further errors later on in the code; so always work on the first error message. If that error can be corrected, the other error messages may disappear. Also, if you cannot see why a failure message is being generated at a particular point in the program, look backwards through the code. The error could exist in an earlier line.

In small programs such as the one used in our example, it is fairly easy to relate the failure messages back to the original program text. However, in a larger program, this may not be so. It would be better to be able to view the failure message embedded in a listing of the program. This can be achieved using the −l option:

```
% pi -l greet.p            Compile illegal Pascal program with listing
Berkeley Pascal PI -- Version 2.0 (Wed Aug 19 10:00:15 1981)

Wed Jan 11 15:55 1984  greet.p

    1   program greet(output);
    2   {output a greeting}
    3
    4       writeln('Hello there')
E  ----------^--- Malformed declaration
    5   end.
E  ------^--- Malformed declaration
E  ------^--- Unrecoverable syntax error - QUIT
%
```

Now you can see much more clearly what the problem is. Both the listing and error messages are sent to standard output and hence:

```
% pi -l greet.p > listing      Redirect compiler output
%
```

will produce a file *listing* which can be examined at leisure via **pg** or **more**.

The errors detected by **pi** in the above examples are syntactic errors. The rules of the grammar were not followed in constructing the programs and they contain sentences that are not legal in the Pascal language. There are other ways in which the language can be used illegally and some of these errors can also be detected by **pi** at compile time. They are often referred to as *semantic errors* since, although the program is syntactically correct, it is a meaningless one. Let us look at some examples of this kind of error.

Suppose we want to construct a program which will read in an integer from the terminal and output the value of the number and its square root. Create the program shown in Figure 4.1 in a file *root.p*. Now compile this program and see what happens:

```
% pi root.p                    Compile Pascal program
Tue Dec 13 11:20 1983  root.p:
    5       read(i);
E  ---------------^--- Undefined variable
In program root:
  E - i undefined on lines 5 6
%
```

A fatal error occurs and the system indicates that the variable i has not been defined. In fact, it even tells us that i is undefined on both lines 5 and 6. In

```
program root(input,output);
{compute square root of an integer}

begin
    read(i);                        Read integer
    writeln(i,sqrt(i))              Output integer and square root
end.
```

*Figure 4.1*

Pascal unlike in FORTRAN and BASIC, all variables must be declared in the **var** section of the program before they are used in an executable statement. Therefore modify **root.p** to include a declaration by introducing a line:

```
var i : integer;
```

before **begin** and recompile. This time the program will compile successfully and produce an object file **obj**. Execute this file and the terminal will go into an input state waiting for you to reply. If you type **4**, the program will respond:

```
4   2.00000000000000E+00
```

```
2 statements executed in 0.00 seconds cpu time.
%
```

and the system will return to the command state. The above output represents 2 $\times$ $10^0$ which is the correct result.

### 4.1.3  Run Time Errors

So now you have a little Pascal program which enables you to find the square root of an integer. Of course, it's not a very convenient program to use. It will only handle one value at a time and never tells you what you are supposed to do — you have to know that it expects to read an integer when it goes into the input state. Further, it is not protected against invalid data. For example, if you execute **obj** and supply **−1** as input, the following output will occur:

```
-1
```

```
Negative argument to sqrt
```

```
Error in "root"+2 near line 8.
```

```
2 statements executed in 0.02 seconds cpu time.
%
```

This illustrates another type of error called a *run time* error since it is detected by the interpreter. As you cannot compute the square root of a negative number, the system has no option but to fail the program and terminate execution whenever any such attempt is made. The error message indicates that the failure occurred in the second executable statement of `root` near line number 8 (note that blank lines are counted). Let us rectify this situation by introducing a conditional `if` statement to check that the input number is positive and output a failure message if it is not. Modify **root.p** to produce the program shown in Figure 4.2.

```
program root(input,output);
{compute square root of an integer}

var i : integer;

begin
    write('Enter number:');      Output prompt
    read(i);                     Read integer

    {check for positive input}
    if i >= 0 then
        writeln(i,sqrt(i):10:4)   Output integer and square root
    else
        writeln('Negative argument supplied.')
end.
```

*Figure 4.2*

Let us experiment with our modified program a little to see if it works correctly. Use **pix** and supply a positive number as input in response to the prompt:

```
Execution begins ...
Enter number: 5
        5      2.2361
Execution terminated.

4 statements executed in 0.00 seconds cpu time.
%
```

However, if a negative number is supplied as input, the output will be:

```
Execution begins ...
Enter number: -1
Negative argument supplied.
Execution terminated.

4 statements executed in 0.00 seconds cpu time.
%
```

The program is now protected against invalid input data.

## 4.1.4 Testing for end-of-file

The program `root` for calculating the square root of an integer is still not very convenient to use since it only processes one number before terminating. What would be more convenient would be to have it process as many numbers as you wish and then tell it somehow that it is to terminate. As end-of-file (^D) is a common terminator in UNIX, let us try that in conjunction with the **repeat** statement which causes a program to loop until some condition becomes true. The predefined function **eof**(*file*) enables you to test whether *file* is at end-of-file or not. If **eof** is used on its own without an argument, the file tested by default is *input*. So extend *root.p* to include these statements as shown in Figure 4.3.

```
program root(input,output);
{compute square root of an integer; terminate with EOF}

var i : integer;

begin
    repeat
        write('Enter number:');        Output prompt
        read(i);                       Read integer

        {check for positive input}
        if i >= 0 then
            writeln(i,sqrt(i):10:4)     Output integer and sq. root
        else
            writeln('Negative argument supplied')
    until eof
end.
```

*Figure 4.3*

This program should loop until you type ^D in response to the Enter number: prompt. Compile *root.p* suppressing execution statistics and try it. It will behave correctly. However, when you type ^D, it will fail:

```
Enter number: 5
        5      2.2361
Enter number: -1
Negative argument supplied
Enter number: ^D

Bad data found on integer read

        Error in "root"+3 near line 9.
%
```

Although the program stops, it is a very clumsy and inelegant way of achieving the desired effect.

Let us see whether you could make the program a little more elegant so that it terminates cleanly when you want it to do so. The problem with the previous example is that the test for termination comes after you supply input. When you respond with ˆ**D** to the read request, there is no valid integer on the input stream; the Pascal run time system detects this and fails the program. What you need to do is place the test for end-of-file before the read statement. To do this, you can make use of the **while** statement. Modify **root.p** as shown in Figure 4.4.

```
program root(input,output);
{compute square root of an integer; terminate with EOF}

var i : integer;

begin
while not eof do
    begin
    write('Enter number:');         Output prompt
    read(i);                        Read integer

    {check for positive input}
    if i >= 0 then
        writeln(i,sqrt(i):10:4)   Output integer and square root
    else
        writeln('Negative argument supplied')
    end
end.
```

*Figure 4.4*

The condition that needs to be true is that input is not at end-of-file. Hence the logical operator **not** is applied to the value of the function **eof**. Now compile the program using **pix −p**. What happens? Nothing very much, it seems! The system just hangs. If you respond by typing a number, the prompt appears followed immediately on the same line by the value of **i** and **sqrt(i)**; a second prompt is then output on the next line and the program waits for you to respond. Further, if you respond ˆ**D**, the program fails just as it did before. Not only have you failed to correct the previous error but you seemed to have introduced another one. The behaviour of the program is illustrated below:

```
5
Enter number:          5     2.2361
Enter number:6
          6    2.4495
Enter number:^D
```

```
Bad data found on integer read
```

```
          Error in "root"+4 near line 10.
%
```

The need to supply input before the first prompt appears is due to the fact that the system cannot determine the initial value of **eof** until after something has been read. It therefore waits at this point in the program until some input has occurred. Hence, the first occurrence of the prompt is output after the first input has been completed. The only way to solve this problem would be to output the prompt before the **while** statement is executed and to move the **writeln** statement in the controlled statement from before the **read** statement to after the statement which outputs the results. This would still not correct the erroneous behaviour which occurs when ^**D** is entered. The problem here is that **RETURN** used to terminate the previous number is still sitting in the input buffer and hence, even though end-of-file has been signalled, the system has not detected it as yet. It tries to read an integer, finds nothing there and fails. The solution is to use another version of the **read** statement, **readln** which reads a line including the terminating **RETURN**. The correct program is shown in Figure 4.5. If this is compiled and executed, it behaves as follows:

```
Enter number:5
          5    2.2361
Enter number:6
          6    2.4495
Enter number:^D
%
```

which is what is wanted i.e. the program terminates rather than fails.

## 4.1.5  Testing for end-of-line

Consider now a program which will read in a line of characters and then output the line in reverse order. Suppose the program is to perform this function until end-of-file is detected. Create the program shown in Figure 4.6. Now let us have a look at some aspects of this program before it is compiled. The executable section consists of a single **while** statement which will terminate at end-of-file. The second statement controlled by the **while** is also a **while** statement which will terminate at end-of-line when the predefined function **eoln** returns the value **true** after the last character in the current line has been read. We need to be able to test for end-of-line since the input lines will be of variable length with a maximum length determined by **maxsize** which, for testing purposes, has been

```
program root(input,output);
{compute square root of an integer; terminate with EOF}

var i : integer;

begin
write('Enter number:');          Output prompt
while not eof do
    begin
    readln(i);                    Read integer

    {check for positive input}
    if i >= 0 then
        writeln(i,sqrt(i):10:4)   Output integer and square root
    else
        writeln('Negative argument supplied');
    write('Enter number:');       Output prompt in loop
    end
end.
```

*Figure 4.5*

set to 6 in this example. As long as end-of-line has not been reached, a character is read into the next element of the array as determined by the index i which is then incremented by 1. When end-of-line is reached, the **while** statement terminates and the **for** statement is executed. Since i has been incremented in readiness for the next character, the control variable j is assigned the value i−1 initially and the controlled statement is executed to write out the elements of the array in the reverse order. Finally, **writeln** is used to terminate the line with a **RETURN** and control goes back to check whether end-of-file has been reached. Looks very simple and straightforward, doesn't it? Well, let's see.

Compile and execute the program and you should observe that it will go into an infinite loop after the first line has been input and output in reverse order. But not to worry — you are sitting at a UNIX terminal and can interrupt the program to bring it to a halt by hitting **RUBOUT** or **DELETE** or whatever your interrupt key is. You should see a message which looks something like the following:

> Interrupted in "rev"+15 near line 25.
> Execution terminated abnormally.
> %

The problem lies with **eoln** and the way in which the system reads characters ahead of time. When the last-but-one character in the first input line is supplied to the program issuing the read request, the system has already read the next character (the end-of-line character) and knows that it has reached the

```
program rev(input,output);
{ reverse lines of a file }

const maxsize = 6; {maximum size of input line}

var i,j : integer;
    line : array[1..maxsize] of char;

begin
while not eof do                    Loop until end-of-file
    begin
    i := 1;                         Initialize array index

    {input line}
    while not eoln do               Loop until end-of-line
        begin
        read (line[i]); i := i + 1
        end;

    {output line in reverse order}
    for j := i - 1 downto 1 do
        write(line[j]);
    writeln
    end
end.
```

*Figure 4.6*

end of the line. It therefore sets **eoln** to be true. The **while** statement terminates, the **for** statement is executed to output the line in reverse order which is then terminated by the newline from the **writeln** statement. Control then returns to the enclosing **while** to test for end-of-file and, since this is not set, the inner **while** statement is executed again. However, **eoln** is still true i.e. no statement has been executed which will reset this to false. The **while** terminates immediately, the **for** produces no output since the initial value of **j** is less than 1 and the **writeln** is executed again. This sequence is repeated continuously until the program is interrupted.

To correct the erroneous behaviour of this program, it is necessary to understand that not only is **eoln** set true when the penultimate character is supplied to the program but also that there is still another character that has to be processed. This is the end-of-line character itself which can actually be read into the program, if required, in which case it is supplied as a space. In your program, you are not interested in it and, hence, can use a **readln** statement which throws away any remaining characters in a line and resets **eoln** to false.

So add ; `readln` to the program after the final **writeln** statement, recompile and try again. This time, the program works correctly until you try an input line of 7 characters:

```
asd
dsa
q
q
1234567

Subscript out of range

        Error in "rev"+8 near line 1>.
Execution terminated abnormally
%
```

The program failed because it attempted to access the array with a subscript outside the range 1-6. This illustrates a particularly useful feature of the Pascal system — there are a number of run time checks including one for array subscripts out of bounds.

**eof** and **eoln** are traps for beginners when a program is being used interactively, so be wary of them. Points to remember are:

(i) at the beginning of a program where input is coming from a terminal, the Pascal system does not know whether the input file is at end-of-file or end-of-line or not. If it encounters **eof** or **eoln** before any read has taken place, it waits there until the user has typed a line. Any prompt following the end-of-file or end-of-line test will not appear until some input has occurred.

(ii) **eoln** becomes true when the penultimate character in the line (the one before the end-of-line character) is supplied to the program.

(iii) the end-of-line character is supplied to the program as a space.

(iv) **readln** discards any unused characters in a line including the end-of-line character and sets **eoln** to false.

## 4.1.6 Accessing UNIX Files

The program **rev** that you have developed almost replicates the behaviour of a standard UNIX command **rev** which copies files to standard output, reversing the order of characters in every line. If no file is specified as an argument, standard input is copied. Your program, however, will only handle standard input. You could of course use **cat** to pipe in one or more files. If you renamed *obj* as *revpi*, then:

```
% cat f1 f2 f3 | revpi > rf      Pipe 3 files to revpi
%                                And redirect output to rf
```

would produce the same effect as:

```
% rev f1 f2 f3 > rf          Reverse lines from f1 f2 f3
%                            And redirect output to rf
```

where *f1*, *f2* and *f3* are input files and *rf* is the output file containing the
reversed lines. But suppose you wanted to use **revpi** directly on a UNIX file
without using **cat**. One way to do this would be to include the name of the file in
the program statement. If you modify `rev` as shown in Figure 4.7, lines would be
read from *f1* rather than from standard input:

```
program rev(f1,output);
{ reverse lines of a file }

const maxsize = 80; {maximum size of input line}

var i,j : integer;
    line : array[1..maxsize] of char;
    f1 : text;

begin
reset(f1);
while not eof(f1) do          Loop until end-of-file
    begin
    i := 1;                   Initialize array index

    {input line}
    while not eoln(f1) do     Loop until end-of-line
        begin
        read(f1, line[i]); i := i + 1
        end;

    {output line in reverse order}
    for j := i - 1 downto 1 do
        write(line[j]);
    writeln; readln(f1)
    end
end.
```

*Figure 4.7*

f1 has been included as an argument in the program statement and this indicates
that it is to correspond to the UNIX file of the same name. The file must be
declared as a variable of type **text**, that is, one internally structured as possibly
variable length lines, each one of which is terminated by an end-of-line character.
The filename must also be supplied as an argument to **read**, **readln** and **eoln**
as indicated. Further, you must arrange for the Pascal system to open the UNIX
file ready for reading by executing the statement `reset(f1)`. In a like manner,

if you want the program to send its output to the file *rf*, you would need to replace output by rf, declare rf to be a file of type text, include rf as an argument to write and writeln and execute the statement rewrite (rf) at the beginning of the program. These statements, reset and rewrite, are not necessary if the program reads from standard input or writes to standard output since opening the files *input* for reading and *output* for writing are carried out automatically by the Pascal system. If you compile and execute the above program, it will write the lines from the file *f1*, reversing the order of characters onto standard output. Unfortunately, if you then wanted to process *f2*, you would have to modify the program again and recompile it to achieve the desired result which would not be a very convenient process. Further, the program would still only handle one input file at a time, whereas what you would like to be able to do is say:

```
% revpi f1 f2 f3 > rf      Reverse lines from f1, f2 and f3
%                          And redirect output to rf
```

i.e. use **revpi** in exactly the same way as you would use **rev**. Therefore you need to be able to access, from a Pascal program, the arguments associated with a UNIX command.

Whenever a UNIX process is started up, the command line which initiated it (including the command name) is made available to the process as an array of characters together with a count of the number of arguments (again including the command name). In the previous example, the program revpi would be invoked with 4 as the count of the number of arguments and revpi as the 0th element of the array, f1, as the 1st element, f2, as the 2nd element, and so on. i.e. the array is indexed from 0 up to one less than the number of arguments. In the Berkeley Pascal system, a program can gain access to its arguments via a built-in non-standard function argc whose value is simply the number of arguments and a built-in non-standard procedure argv(i,a) which extracts the ith argument and makes it available to the program in a, a packed array of characters. Once the argument has been transferred to the program, it can then be used in further computations and control the subsequent course of action. The array could be unpacked so that individual characters could be tested or it could be supplied as an input parameter to another procedure. In your program, the arguments will simply be filenames and you can associate a UNIX filename with a Pascal file variable by using an extended (and non-standard) form of the reset statement reset(f,a) where a is a string and f, a file identifier which causes any reference to f in the program to be interpreted as a reference to a UNIX file with pathname a.

You are now in a position to modify the program rev so that it will behave in exactly the same way as the command **rev**. The modified program is shown in Figure 4.8. name has been declared to be a packed array capable of holding 100 characters (on the assumption that no filename will be longer than this limit). In

```
program rev(input,output);
{ reverse lines of a file }

const maxsize = 80; {maximum size of input line}

var i,j,k : integer;
    line : array[1..maxsize] of char;
    name : packed array[1..100] of char;

begin
k := 1;                              Initialize argument count
repeat                               Loop until no more arguments
    if k < argc then
        begin
        argv(k,name); reset(input,name); k := k + 1
        end;
    while not eof do                 Loop until end-of-file
        begin
        i := 1;                      Initialize array index

        {input line}
        while not eoln do            Loop until end-of-line
            begin
            read(line[i]); i := i + 1
            end;

        {output input line}
        for j := i - 1 downto 1 do
            write(line[j]);
        writeln; readln
        end;
until k >= argc
end.
```

*Figure 4.8*

the main body of the program, **k**, the argument index, is initialized to 1 and the **repeat** statement is executed until all arguments have been processed. If no filename has been supplied as an argument, i.e. **argc** has a value of 1, the program behaves as it did before, reading from standard input. If, on the other hand, one or more filenames have been given as arguments, these are selected in turn by **argv**, stored in the packed array **name** and associated with the file variable **input** by the **reset** statement. Input then takes place from each file supplied as an argument with output going to standard output. Compile the program as follows:

```
% pi -p rev.p        Compile suppressing execution statistics
% mv obj revpi       Rename obj as revpi
%
```

using the −p option to turn off execution statistics and rename *obj* as **revpi** using **mv**. You now have a command **revpi** which will behave in exactly the same manner as **rev**. Try it on standard input and then on one or two small files to see that it functions correctly. Of course, it is a little tedious checking every line to see that it has been reversed correctly so we are immediately led to ask whether there is a better way to test the program. Suppose you were to apply **revpi** to a file and then apply **rev** to the output. You should get back the original file and could then use **diff** to check that this is so. (**diff** is a command which compares two files and outputs the differences, if any. It is described in detail in Section 5.2.) Hence, if you execute the following pipeline using your source file *rev.p* as input:

```
% revpi rev.p | rev | diff - rev.p     Difference output
%                                       of revpi and rev
```

and get no output, you could be fairly confident that **revpi** is working correctly. The − argument to **diff** indicates that one of the files to be used in the comparison will come from standard input. Try it and if you get some diagnostic output from **diff**, you've got a problem!

One final test you could apply is to see whether **revpi** handles non-existent files correctly. Try:

```
% revpi xxxx          Execute revpi on non-existent file
```

and assuming that *xxxx* does not exist in your current working directory, you will get the failure message:

```
Could not open xxxx: No such file or directory
```

Finally, just for interest, let us compare the speed of Pascal and C programs. First of all, recompile *rev.p* using **pc** to produce an executable file *revp*:

```
% pc -o revp rev.p    Compile program to produce revp
%
```

Now run each of **rev**, **revp** and **revpi** separately on some file *alpha* which contains lines of text redirecting output to another file. Precede the command name with the **time** command:

```
% time rev alpha > beta     Time the rev command
```

When the command finishes, the user time and system time in seconds and the elapsed time in minutes and seconds will be output. You will observe that **rev** which, of course, was written in C is by far the fastest and most efficient program; the slowest is **revpi** because the program output by **pi** is being interpreted. **revpi** and **revp** are simply no match for **rev** and hence there is no need to retain them. **rev** does the job very nicely. However, what we hope you have learnt from this exercise is how to integrate a Pascal program conveniently into the UNIX system so that it behaves like any other UNIX command. If you write programs in Pascal for subsequent use, you should compile them using **pc** unless, of course, you are short of file storage space. The object file produced by **pi** for a given Pascal program is much, much smaller than that produced by **pc**. It is simply a question of trading space for speed.

### 4.1.7  Portability of Berkeley Pascal Programs

The Pascal language is now defined by an International Standard (ISO 7185) which is based on a British Standard (BS 6192). At the time the Berkeley Pascal system was written, this standard did not exist and the language was defined by Wirth's Pascal Report. The implementation was based on this report but some extensions were made to the language. For full details of these, we refer you to the Berkeley Pascal User's Manual Version 2.0. We have already made mention of some of them e.g. `argc` and `argv`, the extensions to `reset` and `rewrite`. If you make use of such extensions, it is unlikely that your program will run correctly in some other Pascal systems. To guarantee that your program can be moved easily to another computer, you must adhere to the standard and not make use of extensions. To check if a program conforms to the standard, you can use the –s option with either **pi** or **pc**:

```
% pi -s rev.p        Check Pascal program for non-standard constructs
Mon Jan 23 17:31 1984  rev.p:
s 13 - argc is a nonstandard function
s 15 - argv is a nonstandard procedure
s 15 - Two argument forms of reset and rewrite are nonstandard
s 33 - argc is a nonstandard function
%
```

Appropriate warning messages have been generated indicating that *rev.p* contains non-standard features as you expected.

There are a number of other non-standard features in the Berkeley Pascal system which you might find useful but, beware, use them with caution. Some of these are automatic padding of string constants when assigned to a variable of type **packed array**, reading and writing of enumerated types, functions returning a structured type, comments delimited by (* and *), an include facility similar to that in C, listing control and non-standard predefined procedures and functions.

---------------------------------------------------------------------

## 4.2  Using FORTRAN

FORTRAN was the first of the high level programming languages i.e. one that is more akin to natural language and mathematics than the language of the machine itself. The first version appeared in the early 50s and the language has been used extensively throughout the world since then for scientific programming. Over the years, it has undergone a number of revisions, and, until recently, was defined by an American National Standard published in 1966. This version of the language is therefore known as FORTRAN 66. However, in 1978, a new language known as FORTRAN 77 became an official American standard supplanting FORTRAN 66. It includes almost all of FORTRAN 66 as a subset but with minor differences, some of which we will discuss later. One of the first complete FORTRAN 77 systems was implemented at Bell Laboratories and is available under UNIX. For full details of the compiler and the language that it supports, you should consult "A Portable FORTRAN 77 Compiler" by S.I. Feldman and P.J. Weinberger. What we will do in this book is show you how to run some simple FORTRAN programs under UNIX and illustrate some of the problems.

Because FORTRAN 77 is based on an early language used widely before timesharing terminals and personal computers came into existence, it is still heavily oriented towards the input medium that was in vogue then, namely, the punched card. Thus, to create a FORTRAN 77 program, you must first put it in a file, just as you did for Pascal, and then supply that file as input to the compiler. Any errors must be corrected via an editor until ultimately an executable version of the program is obtained. Further, FORTRAN is nowhere near as convenient a language as Pascal for writing structured programs although the latest version of the language is much better in this regard than were the earlier ones. Nevertheless, you must be extremely careful when writing in FORTRAN since it is all too easy to produce incomprehensible programs containing residual errors that are extremely difficult to detect.

### 4.2.1 A Simple FORTRAN Program

First of all, let us try producing our little greeting program again, this time, in FORTRAN. Create a directory *fex* in your home directory, change to it and input the program shown below:

```
$ cd; mkdir fex; cd fex      Make directory and change to it
$ ed  greet.f                Create FORTRAN program
?greet.f
a
        program greet        Use tab to start line
c output a greeting

        print *, 'Hello there'
        stop
        end
.
w
71
q
$
```

Notice that the file has been named *greet.f* with a suffix *.f* which indicates that it contains source code written in FORTRAN. Without that suffix, the FORTRAN compiler will refuse to process it as input. The first thing you observe about the program is that all the lines are indented except the comment line which has a c in column 1. The format of the remaining lines reflects the historical dependence on card input. The standard FORTRAN format is: columns 1–5 for a statement number, column 6 for a continuation marker indicating that the statement from the previous card is continuing on the current one and columns 7–72 for the statement itself. Columns 73–80 are ignored and were often used to contain a card sequence number. This format is still acceptable to UNIX but would be very inconvenient to input from a terminal. Thus, an alternative is available which permits a tab character either at the start of a line or immediately after a statement number. Tabs may be used elsewhere in the line and are treated as just another blank i.e. a tab character only adds 1 to the character count. Thus the indented lines in the above program commence with a tab and not a number of spaces. An ampersand (**&**) at the start of any line indicates that it is a continuation line.

Notice that lower case has been used throughout the program for convenience (except for the first letter of the greeting). If you had used upper case anywhere apart from in a character string, it would have been converted to lower case since FORTRAN is a 'one-case' language.

| **f77**  -  FORTRAN 77 compiler |
| --- |

Now let us compile the program as follows:

```
$ f77 greet.f        Compile FORTRAN program to produce a.out
greet.f:
    MAIN greet:
$
```

After some delay, the system will return to the command state (**f77** is not a fast interpretive compiler like **pi**) and, if there are no error messages, there should be a file *a.out* in your current working directory. Check this using **ls –l** and you should also see a file *greet.o*. This is the output of the compiler. *a.out* is formed by combining .o files with the run time system to produce an executable program. Observe that *a.out* is much, much bigger than *greet.o*; in fact, it is quite a large program. Execute *a.out* as follows:

```
$ a.out               Execute object file
  Hello there
$
```

The expected greeting is produced but immediately you notice that it is preceded by one or more spaces which displaces it to the right. If you want to get rid of these spaces, you will have to specify an output format explicitly. Modify the program as follows:

```
        program greet
c output a greeting

        print 10
10      format('Hello there')
        stop
        end
```

Compile and execute this program. You will now find that the greeting commences in the first position on the line.

A couple of other points worth noting: if you wanted to write a program containing upper and lower case letters and have these differentiated, you would have to compile the program using the **–U** option. If you want to preserve *a.out* as say *grf*, you could do so using **mv** or the **–o** option. The command:

> **$ f77 -o grf greet.f**        *Compile program to produce grf*
> **$**

would do the trick.

## 4.2.2  Compile Time Errors

While the **f77** compiler is quite reasonable at detecting syntactic errors, the failure messages are often far from enlightening and, in this regard, it is not as easy to use as **pi**. Modify the last version of **greet.f** by removing the right parenthesis from the format statement and recompile:

> **$ f77 greet.f**        *Compile illegal FORTRAN program*
> **greet.f:**
> **MAIN greet:**
> **Error on line 5 of greet.f:**
> **unbalanced parentheses, statement skipped**
> **Error on line 5 of greet.f:**
> **Execution error unclassifiable statement**
>
> **Error.  No assembly.**
> **$**

The compiler detects the unbalanced parentheses but then cannot determine what type of statement it is and signals a fatal error. Unlike **pi**, it does not attempt to repair the program so that execution may still be possible. Often you will simply get the message **syntax error** with no help at all as to where in the line the error actually occurred. For example, modify the program by removing the format statement and replacing the **print** statement by:

>     print '('Hello there')'

instead of the correct one:

>     print '(''Hello there'')'

Now, compile the program:

```
$ f77 greet.f              Compile illegal FORTRAN program
   MAIN greet:
Error:line 4 of greet.f:
name hellothere too long, truncated to 6
Error:line 4 of greet.f:
syntax error

Error.  No assembly.
$
```

To say the least, such error messages could hardly be described as being highly informative.

Sometimes you may get an error message a line or so after the actual line which contains the error. All you can do is check your code very carefully. Since there is no listing option available in **f77**, you cannot produce a file containing both a listing and error messages. As error messages refer to line numbers, you can save yourself a lot of tedious counting if you produce a copy of your program in which lines are numbered via the **nl** command (use **cat –n** in 4.2):

```
$ nl greet.f               Output file with line numbers
1              program greet
2          c output a greeting
3
4              print '('Hello there')'
5              stop
6              end
$
```

Let us explore the problem of compile time errors a little further by attempting to develop again a program to compute the square root of an integer. Let us repeat the same mistake that was made for Pascal by not declaring any variables even though you need one in the program. Create the program shown in Figure 4.9 in a file **root.f**.

```
      program root
c compute square root of an integer

      print *, 'Enter number:'
      read *, i
      print *, i, sqrt(i)
      stop
      end

                Figure 4.9
```

We'll stick to the **print** statements with list-directed output and live with the extra space. The **read** statement specifies the default input device which corresponds to standard input in UNIX.

Now let us see what happens when you compile this program:

```
$ f77 root.f              Compile FORTRAN program
root.f:
    MAIN root:
Error on line 6 of root.f:
bad argument type to intrinsic sqrt

Error.  No assembly.
$
```

The program fails to compile because i supplied as an argument to **sqrt** has the wrong type and not because it hasn't been declared. The implicit type declaration facility of FORTRAN permits a variable to be declared just by using it in a program. Unfortunately, this is a frequent source of errors. You may misspell an identifier whereupon FORTRAN will create another variable for you, different from the one you assumed it to be. As a safeguard, you can use the −**u** option of the compiler. This turns off the automatic data type mechanism and the compiler will complain about any variable which has not been declared in a type statement. So try:

```
$ f77 -u root.f           Compile without automatic data types
root.f:
    MAIN root:
Error on line 5 of root.f :
Declaration error for i :
attempt to use undefined variable
Error on line 6 of root.f:
bad argument type to intrinsic sqrt

Error.  No assembly.
$
```

Let us add a declaration for i to the program **root** and correct the problem with the argument to **sqrt**. This standard function expects a real number as an argument and not an integer. To convert from **integer** to **real**, you will need to use the mode conversion function **real** as shown in the modified program in Figure 4.10. Compile and test the program with a positive number. It will now perform as expected and output a correct square root.

### 4.2.3 Run Time Errors

Let's try our square root program again, this time supplying a negative number as input:

```
      program root
c compute square root of an integer

      integer i

      print *, 'Enter number:'
      read *, i
      print *, i, sqrt(real(i))
      stop
      end
```

*Figure 4.10*

---

$ **a.out**                    *Execute object file*
 Enter number:
−1
 −1  0.
$

So the **f77** system does not protect the user against invalid data being supplied as an argument to **sqrt**. It proceeds quite happily without generating any failure message and always returns 0 as a result. It is up to you to protect yourself by using a conditional **if** statement that checks to see if the input data is positive. So modify **root.f** to produce the program shown in Figure 4.11.

```
      program root
c compute square root of an integer

      integer i

      print *, 'Enter number:'
      read *, i

c     check for positive input
      if (i .ge. 0) then
          print *, i, sqrt(real(i))
      else
          print * 'Negative argument supplied.'
      end if
      stop
      end
```

*Figure 4.11*

Try the program again on negative input data and, this time, the appropriate failure message will appear.

Now extend the program to produce a table of square roots from 1 to the number input from the terminal by adding a **do** statement to control execution of the loop. Store the program shown in Figure 4.12 in a file **roots.f** as you will return later to continue modifying **root.f**.

```
        program roots
c compute table of square roots from 1 to i

        integer i, j

        print *, 'Enter number:'
        read *, i

c       check for positive input
        if (i .ge. 0) then

c   output table of square roots
        print *,'n   sqrt(n)'
        print *,''
        do 10, j = 1, i
            print *, j, sqrt(real(j))
10      continue
        else
            print *, 'Negative argument supplied.'
        end if
        stop
        end
```

*Figure 4.12*

Compile **roots.f** and test it to see that it works correctly for both positive and negative input. Now try one more test, supplying 0 as input:

```
$ a.out                          Execute object file
  Enter number:
0
  n   sqrt(n)

$
```

No output other than the heading occurs. This behaviour differs from what would have happened in FORTRAN 66 where the body of a **do** loop is executed at least once irrespective of the initial values of the loop variable and the limit. This is therefore a potential source of error for programs developed under a FORTRAN 66 compiler which are being recompiled using **f77**. To allow for this situation, **f77** recognizes a flag **–onetrip** or **–1** which causes it to generate code for **do** statements which will ensure that the body of the loop is executed at least once:

```
$ f77 -onetrip roots.f    Compile FORTRAN program
$ a.out                   And execute it
  Enter number:
0
  n    sqrt(n)
  1    1.0000
$
```

The program now outputs a line for 1 and its square root before terminating.

## 4.2.4  Testing for end-of-file

Let us return to the file **root.f** and modify the program so that it reads a sequence of integers from the terminal and computes their square roots until end-of-file is encountered. To do this, it is necessary to add another argument of the form **end** = *label* to the **read** statement. When end-of-file is detected by **read**, control will be transferred to the statement designated by the label instead of the next statement in sequence.

In the first instance, modify **root.f** as shown in Figure 4.13.

```
      program root
c compute square root of an integer
c terminate with end-of-file

      integer i

20    continue
      print *,'Enter number:'
      read (*, end = 10) i

c    check for positive input
      if (i .ge. 0) then
          print *, i, sqrt(real(i))
      else
          print *,'Negative argument supplied.'
      end if
      go to 20
10    continue
      stop
      end
```

*Figure 4.13*

Notice that the **print** statement has been preceded with a labelled **continue**
statement rather than labelling the **print** statement itself. We will follow this
convention in our examples and recommend that you do likewise. In the above
example, we have modelled in FORTRAN the **while not eof** construct of
Pascal. In general, to implement:

> **while** *condition* **do** *action*

use:

```
label    continue
         if ( condition ) then
             action
             go to label
         end if
```

Similarly for:

> **repeat** *actions* **until** *condition*

use:

```
label    continue
             actions
         if ( negated condition ) go to label
```

Let's see what happens when the program is compiled:

```
$ f77 root.f              Compile FORTRAN program
root.f
   MAIN root:
$
```

No objections from **f77** — the program compiles successfully which is a little
strange since it contains an erroneous statement:

```
read (*, end=10) i
```

instead of the correct one:

```
read (*, *, end=10) i
```

However, when you come to execute it:

```
$ a.out                   And execute it
   Enter number:
sue:(103) unformatted io not allowed
logical unit 5, named 'stdin'
lately: reading sequential unformatted external IO
Illegal instruction(core dumped)
$
```

there is a slight problem! The program fails and the system complains that
unformatted input-output is not allowed implying that, for this type of **read**
statement, you must supply a format specification. Hence, the **\*** you included
has been taken by the compiler to specify device 5, the standard input stream as

indicated by the failure message. The keyword **end** has been detected as such and hence there has been no format specified. You can still use **\*** for list-directed input but it must be included explicitly.

What we have attempted to illustrate with this example is that **f77** will pass as syntactically correct an erroneous program which will produce quite catastrophic results when an attempt is made to execute it. Refering back to the last set of failure messages, you will notice that UNIX has "dumped core". This means that a file *core* now exists in your current working directory. It is an image of your program as it existed in memory. This can happen from time to time with programs that you write yourself. If UNIX detects that a program is trying to do something illegal, it aborts the program and preserves a memory image in the file system. The term "core" is a hangover from the past when computer memories were constructed from tiny magnetic cores rather than from silicon chips as they are today. There are various debugging tools in UNIX such as **sdb** which make use of *core* and *a.out* to help you find out what went wrong with your program. However, we will not be treating such tools in this book. Use **ls** to check that *core* exists and then remove it since it is just wasting space.

Finally, modify your program to include the correct **read** statement, compile and test it. This time it will behave correctly, outputting a square root for each integer input until **^D** is used to signal end-of-file.

## 4.2.5  Testing for end-of-line

The problem with testing for end-of-line in FORTRAN is that the language does not include the concept of an end-of-line character. Historically, FORTRAN was developed at a time when most computer input came from 80 column punched cards rather than from terminals. When a card was read, all 80 characters were input to the machine i.e. there were no variable length lines as there are with terminal input. In **f77**, if characters are read into an array from a terminal, they are stored one per array element and, when end-of-line is detected by the system, the remaining unused elements of the array are set to contain spaces. Thus, if a 6 character input line is read into a 256 element character array, each of the last 250 elements will contain a space.

Let us now try to develop a program in FORTRAN 77 to reverse lines in a file. If you simply follow the logic used in the Pascal version, you will have a problem since, if you read characters into an array and output them in reverse order, each line will be preceded by however many spaces were generated by the system which is not what you want the program to do. To get around this difficulty, the program must first locate the last non-blank character in the line before outputting the remaining characters in reverse order. A program to do this for standard input and output is shown in Figure 4.14.

When the **read** statement terminates, j has a value n+1 irrespective of how many characters were supplied from the terminal. Hence, you must make

```
      program rev
c reverse lines in a file

      parameter(n = 6)
      integer i, j
      character line(n)

c input line
10    continue
      read(*, '(256a)', end = 20) (line(j), j = 1, n)

c scan backwards for first non-blank character
      do 30 i = n, 1, -1
         if (line(i) .ne. ' ') go to 40
30    continue

c output line in reverse order
40    continue
      write(*, '(256a)') (line(j), j = i, 1, -1)
      go to 10
20    continue
      stop
      end
```

*Figure 4.14*

use of a do loop to search backwards from the end of the array for the first non-blank character. Once this has been located, the remaining characters are output in reverse order using a **write** statement with an implied **do** loop. Control then returns to read the next input line. This process continues until end-of-line is detected and the program then terminates. Compile and test the program to see that it works correctly:

| | |
|---|---|
| **$ a.out** | *Execute object file* |
| 123 | *Your input line* |
| 321 | *Input line reversed* |
| 1 | |
| 1 | |
| 1234567 | |
| 654321 | |
| ^D | |
| $ | |

Well, it appears to do what you expect. Lines of up to 6 characters are reversed and excess characters are ignored although no failure message is generated as it was in the Pascal system. But suppose you type **12** followed by a space. What you should see is:

```
$ a.out                 Execute object file
12⑤                     Input line is 12 followed by space
  21                    Output line is space followed by 21
$ ▒
```

but what you will observe, if you try it, is:

```
$ a.out                 Execute object file
12⑤                     Input line is 12 followed by space
21                      Output line is just 21
$ ▒
```

i.e. the program does not handle lines with trailing blanks correctly. FORTRAN is just not a language well suited to manipulating characters.

## 4.2.6  Accessing UNIX Files

In spite of the deficiencies in the character handling abilities of FORTRAN, let us extend the program for reversing lines to process files supplied as arguments as well as standard input. You can readily adapt the algorithm used for this exercise in the previous section on Pascal since the **f77** compiler supports additional functions for accessing the UNIX command arguments. The first of these iargc() is a function which returns a count of the number of arguments while the second is a subroutine getarg which takes, as arguments, the number of the required argument and the identifier of an array to receive the character string. Once the filename is available to the program, it can be used as an argument in an **open** statement to connect the file with a unit. After the unit has been rewound, lines may be read from the file and output in reverse order until end-of-file is encountered  using the appropriate portion of the program developed in the previous section.

The complete program which processes one or more files containing lines up to a maximum length of 256 characters is shown Figure 4.15. When execution of the program commences, the number of arguments is obtained through a call on the function iargc and, if no arguments have been supplied, the program behaves as it did in the previous section reading from standard input. However, if one or more filenames have been specified, each is extracted in turn, stored in argv and then connected as standard input via the **open** statement. Its contents are then processed as before with the reversed lines being written to standard output. When the argument list is exhausted, the program terminates.

Compile the program and execute **a.out** without any arguments to check that it still functions correctly taking input from the terminal. Now try it once again, this time supplying an argument:

```
$ a.out rev.f                   Execute object file on rev.f
```

Problems! No output occurs, the program is still trying to read from the terminal and you will have to respond with ^D to return to the command state.

```
        program rev
c reverse lines in a file

        parameter(n = 256, input = 5)
        integer i, j, k, nargs
        character line(n)
        character*100 argv

c assign number of arguments to nargs
        nargs = iargc()

c initialize argument index
        k=1

50      continue
        if (k .lt. nargs) then

c connect next filename argument to input unit
           call getarg(k, argv)
           open(input, file = argv)
           rewind(input)
           k = k + 1
        end if

c input line
10      continue
        read(input, '(256a)', end = 20) (line(j), j = 1, n)

c scan backwards for first non-blank character
        do 30 i = n, 1, -1
           if (line(i) .ne. ' ') go to 40
30      continue

c output line in reverse order
40      continue
        write(*, '(256a)') (line(j), j = i, 1, -1)
        go to 10

c end-of-file, check if any more arguments
20      continue
        if (k .lt. nargs) go to 50
        stop
        end
```

*Figure 4.15*

The behaviour of the above program would lead one to suspect that the argument count returned by `iargc()` is 1 and not 2 as was the case in Pascal. You could introduce a diagnostic print statement to output the value of **nargs** to verify that, indeed, this is the case. Thus, `iargc()` in FORTRAN differs from **argc** in Pascal in that it returns a count of the number of arguments excluding the command name — an annoying difference but one that you will just have to remember. To correct the program, simply add 1 to the value returned by `iargc()` before assigning it to **nargs**. Now it will behave as expected and function just as the Pascal version did. Compile the corrected program to produce an executable file **revf** and test it with and without arguments. You could repeat the exercise with **diff**, this time using **revf** instead of **rev**. But remember, don't use, as input, any file that contains lines with trailing blanks — that's a problem that won't go away unless you are prepared to use further UNIX-dependent features.

If you really must process characters in FORTRAN, there is a function **getc** available in UNIX which will read a character into a variable supplied as an argument just as if it had been input with conversion mode **a**. The function returns a non-zero value on detecting end-of-file and zero otherwise. Further, the end-of-line character may be defined by a character constant of the form `'\n'`. Hence if the FORTRAN fragment shown below is incorporated in your program `rev`, it will process trailing blanks correctly:

```
10      continue
        do 30 i = 1, n
           if ( getc(line(i)) .ne. 0 ) go to 20
           if ( line(i) .eq. '\n' ) go to 40
30      continue
40      continue
        write (*, '(256a)') (line(j), j = i-1, 1, -1)
        go to 10
20      continue
```

But remember, because you have used features like `iargc`, `getarg` and `getc`, your program is not written in standard FORTRAN and you could have difficulty moving it to other computing environments which do not support UNIX.

## 4.3  Using C

C can best be described as a high-level systems programming language. It has been used to write most of the UNIX operating system and many of its commands. Prior to the advent of languages like C, operating systems and systems software in general were written in assembly language because it was believed that this was the only way to achieve reasonable efficiency with regard to both memory occupancy and CPU utilization. It was considered unthinkable that such software could be written in a high level language and hence be less efficient. However, assembly language programs are not *portable*, that is, they will only execute on the machines (or family of machines) for which they were written and they cannot be moved to other machines with a different architecture and instruction set. C and other languages with similar characteristics have altered all of this. They provide sufficient of the high level language constructs to facilitate the production of well-structured programs while still retaining low-level features which enable a programmer to exercise some control over the efficiency of the generated code.

C has sometimes been described as a "portable assembler". While such a description might appear to be a contradiction in terms, it does give some insight into the characteristics of the language. Of course, there are some inefficiencies associated with the use of C — the generated programs are sometimes not as small or as fast as they would be if they had been written in assembly language. However, the advantages gained from using the high level control and data structures and the fact that the programs can be moved from one machine to another far outweigh the disadvantages. Further, falling hardware costs and the development of faster CPU's and larger memories has meant that today there is far less emphasis on efficient utilization of machine resources than was the case 10 years ago. Software costs are now the dominant ones in the industry and the goal of the systems programmer is to produce well-structured programs free of errors which can be used on a wide variety of machines rather than to squeeze the last ounce of power out of a particular computer.

The development of C has been very closely linked with the development of UNIX. In fact, the second version of UNIX was rewritten in 1972 in C which was designed for that purpose. However, because it is a relatively small language and compilers for it are not difficult to produce, it has spread very widely and today is available on many mainframes, minis and even micros. Programs written in C can easily be transported from a UNIX environment to that of another operating system provided they do not contain UNIX dependencies, that is, have built-in knowledge of the structure of the file system or make direct use of specialized facilities of the operating system. The portability of C programs has been aided by the development of a C compiler which is itself portable and which does not require a great deal of effort to transport it to a new machine. The continuing increase in the use of C for a wide variety of programming tasks means that it has become a very important language in the computer field, a position it will retain throughout the remainder of this decade and beyond.

## 4.3.1 A Simple C Program

Traditionally, books on programming in C have used, as their first example, a program to produce a greeting. So let us continue, since we already have developed two of them anyway. Create the following program in a directory *cex*:

```
$ cd; mkdir cex; cd cex    Create directory and change to it
$ ed  greet.c              Create C program
?greet.c
a
/* outputs a greeting */
main ()
{
    printf("Hello there\n"); /*output greeting*/
}
.
w
86
q
$
```

The filename has been given a suffix **.c** to indicate that it contains source code written in C. The C compiler will not process a source file unless it has such a suffix.

| **cc** - C compiler |
| --- |

Now let's compile the program. If it contains no syntactic errors, you should observe the following behaviour:

```
$ cc greet.c              Compile C program
$
```

**cc** is the command to execute the C compiler. It takes as its arguments one or more files containing C source code, compiles them and, if they constitute a complete program, produces an executable file *a.out* in the current working directory. Check with **ls** that such a file exists, once you have managed to get your program to compile successfully. Now execute *a.out* and once again you will be greeted:

```
$ a.out                   Execute object file
Hello there
$
```

You could rename this file as *grc* using **mv**; alternatively, you could use the **−o** option of the compiler to supply the name of the object file:

```
$ cc −o grc greet.c       Compile C program to produce grc
$ ls
greet.c
grc
$
```

The above output assumes that *a.out* has been removed. So now, if you are a glutton for punishment (or being greeted), execute **grc**:

```
$ grc                          Execute grc
Hello there
$
```

The interface to UNIX provided by the C language system is simple and straightforward just as it is for the other languages we have already considered.

If the C program is not a complete one, each source file is compiled into a corresponding object module with a suffix **.o**. Files with this suffix may also be included as arguments to **cc** to avoid having to recompile source files each time.

## 4.3.2 Compile Time Errors

The C compiler has been designed so that its error messages are self-explanatory. However, some are more "explanatory" than others. Make the same change to *greet.c* that you made to your previous examples of *greet* by removing the right parenthesis from the printf statement and compile again:

```
$ cc greet.c                   Compile illegal C program
"greet.c", line 4: syntax error
$
```

Not all that informative but at least you know that the problem is in line 4 since a statement terminator was encountered before a legal expression was recognized. If you now remove the semicolon and compile again, you will see the same failure message for a different line:

```
"greet.c", line 5: syntax error
```

since the compiler is still looking for an expression as part of a statement when it encounters the terminating }. Again, as with **f77** and **pc**, no attempt is made to repair the program as was done by the interpretive Pascal system.

To explore further the error detecting capabilities of **cc**, let us rewrite in C the program to calculate the square root of an integer. The input analogue of printf is scanf. It takes as arguments format specifications and the addresses of variables which will receive the data read from the input medium. The address of a variable is generated by prepending **&** to its identifier. Now create the program shown in Figure 4.16 in a file *root.c*.

```
/* compute square root of an integer */
main ()
{
        scanf ("%d", &i);
        printf ("%f\n", sqrt (i));
}
```

*Figure 4.16*

The function **scanf** reads a decimal integer from the input stream into i; **printf** now has two arguments — a floating point format specification terminated by newline and a call on the standard function **sqrt** with i as an argument. Now compile the program:

```
$ cc root.c                      Compile illegal C program
"root.c", line 4:  i undefined
$
```

So, like Pascal, C requires variables be declared before they are used. Modify the program to include a declaration for an integer variable by adding:

```
    int i;
```

before the first executable statement and immediately after the left brace. Now recompile:

```
$ cc root.c                      Compile illegal C program
Undefined:
_sqrt
$
```

The program contains a reference to an identifier **_sqrt** of a standard library function (as indicated by the underscore) which has not been defined. Unlike Pascal where standard functions are included as part of the overall system, it is necessary in C to specify where functions external to the program you have written may be found.   **_sqrt** is part of a package of mathematical subroutines which are stored in a library file */usr/lib/libm.a* and it is necessary to state this explicitly when any program which uses one of these routines is to be compiled to form an executable module.   **printf** and **scanf** are part of the standard I/O library which is loaded automatically  by the C compiler and you don't have to worry about them.  But you do have to ensure that definitions associated with any  library are available to your program in case you want to make use of them. You do this by using the directive **#include** followed by  a filename to include them in your source file.  So add the statements:

```
    #include <stdio.h>
    #include <math.h>
```

at the beginning of your file *root.c*.  The suffix *.h* indicates that the file contains header information.  To specify the required library file, you use the flag −l followed by a string.  −l*x* causes the library file */lib/libx.a* to be searched; if this file does not exist, a file of the same name is searched for in */usr/lib*.  So try **cc** again:

```
$ cc root.c -lm     Produce executable object file using /lib/libm.a
$
```

Finally, you will have produced an executable file *a.out*.  The **−lm** argument occurs at the end of the command because it is passed on to the loader which only searches a library file for unresolved references once at the point at which it occurs in the argument list.  So now try the program:

```
$ a.out                    Execute object file
4
0.00000
$
```

Doesn't look quite right — you still have a problem!

### 4.3.3  Run Time Errors

The program in **root.c** compiles successfully to produce an executable module but does not give the correct result.  How can you find out what the problem is?

**lint** - a C program checker

Fortunately, there is a useful tool called **lint** which will apply much more stringent checking to a C program than is carried out by the C compiler itself; for example, it checks type usage much more strictly.  It requires access to the whole program including libraries and recognizes the same type of flags as does **cc**.  So try it and you will see something like:

```
$ lint root.c -lm                Check C program
root.c:
sqrt, arg.1 used inconsistently
scanf returns value which is always ignored
$
```

The last comment refers to the fact that you are using a statement to call the function **scanf** and not making any use of the value it returns.  This is not the problem.  The more interesting comment is that there is something wrong with the argument in the call on **sqrt**.  So you had better take a closer look at this function.  List the file **/usr/include/math.h** and you will see a line that looks something like:

```
extern double sqrt(), hypot(), atof()
```

This specifies that **sqrt** is an external function which returns a double length floating point number of type **double** as a result.  It also expects an argument of this type. Although some automatic type conversion occurs when arguments are passed to a function e.g.  **float** is converted to **double**, there is no such conversion from integers to double length floating point numbers.  This has to be carried out explicitly using a *cast* operator which takes the form of the target type enclosed in parentheses.

Returning now to the example, the final form of the program is shown in Figure 4.17.  The function call **sqrt((double) i)** ensures that the input argument to **sqrt** is in the correct form.  Compile the program and try it:

```
/*compute square root of an integer */
#include <stdio.h>
#include <math.h>

main ()
{
    int i;
    scanf("%d", &i);
    printf("%f\n", sqrt((double) i));
}
```

*Figure 4.17*

$ **cc root.c -lm**       *Compile C program specifying a library file*
$ **a.out**
4
2.000000
$ ░

At last, it appears to work correctly! So now try it on a negative number:

$ **a.out**                    *Execute object file*
−1
0.000000
$ ░

Clearly, you will have to be a lot more careful using C than you were when programming in Pascal.

Let us improve **root.c** by prompting for input and checking for invalid data with an **if** statement. Modify the program as shown in Figure 4.18. Compile it as before and execute **a.out** for positive and negative values. It is now protected against invalid input data.

Let us now extend the program to compute a table of square roots from 1 to i where i is input from the terminal. To do this, you need to make use of the **for** statement. Copy the file **root.c** to **roots.c** and edit the latter to produce the program shown in Figure 4.19.

There is a problem with this program, namely, if you redirect output, everything written to standard output will be sent to the file including the prompt which you will therefore never see. To avoid this difficulty, you could arrange to write the prompt on standard error output rather than on standard output. However, **printf** only writes on standard output and you must therefore use **fprintf** to output the prompt. This takes, as its arguments, a file pointer and a format specifier. The second argument may simply be the actual string to be output. Hence, the **printf** statement which outputs the prompt may be replaced by:

```
#include <stdio.h>
#include <math.h>

/*compute square root of an integer */

main ()
{
    int i;
    printf("Enter number:");
    scanf("%d", &i);

    /* check for positive input */
    if (i >= 0)
        printf("%f\n", sqrt((double) i));
    else
        printf("Negative argument supplied\n");
}
```

*Figure 4.18*

```
#include <stdio.h>
#include <math.h>

/* compute table of square roots of integers */

main ()
{
    int i, j;
    printf("Enter number:");
    scanf("%d", &i);
    printf("\n n    sqrt(n)\n\n");

    /* check for positive input */
    if (i >= 0)
        for(j = 1; j <= i; j++)
            printf("%3d   %6.3f\n", j, sqrt((double) j));
    else
        printf("Negative argument supplied\n");
}
```

*Figure 4.19*

```
        fprintf (stderr, "Enter number:");
```

Make this change to *roots.c*, recompile and try redirecting output:

```
$ cc -o roots roots.c -lm          Compile to produce roots
$ roots > table                    Execute roots
Enter number: 10
$
```

Inspect *table* to check that the program has functioned correctly.

As you will need this program later for another exercise when you will be working in another directory, it would be a good idea to create a *bin* sub-directory of your home directory (if you don't already have one) and move *roots* to it. Usually, people store commands they have developed themselves in their own *bin* directory. Make sure that this directory is in your search path so that you can execute the command irrespective of what your current directory is:

```
$ mkdir ../bin                     Make bin in home directory
$ PATH=$PATH:$HOME/bin             And add it to the search path
$ mv roots ../bin                  Move roots to bin
$
```

================================================

In the C-shell, the command required to add the new directory to the search path (if it is not already there) is:

```
% set path=($path $HOME/bin)       Add bin to search path
```

There is still a slight difficulty, however, in that if you now issue the **roots** command, the system will complain that it cannot find it:

```
% roots                            Execute roots
roots: Command not found.
%
```

The reason is that the C-shell maintains a hash table of the commands in your search path so that it can find a command quickly when you issue one. This table is computed when the C-shell is first invoked. Since *roots* did not exist in *bin* at that time, the shell has no record of it.

> **rehash** - recompute hash table

To recompute the hash table, it is necessary to issue the **rehash** command. Try it now and then issue **roots** once more. This time, it will respond to you.

--------------------------------------------------------------------

## 4.3.4  Testing for end-of-file

As we did with the previous versions in other languages, let us modify **root.c**
so that it reads in numbers and calculates the square root until terminated with
end-of-file, **^D**. There are no tests for end-of-file in C as there are in Pascal and
FORTRAN. Rather a special symbol called **EOF** is returned by the various input
routines including scanf. The value of **EOF** is defined in the header file **stdio.h**
and one of the reasons why you include such files in your program is to be able to
make use of these definitions. Look in the file **/usr/include/stdio.h** and you will
see:

```
#define EOF (-1)
```

Now, modify **root.c** as shown in Figure 4.20 to produce the desired program.

```
/*compute square root of an integer */
#include <stdio.h>
#include <math.h>

main ()
{
    int i;
    printf("Enter number:");
    while(scanf("%d", &i) != EOF)
    {
        /* check for positive input */
        if (i >= 0)
            printf("%3d  %f\n", i, sqrt((double) i));
        else
            printf("Negative argument supplied\n");
        printf("Enter number:");
    }
    printf("\n");
}
```

*Figure 4.20*

Notice that, once again, you had to include statements to output the prompt
twice, once before the loop starts and again inside the loop. The final printf
statement simply outputs a new line to ensure that, when the program exits, the
shell prompt will be output on the left hand side of the screen. Compile and
execute the program to check that it behaves as predicted.

## 4.3.5  Testing for end-of-line

Handling end-of-line is much easier in C than it is in Pascal or FORTRAN
since you can actually access the newline character itself. To illustrate this point,
let us once again develop, in C this time, a program to reverse lines in a file. The

logic of the program will still be basically the same as before — as long as end-of-file does not occur, read in a line terminated by newline, store it in an array and then output the characters of the line in reverse order. Create the program shown in Figure 4.21 to carry out this operation.

```
#include <stdio.h>

/* reverse lines of a file */

#define N 256
char line[N];

main()
{
    register int i, c;

    i = 0;
    while ((c = getchar()) != EOF)
        if ((line[i++] = c) == '\n')
        {
            while (--i >= 0)
                putchar(line[i]);
            putchar('\n');
        }
}
```

*Figure 4.21*

In this program, we have declared a character array line of size N which is currently defined to have a value of 256. The integers i and c have been declared as **register** variables which advises the compiler that they will be used frequently in the program. The compiler will allocate these variables to machine registers if it is able to do so to improve the efficiency of the object code.

In the executable part of the program, i is initialized to 0 and then the **while** statement is executed. Let us first of all analyse the expression controlling the while loop. The function **getchar** reads a character from standard input and returns an integer representation of the character. This is assigned to c and compared with **EOF**. If equal, the while loop terminates and the program exits; if not, the **if** statement is executed. The character in c is stored in the array element line[i] and the index is incremented by the postfix operator ++. Then a test is applied to see if the current character is newline. If it is not, the next iteration of the loop is executed; if it is, a second **while** loop is initiated to output the characters from the array in reverse order. The prefix operator -- decrements i before it is used as an index since it will have already been incremented in readiness for the next input character. The function **putchar** outputs its argument as a character on standard output. Finally, a newline is output to terminate the reversed line and control returns for the next iteration of the loop. Compile the program and try it:

```
$ cc rev.c               Compile C program
$ a.out                  And execute object file
12345

54321
12345

5432
^D
$
```

Doesn't work, does it! Clearly, we have forgotten to discard the newline at the end of the input line (hence the blank lines in the above output). However, the other error is a little more subtle. The first input line is reversed correctly but thereafter the first input character is lost. The problem lies with the expression `--i >= 0`. The output loop will terminate only when `i` takes on the value –1 and it will still have this value when the next input line is processed. Thus, the first character will be stored at `line[-1]` i.e. in the memory location before the start of the array `line`. It will never be seen by the output loop and the output line will be truncated. The moral of this story is that, unlike Pascal, C does not check whether array bounds have been exceeded. So you have to be much more careful when programming in C.

You can easily correct the errors by applying the prefix operator `++` to `i` when it is used to store an input character. It will then be reset to 0 before the first input character is stored in the array. Also, `i` will always point to the last array element referenced and the output loop will commence at the penultimate character, ignoring the terminating newline. To handle the situation for the first input line, all you need to do is to initialize `i` to –1 rather than to 0. Make these changes to produce the program shown in Figure 4.22. Compile and execute it, supplying some text lines from the terminal. This time, it will work correctly! To convince yourself even more, try:

```
$ cc -o revc rev.c              Compile to produce revc
$ revc < rev.c | rev | diff - rev.c   Compare revc with rev
$
```

as you did before and no output should occur from **diff** indicating that your program **revc** behaves in exactly the same way as the system command **rev**, at least, for standard input.

```
#include <stdio.h>

/* reverse lines of a file */

#define N 256
char line[N];

main()
{
    register int i, c;

    i = -1;
    while ((c = getchar()) != EOF)
        if ((line[++i] = c) == '\n')
        {
            while (--i >= 0)
                putchar(line[i]);
            putchar('\n');
        }
}
```

*Figure 4.22*

## 4.3.6  Accessing UNIX Files

Let us now extend **revc** to behave exactly like **rev**, that is, accept filenames as arguments but still read from standard input if no arguments are supplied. By convention, when **main** is called to begin execution, it is supplied with two arguments, **argc**, the count of the number of command line arguments (including the command name itself) and **argv**, the address of an array of addresses, each of which points to an array of characters comprising the argument.

To access a file other than standard input, standard output or standard error output, a program might first open the file by calling a library function **fopen** supplying as arguments the filename and the mode. The latter indicates how the program intends to use the file. If **fopen** cannot open the file, it returns an indicator called **NULL** so that the calling program can take some corrective action such as outputting a failure message. If, on the other hand, the file can be opened, a file pointer is returned which can be assigned to some internal name in the program. If, for example, the internal name was **input**, this would be declared as follows:

　　　FILE *input

Once the file pointer has been assigned to **input**, it can be used as an argument in calls on other system functions for reading and writing characters or lines, e.g. the statement:

```
ch = getc(input)
```

reads the next character from the file **input** and assigns it to **ch**.  EOF is returned if end-of-file is encountered.  Similarly:

```
putc(ch, output)
```

writes the contents of **ch** on the file **output** as well as returning it as a value. Finally, when the program has finished with a file, it should close it by calling **fclose**, again supplying the file pointer as an argument.

You can now extend the program **rev.c** to process filenames as arguments. The new version is shown Figure 4.23.  **main** now has two arguments **argc** and **argv**, the latter being declared as an array of pointers to objects of type **char**. Initially, the file pointer **stdin** is assigned to **input**.  Standard input along with standard output and standard error output have already been opened by the system before the program is called and their corresponding file pointers are **stdin**, **stdout** and **stderr**.  The main body of the program is controlled by a **do-while** loop which causes it to be executed at least once and continues execution as long as there are more arguments to be processed.  The first **if** statement checks to see if there are any arguments and, if not, the program behaves as it did previously, reading from standard input. If there are arguments and **argc** is greater than 1, the program attempts to open a file for reading by calling **fopen** supplying **argv[1]** and **"r"** as arguments. The former is a pointer to a character string array containing the argument; the latter indicates that the file will only be used for reading. At the end of the enclosing **do-while** loop, **argv** is incremented and hence, during the second traversal of the loop, **argv[1]** points to the second argument, during the third, to the third argument and so on.

If **fopen** cannot open the file, it returns **NULL** and the program outputs a failure message on standard error output using **fprintf** which prints formatted output on a specified file.  The program then exits returning an error code of 1, the argument of the function **exit**. If the file can be opened, the file pointer returned by **fopen** is assigned to **input**.

The next section of the program is code you have already developed with **getchar** and **putchar** changed to **getc** and **putc** respectively, each of which takes an extra argument, the file pointer **input** for reading and **stdout** for writing.  Finally, the file currently opened for input is closed, **argv** is incremented and **argc** decremented. Once **argc** reaches 1, all arguments have been processed and the program exits.

Compile the program and test it both from the terminal and using **rev**. Also remember to try it on a non-existent file.  You might also like to  measure the execution speed of **revc** and **rev** again.  You won't find much difference this time since both programs are written in C.

```
#include <stdio.h>

/* reverse lines of a file */

#define N 256
char line[N];
FILE *input;

main (argc, argv)
int argc;
char *argv[];
{
    register int i,c;
    input = stdin; /* initialize input */
    do
    {   /* repeat until no more arguments */
        if (argc > 1)
        {   /* open file supplied as argument */
            if ((input = fopen (argv[1], "r")) == NULL)
            {
                fprintf (stderr,
                    "rev: cannot open %s\n",argv[1]);
                exit (1);
            }
        }
        i = -1;
        while ((c = getc (input)) != EOF)
            if ((line[++i] = c) == '\n')
            {
                while (--i >= 0)
                    putc (line[i], stdout);
                putc ('\n', stdout);
            }
        fclose (input);
        argc--; /* decrement argument count */
        argv++; /* increment index to array of pointers
                    to arguments */
    } while (argc > 1);
}
```

*Figure 4.23*

## 4.4  Using the Shell

To this point, we have used the shell primarily as a command language interpreter, that is, as a systems program which reads a command line from the terminal, performs filename expansion, sets up input-output redirection if required, locates the command and, if it exists, initiates its execution. When it terminates, the shell tidies up and returns control to the terminal, prompting for another command line. However, the shell also provides a programming language which enables you to tailor your interface to the system to one of your own choosing. You can create new commands, modify or enhance the behaviour of existing ones or even replace them if you so desire. You can program small tasks in the language provided by the shell without resorting to conventional programming languages like Pascal or C.

The syntax of the shell programming language is rather strange at times and often leaves a lot to be desired. Like Topsy, it has "growed" over the years; there probably never was a complete design specification in the beginning. Your reaction to some particular idiosyncrasy might be "Ugh! why do I have to learn this?" But persevere, your reward will come when you master the language and can quickly modify your interface to UNIX.

As we have already mentioned, there are two shells in common use in UNIX systems − the standard shell (**sh**), sometimes called the Bourne shell after its creator, and the C-shell (**csh**) developed by Bill Joy and others at the University of California at Berkeley. We prefer the syntax of **sh** for shell programming. However, for interactive use, **csh** provides superior facilities to those in **sh**.

### 4.4.1  A Simple Shell Program

At the risk of being boring, let us write once again, for the last time (that's a promise), a program to output a greeting. This time, we will use shell commands in a file which is often called a *shell script* or a *shell procedure*. Make a directory *shex* in your home directory, transfer to it and create the script shown below:

```
$ cd; mkdir shex; cd shex        Create directory and change to it
$ ed gr                          Create a shell program
?gr
a
:  'outputs a greeting'
echo Hello there  # output greeting
.
w
59
q
$
```

Like any good programming language, the shell provides facilities for including comments in the program text. Two methods are illustrated above. The  :  command does nothing and hence its arguments may be used as a comment. Remember to use one or more spaces to separate the  :  from its arguments. It is best to enclose the comment in quotes as we have shown to prevent any metacharacters being interpreted by the shell. The second method allows a comment to be placed at the end of a line. The # character causes the remainder of the line to be ignored and hence treated as a comment. (Note that the latter facility is not available in Version 7 UNIX.)

The simplest way of executing a shell program is to cause the shell to read commands from a file instead of from the terminal. This can be achieved by issuing the "dot" command.

> | **.** - read and execute commands from a file |

This command takes a filename as an argument and uses the search path defined in the shell variable PATH to locate the file. The shell then executes the commands read from the file as though they had come from the terminal:

```
$ . gr                    Read and execute commands
Hello there
$
```

If any command alters the environment of the shell, the changes will persist after execution of the commands from the file ceases.

=============================================

> | **source** - read and execute commands from a file |

This command is the C-shell equivalent of the "dot" command. The file being read may itself contain **source** commands. Note that commands executed in this manner are not placed on the history list.

-----------------------------------------------------------------

It is not always convenient to execute a command file which results in permanent changes to the environment of the shell. There are times when it would be preferable to have such changes as temporary ones only. To achieve this, you need to issue **sh** as a command itself.

> | **sh** - command language interpreter |

To cause a shell program to be executed, you simply supply the name of the file containing shell commands as an argument to **sh**:

```
$ sh gr                   Execute a shell program
Hello there
$
```

The shell initiates a new process which is itself a shell called a *sub-shell* and this reads the commands from the file instead of from the terminal. As each command is read, it is executed. The shell is therefore behaving as both a compiler and an interpreter. When end-of-file is encountered, the sub-shell exits back to the login shell which outputs the command prompt and waits for further instructions. Any changes made to the environment of the sub-shell will be lost.

As you will see shortly, you can write quite complex shell programs and hence you may need some assistance with debugging them. It is possible to cause the shell to operate in a verbose mode by supplying **−v** as an argument so that each command line is printed out after it has been read:

```
$ sh -v gr                    Print each command as it is executed
: 'outputs a greeting'
echo Hello there  # output greeting
Hello there
$
```

Further, the **−x** option causes the shell to produce an execution trace, printing out each command with its arguments before it is executed:

```
$ sh -x gr                    Output execution trace
+ : outputs a greeting
+ echo Hello there
Hello there
$
```

Since the file *gr* contains the commands you want to execute, it would be more convenient to be able to give the name of the file as a command. So try it:

```
$ gr                          Try to execute shell program
gr:  cannot execute
$
```

Not so good, eh! The problem is that, although you know that *gr* contains executable statements, the system doesn't since you created the file via output redirection and the permissions are therefore the default ones. Hence, you will have to use **chmod** to turn on execute permissions:

```
$ chmod 755 gr                Make gr executable
$ gr
Hello there
$
```

Everything now works as you wanted it to do.

====================================================

┌─────────────────────────────────────────┐
│ **csh** - command language interpreter │
└─────────────────────────────────────────┘

There is, however, one slight problem if your login shell is **csh**. All we have said so far about shell scripts for **sh** applies equally well for **csh** except for an executable script. If you want this to be executed by **csh** rather than by **sh**, the first line must commence with **#**, that is, be a comment. Since the file *gr* does not start with such a line, then, if your interactive shell is **csh** and you issue the command **gr**, **sh** will be invoked as a sub-shell to execute it. If, on the other hand, *gr* contains:

```
# outputs a greeting
echo Hello there  # output greeting
```

then **csh** will invoke **csh** as a sub-shell rather than **sh**.

------------------------------------------------------------------------

## 4.4.2  Run Time Errors

What happens if an error is made in a shell program? Let's introduce one and find out. Using an editor, change `echo` in *gr* to `ech` and then execute **gr** again:

```
$ gr                    Execute an invalid shell program
gr:  ech:  not found
$
```

The fact that the command **ech** does not exist is reported together with the name of the command file in which the error occurred. In this respect, shell scripts are similar to ordinary programs — syntax errors are detected and reported to the user. But just how well is this done? Modify your program as shown below and introduce the shell variables H and `t` :

```
:  'outputs a greeting'
H=Hello   t=there
echo  $H $t  # output greeting
```

Convince yourself that **gr** still works and then introduce an error by converting the identifier `t` to `T` in the second line. Now, execute **gr** again:

```
$ gr                    Execute shell program
Hello
$
```

**sh** does not report that `t` has not been declared. Instead, it simply takes its value as the null string. So you will have to be a little careful when using shell variables that you do not misspell their identifiers or forget to give them an initial value.

========================================================================

**csh**, on the other hand, applies more stringent checks. If *gr* contains:

```
# outputs a greeting
set H=Hello set T=there
echo $H $t  #output greeting
```

**csh** will report  `t: Undefined variable`.

------------------------------------------------------------------------

So now you are in a position to create your own commands and tailor your interface to UNIX to suit your own tastes.

### 4.4.3  Input-Output

Unless you are overly narcissistic, let us finally give up asking the computer to greet you and try something a little more useful. A command that comes to mind is one which outputs a count of the number of users currently logged in. Let's call it **uc** (user count). It may be that, if the count is too high in a multi-user system, the response will be poor and you may as well logout and try again later. So create a file *uc*, make it executable and try it:

```
$ echo 'who | wc -l' > uc   Create a shell program to count users
$ chmod +x uc               Make uc executable
$ uc                        Try it
    5                       5 users are logged in
$
```

Since **uc** is a command that you might want to use at any time, you should place it in the *bin* sub-directory of your home directory.

```
$ mv uc ../bin              Move uc to bin
$
```

After all, even though it is not a binary file, it is executable and is therefore indistinguishable from an object binary as far as its behaviour is concerned.

In the two examples we have considered so far, output from a shell program has appeared on the terminal, that is, it has been sent to standard output. It could therefore be redirected just as if it had come from a system command. But what about input? By analogy, one would expect that, if a command in a shell program reads from standard input, the user at the terminal could respond or input could come from a file through input redirection. To illustrate this facility, let us construct a command **un** which outputs only the usernames of those users currently logged in and does so on one line. You need to select the usernames from the output of **who** and discard the remaining information. Sounds like a job for **ed**! (There are more elegant ways of doing this but this will serve for the moment.) First, construct **un** as follows and then make it executable:

```
$ ed un                     Create shell program to output usernames
?un
a
who > temp                  Preserve who output
ed - temp                   Edit who output
echo 'cat temp'             Output on one line
rm temp                     Tidy up
.
w
45
q
$ chmod +x un               Make un executable
$
```

(The − argument to **ed** supresses the output of character counts and some of the more trivial error indicators.) Now, when you issue the **un** command, you will have to supply input from the terminal to instruct **ed** to delete the unwanted information in each line and to quit after rewriting *temp*. The commands **echo** and **rm** will then be executed:

```
$ un                          Execute un to output usernames
1,$s/ .*//                     Truncate all lines
w                             Preserve changes
q                             Exit
mcf pcp eas yew               List of users logged in
$
```

Naturally, being very observant, you will have realized that the directives you must supply to **ed** are the same every time. Hence, they could be placed in a file, say *edcoms*, and accessed by input redirection:

```
$ un < edcoms                  Redirect input and execute un
mcf pcp eas yew
$
```

but, really, the whole thing is becoming rather clumsy. What we would much prefer to do is be able to include the edit directives in the shell script itself. Fortunately, there is a way of doing just this using the metacharacter **<<**.

The shell supports a facility known as a *here document* whereby standard input for a command can be placed in a file along with the command itself. As its name implies, the input is right *here* rather than somewhere else, for example, in another file. The command line containing the command which requires the input is extended by **<<** followed by a character string. Subsequent lines are then taken as standard input up to but not including a line which contains only the specified character string. This acts as a terminator. So let's modify *un* as shown in Figure 4.24 and try this facility.

```
who > temp                    Preserve who output
ed - temp <<end               Edit who output using here document
1,$s/ .*//                     Truncate all lines
w                             Preserve changes
q                             Exit
end                           Here terminator
echo `cat temp`               Output on one line
rm temp                       Tidy up

                              Figure 4.24
```

The character string being used to signal the end of standard input is **end**. So now, try the new command and, much to your annoyance, you will find that it doesn't work. What you will see is a **?** complaint from **ed** followed by all the output of **who** on one line. So **ed** must have failed! If you want to see why, try

**sh −x un** and observe that the substitute command has been altered. The problem is that the here document has been subjected to shell expansion; the string **$s** has been treated as a shell variable and replaced by its value, probably the null string. To prevent this happening, it is necessary to quote the terminating character string which follows << either by using backslash or enclosing it in single quotes. So change the first **end** to ´end´ and try again:

```
$ un                        Execute un to output usernames
mcf pcp eas yew
$
```

You have a new command! The moral of this little saga is that shell programming can be tricky. The shell is always doing things behind your back and you had better be on your guard!

So now you know how to make one of your own shell programs read from standard input. But is this facility powerful enough to handle all situations? Let us explore this for a moment. Suppose you want to build a private directory enquiry service based on a command which searches a file for a string and a file containing names and telephone numbers. The command you will need to use is **grep** which takes a string and a filename as arguments. (We will discuss this command in detail later in Section 5.2.) You could create a command file **de** containing the names and numbers as a here document but the thing which changes each time you make an enquiry is the search string which **grep** expects as an argument, that is, it cannot read the string from standard input. So you have a problem which, on inspection, looks very similar to one that might occur in a programming language like Pascal. If you want to calculate, say, the square root of a number, you write a program using variables which are initialized by means of a read statement. So, if the shell provides a **read** command, which it does, the problem is solved.

| **read** - read one line from standard input |
| --- |

The built-in command **read** which takes as arguments one or more variable names, reads a line of text from standard input and assigns one word to each variable in turn. Any remaining words are assigned to the last variable. Note that the end-of-line character is discarded. So create the script shown in Figure 4.25 in a file **de** varying the names and phone numbers to suit your own requirements. (In **csh** and earlier versions of **sh**, use **echo −n** ´name?´ to suppress output of newline.) Now try it:

```
$ de                        Execute directory enquiry program
name?jack jones             Supply name to be located
jack jones    519-3723
$
```

Notice that the argument for **grep** has been enclosed in double quotes so that

```
echo 'name?\c'            Output prompt without newline
read string               Input name to variable string
grep "$string" <<'end'    Search here document
bill brown     347-6851
jack jones     519-3723
mary smith     059-62-9817
end                       Here terminator
```

*Figure 4.25*

variable substitution is performed but you can still search for a string containing blanks. If you replied **bill brown** to the input query, then, without the double quotes, **grep** would look for the string **bill** in the file *brown* which is not what you want it to do.

By now, the similarities between shell programming and writing programs in a high level language should be fairly obvious. You can write to standard output using **echo**; you can read from standard input using **read**. Input and output also occur for commands much as they would with high level language procedures. Later, we will see that there are even more similarities.

## 4.4.4 Accessing Arguments

Now let us investigate how we can create a shell command file that behaves just like an ordinary system command, that is, one to which you can supply arguments. When a new shell is invoked by the current shell, any arguments on the command line are made available to it. The first argument (not counting any options) is the name of the file containing the shell commands to be read and executed. The remaining arguments may be thought of as data which may be used by the commands as they are executed. The notation used to access an argument is $ followed by a single digit indicating the position in the argument list. Thus **$1** references the 1st argument, **$2**, the second and so on up to **$9**. The interpretation of **$0** is that it gives access to the name of the file containing the shell commands. Let us create a shell command file to enable you to examine this mechanism a little more closely:

```
$ echo 'echo $0 $1 $2 $3' > tsp    Create tsp
$ sh tsp a b c                      Execute tsp with 3 arguments
tsp a b c                           3 arguments echoed
$ sh tsp a b c d                    Execute tsp with 4 arguments
tsp a b c                           4th argument ignored
$ sh tsp a                          Execute tsp with 1 argument
tsp a                               2nd and 3rd arguments null
$
```

Notice that, if more arguments are supplied than are needed, the extra ones are ignored; conversely, if an argument is not supplied, its value is the null string. Now make the file *tsp* executable and try again:

```
$ chmod +x tsp              Make tsp executable
$ tsp a                     And execute it
tsp a                       Command and argument echoed
$
```

**$0** is still the name of the file containing the commands to be executed.

If you wish to create a command which has a variable number of arguments (up to a maximum of 9), then, obviously, you could do so using **$1, $2 ... $9** to reference them. However, this could become a little tedious. Fortunately, you can make use of the notation **$\*** to mean "all arguments including the null string". Add **echo $\*** to the end of the file *tsp* and try it again:

```
$ tsp 1 2 3 4               Execute tsp with 4 arguments
tsp 1 2 3                   Command and 3 arguments
1 2 3 4                     4 arguments
$
```

Notice that **echo $\*** does not produce the name of the command.

We are now in a position to modify the directory enquiry command so that the name to be retrieved can be supplied as an argument. The modified form is shown in Figure 4.26.

```
grep  "$*" <<'end'                Search here document
bill brown     347-6851
jack jones     519-3723
mary smith     059-62-9817
end                               Here terminator

                 Figure 4.26
```

The command now behaves as follows:

```
$ de mary                   Execute de to locate mary
mary smith     059-62-9817
$
```

So now you know how to write a shell script and make it behave just like any of the other commands in the system. Install the file in your *bin* directory replacing the previous one if you had moved it there and you have added a new tool to your repertoire.

## 4.4.5  Repetition

The directory enquiry program has one major limitation, namely, it can only retrieve one telephone number at a time. Obviously, there will be times when you want to make a number of calls and you may wish to supply more than one name as an argument to **de**. You therefore need a mechanism that will allow you to process a variable number of arguments and repeat the commands for each one.

| **for** - execute commands repeatedly |
| --- |

To repeat commands, you use the **for** command which has the following syntax:

```
for name in word_1 word_2  ...
do
        command-list
done
```

*name* is a shell variable which takes on successive values *word_1*, *word_2*, ... as execution of the loop progresses. The loop terminates when the list of words is exhausted. If **in** *word_1 word_2...* is omitted, the default list is the arguments equivalent to **$*** and the loop is executed once for each such argument.

You can now modify **de** to handle more than one name by adding a **for** command as shown in Figure 4.27.

```
for i                          For each argument
do
grep "$i" <<'end'              Search here document
bill brown        347-6851
jack jones        519-3723
mary smith        059-62-9817
end                            Here document terminator
done
```

*Figure 4.27*

By retaining the double quotes, you can still look for a first name and surname provided they are enclosed in single quotes in the argument list:

```
$ de mary 'jack jones'         Execute de to locate 2 entries
mary smith        059-62-9817
jack jones        519-3723
$
```

In setting out a **for** command, you must be careful that the **do** and **done** follow immediately (not counting white space) after a newline or a semicolon. Try:

```
$ for i in *; do echo $i ; done
```

and you will obtain a listing of your current directory. Of course, it would not be very sensible to use this command since **ls** does the same job much more efficiently. Be careful that you do not use a **for** command in situations where a command processes multiple arguments which can be generated by filename expansion. Only use **for** to control multiple commands or where an individual command cannot handle multiple arguments.

Suppose, for example, that in a certain directory you keep source text for Pascal programs each with a suffix *.p*. From time to time, before you modify a file, suppose that you save it in the same directory with a suffix *.p_old*. At any time, if you want to know what the differences are between the current and previous versions of a file, you would use the **diff** command:

```
$ diff file.p  file.p_old
```
    *Output differences between 2 files*

If there are a number of files in the directory, what you would like to be able to do is say:

```
$ diff *.p  *.p_old
```
    *Can't be done!*

but you can't since the arguments for **diff** must be single filenames. In such a situation, you must use the **for** command. Create an executable file *diffold* containing the commands shown in Figure 4.28.

```
for i in *_old                    Iterate over suffix _old
do
  base=`basename $i  _old`        Remove suffix
  echo $base                      Output basename
  diff $base ${base}_old          Compare old and new files
done

                  Figure 4.28
```

The loop variable `i` takes on, successively, the filenames in the current directory which have a suffix `_old`.

**basename** - deliver base of pathname

This command will remove any prefix ending in **/** from its first argument and any suffix specified by its second argument. Hence, it strips the suffix *_old* and the resulting basename is assigned to the variable **base**. The basename is then output and the files are compared. Install *diffold* in your *bin* directory, create a few files in a directory with and without the suffix *_old*, **cd** to that directory and test **diffold**. Works nicely or does it really? Well, it does work correctly but only in your current directory which is hardly in keeping with the

UNIX philosophy. What you would really like to be able to do is specify a directory or, better still, a list of directories as an argument. The command could iterate over the directory names and then, within each directory, iterate over those files with a suffix _old, that is, you need a loop within a loop. So enclose the previous loop in an outer loop and precede the basename with the directory name as a prefix. The modified script is shown in Figure 4.29.

```
for j                              Iterate over argument list
do
    for i in $j/*_old              Iterate over suffix _old
    do
        base=`basename $i  _old`   Remove suffix
        echo $j/$base              Output base name
        diff $j/$base $j/${base}_old  Compare old and new
    done
done
```

*Figure 4.29*

So now it doesn't matter what your current working directory is — you can issue the command with one or more directories as arguments. Nested **for** commands are a powerful feature of shell scripts just as they are in high level language programs. One slight problem, though — if your current working directory is the directory in which you are interested, you have to issue the command:

$ **diffold** .          *Compare old and new files in current directory*

whereas the typical UNIX convention assumes that the current directory is the default. However, if you issue the command **diffold** without an argument, no output will be generated since the outer loop, in the absence of any names over which to iterate, will terminate immediately. So you need to be able to determine whether or not there are any arguments.

There is also another problem which we have carefully avoided mentioning. If there are no filenames in the directory ending with the suffix _old, then, according to the rules of filename expansion, the original string will be left untouched. So i will initially take on the value $j/*_old where $j is the directory name. Things will then go haywire. **base** will be assigned a value *, **echo** will output all the names of files in the current directory and **diff** will complain about having too many arguments. We will return to these problems again later and show you how to improve the command still further.

> **while** - execute commands repeatedly

The shell provides two other iterative commands. The **while** command has the following syntax:

```
while command-list_1
do
      command-list_2
done
```

> **until** - execute commands repeatedly

The syntax of another iterative command is defined as follows:

```
until command-list_1
do
      command-list_2
done
```

So clearly **while** and **until**, by analogy with similar constructs in other programming languages, must be testing the value of a boolean expression to see whether it is `true` or `false`. In the case of **while**, the second command list is executed repeatedly as long as the boolean expression is `true`; the reverse holds for **until**. Now we have to ask where the boolean value is being generated.

You will have noticed by now that commands work successfully sometimes and, at other times, they fail, perhaps because you have given them incorrect data to process. When a UNIX command terminates, it returns an *exit status* which tells something about what happened. If it returns a zero, this is taken to mean that everything worked as expected; conversely, non-zero implies that there were deviations from the expected behaviour. The value returned can be used by the shell program to determine its subsequent course of action. By convention, zero stands for `true` and non-zero for `false` (which is the reverse of the convention in the C programming language). The exit status tested by the **while** and **until** commands is that produced by the last command in the first list of commands. The second command list will be executed if the exit status is zero for **while** and non-zero for **until**.

### 4.4.6  Testing for end-of-file

To illustrate the use of the **while** command, let us develop a shell command called **arem** which enables you to add one-line reminders to a file *rems* in your home directory. The format of each reminder is a sequence number in the range 1 to 999 followed by the date and time at which it was added and the text of the reminder itself. The current maximum sequence number is to be kept in a file *remno*, also in your home directory. The command is to accept the text of the reminders from standard input until end-of-file is encountered. Once this happens, **remno** is to be updated before exit occurs. The logic of the command is shown in Figure 4.30. The text of the command file corresponding to this is shown in Figure 4.31.

```
Retrieve current maximum sequence number
Add colon to list of input field separators (IFS)
Split output of date into separate arguments
DOWHILE not end-of-file
    Read reminder
    Output sequence number, date, time, reminder text
    Increment sequence number
ENDWHILE
Preserve new maximum sequence number
```

*Figure 4.30*

```
: initialize remno in your home directory before
: running this script
: adds one line reminders to reminder file rems
seqnum=`cat $HOME/remno`          Initialize sequence number
IFS=' (T)                          Add : to internal field separators
:'
set `date`                         Assign date output to arguments
while read rem                     Input reminders until EOF
do
    echo $seqnum':' $2 $3 $4':''$5 $rem >> $HOME/rems
    seqnum=`expr $seqnum + 1`     Increment sequence number
done
echo $seqnum  > $HOME/remno        Preserve new sequence number
```

*Figure 4.31*

IFS is redefined to include a colon as well as space, tab and newline. We have shown the tab as (T) in the figure just so you won't forget to include it. Now, whenever a command line is broken up into its components, a colon will have the same effect as a space. You encountered the **set** command earlier in Chapter 2 where it was used to output the values of shell variables. However, it can also be used in System V to turn shell flags on or off and to assign values to the positional parameters. Thus, **set −v** turns on a diagnostic mode which causes all input lines to be printed as they are read and **set +v** turns it off. Any remaining arguments after the flags are assigned in turn to **$1**, **$2**, ... etc. Hence, after the **set** command has been executed, the month, day number, hours and minutes are available as positional parameters 2, 3, 4 and 5 respectively. The command **read** returns zero if a line of text is input and non-zero if end-of-file is detected. As long as you supply reminder text lines, the body of the **while** loop is executed causing the new reminder line to be appended to *rems* and the sequence number to be incremented.

> **expr** - evaluate arguments as an expression

The command **expr** evaluates its arguments as an expression and writes the result on standard output. The integer arithmetic operators + − * / % (the remainder operator) are recognized, as are the relational operators < <= = != >= >. For the latter operator set, the expression yields a value of 1 if the comparison is true, otherwise 0. Notice that both operators and operands have to be delimited in some way e.g. + is separated from its operands by spaces. When end-of-file occurs, the current value of the sequence number is preserved in *remno* and the command terminates. Set up the command as shown and experiment with it. You can look at *rems* using **cat, more, pg** or an editor; the latter command will also enable you to delete reminders, once they are no longer required.

There are a number of things not quite right with your new command **arem**. If, for example, you forget how to use it correctly and supply some arguments, it simply ignores them and says nothing about it; if the file *remno* does not exist or has been corrupted, execution of the commands in the file *arem* proceeds regardless, possibly causing some corruption of *rems*. You need to be able to protect yourself from your own mistakes, a good design philosophy for any command. We will return later to consider how this goal could be achieved.

Sometimes it is necessary to escape from a loop before the end conditions are satisfied. The shell does not recognize a **goto** command but it does provide **break** and **continue** which function in much the same way as statements of the same name in C.

> **break** - exit from the enclosing loop

This command causes exit from the enclosing **for, while** or **until** loop. Since you can have loops within loops within loops and so on, so you can attach a level number as an argument to **break**. Thus, **break** causes exit from the current loop and **break 1**, from the enclosing loop.

> **continue** - advance to next iteration

This command resumes at the next iteration of the enclosing **for, while** or **until** loop. It can also take a level number as an argument. Structured programming is available in the shell as it is in other modern programming languages.

## 4.4.7 Selection

The shell executes commands in a command file in sequence, one after the other, until the sequence is broken either by a repetition which causes one or more commands to be executed repeatedly or a selection which causes one or more commands to be executed out of a number of possible alternatives. There are two forms of selection available in **sh**, namely **case** and **if**. The former selects a command via a pattern match, the latter on the basis of the exit status of a command.

| **case** - execute one of a number of alternative commands |
| --- |

The syntax of the **case** command is:

```
case word in
    pattern_1 )  command-list_1  ;;
    pattern_2 )  command-list_2  ;;
            .
            .
            .
    pattern_n )  command-list_n  ;;
esac
```

The command compares *word* with each of the patterns in turn, from top to bottom. The first pattern which produces a match causes the associated command list to be executed. After this has been completed, the next command obeyed is the one following **esac** even if a subsequent pattern would also have produced a match. If no pattern is matched, then the effect of the **case** is the same as the null command. The patterns are those with which you are already familiar from file name generation with one useful extension. The pattern **x|y** will match **x** or **y**. Additional alternatives may also be specified e.g. [1-9]|10|11|12 will match the integers 1 to 12.

To try out the **case** command, let us add some commands to **arem** to guard against the situation in which the user forgets how to use the command and supplies some arguments. What you would like to do if this occurs is output a usage message. The special shell variable $# is set to the number of input arguments and, if this is non-zero, you could warn the user of this fact. The value of $# could therefore be used as a selector in the **case** command. Create a file *ctst* as follows:

```
$ cat > ctst              Create shell program
case $# in
    0) ;;
    *) echo 'usage: arem' 1>&2; exit 1;;
esac
^D
$
```

| **exit** - exit from shell |

This command causes the shell to terminate. If used without an argument, the current exit status is left unchanged. However, if an expression is supplied as an argument, it is evaluated and its value becomes the new exit status.

The notation `1>&2` used in the preceding example causes the failure message to be sent to standard error output. If `$#` is equal to 0, no commands are obeyed and the shell command just exits normally. However, if any arguments are supplied, the value of `$#`, irrespective of what it is, matches the pattern `*`. The usage message is printed and the shell command returns an exit status 1. Obviously, this pattern must be the last one in the **case** command, otherwise it would also match 0. Now try the command file:

```
$ sh ctst          Execute shell program with no arguments
$ sh ctst 1        Execute shell program with 1 argument
usage: arem
$
```

Add the contents of **ctst** to the beginning of **arem** and your new command is starting to take shape.

You could also use a **case** to improve the **diffold** command. Remember that it did not work correctly in the absence of any arguments. If, however, you add to the beginning of this command the statements:

```
case $# in
    0)  set . ;;
esac
```

then, if no arguments are supplied, . is made positional parameter 1, that is, the default is now the current working directory.

| **if** - conditional execution |

Now let us consider the **if** command which has the following syntax:

```
if command-list_1
then
    command-list_2
else
    command-list_3
fi
```

The layout of the command is important. **if**, **then** and **else** are only recognized after a new line or semicolon, (not counting, of course, any preceding white space). The **else** *command-list_3* part of the **if** command is optional. If the last command in *command-list_1* returns exit status 0 (**true**), the commands in *command-list_2* are executed and those in *command-list_3* are ignored; if the exit status is non-zero (**false**), the reverse occurs. Control then passes to the next command in the file. If **else** is omitted, the commands in *command-list_2* are executed only if the last command in *command-list_1* returns 0; otherwise, the **if** command has the same effect as a null command.

Let us now see if we can use the **if** command to improve **diffold** and **arem**. To carry out such checks as determining whether a directory contains a file with a specific suffix or whether a file exists and contains an integer in a specific range, you will need to make use of the **test** command.

$$\boxed{\textbf{test} \ - \ \text{evaluate a condition}}$$

The **test** command is designed for use in shell programs rather than from a terminal. There are three main types of tests that can be carried out:

(i) *tests on numerical values* : two integers may be compared using the standard relational operators **–eq**, **–ne**, **–gt**, **–ge**, **–lt** and **–le**. If the value of the expression is true, **test** returns an exit status of zero. Otherwise, it returns non-zero. To see this, try the following sequence (**$?** is a special shell variable which is always set to the exit status of the last command obeyed):

```
$ test 3 -eq 6        Compare 3 with 6
$ echo $?             Inspect exit status
1                     Numbers are not equal
$ echo $?             Output exit status
0                     Echo command worked correctly
$
```

Since 3 is not equal to 6, **test** returns non-zero, in this case, 1 and **echo** prints it on the terminal. Since **echo** executed successfully, it returns zero and this becomes the new value of **$?** as illustrated by the output of the second **echo** command. Note that the comparisons are carried out on numeric values and not character strings. Thus, 00001 has the same value as 1.

(ii) *tests on character strings* : two character strings may be compared using the operators **=** and **!=** which stand for "equal" and "not equal" respectively:

```
$ test 00009 = 9      Compare 2 strings
$ echo $?             Inspect exit status
1                     Strings are not equal
$
```

Because the equality of two strings is being tested, **test** returns non-zero since the strings 00009 and 9 are different.

Another test that can be performed is whether the length of a string is zero or not using the operators **–z** and **–n**:

```
$ test -z abc ;  echo $?   Check length of string
1                          String is non-null
$
```

Exit status 1 is printed since the length of **abc** is not zero. You can also check for the presence or absence of a string using the **test** command without any operators:

```
$ test $HOME; echo $?      Does HOME have a value?
0                          Yes
$
```

**test** returns exit status 0 since the shell variable HOME contains a string.

(iii) *tests on files* : it is often convenient in a shell command to be able to determine whether a file exists and, if it does, to test some of its characteristics. The form of the argument for **test** is an operator followed by a filename. The more commonly used operators are **-f** or **-d** to test whether a file is an ordinary one or a directory, **-r**, **-w** or **-x** to test whether the file is readable, writable or executable respectively. **-s** tests that the file exists and is non-empty. Try:

```
$ test -d . ; echo $?      Is file a directory?
0                          Yes
$
```

which indicates that the current directory exists whereas:

```
$ test -f . ; echo $?      Is current directory an ordinary file?
1                          No
$
```

illustrates that it is not an ordinary file. Arguments for **test** can be combined using the operators **-a**, **-o** and **!** which represent logical **and, or** and **not** respectively. Parentheses may also be used to create groupings. However, remember that parentheses are meaningful to the shell and must be escaped. If you wanted to test that a file *alpha* exists, is not a directory and is readable but not writable, the required command would be:

```
$ test -f alpha -a -r alpha -a ! -w alpha
```

Not particularly elegant, is it — in fact, it is downright clumsy but that is the way it is, so you'll just have to get used to it.

So now back to improve the commands **diffold** and **arem**. The final version of the first one is shown in Figure 4.32. A test has been added inside the inner **do** to check that a file with suffix *_old* exists in the directory being searched. If it does not, a warning message to this effect is written on standard error output. Use has also been made of the fact that **diff** returns exit status 0 if no match occurs to reduce the amount of output. The directory name is only printed for those directories in which differences occur between old and current files. The

```
: compare old and current versions of files in a directory
: old versions have suffix _old
: usage: diffold [ name ...]
case $# in
    0) set . ;;                                    $1 is current directory
esac
for j in $*
do
    for i in $j/*_old                              For each suffix _old
    do
        if test $i != "$j/*_old"                   At least 1 file
        then
            base=`basename $i _old`                Remove suffix _old
            if diff $j/$base $j/${base}_old   Compare
            then :
            else echo $j/$base                     Output basename
            fi
        else
            echo "no _old suffixes in $j"  1>&2
        fi
    done
done
```

*Figure 4.32*

command could be further improved by adding a test to check that the filename supplied as an argument is indeed the name of a directory. We will leave that to you as an exercise.

Now for **arem**. The problem here was to incorporate a test that **seqnum** contains an integer in a specified range. The best way to do this is to assign the contents of *remno* to **seqnum** after checking that *remno* exists and then test that **seqnum** contains an integer in the range 1 to 999. The final form of the command is shown Figure 4.33. If *remno* does not exist, a failure message is printed and exit 2 occurs; if its contents are illegal, this is reported to the user before the command exits with exit status 3. Thus, any commands which make use of *arem* could determine why it failed. The command has also been extended to incorporate commands to reset the sequence number to 1, once it reaches 1000.

There are some other improvements that you could make to the reminder system. Since you are not really interested in the file *remno*, you could make it invisible to normal examination of your home directory by changing its name to *.remno*. We will leave you to implement this if you wish. You could also

```
: initialize remno in your home directory before
: running this script
: adds one line reminders to reminder file rems
case $# in
    0) ;;
    *) echo 'usage: arem' 1>&2; exit 1;;
esac
if test ! -f  $HOME/remno              Sequence no. file exists?
then echo "$HOME/remno does not exist"; exit 2
fi
seqnum=`cat $HOME/remno`               Initialize sequence number
if test $seqnum -lt 1 -o $seqnum -gt 999        Seq. no. valid?
then echo 'invalid sequence number'; exit 3
fi
IFS=' Ⓣ                                Add : to internal field separators
: '
set `date`                            Assign date output to arguments
while read rem                        Input reminders until end-of-file
do
    echo $seqnum':' $2 $3 $4':'$5 $rem >> $HOME/rems
    seqnum=`expr $seqnum + 1`         Increment sequence number
done
if test $seqnum -eq 1000
then echo 1  > $HOME/remno            Reset sequence number
else echo $seqnum > $HOME/remno      Preserve new sequence number
fi
```

*Figure 4.33*

develop commands **srem** and **drem** to show or delete various reminders.

======================================

## 4.4.8  C-shell Aliases

It would clearly be convenient, in many instances, to be able to replace a long command by a much shorter one. Such a facility is called an *alias* and is supported by the C-shell. It enables you to rename commands, to supply default arguments and to apply transformations to a command line.

**alias** - define or print command aliases

To illustrate the use of aliasing, consider the command **ls** that we have used many times already in this book with arguments −l, −a and −al. You can alias these as follows using the **alias** command:

```
% alias ll ls -l          Define ll as an alias
% alias la ls -a          Also la
% alias lal ls -al        And lal
%
```

Then any time you type **ll**, you will get a long listing of your current working directory. Since the characters `ll` in the line you type are replaced by `ls -l`, further arguments can be supplied. So, after creating the aliases shown above, try:

```
% ll /etc/motd            List directory entry in long format
```

and you will obtain the long format of the directory entry for */etc/motd*.

Aliasing and history substitution can be combined to enable arguments to be extracted from the line you type (which becomes the previous event) and incorporated into the current command line (the aliased command). If you wanted to find more details about the person associated with a given username, you could use **grep** to search the password file. You could also set up an alias **whois** for this operation:

```
% alias whois 'grep \!$ /etc/passwd'    Define whois as an alias
% whois yew                             Output password file entry for yew
yew:jOVpBYJYP2TF6:8:1:Yorick Whiffle:/usr/staff/yew:/bin/sh
%
```

The string defining **whois** is enclosed in quotes to prevent any shell expansion but notice that ! has to be escaped with \ to prevent it being interpreted when the alias for **whois** is defined. When the **whois** command is issued, it is first of all replaced by its alias and the command line is then substituted. The last parameter in the previous command, in this case, **yew**, is substituted as the first argument of **grep** before the current command is obeyed to produce the desired result.

Aliasing is a particularly convenient facility since one can alias short commands to long commands, multiple commands and even pipes. But you have to be a little careful not to get carried away. Too many may slow the system down a little and your response times will increase. If you want to see at any time what aliases you have set, simply issue the **alias** command without any arguments:

```
% alias                    List currently defined aliases
     ll    (ls -l)
     la    (ls -a)
     lal   (ls -al)
     whois grep !$ /etc/passwd
%
```

> **unalias** - remove command aliases

Finally, if you want to get rid of an alias that is no longer required, use the **unalias** command with the alias as an argument.

------------------------------------------------------------------

## 4.4.9 Shell Initialization and Termination

It should be clear now that there are a number of ways in which you might wish to tailor the behaviour of the shell to suit your own particular requirements. You might wish to set shell variables or even execute certain commands. It would be a pain if you had to do this every time you logged in. Consequently, each time a shell starts up after login, it looks in your home directory for specific files and, if it finds any, executes the commands they contain before calling for commands from the terminal. For the standard shell, there is only one such file called *.profile*.

=====================================================

For the C-shell, there are two files, *.cshrc* and *.login*. In fact, any time the C-shell is initiated whether immediately after login or not, it executes any commands in *.cshrc*.

------------------------------------------------------------------

If you store in these files the commands you want executed, the environment that suits you will be configured automatically each time you login.

Let us create a file *.profile* in your home directory if one does not already exist. Sometimes such a file is put there by the system administration when your account is established. Check your home directory with **ls −a**. If no such file exists, you can use **ed** to create one:

```
$ ed .profile          Create file for sh initialization
?.profile
a
TERM=vc404             Define terminal type
export TERM            And export it
date
who
.
w
32
q
$
```

To test this facility, you must login again by responding **login** to the command prompt and supplying your password in the usual fashion. You should then see the output from these commands. If you start up another shell by issuing the **sh** command, no output will occur since *.profile* is only examined by the login shell.

To avoid having to logout and login again, you can simply issue the "dot" command which will cause the shell to read commands from the file and execute them.

======================================================

If you are using C-shell, create a *.login* and a *.cshrc* (if these files do not exist already):

```
% ed .login              Create file for initialization after login
?.login
a
set TERM=vc404           Define terminal type
date
who
.
w
24
q
% ed .cshrc              Create file for csh initialization
?.cshrc
a
set history=10           Define size of history list
alias ll  ls -l          Define ll as an alias
.
w
30
q
%
```

Now you can login again. You will receive the output from the commands in *.login* and will find that ll and the history list are available to you. As an alternative to logging out and logging in again, you can use the command **source** to cause the shell to read and execute commands from *.login* and *.cshrc*. Remember that *.login* is read after *.cshrc*. You can make use of variables set by commands in *.cshrc* in the commands you place in *.login* but not the other way around. Also you must be careful where you place aliases and set variables, since if you initiate another shell only *.cshrc* is read and executed.

The C-shell also looks for the existence of a special file called *.logout* in your home directory when you logout. If it exists, commands in this file are executed, thereby enabling you to tidy up your terminal session, if you so desire. You might arrange to delete temporary files, output your disk space usage or even send yourself a little message to cheer yourself up. Try:

```
% /usr/games/fortune           Let UNIX tell your fortune
```

and see what you get. If you like that sort of thing, you could incorporate it in your *.logout* file.

------------------------------------------------------------------

## *SUMMARY*

- Pascal, FORTRAN and C are high level programming languages which are more akin to natural language and mathematics than is machine language.

□ Pascal is a general purpose language that can be used to create structured programs, that is, programs whose structure makes them understandable by people as well as machines.

□ A Pascal program must be placed in a file with a **.p** suffix before it can be compiled and executed.

□ To compile a Pascal program, supply the filename of the file that contains it as an argument to **pi**, the Pascal interpreter code translator which, if no errors are detected, will produce a file of interpretive code called *obj*.

□ To execute a Pascal program, supply the filename of the file that contains the interpretive code (the default is *obj*) as an argument to **px** which, if there are no errors, will read from standard input and write results and various execution statistics on standard output.

□ A Pascal program may also be executed simply by issuing the name of the object file as a command.

□ To remove the execution statistics from the output of **px**, recompile the program using the −**p** option of **pi**.

□ To produce a listing of the Pascal source, use the −**p** option of **pi**.

□ **pix** is the "load and go" system and is a combination of **pi** and **px** which does not produce an object file *obj*.

□ The −**p** and −**l** options of **pi** are also available for **pix**.

□ Compile time errors may be syntactic errors or semantic errors.

□ If a syntactic error is detected by **pi**, it issues an error message consisting of an error class code, a line number, a diagnostic message and a pointer to the position in the line where the error was first detected.

□ For semantic errors, **pi** issues an error message consisting of an error class code, a diagnostic message and an indication of the line in the source text near the point of error.

□ Error class codes are **E** for a fatal error, **e** for a non-fatal error, **w** to warn about a potential problem and **s** to mark a non-standard construct.

□ For non-fatal errors, **pi** attempts to repair the program and continues processing to produce an object file.

□ For fatal errors, no object file of executable code is produced.

□ Run time errors may be semantic errors or logical errors.

□   If a semantic error is detected by **px**, execution is terminated, a diagnostic message is generated and an indication given of the line in the source text near where the error occurred.

□   If a logical error occurs, the output will be incorrect and it is then necessary to examine the source code to determine why the program is misbehaving.

□   **pc** is a Pascal compiler which produces directly executable object code in a file with the default name *a.out* which can be renamed using the **–o** option.

□   To execute the Pascal program, issue the name of the file that contains the compiled program as a command.

□   The Pascal function **eof** returns **true** if end-of-file is set, otherwise **false**.

□   A test for end-of-file on standard input from a terminal can only be made after some input has occurred.

□   To ensure that a prompt for input appears on a terminal, it is necessary to place it before the first test for end-of-file in the code.

□   Use **readln** instead of **read** to input a line of data including the terminating newline.

□   The Pascal function **eoln** returns **true** when the last character in the current line immediately before the newline has been read into the program.

□   The terminating newline may be read into a program and is supplied as a space.

□   **readln** without arguments can be used to discard the remainder of an input line including the terminating newline.

□   To be able to read from a file other than standard input or write to a file other than standard output, it is necessary to include the filename as an argument in the **program** statement and declare the file to be a type **text**.

□   Such a file must be opened for reading or writing by executing a **reset** or **rewrite** statement respectively and any input-output statement or test for end-of-file or end-of-line must include the filename as an argument.

□   Command line arguments may be accessed from a Pascal program using **argc**, a function which returns the number of arguments and **argv**, a procedure which loads a specific argument as a character string into a packed array.

●   FORTRAN 77 is a general purpose programming language for scientific computations which can be used for writing structured programs if the programmer exercises some discipline.

●   A FORTRAN program must be created in a file with a suffix *.f.*

●   Comment lines start with a **c** in column 1.

●   Statement numbers start in column 1 and are followed by a tab.

- All other lines commence with a tab.

- Tabs may be used elsewhere in a line and are treated as the equivalent of one blank character.

- An ampersand at the start of a line indicates that it is a continuation line.

- Lower case characters may be used for the entry of program text and upper case is converted into lower case automatically (except in character constants).

- Standard input, standard output and standard error output are FORTRAN devices 5, 6 and 0 respectively.

- To compile a FORTRAN program, supply the name of the file that contains the source code as an argument to **f77** which will produce an executable program in a file *a.out* in the current working directory if no errors are detected.

- To execute a FORTRAN program, issue as a command the name of the file that contains the executable code.

- Use the −**o** option of **f77** to rename the object file.

- If an error is detected by **f77**, a message is generated indicating the line at which the error was detected and output of object code is suppressed.

- The −**u** option of **f77** should always be used to make the default type of a variable **undefined** rather than using the default rules of FORTRAN.

- If an error is detected during execution, the program will stop and in most cases produce an appropriate failure message.

- In FORTRAN 66, a **do** loop is executed at least once and the program may not behave correctly if compiled with **f77** unless the −**onetrip** or −**1** option is selected.

- To test for end-of-file, include an argument **end=** *label* as an argument in a **read** statement as part of the control list.

- End-of-line cannot be detected simply in FORTRAN unless use is made of a non-standard function **getc** only available in UNIX.

- Command line arguments may be accessed from a FORTRAN program by using the function **iargc** which returns a count of the number of arguments (not including the command) and the subroutine **getarg** which transfers a specified argument string into a character array.

- C is a general purpose language which supports structured programming.

- C is often referred to as a high level assembler since it enables programmers to access low-level features of the machine and has been used to write systems software including the UNIX system.

- A C program must be placed in a file with a **.c** suffix before it can be compiled and executed.

- **cc** is the command to execute the C compiler and takes as its arguments various options and the filenames of one or more files containing C source code.

- If no errors are detected, **cc** produces an executable object file with the default name *a.out.* which may be renamed using the –o option.

- To execute a C program, issue as a command the name of the file that contains the executable code.

- If errors are detected by **cc**, it generates an error message consisting of the filename containing the incorrect source code, a line number within the file and a reason.

- If an error is detected during compilation, no object file is produced.

- To make a C program compile successfully, it may be necessary to include certain header files such as *stdio.h* and indicate which subroutine libraries are to be searched using the –l option in the command line.

- Use **lint** to apply more stringent syntax and type checking to a C program than is carried out by **cc.**

- Explicit type conversion is performed in C using the `cast` operator.

- End-of-file is detected when the current input character is equal to EOF, a constant defined in *stdio.h.*

- End-of-line is detected when the current input character is equal to \n, the representation in C of newline.

- Files other than standard input, standard output and standard error output must be declared using `FILE` which defines a file pointer to be used in subsequent input-output operations.

- Command line arguments may be accessed from a C program by using as arguments to `main` the integer `argc`, a count of the number of arguments (including the command) and `argv`, an array of pointers to the arguments.

- The shell provides a programming language which supports variable declaration, assignment statements, conditional statements, repetition statements, input-output statements, comments and procedures with parameters.

- Shell programs are often called shell procedures or shell scripts.

- To execute a shell program, first create it in a file, then supply the filename as an argument to **sh** or **csh**.

- Another method of executing a shell program is to make the file executable and then issue the filename as a command which causes the automatic invocation of a sub-shell.

- To help with the debugging of a shell program, use the –v option to print each command as it is executed or the –x option to provide an execution trace.

- Comments may be included in a shell program by preceding them with **#** which causes the remainder of the line to be ignored or as quoted arguments to :, the null command which does nothing.

- Both **sh** and **csh** automatically invoke **sh** as a sub-shell to execute a command file unless the first line in the file starts with **#** in which case **csh** will invoke itself.

- Both shells report syntax errors but **sh** is more forgiving than **csh**, e.g. **sh** takes the value of an undefined variable as null whereas **csh** flags it as an error.

- Shell programs can be used to create commands tailored to your own requirements and these should usually be stored in your *bin* directory.

- A basic input facility is provided by **read** which takes a line of text from standard input, breaks it up into words and assigns these in turn to its arguments.

- A basic output facility is provided by **echo** which writes its arguments separated by a space and terminated by a newline on standard output.

- Input-output can also be performed by commands in the program which read from standard input and write to standard output.

- If a command line in a shell program is terminated by the shell metacharacter **<<** followed by a character string, the subsequent lines up to but not including a line consisting only of the specified string are taken as standard input to the command in what is called a "here" document.

- The lines in a here document are subjected to shell processing unless the terminator string is escaped or enclosed in quotes.

- Arguments to a shell program may be accessed using the notation **$1**, **$2** ... **$9**; **$0** is the name of the command file.

- All arguments from **$1** onwards can be referenced by **$\***, the total number of arguments by **$#**, the exit status of the last command executed by **$?** and the process number of the current shell as a decimal string by **$$**.

- Repetition is provided by the command:

    **for** *variable* **in** *list* **do** *commands* **done**

    which causes *commands* to be executed once for each word in *list* assigned to *variable*.

- If **in** *list* is omitted from the **for** command, the values used are the positional parameters.

- Repetition is also provided by the command:

    **while** *commands-1* **do** *commands-2* **done**

    which causes *command-2* to be executed as long as the last command in *commands 1* returns an exit code of 0 meaning **true**.

- **while** may be replaced by **until** to cause *commands-2* to be executed as long as the last command in *commands-1* returns non-zero meaning `false`.

- Note that in the **for**, **while** and **until** commands, **do** and **done** must be preceded by ; or start a new line.

- Selection is provided by the command:

    **case** *word* **in** *case-parts* **esac**

    where *case-parts* is a sequence of alternatives of the form:

    *pattern* **)** *commands* ; ;

    which causes *commands* to be executed for the first alternative for which *pattern* matches *word*.

- A conditional statement is provided by:

    **if** *commands-1* **then** *commands-2* **else** commands-3 **fi**

    which causes *commands-2* to be executed if the last command in *commands-1* returns a zero exit code, otherwise *commands-3* is executed.

- An alias in the C-shell is a short hand name for a command and its arguments.

- To define an alias, use **alias** which, in the absence of arguments, will list out existing aliases; use **unalias** to remove aliases.

- When the standard shell is first invoked as the login shell, it reads and executes commands from *.profile* in your home directory.

- The C-shell executes commands from *.login* in your home directory when first invoked as the login shell after it has processed the commands in *.cshrc.*

- Whenever the C-shell is invoked as a sub-shell, it will execute commands from *.cshrc.*

- When you logout, C-shell will execute commands from *.logout* in your home directory if such a file exists.

## Chapter 5

# MANAGING

The management of information in a computer system implies the ability to keep it under control, that is, to know where it is, to transform it as required, to minimize the cost of the system resources it needs and to communicate it to other people. UNIX provides many tools to help with these functions and we will now consider, in more detail, a selection of them. However, remember that you can always add to the basic set by developing tools of your own if the characteristics of those supplied are not exactly to your taste.

## 5.1 Managing Files

There are a number of tools available to assist you in managing your files. We have already seen some of them — **ls** to list a directory and **du** to summarize disk usage. The additional tools can very roughly be divided into two main categories — those which help you manage individual files and those which help you optimize your use of disk space.

### 5.1.1 Locating Files

The first command we will consider is **find** which will locate lost files. "What's that?" you say, "UNIX loses files!" Not so, but, from time to time, *you* will lose them. Since the organization of the file system encourages users to create many small files rather than perhaps just a few large ones, you will have created many directories and files after you have been using the system for a while. You know you have a file with a certain name somewhere in your collection, but for the life of you, you can't remember where it is. You could start looking with **ls** but that could become a little tedious.

| **find** - find files |

Instead of using **ls**, just use **find** which, starting at a directory that you specify, will recursively descend the directory hierarchy looking for the missing file. If it can be found, you can arrange for **find** to print out its pathname relative to the starting directory. Your "lost sheep" will have been returned to the fold.

Let us use **find** to search for the file *arem* which you should have stored in your *bin* directory. Unfortunately, **find** is one of those annoying commands in UNIX which is very powerful, does many useful things but has a rather clumsy syntax for its arguments. The synopsis of the command is:

> find *path-name-list expression*

where the elements in the list specify the starting points for each search and the expression defines the files which are to be located. The components of the expression have values `true` or `false` and, if the whole boolean expression is true for a given file, the file is said to match the expression. Components are available which match a filename, cause the filename to be printed, check permissions, match the username of a file owner and check how long since the file was modified or accessed. The list is long and we will not cover all the possibilities in detail here but, instead, refer you to the glossary and the documentation.

To locate the file you are looking for, execute **find** as follows from your home directory:

```
$ find . -name arem -print       Find and print arem pathname
./bin/arem
$
```

Notice that the components of the expression are introduced by a keyword preceded by a minus sign and that concatenation implies logical **and**. The component **-print** is always true and simply causes the name of the matched file to be printed. The negation operator is ! and logical **or** can be specified by **-o** . To find both *arem* and *de*, you would execute:

```
$ find . \( -name arem -o -name de \)    \ Find arem or de
> -print                                 And print pathnames
./bin/de
./bin/arem
$
```

Parentheses provide a grouping facility but notice how they had to be escaped since they are significant to the shell. Also, as they are arguments to **find**, they must be preceded and followed by white space.

Another useful component is **-exec** which causes the command which follows to be executed. The command must be terminated by an escaped semicolon. Try:

```
$ find . -name arem \            Find arem
> -exec ls -l {} \;              And inspect directory entry
-rwxr-xr-x  1 yew             247 Apr 17 08:18 ./bin/arem
$
```

The adjacent braces are replaced by the current pathname before the command is executed. Notice that the escaped semicolon must be preceded by at least one space. One very useful application of this facility is to remove unwanted *a.out* and *.o* files which have not been accessed for some time so that the disk space they occupy is set free. The required command is:

```
$ find . \( -name a.out \        Find a.out files or files
> -o -name '*.o' \) \            with .o suffix and remove those not
> -atime +7 -exec rm {} \;       accessed within the last 7 days
$
```

**−atime** specifies a component which is true if the file was last accessed exactly $n$ days ago. If +$n$ is used instead of $n$, it is interpreted to mean more than $n$ days ago. Similarly −$n$ means less than $n$. Notice the use of primes to prevent *.o being expanded by the shell. There is only one filename associated with **−name** but it may include shell metacharacters if they are escaped. Filename expansion is carried out later by **find**. If you would like the removal to be carried out interactively, you can use **−ok** instead of **−exec** in which case the generated command line will be printed followed by a query and will only be executed if you respond with a **y**.

================================================================

| **whereis** - locate source, binary and/or manual for program |

A more restricted command than **find**, but one which is easier to use, is to be found in the Berkeley system. It is called **whereis** and its function is to locate source, binary and manual entries for a program. Hence, it only searches certain system directories. Let us see what it will locate for the **cp** command:

```
% whereis cp                     Output directory entries for cp command
cp : /usr/src/bin/cp.c /bin/cp  /usr/man/man1/cp.1
%
```

Various options are available to restrict the search even further. Thus, **−m** causes only the manual entry to be returned and **−b**, the binary:

```
% whereis -b cp                  Output entry for cp binary
cp: /bin/cp
%
```

-----------------------------------------------------------------

| file | - determine file type |
|------|------------------------|

Having found the missing file, it may be that you have also forgotten what it contains. You could of course use **cat** or **more** but, if it's a binary file, your screen will be corrupted. Instead, you can use the **file** command which attempts to determine the file type according to the information stored in the file:

```
$ file bin  bin/arem  /etc/passwd  cex/greet.c  cex/grc
bin:            directory
bin/arem:       commands text
/etc/passwd:    ascii text
cex/greet.c     c program text
cex/grc:        pure executable not stripped
$
```

If **file** thinks that the file contains ASCII characters, it tries to guess the language. Unfortunately, it is not foolproof and sometimes reports that a command file contains a C program. Also, it does not know anything about FORTRAN or Pascal:

```
$ file pex/greet.p fex/greet.f          Output file type
 pex/greet.p     c program text
 fex/greet.f     ascii text
$
```

## 5.1.2  Linking Files

Sometimes, you may want to access a file in a particular directory from another directory using a different name. You could, of course, simply make a copy of the file but that would be wasteful of space. Instead, what you can do is establish a *link*. This is just a directory entry for a particular file made after the file has been created. You can think of it as another name for the file. There is in fact no way of distinguishing a link to a file from its original directory entry.

| ln | - make links |
|----|---------------|

The command **ln** is used to make links to existing files. If given two filenames as arguments, it creates a link to the first file with the second one as the name of the link.

Create two directories, *int* and *ext*, in your home directory and two files, *mon* and *tue*, in the latter directory:

```
$ mkdir int ext              Make two directories
$ tee ext/mon ext/tue        And two files
^D
$
```

Change your working directory to *int* and create a link to *mon* in *ext:*

```
$ cd int                          Change working directory
$ ln ../ext/mon mon               Create a link
$ ls -l                           And list directory
-rw-r--r-- 2 yew          0 Mar  2 17:23 mon
$
```

The file **mon** now has two links, one in **int** and the other in **ext** as indicated by the second field in the output of **ls**. Next create a link to **tue** in **ext** but this time using a different name:

```
$ ln ../ext/tue tuesday           Create a link
$ ls -l                           And inspect the directory
-rw-r--r-- 2 yew          0 Mar  2 17:23 mon
-rw-r--r-- 2 yew          0 Mar  2 17:24 tuesday
$
```

Again you will observe that **tuesday** has 2 links as has **tue** if you listed the entry for that file in its directory:

```
$ ls -l ../ext/tue                Inspect directory entry for tue
-rw-r--r-- 2 yew          0 Mar  2 17:24 ../ext/tue
$
```

Now remove **mon** from the current directory and **tue** from **ext**:

```
$ rm mon ../ext/tue               Delete 2 files
$ ls -l                           And inspect current directory
-rw-r--r-- 1 yew          0 Mar  2 17:24 tuesday
$
```

Although the original file has been deleted, **tuesday** still remains with a link count of 1. So even if you link to a file belonging to someone else and that file is removed by its owner, it is only that directory entry which disappears. Your directory entry remains still pointing to the file.

Now change directory to **ext** and list its contents:

```
$ cd ../ext                       Change to new directory
$ ls -l                           And inspect it
-rw-r--r-- 1 yew          0 Mar  2 17:23 mon
$
```

As expected, **tue** has gone but you could get it back again if you wished using **ln**:

```
$ ln ../int/tuesday tue           Create a link
$ ls -l                           And inspect result
-rw-r--r-- 1 yew          0 Mar  2 17:23 mon
-rw-r--r-- 2 yew          0 Mar  2 17:24 tue
$
```

## 5.1.3  Splitting Files

Sometimes, you might have to deal with an inordinately large file, so large that programs like **ed** and **vi** just can't handle it. Remember that they use a buffer to hold the file being edited and it may be that the large file simply won't fit into the buffer. You might say "Well, I won't get myself into that bind and will keep all my files relatively small." However, perhaps a program you run will generate a very large output file or you may receive a file from another installation which you want to edit.

> **split** - split a file into pieces

The command which breaks up files into smaller chunks is called, as you might expect, **split**. It will read a file and write out *n*-line chunks on to a set of output files. The default value of *n* is 1000 but this may be redefined by supplying −*n* as an argument.

To experiment a little with **split**, let us first create a large file of, say, approximately 5000 lines called *big* in a directory *spex*. You could do this from the keyboard but you would be rather tired and fed up by the time you finished. Instead, let us use the C program **roots** you have already developed which will output a table of square roots one per line. Make *spex* your current working directory and create *big* by output redirection:

```
$ cd; mkdir spex          Create directory
$ cd spex                 And change to it
$ roots > big             Execute roots to create big
Enter number: 5000
$
```

Now execute **split** on *big* and list the directory:

```
$ split big               Break up big
$ ls                      And list directory
big   xaa   xab   xac   xad   xae   xaf
$
```

Six new files have been created with filenames *x* (the default stem) to which has been appended the letter pairs *aa*, *ab*, etc. Thus, **split** has the capability of generating 676 output files. In our example, each of the first five files contains 1000 lines and the last one, 3 lines since **roots** outputs a 3-line heading before generating the table:

```
$ wc -l x*                Count lines in files xaa, xab, etc.
   1000 xaa
   1000 xab
   1000 xac
   1000 xad
   1000 xae
      3 xaf
```

```
$ cat xaf                    Output file xaf
4998   70.697
4999   70.704
5000   70.711
$
```

You can supply your own stem as the final argument in the command line, if you wish, providing the name you choose is no longer than 12 characters. Let's try **split** again, this time creating 2000-line chunks and using **section** as the stem:

```
$ split -2000 big section    Break up big into sections
$ ls s*                      List entries for sections
sectionaa sectionab sectionac
$
```

As expected, three output files have been created. If, at some future time, you wanted to recombine the sections, say, after they had been modified, all you would need to do is use **cat**:

```
$ cat section* > big         Concatenate sections to form big
$
```

In System V, there are two other commands available for handling large files, **bfs** and **csplit**. The latter is similar to **split** except that it sections the file by context rather than by number of lines, that is, it accepts regular expressions or patterns similar to those of **ed** as defining section boundaries. **bfs** (big file scanner) also bears a close resemblance to **ed** but cannot be used to modify a file. It handles much larger files and is useful (and more efficient than **ed**) for scanning a large file to determine how it should be split using **csplit**.

## 5.1.4  Archiving Files

Now let us consider the tools that can help you manage your use of disk space. By the very nature of things, it seems that file systems will grow in size to occupy the space available. People are loathe to throw away old files, even though they have not been accessed for a long time. Hence, unless you are using some version of UNIX which enforces disk quotas, it may be that, from time to time, you will be working with a very full disk (or file system) and programs that you execute which require additional file space will fail because there is none available. Also, you may find that you cannot create any files because the system has run out of i-nodes.

> **df** - disk free

Most UNIX systems include a command **df** (disk free) which will output a table showing how big each file system is and how much space has already been used:

```
$ df                    How much free disk space is there?
Filesystem     kbytes     used    avail capacity  Mounted on
/dev/msm0a      6375      5421      316    94%     /
/dev/msm1ra     6375      3915     1822    68%     /tmp
/dev/msm1e     35643     33292      568    98%     /usr
/dev/msm1d      4487      1455     2807    34%     /usr/adm
/dev/msm1f      8255      5421     2008    73%     /usr/spool
$
```

The filesystems are devices in **/dev** and, for each system, there is an entry in the table showing its size in kilobytes and the percentage utilization. The last column gives the pathname of each filesystem. If **df** is supplied with either the device or the pathname as an argument, it will output the table entry for just that system:

```
$ df /usr               How much free disk space is there in /usr
Filesystem     kbytes     used    avail capacity  Mounted on
/dev/msm1e     35643     33292      568    98%     /usr
$
```

===============================================

```
┌─────────────────────────────────────────┐
│ quota  - display disk usage and limits   │
└─────────────────────────────────────────┘
```

This command enables you to find out just how much disk space you are using and how much you are entitled to use:

```
% quota                    What is my disk quota and usage?
Disk quotas for yew (uid 8):
Filsys  current quota limit #warns  files quota limit #warns
/usr        12    23   109            9    14    29
%
```

The output shows the number of files you currently own and your usage of disk blocks. The quota defines the maximum number of these that you should have at any one time. However, you are allowed to exceed your quotas temporarily during a session up to the values defined by the limits. If you are over quota when you logout, you will be warned then and again when next you login. If you ignore some number of warnings as preset by the system administrator, you will be prevented from using any more disk space. Thus, it's a good idea to reduce the number of files and blocks you are using back to your quota before you logout.

--------------------------------------------------------------------

Given that you have to economize on your use of disk space and that you do not wish to delete any files, you can either use your existing space more efficiently or remove files from disk on to some other storage medium such as magnetic tape. This process is called *archiving*. We refer to the reverse process, in which files are recovered from the archives, as *restoring*.

| **ar** - archive and library maintainer |

The first command we will consider is **ar** which maintains groups of files combined into an archive file. The space occupied by the single file is usually less than the total required for the individual files of the group. Further, there is only one directory entry (and hence one i-node) rather than many. **ar** can also be used to create and update library files of functions used by the *loader* or *link editor* when it is creating an executable binary.

Create a directory *arex* in your home directory and **cd** to it. Now use **ar** to extract files from one of the library files we have seen before, *libm.a*, which contains the standard mathematical functions:

```
$ ar x /usr/lib/libm.a          Extract files from archive
$ ls
__.SYMDEF   erf.o    gamma.o   j1.o    pow.o   sqrt.o
asin.o      exp.o    hypot.o   jn.o    sin.o   tan.o
atan.o      floor.o  j0.o      log.o   sinh.o  tanh.o
$
```

Eighteen files have been recovered from the archive and set up in your current working directory. The synopsis of **ar** is:

**ar** *key* [ *posname* ] *afile* [ *name* ... ]

where *key* is a string of characters (optionally preceded by minus) which selects the various options available in the command. *afile* is the name of the archive file and *name*, the filename of a component file. *posname* specifies a position in the archive file. In the example, you instructed **ar** to extract (**x**) files from */usr/lib/libm.a* and restore them to the current directory. Since no component filenames were mentioned, all files were recovered. Now, use **du −s** to determine the number of blocks occupied by the files in this directory and make a note of this figure.

Now build your own copy of *libm.a* in the current directory:

```
$ ar r libm.a *                 Create an archive file
ar : creating libm.a
$
```

Here, the key used is **r** indicating that the files in the archive are to be replaced by the named files. If no archive file exists, one is created. Use **du −s** again to determine how many blocks are occupied by the files in this directory. It should be less than twice the original figure showing that an archive file occupies less space than its components. If you now removed these, there would be some saving of disk space as well as, of course, a reduction in the number of occupied i-nodes.

In addition to extraction and replacement, **ar** also enables you to **delete** files from an archive and print a table of contents. Remove all *.o* files from *libm.a* using the **d** key and list what remains with the key **t**:

```
$ ar d libm.a  *.o           Delete files from archive
$ ar t libm.a                And list remainder
__.SYMDEF
$
```

If you now return, say, two files to the archive, they will be appended to whatever is already there in the order in which they are specified in the argument list:

```
$ ar r libm.a  atan.o   asin.o  Append files to archive
$ ar t libm.a                And list current contents
__.SYMDEF
atan.o
asin.o
$
```

The command **ar** has a number of other functions which will help you manage your archives and these are described in the glossary.

Although small savings in disk utilization can be made using **ar**, large reductions can only be achieved by first copying the files to some other storage medium and then deleting the original ones. Usually, the other medium is magnetic tape although, on some of the smaller UNIX machines, it might be floppy disk or cartridge tape. For the sake of this discussion, let us assume that you plan to archive files to magnetic tape. First, you have to mount a tape on a magnetic tape unit and then say which files you wish to archive. Since UNIX treats devices as files, you could use **cat** to copy a file to tape. Assuming that the magnetic tape has been mounted on unit 1 to be used at medium density, then:

```
$ cat file > /dev/mt/1m   Write file to magnetic tape
$
```

would accomplish the desired action. However, if you then wanted to add other files to the tape at some later time, you could have problems since you would have to ensure that the tape was positioned correctly to prevent previously archived files from being overwritten. Instead, the appropriate utility program to use is **tar**, the **t**ape **ar**chiver, which saves and restores files on magnetic tape.

| **tar** - tape archiver |
|---|

The synopsis of the **tar** command is:

> **tar** [*key*]  [*file*...]

where *key* selects one of the available functions which are very similar to those of **ar** i.e. **r** to archive files to tape, **x** to extract them and **t** to list the current contents of an archive tape. A key of **c** causes a new archive tape to be created and implies **r**. However, files are written from the beginning of the tape instead of being appended to the files already there.

As well as specific files, **tar** also accepts directory names as arguments. In this case, not only is the directory archived to tape but also all the files it contains. This applies to sub-directories as well and, in turn, to their contents and so on recursively through the directory hierarchy. Similarly, when files are being restored, a directory name in the argument list causes the contents of that directory and any sub-directories to be extracted from the archive tape. In the extract mode, if no file arguments are given, the entire contents of the tape are restored.

In addition to the letter which selects the function, the key may also contain other characters which modify the behaviour of **tar**. For example, a verbose mode is activated by the modifier **v** while **f** instructs **tar** to use the next argument as the name of the archive. If some device such as a floppy disk is to be used as the archive medium, its name must be specified explicitly e.g. */dev/fl6*. It could also be the name of a file and this facility enables us to experiment a little with **tar** without actually using any external devices.

Create a directory *tarex* in your home directory and three files *f1*, *f2* and *f3* in that directory, each containing a few characters:

```
$ cd; mkdir tarex        Create directory tarex
$ cd tarex               And change to it
$ tee f1 f2 f3           Create 3 files
abcd
abcd
^D
$ cd                     And go back home
$
```

Now, issue the following commands:

```
$ tar cf arch tarex      Create archive file arch
$
```

The **cf** option causes the file *arch* to be created and used as the archive file. Now remove *tarex* with its component files and then restore them using **tar**:

```
$ rm -r tarex                 Remove directory and its files
$ tar xvf arch                Restore files from archive verbosely
x tarex/f1, 5 bytes, 1 tape blocks
x tarex/f2, 5 bytes, 1 tape blocks
x tarex/f3, 5 bytes, 1 tape blocks
$
```

Check with **ls** and **cat** that the directory, its component files and their contents have been restored correctly. (You can look at the contents of *arch* if you wish but because **tar** calculates a check sum, it will probably contain some non-printable characters.) Now add *bin/uc* to the archive and check the current table of contents using the **t** option:

```
$ tar rvf arch bin/uc        Add file to archive verbosely
a bin/uc 1 blocks
$ tar tf arch                And list contents of archive
tarex/
tarex/f1
tarex/f2
tarex/f3
bin/uc
$
```

In addition to creating and maintaining archive files, **tar** can also be used to move file hierarchies from one position in the filing system to another. To do this, you make use of the fact that, if the archive file is specified as −, **tar** writes to standard output or reads from standard input depending on what function it is carrying out. Hence, if you create an archive on standard output and pipe it as input to **tar** in the restore mode, the net effect is to copy files and directories. Let's try moving *arex* into *tarex*:

```
$ tar cf − arex | (cd tarex; tar xf − )    Move file hierarchy
$ ls tarex                                 And list directory
arex f1 f2 f3
$
```

As you see, **tar** is quite a versatile command and one you may need to use frequently if disk space is at a premium.

## 5.1.5  Packing Files

There is another way in which disk space can be saved without actually removing the file, namely, by compressing its contents. Now, this is not as strange as it might sound. If you think about it for a moment, the space required by a file which contains sequences of repeated characters could be reduced by replacing each run by a special symbol which specified not only what the repeated character is but also the length of the run. A file which contained lots of spaces could be reduced in size quite considerably  using this technique.

```
┌─────────────────────────────┐
│ pack - compress files       │
└─────────────────────────────┘
```

The UNIX command to compress a file is **pack**. It uses a different and much more complex algorithm than the one mentioned above. This works by encoding the most frequently occurring characters in less than the 8 bits normally required to represent a character. The amount of compression obtained depends on the size of the file and the distribution of characters. It is usually not worthwhile to pack files which occupy less than 3 disk blocks. Typically, text files are compressed to 60–75% of their original size. Binary files, on the other hand, may only show a 10% reduction in space.

Let us try **pack** on *gamma.o* in the directory *arex* after first determining its size:

```
$ cd arex; ls -l gamma.o            List file details
-rwx--x--x  1 yew           1265 Jan  1 1970 gamma.o
$ pack gamma.o                      Compress file
pack: gamma.o: 18.9% Compression
$ ls -l gamma*                      And list details again
-rwx--x--x  1 yew           1026 Jan  1 1970 gamma.o.z
$ ▒
```

A reduction in space of almost 20% has been achieved. Notice that the file has been renamed with the addition of a further suffix, **.z**. Now try the command again on one of the smaller files in the directory:

```
$ ls -l exp.o                       List file details
-rwx--x--x  1 yew            690 Jun 25 10:49 exp.o
$ pack exp.o                        And try to compress it
pack: exp.o: no saving - file unchanged
$ ▒
```

---

| **unpack** - expand compressed files |

The compression produced by **pack** is reversed by the **unpack** command:

```
$ unpack gamma.o                    Expand file
unpack: gamma.o: unpacked
$ ls -l gamma*                      And list details
-rwx--x--x  1 yew           1265 Jan  1 1970 gamma.o
$ ▒
```

For both **pack** and **unpack**, the time of last modification remains as it was before the file was packed. Packing and unpacking are not considered to be modifications of a file.

Now let us see how effective **pack** is on a text file. In order to make a large enough file, concatenate the source files that you created earlier in the directories *cex* and *pex* into a file *text*:

```
$ cat ../cex/*.c ../pex/*.p > text  Create text
$ pack text                         And compress it
pack: text: 38.7% Compression
$ ▒
```

So the savings in space are quite substantial! To look at the contents of *text.z*, you can either unpack it or use **pcat** which unpacks a *.z* file without renaming it and writes to standard output. After you have done this, you can remove the file *text* since you will not be using it again.

## 5.2  Managing Data

Having surveyed some of the commands which can help you manage your files, let us now look at what tools are available to help manage the data you have stored in these files. Obviously, you have already used many of these in earlier chapters — **cat** and **pg** to look at the contents of a file, **pr** and **lp** to print it, **ed** and **vi** to change it, **cp** to make a copy of it and so on. But there are many more operations that you may wish to carry out on your data. You may want to compare the contents of one file with another or you may want to organize the data into some particular order. Sometimes, it may be desirable to encrypt the data in a file so that no one else can read it. At other times, you may wish to search through many files looking for the occurrence of some particular character string. UNIX provides tools to carry out these operations and many more.

### 5.2.1  Comparing

It is often necessary to compare two files to see whether they are the same or not. For example, you may have modified a program and want to know whether its output is the same as that from the original one. It could be rather tedious to do this by eye. There are a number of commands available in UNIX which enable you to compare files and determine what the differences are if any exist.

To create some files to compare, change directory to *cex*, copy *root.c* to *root1.c* and  make the following modifications to the latter file:

(i)   add the comment `/*one input only*/` after line 1

(ii)  replace the line beginning with `while` by `scanf("%d", &i);`

(iii) remove the next line containing a single left brace

(iv)  remove the second occurrence of the statement `printf("Enter number:")` and the following line containing a single right brace.

The modifications are such that now the program will process only one input number before terminating. Compile and execute it to check that this is so.

| **cmp** - compare two files |
| :---: |

The first command we will try is **cmp** which compares two files whose names are supplied as arguments and outputs the byte and line number at which the first difference occurs:

```
$ cmp root1.c root.c              Compare 2 files
root1.c root.c differ: char 40, line 2
$ 
```

This is what you would expect given the changes you made to *root.c*. If the files are the same, nothing is printed. If an argument is − instead of a filename, standard input is used. Hence, the command can be incorporated in a pipe.

$$\boxed{\textbf{diff} \text{ - differential file comparator}}$$

Although **cmp** is quite useful at times, it does not tell you about all the differences between two files, merely that they are different. A more powerful command is **diff** which we have already encountered in an earlier chapter. It not only informs you that the files are different but also prints out what those differences are:

```
$ diff root1.c root.c        Find differences between 2 files
2d1
< /*one input only*/
10c9,10
<     scanf("%d", &i);
---
>     while(scanf("%d", &i) != EOF)
>     {
15a16,17
>         printf("Enter number:");
>     }
$
```

The output resembles **ed** commands that would convert the first file into the second one. The letters **a**, **c** and **d** stand for **append**, **change** and **delete** respectively. The numbers before the letters refer to the first file and those after, to the second. The subsequent output then shows the lines that are affected in both files. Those in the first file are preceded by < and those in the second by >. If lines in both files are output, the respective outputs are separated by a line consisting of minus signs. In the above example, you will observe that, to convert *root1.c* to *root.c*, line 2 must be deleted, line 10 changed into the two lines following the line of minuses (which would then have numbers 9 and 10) and two lines numbered 16 and 17 must be added after line 15. In fact, it is possible to cause **diff** to generate an editor script which will convert *root1.c* to *root.c* by specifying the –e option:

```
$ diff -e root1.c root.c          Output edit script
15a
        printf("Enter number:");
    }
.
10c
    while(scanf("%d", &i) != EOF)
    {
.
2d
$
```

Clearly, this should work but let us just check it by applying the script to *root1.c* and then looking for any differences between the modified file and *root.c*:

```
$ (diff -e root1.c root.c;\        Produce edit script
> echo '1,$p') |                   Output modified file
> ed - root1.c |                   Apply edit script
> diff - root.c                    Check differences again
$
```

No output occurs! The command **echo** `'1,$p'` writes the modified file on standard output which then becomes input to the second occurrence of **diff**.

A useful application of this facility for generating an edit script to convert one file into another is to maintain a number of different versions of a program without having to store each one in a separate file. Instead, one need store only the initial version and the various edit scripts to create other versions. By concatenating together the appropriate sequence of scripts and applying these to the base program, a given version may be regenerated. There are commands in System V called the Source Code Control System (**sccs**) which will perform such functions. However, if you don't have these available, you can still use **diff**.

---

**comm** - select lines common to two files

---

Sometimes you want to know something about the similarity of files, for example, what lines are common to two files. The command to use in this case is **comm** which takes as its arguments two files containing lines that have been sorted into the same order and outputs those lines which occur in both files together with those which only occur in each of the individual files.

To illustrate the use of **comm**, suppose that we are producing versions of the same program written in two different languages, say, C and Pascal. We would like to be able to compare the contents of the two directories to ensure that desired correspondences are being maintained. First of all, we will need a shell script which will list a directory and remove one or more suffixes supplied as parameters. Create the following script to list files without their suffixes:

```
$ cd; cat > lsws                   Create file
: 'list directory removing'
: 'specified suffixes from filename'
files=`ls $1`                      Store filenames in files
shift                              Rename positional parameters
for name in $files                 For each filename
do
    for suffix                     For each argument
    do
        name=`basename $name $suffix`   Remove suffix
    done
    echo $name                             Output basename
done
^D
$
```

The built-in shell command **shift**, which may take an optional argument *n* (default is 1), renames the positional parameters $n+1$, $n+2$ ... as **$1**, **$2**.... The effect of **shift** in the above example is to make any suffixes supplied as arguments the positional parameters **$1**, **$2**, etc. so that they can be used to control the extent of the **for** loop. When you have satisfied yourself that **lsws** is working correctly, install it in your **bin** directory:

```
$ mv lsws bin              Move lsws to bin
$
```

Now in Chapter 4, we developed programs in C and Pascal with similar names and the contents of the directories should be something like the following:

```
$ ls pex cex              List directories
cex:
grc        greet.c  revl.c    root.c    root1.c  roots.c

pex:
greet.p  grp        revl.p    root.p    roots.p
$
```

Ensure that *lsws* is executable and run it on each of these directories redirecting output to the files *pexl* and *cexl*:

```
$ lsws pex .p > pexl       Remove .p suffixes from files in pex
$ lsws cex .c > cexl       And .c suffixes from files in cex
$
```

Since **ls** produces its output sorted into alphabetical order, the files *pexl* and *cexl* can now be processed with **comm**:

```
$ comm pexl cexl          Output unique and common lines
      grc
                  greet
grp
                  revl
                  root
      root1
                  roots
$
```

The output occurs in 3 columns. The first contains only those lines which occur in *pexl*, the second, only those found in *cexl*, while the third lists the lines common to both files. You can suppress the printing of any column by including the column number as a flag in the argument list preceded by a minus:

```
$ comm -12 pexl cexl      Output common lines in 2 files
greet
revl
root
roots
$
```

The only column printed is the third one containing the basenames which are common to both directories. If − occurs on its own, it is interpreted as a filename argument implying standard input.

$$\boxed{\textbf{uniq} \ \text{-  report repeated lines in a file}}$$

Another form of comparison which is often quite useful within a single file is where the lines themselves are compared. The question you would like to ask is "Are there lines in the file which have been replicated?" or putting it another way "What are the unique lines in this file?". The command to do this is called **uniq** and, again, it requires the input file to be sorted.

In the previous example, you determined the common basenames used in two different directories. Suppose, instead, you wanted to know the unique basenames used in a particular directory. Again, you would have to strip off suffixes using **lsws** and then use **uniq** to remove replicated lines. To obtain some files with which to experiment, compile all the *.c* files in *cex* to produce corresponding *.o* files:

```
$ cd cex                          Change directory
$ cc -c *.c                       Compile C programs
cex/greet.c:
cex/revl.c:
cex/root.c:
cex/root1.c:
cex/roots.c:
$ ls                              List directory
grc       greet.o     revl.o    root.o    root1.o    roots.o
greet.c   revl.c      root.c    root1.c   roots.c
$
```

The −**c** flag forces *.o* file to be produced and suppresses the link edit phase. Now remove the *.o* and *.c* suffixes and pipe the output into **tee** to capture it in the file *cexb*, then pipe the output into **uniq**:

```
$ cd; lsws cex .c .o |            Remove suffixes
> tee cexb | uniq                 Output each basename once
grc
greet
revl
root
root1
roots
$
```

The output is the required list of unique basenames.

There are a number of options available with **uniq**. The −**u** flag produces as output only those lines which are not repeated at all in the file i.e. ones that are really unique; −**d**, on the other hand, produces one copy of the lines which are repeated. The normal output is just the union of these two:

```
$ uniq -u cexb          Output non-replicated basenames
grc
$ uniq -d cexb          Output replicated basenames
greet
revl
root
root1
roots
$
```

The **−c** option produces the same default output for **uniq** but precedes each line
with a count:

```
$ uniq -c cexb     Output each basename once preceded by count
   1 grc
   2 greet
   2 revl
   2 root
   2 root1
   2 roots
$
```

In the default mode, **uniq** reads from standard input and writes to standard
output. As illustrated above, the first file argument is taken as an input file. If a
second file argument is supplied, **uniq** writes its output to that file.

## 5.2.2  Sorting

A common operation required in data processing is to sort a file so that the
records are in a particular sequence. For example, a file of employee records
might be sorted into alphabetical order on the employee surname. If another file
containing the number of hours worked this week is similarly ordered, the two
files can be merged to generate data for the weekly payroll.

Examples of sorted output have already been seen in some of the UNIX
commands we have been using. For example, **ls** produces its listing of filenames
sorted into alphabetical order as the default. Commands like **comm** and **uniq**
require their input to be sorted in order to function properly. The command
provided in UNIX to perform sorting and merging is **sort** which sorts lines in one
or more named files and writes its results on standard output.

> **sort** - sort or merge files

We have already met **sort** as part of a pipe in Chapter 2 where it was used
to produce a list of users currently logged in, ordered alphabetically on the
username. From this we infer, that if no input files are specified in the argument
list, **sort** reads from standard input. In the default mode, the sort key, that is,
the section of the line on which the sorting is based, is the whole line. The

default ordering is lexicographic, based on the value of each character stored in a byte. This produces what is known as the *machine collating sequence*. It is machine dependent and varies from computer to computer. The examples used in this book were prepared on a machine based on the ASCII character set and hence the results may be different from what you see if your machine uses a different character set. To check this out, execute **sort** and input the data shown in the left hand column (the output produced is shown in the right hand column):

```
$ sort                      Sort standard input
z                    tab
a                    space
Z                    +
A                    -
-                    0
+                    9
 space               A
Ⓣtab                 Z
{                    a
}                    z
~                    {
9                    }
0                    ~
^D                   $
```

The input lines have been sorted into ascending order. Thus, of those characters supplied as input, tab has the lowest value and tilde the highest. The letters of the alphabet are ordered with lower case having higher values than upper case which in turn exceed those of the digits. You can verify this if you are using an ASCII machine by inspecting */usr/pub/ascii* which we looked at earlier in Chapter 2.

There are many options available with **sort** which make it a very powerful and versatile command. **−r** causes the sense of the comparisons to be reversed:

```
$ sort -r        Sort standard input in reverse order
a                    c
b                    b
c                    a
^D                   $
```

**−f** causes the upper and lower case letters to be treated as having the same value, that is, upper case letters are folded onto lower case:

```
$ sort -f        Sort standard input ignoring case
Z                    a
a                    Z
^D                   $
```

If **−u** is specified as an argument, all but one in each set of equal lines is suppressed:

```
$ sort -u          Sort standard input ignoring replicated lines
a                  a
b                  b
a                  $
^D
```

If a file contains non-printable characters, it may still be sorted by specifying the −i flag in which case characters outside the ASCII range 040−0176 are ignored in non-numeric comparisons. A −d flag specifies dictionary order and only letters, digits and blanks are significant in the comparison:

```
$ sort -d          Sort standard input in dictionary order
ab                 a{
a{                 ab
^D                 $
```

If −n is specified, the sorting is based on the arithmetic value of an initial numerical string consisting of optional spaces, an optional sign (+ or −), zero or more digits with an optional decimal point:

```
$ sort -n          Sort standard input by arithmetic value
 2                 1
1                  2
^D                 $
```

Notice the use of the word "initial" in the above definition. After sorting numerically on the first arithmetic value, the command reverts to lexicographical sorting:

```
$ sort -n          Sort standard input by arithmetic value
23.7b
23.7a
^D
23.7a
23.7b
$ sort -n          Sort standard input by arithmetic value
6 7
6  8
^D
6  8
6 7
$
```

In addition to using the whole of the line as the sort key, you can tell **sort** to use fields within a line where a field is a non-empty non-blank string separated by blanks. To illustrate the use of this feature, create a file **phys** in a directory **grades** which contains the marks out of 20 obtained by students in a physics examination (use spaces rather than tabs as separators in the following example):

```
$ mkdir grades; cd grades          Create directory and change to it
$ cat > phys                       Create file for physics students
Mary White         f      P 19
Sam Brown          m      P  6
Janet White        f      P 16
Bill Brown         m      P  6
Sam Black          m      P 16
^D
$
```

The first two fields are the student's first name and surname, the third indicates whether the student is male or female, the fourth is the letter P for "Physics" while the fifth contains the actual mark.

If you sort without specifying any options or fields, the entire line is used:

```
$ sort phys                        Sort on whole lines
Bill Brown         m      P  6
Janet White        f      P 16
Mary White         f      P 19
Sam Black          m      P 16
Sam Brown          m      P  6
$
```

In this example, the filename is supplied as an argument and the contents of the file rather than standard input are sorted. The lines are ordered alphabetically with the relative position of the 4th and 5th lines being determined by the second character of the surname. If you wanted the output ordered on the surname, you could instruct **sort** to skip the first field before it starts sorting:

```
$ sort +1 phys                     Sort on 2nd field onwards
Sam Black          m      P 16
Sam Brown          m      P  6
Bill Brown         m      P  6
Mary White         f      P 19
Janet White        f      P 16
$
```

Now the file is ordered on surnames but notice that the students named White are out of sequence on their first names since the first field has been ignored during the sort. You can rectify this by instructing **sort** to stop sorting at the end of field 2, whereupon it will resume from the beginning of the line and produce the correct order of first names:

```
$ sort +1 -2 phys                  Sort on 2nd field, then whole line
Sam Black          m      P 16
Bill Brown         m      P  6
Sam Brown          m      P  6
Janet White        f      P 16
Mary White         f      P 19
$
```

Suppose now, you wanted to order the list on the third field, that is, results for
the girls first, then those for the boys:

```
$ sort +2 phys              Sort on 3rd field onwards
Sam Brown       m     P  6
Sam Black       m     P 16
Mary White      f     P 19
Bill Brown      m     P  6
Janet White     f     P 16
$
```

Didn't work, did it? A moment's examination of the output shows that it is
ordered on the number of blanks between the end of the surname and the sex
code. What you need to do is to tell sort to ignore leading blanks in the field by
attaching the flag **b** to the position specifier. Suppose, at the same time, you
want to order the surnames, then the first names:

```
$ sort +2b +1 -2 phys       Sort on 3rd field onwards
Janet White     f     P 16    ignoring blanks, then 2nd field,
Mary White      f     P 19    then whole line
Bill Brown      m     P  6
Sam Brown       m     P  6
Sam Black       m     P 16
$
```

The ordering on the sex code is now correct but the surnames have not been
sorted correctly. What you forgot to do is to tell **sort** to stop sorting after it used
the third field and go back to sort the surnames. Instead, it used the remainder of
the line and P **6** must precede P **16**. This is easily corrected as follows:

```
$ sort +2b -3 +1 -2 phys    Sort on 3rd field ignoring blanks,
Janet White     f     P 16    then 2nd field, then whole line
Mary White      f     P 19
Sam Black       m     P 16
Bill Brown      m     P  6
Sam Brown       m     P  6
$
```

The file is now ordered as you wanted it to be.

One would normally expect that a file containing marks would be ordered on
those marks with the highest first. You can use the **r** flag to indicate reverse sort
and **b** to ignore the blanks:

```
$ sort +4rb phys            Sort in reverse order on 5th field
Bill Brown      m     P  6    ignoring blanks, then the whole line
Sam Brown       m     P  6
Mary White      f     P 19
Janet White     f     P 16
Sam Black       m     P 16
$
```

Not what you expected! The marks with two digits are ordered correctly but are preceded by the single digit values. The problem is that you are still sorting alphabetically and **6** has a higher lexicographical order than **19**. What you need to do is request the sort to be carried out on numeric values by specifying the flag **n**:

```
$ sort +4nr phys            Sort in reverse arithmetic order
Mary White      f    P 19    on 5th field, then whole line
Janet White     f    P 16
Sam Black       m    P 16
Bill Brown      m    P  6
Sam Brown       m    P  6
$
```

Notice that you did not have to use **b** since **n** implies that leading blanks are ignored. Finally, let us put it all together and sort **phys** first in reverse numeric order, then on the sex code, then on the surname and finally on the first name. Replace the original file by the new one using the **–o** option which specifies that the following argument is the name of the output file:

```
$ sort -o phys +4nr +2b +1 -2 phys    Sort on 5th field
$ cat phys                             in reverse arithmetic
Mary White      f    P 19              order, then on 3rd field
Janet White     f    P 16              ignoring blanks,
Sam Black       m    P 16              then 2nd field,
Bill Brown      m    P  6              then the whole line
Sam Brown       m    P  6
$
```

Notice that when an output file is specified, it may have the same name as one of the input files.

Let us now assume that these students in the physics class also study chemistry. Further, there is an additional student in this class. Create a file **chem** and sort it as you did before to produce the following:

```
$ cat chem                  List file of chemistry students
Janet White     f    C 18
Sam Black       m    C 18
Mary White      f    C 17
Sandra Brown    f    C  9
Bill Brown      m    C  9
Sam Brown       m    C  9
$
```

Since **sort** will handle multiple input files, you could produce a combined list sorted first on surnames and then on first names as follows:

```
$ sort +1 -2 phys chem              Sort on 2nd field,
Sam Black          m    C 18        then the whole line
Sam Black          m    P 16
Bill Brown         m    C  9
Bill Brown         m    P  6
Sam Brown          m    C  9
Sam Brown          m    P  6
Sandra Brown       f    C  9
Janet White        f    C 18
Janet White        f    P 16
Mary White         f    C 17
Mary White         f    P 19
$
```

From the above output, you observe that for each student, the lines are ordered on the subject code.

If you wanted to obtain a class list with unique names, you could do so with the −u option:

```
$ sort -u +1 -2 +0 -1 phys chem     Sort on 2nd field,
Sam Black          m    P 16        then 1st field
Bill Brown         m    C  9        suppressing all but
Sam Brown          m    P  6        one of lines with
Sandra Brown       f    C  9        1st and 2nd fields
Janet White        f    P 16        the same
Mary White         f    P 19
$
```

Notice that fields outside those specified are ignored in the comparisons.

Sometimes, one needs to know whether a file has been sorted according to the specified ordering rules without actually carrying out the complete sort. This can be accomplished using the −c flag:

```
$ sort -c phys                      Check to see if file is sorted
sort: disorder: Janet White    f    P 16
$
```

The exit code returned in this case is non-zero since the file is not in lexicographical order.

In our examples to date, the assumption has been that space or tab is the field separator character. However, situations may arise where you want to sort a file containing fields separated by some other character. In such a case, you can specify the field separator as the character which follows immediately after the −t flag. For example, if you wanted to sort the password file on one of its fields which are separated by colons, you would have to specify −t: before the ordering rules. Thus:

```
$ sort -t: +2n /etc/passwd          Sort numerically on 3rd field
```

would sort the file numerically on the third field.

## 5.2.3  Merging

Merging is the process of combining two or more files which have already been sorted into the same order to produce an output file in which this order is maintained. If the individual files input to **sort** have already been sorted, you can specify a −m flag to inform **sort** of this fact and thereby save some time since, with this option selected, the files are simply merged. If the −m flag is specified and the files are not really sorted into the order expected, the files will still be merged but the ordering will not be correct:

```
$ sort -m phys chem          Merge physics and chemistry students
Janet White      f     C 18
Mary White       f     P 19
Janet White      f     P 16
Sam Black        m     C 18
Mary White       f     C 17
Sam Black        m     P 16
Bill Brown       m     P  6
Sam Brown        m     P  6
Sandra Brown     f     C  9
Bill Brown       m     C  9
Sam Brown        m     C  9
$
```

The first three pairs of lines are simply those from each of the files *phys* and *chem*. The next line from *chem* causes the next two lines from *phys* to be output before it appears. Finally, the remaining two lines from *chem* are appended to the output.

> **join** - relational database operator

Another way in which files can be merged is on a line-by-line basis, that is, a line from one file is joined onto a corresponding line in another file. The command which does this is **join**. It is often referred to as the "relational database operator" since it forms a *join* of relations specified by the lines in the two files. It expects the files to be sorted into lexicographical order on the fields on which they are to be joined. Normally, the output line consists of the common field followed by the rest of the line from the first file, then the rest of the line from the second file.

In the example about student grades, having produced class lists for physics and chemistry, you may wish to combine these into one master file containing names and results from both subjects. First of all, sort *phys* and *chem* into order on the first field to produce *physa* and *chema*, then join them:

```
$ sort phys > physa          Sort phys on whole line
$ sort chem > chema          And again for chem
$ join physa chema           Join lines from each file
Bill Brown m P 6 Brown m C 9
Janet White f P 16 White f C 18
Mary White f P 19 White f C 17
Sam Black m P 16 Black m C 18
Sam Black m P 16 Brown m C 9
Sam Brown m P 6 Black m C 18
Sam Brown m P 6 Brown m C 9
$
```

This is not the output that is wanted but does give some insight into how **join**
works. The first three lines approximate the desired output (although the
surname is replicated unnecessarily). However, the next four illustrate that there
is one line of output for each pair of lines of input that have identical join fields.
Because the first name **Sam** occurs twice in each input file, four possible
combinations are generated. While this could be useful in some situations, it is
not acceptable in this instance. You need to join the files on a field which does
not have replicated values. Similar difficulties would arise if you joined the files
on the second field since surnames are also replicated.

To solve this problem, it is necessary to understand that, in its default mode,
**join** assumes that fields are separated by blank or tab. It is possible to redefine
the field separator using the −t flag where the character immediately following
the flag becomes the new one. If you define this as tab, it will be the only
character recognized as a field separator. What you need to do is create a unique
initial field but use some character other than tab to separate first name and
surname. Suppose you choose space; then the remaining fields must be separated
by a tab rather than spaces. Modify *physa* and *chema* accordingly using an
editor and join them again:

```
$ join -t'(T)' physa chema     Join using tab as a separator
Bill Brown    m      P      6      m      C      9
Janet White   f      P      16     f      C      18
Mary White    f      P      19     f      C      17
Sam Black     m      P      16     m      C      18
Sam Brown     m      P      6      m      C      9
$
```

Notice that you had to quote the tab character since it is significant to the shell.
The output looks a lot better but, if you are observant, you will have noticed that
there is no entry for **Sandra Brown** who is studying chemistry but not physics.
You can rectify this by using the −a flag. This is followed by a file number $n$
which takes the value 1 or 2 and produces an output line for any unpairable line
in file $n$ in addition to normal output. Hence, the full command line required
which will also handle the case of a student studying chemistry but not physics is
as follows:

```
$ join -t'(T)' -a1 -a2 physa chema    Join and output unpairables
Bill Brown      m      P      6      m      C      9
Janet White     f      P      16     f      C      18
Mary White      f      P      19     f      C      17
Sam Black       m      P      16     m      C      18
Sam Brown       m      P      6      m      C      9
Sandra Brown f         C      9
$
```

The output is now correct but contains extraneous information which is not really required. You could improve it still further by using the **–o** flag to introduce a list of the fields of the input lines which will occur in each output line. Each element in this list has the form *n.m* where *n* is the file number and *m* is the field number. Missing fields in the output line can be indicated by supplying a character string in association with the **–e** flag:

```
$ join -t'(T)' -a1 -a2 \          Join with output of unpairables
> -e X \                          Missing field indicator string
> -o 2.1 1.4 2.4 \                Define fields to be included
> physa chema                     Files to be joined
Bill Brown      6      9
Janet White     16     18
Mary White      19     17
Sam Black       16     18
Sam Brown       6      9
Sandra Brown X         9
$
```

If there are files containing marks for other subjects, these could be extracted in a similar way and added to the master list. The process is a little clumsy since prior knowledge is required of the whereabouts of the student's name. In the previous example, you had to specify field 2.1 to ensure that all names appeared in the output. A better approach would be first to produce a unique list of names using the **–u** option of **sort** and then add marks from the individual subject files to the master list using **join**.

The commands **join**, **sort**, **comm** and **uniq** provide a useful but somewhat primitive set of functions for maintaining a database. However, the conventions used in each command differ and sometimes it is difficult to match them.

## 5.2.4  Searching

A commonly occurring requirement in the management of data stored in many files is to be able to search for lines containing a particular character string and to be informed in what files the lines occur and their position in that file. You could of course simply use one of the editors since they possess the ability to search by context for patterns. However, it would be rather tedious to have to search through each of the files individually. Instead, it is preferable to use one of the members of the "grep" family — **grep**, **egrep** or **fgrep**.

You have already encountered **grep** in earlier chapters when you used it to search for simple character strings in a single file. However, it will also handle limited regular expressions which specify a pattern similar to those you have used in **ed**. The name "grep" is an acronym for **g**lobal **r**egular **e**xpression **p**rinter which comes from the **ed** command **g/re/p**. A regular expression may be defined as a rule for generating a set of character strings. For example, if **a** is a regular expression, it generates the string **a** whereas **ab\*** generates the strings **a, ab, abb** ... etc. and [a-z][A-Z], all 676 possible two-letter combinations consisting of a lower case letter followed by an upper case one. **egrep** will handle full regular expressions of which the limited ones available in **grep** are a subset, hence its name, **e**xtended **grep**. On the other hand, **fgrep** (**f**ast **grep** or **f**ixed **grep**) will only accept fixed strings as input but it carries out the search very efficiently and rapidly. Note that the regular expressions processed by these commands cannot be used to match a newline i.e. the character string being searched for must lie entirely within a single line.

> **fgrep** - fast pattern search

Let us now examine some of the facilities available in **fgrep**. Try locating the entries for `Black` in the files **phys** and **chem**:

```
$ fgrep Black phys chem          Output lines containing Black
phys:Sam Black          m     P 16
chem:Sam Black          m     C 18
$
```

The complete line is output and is preceded by the name of the file if there is more than one input file. If the **−n** flag is set, each line is preceded by its relative line number in the file:

```
$ fgrep -n Black phys chem        Output matching lines with count
phys:3:Sam Black        m     P 16
chem:2:Sam Black        m     C 18
$
```

If the **−x** flag is specified, only those lines matched in their entirety are output. This flag is only available for **fgrep**. The **−i** flag causes the case of letters to be ignored when making comparisons. This option is not available in System V and in some of the other versions is called **−y**. The **−h** flag (also not available in System V) suppresses the output of the filename before any matched line:

```
$ fgrep -i -x -h 'sam black       m     p 16' phys chem
Sam Black          m     P 16
$
```

When the **−c** option is specified, only a count of the matching lines is produced whereas **−l** outputs the names of files in which matches occur. The filename is generated once irrespective of the number of matching lines:

```
$ fgrep -c Brown phys chem          Count matching lines
phys:2
chem:3
$ fgrep -l Sam phys chem            Output names of files
phys
chem
$
```

If you want to search through files looking for more than one string, you can
do so using **fgrep** by separating the argument strings with a newline:

```
$ fgrep 'Sandra                     Output lines matching this string
> Bill' phys chem                   Or this one
phys:Bill Brown        m    P  6
chem:Sandra Brown      f    C  9
chem:Bill Brown        m    C  9
$
```

Notice how the argument had to be enclosed in quotes. Alternatively, you could
place the strings in a file, one per line and supply the name of the file using the −**f**
flag:

```
$ cat > strings                     Create file of search strings
Janet
Sandra
^D
$ fgrep -f strings phys chem        Output lines matching strings
phys:Janet White       f    P 16
chem:Janet White       f    C 18
chem:Sandra Brown      f    C  9
$
```

In the examples given so far, the output consists of lines which contain a
string which matches the argument string. If the −**v** flag is specified, the situation
is reversed and only those lines which do not match are output:

```
$ fgrep -v a phys chem              Output lines not matching a
phys:Bill Brown        m    P  6
chem:Bill Brown        m    C  9
$
```

The output consists of those lines in the two files which do not contain the letter
**a**.

---

| **grep** - search a file for a pattern |
| --- |

---

The flags discussed in the above examples for **fgrep** are also available with
**grep** with the exception of −**f** and −**x**. Further, **grep** will only handle one
regular expression at a time as an input argument. If you want to search for
alternatives, you will have to use **egrep**.

We have already presented many examples in the section on **ed** of the use of regular expressions to search for character strings in a file and do not propose to repeat these here. However, it is appropriate to include a more formal description of the regular expressions used by **grep** than rely on the rather informal one presented earlier.

A regular expression defines a set of character strings and members of the set are said to be matched by the regular expression. In constructing regular expressions, the following rules apply:

(i)     a character matches itself unless it is one of the following metacharacters:

$$\backslash \quad . \quad * \quad [ \quad \hat{} \quad \$$$

(ii)    any character, including the metacharacters but excluding the digits, **(** and **)**, preceded by a backslash matches itself. Hence the following are all ordinary single characters:

$$\backslash\mathbf{a} \quad \backslash\backslash \quad \backslash. \quad \backslash* \quad \backslash[ \quad \backslash\hat{} \quad \backslash\$$$

(iii)   a period matches any single character.

(iv)    a non-empty string of characters enclosed in square brackets matches any one of the characters in the string. This includes the metacharacters which lose their special meaning when used in such a string. However, if ⌃ is the first character of the string, any character not contained in the remainder of the string will be matched. If ⌃ is not the first character, it is not considered special and is an ordinary member of the string. Character classes or ranges are indicated by connecting two characters with a minus sign e.g. **a–z** matches any lower case letter. If the minus sign is the last character in the string or occurs immediately after the left square bracket (or the immediately following caret if any), it loses its special significance. In fact, it can be placed in any position where it cannot be mistaken for a range indicator. If a right square bracket occurs in the string, it must occur as the first character in the string. Some examples are given in the first section of Table 5.1.

(v)     regular expressions may be concatenated to form more complex regular expressions as shown in the second section of Table 5.1.

(vi)    a single character regular expression followed by **\*** matches zero or more occurrences of the character that matches the regular expression. The match is the longest possible string. **\*** is called a *closure* operator. Some examples are given in the third section of Table 5.1.

(vii)   a tagged regular expression is one enclosed between **\(** and **\)**. It matches whatever the regular expression matches. The expression **\n** where *n* is a digit matches the same character string as was matched by a tagged regular expression earlier in the composite regular expression. The sub-expression specified is that beginning with the *n*-th occurrence of **\(**

| Table 5.1 | |
|---|---|
| *Regular Expression* | *Matching String* |
| [a9] | a *or* 9 |
| [\.*[^$] | \ *or* . *or* * *or* [ *or* ^ *or* $ |
| [^ab] | *any character except* a *or* b |
| [0-9] | *any digit* 0 *to* 9 |
| [1-30] | 0  1  2  *or* 3 |
| [^A-Z] | *any character except an upper case letter* |
| [] [-] | ] *or* [ *or* − |
| [^^] | *any character except* ^ |
| [^a-z-+A-Z] | *any character except a letter,* + *or* − |
| abc | abc |
| a[0-9]b | a *digit* b |
| [0-9]\.[0-9] | *digit period digit* |
| [A-Z]... | *any three characters after upper case letter* |
| x* | *null string or string of* x |
| xy* | x *followed by string of* y *or null string* |
| [a-zA-Z]* | *null string or alphabetic string* |
| .* | *any string including null string* |
| [+-][0-9]*\.[0-9][0-9]* | *signed real number in Pascal* |
| \(.\)\1 | *repeated character e.g.* bb |
| \(.*\)\1 | *repeated string e.g.* abcabc |
| \([a-z]\)\([a-z]\)\2\1 | *4 letter palindrome e.g.* noon |
| ^[^a-z] | *start of line other than a lower case letter* |
| ^$ | *null line* |
| ^ *$ | *line of spaces* |
| ^\(.*\)\1$ | *line consisting of a doubly repeated string* |

counting from the left. (The tagged regular expression facility is only available in **grep**.) For some examples, see the fourth section of Table 5.1.

(viii)   if a regular expression is preceded by ^, it is constrained to match from the beginning of the line. If a regular expression is followed by $, it is constrained to match up to the end of the line. Some examples are given in the last section of Table 5.1.

---

**egrep** - extended pattern search

---

Now let us consider the facilities available in **egrep**. In addition to those described above (with the exception of tagged regular expressions), it includes two more closure operators, + and ?, permits the specification of alternatives and provides a grouping facility using parentheses.

If a single character regular expression is followed by +, it matches one or more occurrences of the character which matches the regular expression (as compared with zero or more occurrences for *):

```
$ egrep 1+ phys              Output lines containing 1 or 11
Sam Black        m    P 16
Bill Brown       m    P  6
$
```

The first line contains 1 and the second, 11. Hence, they match the regular expression. If ? is used instead of +, 0 or 1 occurrence is matched.

Alternative regular expressions are specified by separating them with | or a newline:

```
$ egrep 'Bill|Mary' phys     Lines matching Bill or Mary
Mary White       f    P 19
Bill Brown       m    P  6
$
```

Notice how you had to quote the argument since | is a significant character to the shell. Regular expressions may also be stored in a file, one per line, and the file can then be specified as an argument using the **–f** flag:

```
$ cat > res                  Create file of search patterns
Brown *f
Black *m
^D
$ egrep -f res phys chem     Lines matching patterns in res
phys:Sam Black       m    P 16
chem:Sam Black       m    C 18
chem:Sandra Brown    f    C  9
$
```

A regular expression may be enclosed in parentheses for grouping:

```
$ egrep 'Sam (Black|Brown)' phys
Sam Black      m    P 16        Output lines containing
Sam Brown      m    P 6         Sam Black or Sam Brown
$
```

The regular expression matches a string which consists of Sam followed by Black or Brown.

The **grep** family provides a powerful set of tools for searching for lines containing specified strings in one or more files. **fgrep** is fast and will look for hundreds of words at the one time. However, it does not interpret metacharacters. **egrep** handles more general regular expressions than **grep** with the exception of tagging. Once it has initialized itself with the strings for which it is to search, **egrep** runs significantly faster than **grep**. Hence, our advice is that, for simple strings, use **fgrep** and, for regular expressions, use **egrep** unless you want to make use of tagged regular expressions.

## 5.2.5 Transforming

From time to time, you will need to transform the data in a file from one format to another. Sometimes, the transformation will be permanent; at other times, it will only be a temporary one. Of course, you have already used commands like **ed** or **vi** to change the contents of a file. Even commands like **sort**, **comm**, **uniq** and **join** could be thought of as file transformers. But there are many more available in UNIX and we will consider some of them here.

> **wc** - word count

You have already encountered the command **wc** (**w**ord **c**ount) and used it to produce a count of the number of lines in a file. This is only one of its options. In fact, in the default mode, it produces a count of the number of lines, words and characters in a file. If more than one file is specified, the filename is appended to the output and the last line contains a grand total for all files:

```
$ wc phys chem              Count lines, words and characters
        5      25      130 phys
        6      30      157 chem
       11      55      287 total
$
```

The first column is the line count, the second, the word count and the third, the character count. The −l flag selects the first column only, the −**w** flag, the second and −**c**, the third:

```
$ wc -wc phys chem              Count words and characters
      25        130 phys
      30        157 chem
      55        287 total
$
```

The default is therefore equivalent to **–lwc**. As a data transformer, the command can be viewed as one which changes a file of lines, words and characters into one which contains only the respective counts of each of these entities.

> **tr** - translate characters

This command is more obviously a data transformer since it copies standard input to standard output with the substitution or deletion of selected characters. It takes two arguments. The first is a string of input characters which are to be mapped into the corresponding characters in the second argument. If the second argument is shorter than the first one, it is padded out to the correct length by repeating the last character:

```
$ tr abc xy                     Translate a→x, b→y, c→y
a
x
aab
xxy
abc
xyy
^D
$
```

In the string **abc**, c has been replaced by **y** because of the automatic extension of the target string. Character classes or ranges are allowable arguments. If, for example, you want to change all lower case characters in **phys** to upper case, you can do so as follows:

```
$ tr a-z A-Z < phys             Translate lower to upper case
MARY WHITE      F       P 19
JANET WHITE     F       P 16
SAM BLACK       M       P 16
BILL BROWN      M       P  6
SAM BROWN       M       P  6
$
```

In some versions of **tr**, it is necessary to enclose ranges in square brackets in which case they must be quoted to avoid shell expansion:

```
$ tr '[A-Z]' '[a-z]' < phys        Translate upper to lower case
mary white       f    p 19
janet white      f    p 16
sam black        m    p 16
bill brown       m    p  6
sam brown        m    p  6
$
```

Any character in either string which has special meaning to the shell may be protected by quoting or escaping:

```
$ tr ' '   \*                      Translate space to asterisk
a b  c
a*b**c
^D
$
```

The first argument is a space and hence the command translates spaces into asterisks. If \ is followed by 1, 2 or 3 octal digits, the combination is taken to stand for the character whose ASCII code is specified by the digits. So let's try converting each space into a newline which has an ASCII code of 012:

```
$ tr ' ' \012                      Translate space to newline?
a b
a0b
^D
$
```

That wasn't what you intended — space has been converted into 0. As you might expect, the shell is the culprit. The quotes correctly protect the space and it is transmitted to **tr** as the first argument. However, \0 becomes just 0 and the second argument is therefore 012. Since space and zero correspond, the observed transformation is correct. What you need to do is enclose the second argument in quotes to prevent the shell seeing the backslash. In fact, it's probably a good idea to always quote arguments to **tr** to avoid unexpected behaviour:

```
$ tr ' '   '\012'                  Translate space to newline
a b
a
b
^D
$
```

There are a number of flags recognized by **tr**. If −**d** is specified, all characters in the first argument string are deleted from standard input (the second argument is redundant). Thus, you could delete all letters and spaces from a file as follows:

```
$ tr -d 'a-zA-Z ' < phys          Delete letters and spaces
19
16
16
6
6
$
```

If **−c** is specified, the set of characters in the first argument is complemented with
respect to the universe of characters whose ASCII codes are **001** through **377**
octal. When combined with **−d**, it means delete all characters other than those in
the argument string:

```
$ tr -cd 'a-zA-Z' < phys      Delete all non-alphabetic characters
MaryWhitefPJanetWhitefPSamBlackmPBillBrownmPSamBrownmP$
```

All non-alphabetic characters have been removed from the file. Finally, **−s**
squeezes strings of repeated characters specified in the second argument into a
single character:

```
$ tr -s 'a-z' 'A-Z'          Translate lower to upper case and squeeze
aabbbbcccc
ABC
^D
$
```

Suppose now you wanted to extract all strings of digits from a file and output
them separated by spaces. What you would need to do is replace all characters
except digits with a space and then squeeze strings of spaces to a single space:

```
$ tr -cs '0-9' ' ' < phys  Replace non-numeric strings by one space
 19 16 16 6 6 $
$
```

Consider now the problem of creating a list of unique lower case words, sorted
into alphabetical order where a word is defined to be a sequence of letters:

```
$ tr 'A-Z' 'a-z' < phys |          Translate upper to lower case
> tr -cs 'a-z' '\012' |            Replace numeric strings by newline
> sort -u                          And sort
bill
black
brown
f
janet
m
mary
p
sam
white
$
```

After upper case has been converted to lower case, all characters other than letters are replaced by new lines and then squeezed. Finally, **sort** is run to produce the list of unique words. Obviously, such a transformation could be quite useful in preparing an index to a document stored in a file.

The possibilities for using **tr** are endless and only limited by your imagination. If, for example, you translate each character in a file into some other character, the file would not be readily understood by other people, yet you could easily recover the original file by reversing the process:

```
$ tr ´ a-zA-Z0-9´ ´a-zA-Z0-9 ´ < phys          Encrypt file
NbszaXijufaaaaaagaaaaQa2
KbofuaXijufaaaaagaaaaQa27
TbnaCmbdlaaaaaaanaaaaQa27
CjmmaCspxoaaaaaanaaaaQaa7
TbnaCspxoaaaaaaanaaaaQaa7
$
```

Such a transformation is called *encryption*. However, this code would be very easy to break. There are better ways of encrypting a file using the **crypt** command as we will see shortly.

| **od** - octal dump |
|---|

Another useful transformer is **od** which will output the contents of a file in a number of different formats including octal (hence its name, **o**ctal **d**ump). It recognizes a number of flags which control the form of the output. If −**c** is specified, each byte in the file is treated as an ASCII code. If the code represents a non-graphic character, it is output as the equivalent C language escape character if one exists e.g. a newline is output as **\n**, a tab as **\t**. Otherwise non-graphic characters which have no such representation appear as 3-digit octal numbers. Let's try the command reading from standard input a line consisting of 0, tab, **abc**, escape, space and newline:

```
$ od -c                    Dump in ascii characters
0(T)abc(E) (R)
^D
0000000    0  \t    a    b    c 033         \n
0000010
$
```

The first column gives the address in octal of the first byte in the line. Notice how escape has been output as **033**, its value in the ASCII character set. Now try the same input string but, this time, use the flag −**b** which causes each byte to be output as a 3-digit octal value:

```
$ od -b                          Dump in octal
0(T)abc(E)  (R)
^D
0000000   060 011 141 142 143 033 040 012
0000010
$
```

Again every byte in the file including newline has been output. If you wanted
hexadecimal output instead of octal, the **-x** flag must be specified:

```
$ od -x                          Dump in hexadecimal
0(T)abc(E)  (R)
^D
0000000   3009 6162 631b 200a
0000010
$
```

Each group of four digits represents two bytes or characters. You should convert
each pair of hexadecimal digits in the above output line into the corresponding
octal value to check that you understand how to convert from one number system
to the other. If you want each 16-bit word output in octal, you can use **od** in its
default mode or with the **-o** flag:

```
$ od                             Dump in words
0(T)abc(E)  (R)
^D
0000000   030011 060542 061433 020012
0000010
$
```

There are other flags recognized by **od** but their effect can vary from one
system to another. You will have to check the documentation available with your
system to see what effect the various flags have.

As you will have realized by now, the command **od** can be very useful for
examining the contents of binary as well as character files since it always produces
printable and hence readable output. If the file is a very large one, it would be
tedious to read through an excessive amount of output to find the region in which
you are interested. Hence, **od** permits the specification of an offset at which
dumping is to start. This is usually expressed as a number of bytes in octal but
may be given in decimal if terminated by a period:

```
$ od -c phys 96.                 Dump in ascii characters with offset
0000096             P       6 \n  S   a   m       B   r   o   w
0000112   n                         m                       P
0000128   6 \n
0000130
$
```

Notice that the addresses in the first column are now expressed in decimal. If the
filename is omitted, the offset must be preceded by a + sign If **b** is appended to

the offset, it is treated as a multiple of 512 bytes making the command more convenient to use for extremely large files.

$$\boxed{\textbf{dd} \; \text{-} \; \text{convert a file}}$$

A somewhat similar and even more powerful command is **dd** which copies a specified input file and converts it from one form to another. It is especially suited to direct input-output on physical devices since it allows for the reading and writing of arbitrary sized records. It is therefore frequently used for the interchange of data with other computer systems which do not operate under UNIX. If a magnetic tape has been written on another system, it can be read and its contents transferred to a UNIX file by specifying its layout to **dd** and indicating what conversions (if any) are to be applied to the data. Conversely, a tape may be written on a UNIX system in a format acceptable to a foreign operating system.

There are many options available with **dd** but we won't go into all the details here. Suffice to say that you can specify the name and block size of both the input and output files, position either or both files before copying commences, specify the number of records to be copied or copy to end-of-file, convert variable length records to fixed length and vice-versa, map from one case to the other and translate from one character set to another. To illustrate some of these facilities, suppose you wanted to produce a file containing characters in EBCDIC (Extended Binary Coded Decimal Interchange Code) rather than in ASCII. The former is an 8-bit code as contrasted with the 7-bit ASCII code and is used by many computer manufacturers, for example, IBM. First of all, create a file *achars* containing some ASCII characters and convert these to produce an output file *echars*:

```
$ echo abcdef > achars                Create achars
$ dd if=achars of=echars conv=ebcdic  Convert ascii to ebcdic
0+1 records in
0+1 records out
$
```

Notice that **dd** is another of the commands which does not conform to the standard UNIX convention for selecting options. The keyword **if** defines the input file name (standard input is the default) while **of** defines the output filename (standard output is the default). The conversions are specified by the keyword **conv** and, if there are more than one, they are separated by commas. In this case, you have requested **dd** to convert characters from ASCII to EBCDIC. After the copying has been completed, **dd** reports the number of whole and partial input and output blocks on standard error output. Now let us look at the contents of *echars*:

```
$ od -x echars                    Dump in hexadecimal
0000000    8182 8384 8586 2500
0000010
$
```

Obviously, a different representation from the values you have seen before for these characters e.g. 25 in EBCDIC for newline as compared with 0a in ASCII. Now, convert the contents of *echars* back to ASCII, specifying at the same time a change to upper case and a reversal of each pair of characters:

```
$ dd if=echars conv=ascii,\     Convert ebcdic to upper case ascii
> ucase,swab                    And swap bytes
BADCFE
0+1 records in
0+1 records out
$
```

The last conversion **swab** (**swa**p **b**ytes) is sometimes needed to be able to transfer information to or from machines such as the DEC VAX 11/780 which stores each pair of bytes in reverse order in a 16-bit word.

---

**crypt** - encode or decode a file

---

In earlier sections, we alluded to the need to encrypt data stored in a file to protect it from prying eyes and the existence of a command **crypt** on most systems to do just this. The command expects to be supplied with a key, and then uses this to transform standard input and write the encrypted form of the file on standard output. If no key is supplied as an argument, **crypt** prompts for one from the terminal but, fortunately, turns off echoing as the characters are typed, thereby helping to preserve its secrecy:

```
$ crypt < phys > cphys           Encrypt file
Enter key:
$
```

You can look at *cphys* if you wish but, as it is likely to contain non-printable characters, you won't learn much from it. The process is, of course, reversible using the same key:

```
$ crypt < cphys | diff - phys    Decrypt file and compare
Enter key:
$
```

Since there is no output, the decryption process has produced exactly the same file as the original one.

The key may also be supplied as an argument, in which case it is visible on the terminal:

```
$ crypt 'a9B-(z)' | crypt 'a9B-(z)'     Encrypt and decrypt
abcdef
^D
abcdef
$
```

Unless some special action is taken, the key is also potentially visible to any user executing **ps** (which you will meet in the next section) since arguments to a command are output in the extended list produced by **ps**. Hence, **crypt** destroys any record of the key as soon as it is entered.

The security of the encryption process depends on how secret you keep the key, how long it is and how easy it would be for some other user to guess it. Don't choose a key that is too short (all combinations of three lower case letters can be generated and applied to a file in just a few minutes of machine time) and don't choose something that is too obvious. A final word of warning — once a file has been encrypted, don't forget what the key is, otherwise, the data may be lost forever.

## 5.3  Managing Jobs

Typically, you will be using a computer system to carry out a number of tasks to achieve a set of goals. You may want to solve some numerical problem, sort or retrieve some data, create a document, communicate with someone else or even just play a game. Between login and logout, you will, from time to time, initiate *jobs*, that is, command the machine to carry out some specific task for you. To enable you to do this effectively and conveniently, UNIX provides a number of commands to help you manage your jobs. Before examining these in some detail, let us take a closer look at just what is meant by the term *process*.

After you have logged in successfully, UNIX activates the shell on your behalf to interpret the commands you issue and supervise the running of the jobs you initiate. To do this, it allocates some memory, loads the instructions and data that constitute the shell and causes it to be executed. We refer to this activity as initiating a process, in this case, the shell. UNIX adds the name of this process to its process table so that it can schedule it along with other processes to ensure that it obtains its fair share of the CPU time. It is important to grasp the difference between a program and a process. The shell exists as a program written in C, also in a compiled form which may be executed by the machine. When it is being executed, it is referred to as a process, that is, an instance of a running program. In a given UNIX environment, there will only be one copy of the shell program (for each of its various forms) but many shell processes, in fact, at least one for each user logged in.

Once a shell process has been activated on your behalf, it will continue in existence until you logout. During this time it will exist in one of a number of discrete states. It may be *running*, in which case it has been allocated the CPU, it may be *ready-to-run* and will eventually be allocated the CPU when its turn comes or it may be *waiting* for some event to happen such as the termination of an input-output transfer. Other possibilities include whether it is resident in high speed memory or swapped out onto backing store.

## 5.3.1  Initiating Jobs

When the shell initiates the execution of a command for you, it does so by creating a new process called a *child* of which it now becomes the *parent*. It allocates some memory, loads in the object program and causes it to be executed, that is, scheduled along with other processes for CPU time. It then waits for the child process to terminate. If the command is a pipe, the shell will create a process for each of the components and wait until the last one has finished before calling for the next command line.

The facilities available to the shell for initiating new processes are also available to any of its children. In turn, they can create processes which can create further processes and so on. It is therefore possible to create a hierarchy of processes with the login shell as the root and a structure very similar to that of the file system.

After a command has been initiated, it executes to completion or until it is aborted via an interrupt. This is known as *foreground* execution. No other jobs can be initiated until the current one completes. This is not always convenient. Sometimes, you may wish to start up a job that you know will take a long time and not be prevented from using the terminal to do other things whilst the job is executing. This is called *background* execution.

A job may be started up in the background by appending an ampersand (**&**) to the end of the command line. The command:

```
$ cal 1984 > c84 &          Initiate background job
3294
$
```

initiates **cal** as a background process that will run in parallel with any foreground activity. The integer output by the shell is the *process identifier* (PID) that allows the user to keep track of the process. The system then returns to command mode.

===========================================

A similar facility exists in the C-shell except that, in this case, a job number is output as well in square brackets at the start of the line:

```
% cal 1984 > c84 &              As above for C-shell
[1] 6150
%
[1]     Done                    cal 1984 > c84
```

A message indicating the job has finished is also output on the terminal when it is no longer in input mode. In the above example, this final message would not appear until the user responded with **RETURN** to the second command prompt. Another variation in the C-shell, is that a process identifier is output for each process in a pipe whereas in the standard shell only the PID of the first process is displayed. The command:

```
% who | wc > cnt &              Initiate background pipe in C-shell
[1] 6119 6120
%
```

illustrates the behaviour of C-shell for background pipes.

------------------------------------------------------------------

## 5.3.2 Suspending Jobs

Sometimes you may wish to suspend a job and resume it at some later time after having executed other commands in between the suspension and the restart.

==================================================================

In the C-shell, a job may be suspended, whether it is executing or waiting for input, via the stop signal, **control–Z**. To experiment with this facility, write a message to yourself and, at some point, stop the job:

```
% write yew                     Write to yourself again

message from yew on ttyj at 10:46 ...
This is a test                  This is what you type
This is a test                  And the machine responds
^Z                              Now suspend write
Stopped
%
```

Here **^Z** was issued at the beginning of an input line; if it had occurred after some input had been typed, these characters would have been lost. The system has returned to the command state ready to accept new commands.

| **jobs** - print list of background and suspended jobs |
| --- |

At any time, you can examine the status of your jobs via the **jobs** command:

```
% jobs                          What jobs do you have?
[1]  + stopped              write yew
%
```

The job has a number (in this case, 1) and a status (stopped). The + sign indicates that it is the current job. Now, create a file using **cat**, stop it also and then examine the status of your jobs:

```
% cat > alpha            Create a file
 Stopping jobs           Input a line
^Z                       Now suspend cat
Stopped
% jobs                   What jobs do you have now?
[1]  - stopped           write yew
[2]  + stopped           cat > alpha
%
```

**cat** has become the current job as shown by the + and the − against job 1 indicates that it is now the previous job. Any number of jobs may be suspended, the most recent one becoming the current and the preceding one, the previous job.

| **fg** - start job in foreground |

Jobs may be restarted in any order using the **fg** command that takes as its argument the name of the job. This is a **%** sign followed by the job number. Let us restart the **write** command and continue the message, terminating it in the normal way with end-of-file:

```
% fg %1                  Restart job 1 in foreground
write yew                write has been restarted
of job control           Continue input of message
of job control
^D                       Terminate input
EOF
%
```

The shell outputs the command line reminding you of the command that is being restarted and the job then resumes from where it left off. Other variations of the job name are **%+** and **%−** referring to the current and previous jobs respectively, **%** followed by a character string that uniquely identifies the start of a command line or **%?** followed by a string that occurs somewhere in only one of the command lines. The job name on its own is sufficient to restart a job. **%−** would have produced the same effect as **fg %1**. **fg** on its own without any arguments will restart the current job by default.

The ability to suspend a job provides a second method in **csh** for executing a job in the background. First of all, you start it in the foreground, then stop it with **^Z** and then restart it in the background. To try out this facility, let us choose a command that produces a lot of output and redirect that output to a file − **du** applied to the root directory will do. Start it up and then suspend it with **^Z**:

```
% du / >& out           Initiate foreground job
^Z                      Suspend it
Stopped
% jobs                  And examine what jobs you have
[2]  - stopped             cat > alpha
[3]  + stopped             du / >& out
%
```

| **bg** - start job in background |
|---|

To restart a background job, you issue the **bg** command with the job name
as an argument. If no name is supplied, the current job is restarted:

```
% bg                    Restart suspended job in background
[3]    du / >& out &
%
```

The shell outputs the command line to remind you of the job that you have
restarted. It will now run to completion or until you stop it again.

| **stop** - suspend a background job |
|---|

However, because it is a background job, you will have to use the **stop**
command supplying the job name as the argument:

```
% stop %3               Stop background job 3
%
```

When the job stops, the shell outputs a message when it can (i.e. when the
terminal is not waiting for input) of the form:

```
[3]  + stopped (signal)      du / >& out
```

You could now resume execution in the background via **bg** or in the foreground
using **fg**. Being able to suspend jobs and move them easily between foreground
and background is a convenient and powerful facility that allows you to optimize
your use of a terminal. You don't have to sit there waiting for a job to finish
even if you started it in the foreground. Since a background job will stop when it
tries to read from a terminal, there is no restriction on the type of job that may
be run in the background. Whenever such a job requires input, it can be
restarted in the foreground and have its read request satisfied. It can then be
continued in either foreground or background mode.

------------------------------------------------------------------------

In the standard shell, you cannot suspend a foreground job as you can in the
C-shell. However, you can obtain approximately the same effect by using a
facility called *shell layers* which is only available in System V.2.

**shl** - shell layer manager

The shell layer manager allows a user to interact with more than one active shell from a single terminal. Only one of these shells called the *current layer* can receive input from the keyboard. Other layers attempting to read from the keyboard are blocked. On the other hand, output from any of the layers will appear on the terminal unless specific action has been taken to block such output.

To experiment with this facility, first of all, issue the **shl** command:

```
$ shl                           Activate shell layer manager
>>>
```

A new and distinctive prompt >>> appears indicating that the shell layer manager is ready to receive commands. The first action you must take is to create a layer:

```
>>> c                           Create new shell layer
(1)
```

The **create** command, which may be abbreviated as shown above, makes a new shell layer with a prompt set to the name of the layer which may be supplied as an argument to the command. If no argument is supplied, **shl** uses one of the names (1) through to (7) (the maximum number of layers that may be created is 7). Once the prompt has appeared, you can issue commands to the shell in the normal way. To get back from a layer to **shl**, you use an **stty** character called **swtch** which has a default value of **^Z**. The effect of this character is therefore somewhat similar to what it is in the C-shell.

```
(1) write yew                   Write to yourself

Message from yew (sxt011) [Sun May 19 11:46:22] ...
Testing shell layers
Testing shell layers
^Z                              Stop job and exit to shl
>>>
```

You are now back in **shl** and can issue any of the commands it understands. To find out what these are, try **help** or **h** or just **?** to output a list of **shl** commands. You will see that one of these is **layers** which will output information about the layers you have created:

```
>>> l                           List layer details
(1) (2223) executing or awaiting input
>>>
```

Only one layer exists with name (1) as expected. The **write** command in this layer is suspended as it is blocked from reading input from the terminal. Now let's create a second layer, then a new file and return to the layer manager to inspect the layers again:

```
>>> c                                    Create 2nd layer
(2) cat > alpha                          Create new file
stopping jobs                            Type input line
^Z                                       Exit to shl
>>> l                                    List layer details
(1) (2223) executing or awaiting input
(2) (2225) executing or awaiting input
>>> ░
```

Now you have 2 layers, each with a suspended foreground job.

To restart the **write** command, you need to return to the first layer by issuing the command **resume 1** or **r 1** or simply **1**. Without an argument, the **resume** command restarts the previously active layer (in this case, layer 2). Since layer 1 was current before the last current layer, you can also reactivate it by using the **toggle** command:

```
>>> t                                    Resume layer 1
resuming (1)
in System V.2                            Continue input to write
in System V.2
^D                                       Terminate input
<EOT>
(1) ░                                    Layer 1 shell prompt
```

You still have a suspended job **cat** in layer 2 which you could restart by returning to **shl** and causing layer 2 to resume. However, if you decide that you don't want to continue with that command, you can remove the layer using the **delete** command which will cause all processes in it to terminate:

```
(1) ^Z                                   Exit to shl
>>> d 2                                  Delete layer 2
>>> l                                    List layer details
(1) (2223) executing or awaiting input
>>> ░
```

Now there is only one layer left. You can either continue operating in it or return to the login shell by issuing the **quit** command:

```
>>> q                                    Exit from shl
$ ░                                      Normal shell prompt
```

The **quit** command, in fact, will terminate all layers and the processes operating within them before exiting from **shl**.

## 5.3.3  Monitoring Jobs

Once a background job has been initiated on your behalf, you may wish, from time to time, to know how it is progressing, how much CPU time it has consumed or even what its PID is (assuming you have forgotten what number was output when the job started). To do this, you use the **ps** command which will list information about the currently active processes (**ps** stands for **p**rocess **s**tatus).

```
┌─────────────────────────────┐
│ ps  -  process status       │
└─────────────────────────────┘
```

Assuming that there are no other processes, **ps** without an argument just outputs a line for itself since it is running while accumulating information to be sent to standard output:

```
$ ps                            Output process status
  PID TT STAT   TIME COMMAND
12528 j  R      0:02 ps
$
```

where:

| | |
|---|---|
| PID | *is the process identification number.* |
| TT | *is the terminal number.* |
| STAT | *is the execution status -* **R** *for running,* **S** *for sleeping, etc.* |
| TIME | *is the cumulative execution time* |
| COMMAND | *is the name of the command.* |

(If your output differs somewhat from our example, don't be concerned — **ps** is very system dependent and there are many variants.)

If you are using shell layers, you can inspect the status of various jobs from within **shl** by using the **layers** command with the −l option. For example, if you had used this command when you had 2 layers with **write** and **cat** both suspended and waiting for input, you would have seen something similar to the following:

```
>>> l -l                        List layer details in long format
(1) (2223) executing or awaiting input
    UID   PID  PPID  C    STIME   TTY TIME COMD
    yew  2222  2221  1 15:49:08   011 0:00 sh
    yew  2223  2222  0 15:49:19   011 0:00 write

(2) (2225) executing or awaiting input
    UID   PID  PPID  C    STIME   TTY TIME COMD
    yew  2224  2221  1 15:49:30   012 0:00 sh
    yew  2225  2224  0 15:49:36   012 0:00 cat

>>>
```

**ps** on its own only lists your processes. However, if −a (or even just **a**) is supplied as an argument, all currently active processes including those belonging to other users are listed. If you use the −g flag, **ps** will print all of your processes including the uninteresting ones such as your login shell:

```
$ ps -g                         Output status for all your processes
  PID TT STAT   TIME COMMAND
11340 j  S      0:05 -sh (sh)
12529 j  R      0:02 ps -g
$
```

The minus sign in front of **sh** indicates that it is your login shell. Notice that its status is **S** meaning that it is sleeping while waiting for **ps** to finish. It is the parent of the child process **ps** but is not executing in parallel with it. You can see this by calling for a long listing with the **–l** flag:

```
$ ps -lg                          Output process status in long format
   F UID    PID  PPID CP PRI NI ADDR   SZ WCHAN STAT TT   TIME COMMAND
   1   8 11340     1  1   5  0  2D7   28 BC804 S    j   0:05 -sh (sh)
   1   8 12531 11340 96  49  0  37A  134       R    j   0:04 ps -lg
$
```

For the meaning of most of this information, we refer you to the manual for **ps**. However, you should be able to interpret some of it. The first column is simply a set of flags which say something about the process. The value **1** in this example indicates that the process is in high speed memory. The UID column contains the *user identifier*, a unique number by which each user is known to the system. Hence, the user identifier for **yew** in our system is **8** which you could verify by extracting the entry for **yew** from the password file using **grep**. As you will observe, the user identifier is the third field. The column headed PID contains the process identifier, a unique number generated by the system when a process is created and by which it identifies the process. The next column is the process identifier of the parent process. Notice that the entry for **ps** in this column is **11340** which is the process identifier of the shell. The process number for the parent of the shell is **1** i.e. the second process started up when the system was initialized. The next column contains a number showing CPU utilization which is used by the scheduler in determining which process will get the CPU next. The column headed PRI contains the priority of the process which is also used by the scheduling algorithm. The higher the number, the lower the priority and the less likely it is that the process will get the CPU. The priority is adjusted dynamically and, in most systems, falls the more demand the process makes on system resources. Since **ps** performs a great deal of computation, its priority is much lower than that of the shell. The next column contains the "niceness" number which is also used in calculating priority.

---

**nice** - run a command at low priority

---

To run a job at a lower priority than normal, you use the **nice** command:

```
$ nice ps -lg        .              Lower priority of job
   F UID    PID  PPID  CP PRI NI ADDR   SZ WCHAN STAT TT   TIME COMMAND
   1   8 11340     1   1   5  0  2D7   28 BC804 S    j   0:05 -sh (sh)
   1   8 12533 11340 118  74 10  37A  134       R N  j   0:04 ps -lg
$
```

You will probably have had to wait a little longer for output to appear since the priority of **ps** was reduced because you were being nice to other users. The default value of the "niceness" number is **10** which now appears in the NI column.

Notice that the number in the PRI column has been increased, thereby reducing the priority of the process. Other values of the "niceness" number up to a maximum of 20 may be supplied as an argument:

```
$ nice -5 ps -lg              Lower priority of job by specified amount
  F UID   PID  PPID  CP PRI NI ADDR  SZ WCHAN STAT TT  TIME COMMAND
  1  8 11340     1   1   1  5 0 2D7  28 BC804 S    j   0:05 -sh (sh)
  1  8 12535 11340 132  68  5 37A 134        R N  j   0:04 ps -lg
$
```

Those readers with devious minds are probably already thinking "What if I supply a negative number as an argument? Then, I can run my jobs at a higher priority than anyone else and be finished more quickly". Well, try it:

```
$ nice --10 ps -lg         Try to run job at high priority
nice: Badly formed number
$
```

Tough luck! Only the superuser can run jobs at a very high priority. If ordinary users were allowed to do this, the ensuing free-for-all would produce chaos.

The last four columns of the long output are also part of the shortened version − status of the process, teletype number, cumulative execution time for the process and name of the command with its arguments. Notice that the status of **ps** is always **R** for "running" while sometimes the shell status is **S** for "sleeping" and at other times **I** for "idle" On our system, a sleeping process becomes idle once it has slept for more than 20 secs.

## 5.3.4 Terminating Jobs

Although **ps** enables you to monitor what other users are doing, it is used most frequently to inspect the state of the processes you have initiated so that you can take some action if necessary e.g. terminate a job if it is stuck or is taking too much time. To experiment with process termination, you need to be able to set up a background process that will stay around for a while. To do this, you can make use of the **sleep** command.

---
**sleep** - suspend execution for an interval
---

If a command is preceded by **sleep** which takes some number of seconds as its argument, execution of the command will be delayed for that period of time:

```
$ sleep 20; date              Delay output of date
Fri June 29 17:16:04 EST 1984
$
```

There should be a delay of at least 20 seconds before the output appears on the terminal. The **sleep** command can be used to execute a command after a certain amount of time or every so often if it is included in a **while** loop in a shell script.

$$\boxed{\textbf{kill} \text{ - terminate a process}}$$

Once a background job has been initiated, it will run to completion or until it is terminated from the terminal. To do this, you can use the **kill** command, supplying the process identifier as an argument e.g. the command:

```
$ kill 3294                    Terminate process
$
```

would terminate the first example of a background job given in Section 5.3.1 above. More than one PID may be supplied as arguments to the **kill** command.

========================================================

In the C-shell, **kill** may also be used to terminate a suspended job and takes as arguments either PIDs or job names. The foreground job **cat** that was suspended earlier and never restarted could be terminated as illustrated below:

```
% jobs                         What jobs do you have?
[2]  + stopped          cat > alpha
% kill %2                      Terminate job 2
% jobs                         And examine your jobs again
[2]   terminated        cat > alpha
%
```

-------------------------------------------------------------------

Now, let us set up a background job using **sleep**, kill it and then examine the status of remaining processes:

```
$ sleep 200 & ps               Initiate background process
12537
  PID TT STAT   TIME COMMAND
12537 j  S      0:00 sleep 200
12538 j  R      0:02 ps
$ kill 12537                   Terminate background process
12537 Terminated
$ ps                           And check that it is dead
  PID TT STAT   TIME COMMAND
12558 j  R      0:02 ps
$
```

The output from the first **ps** shows that a process exists for **sleep 200** and that it is sleeping; the output from the second shows that it has disappeared.

What happens if you initiate a background pipe and how do you kill it? Execute the following command line:

```
$ sleep 200 | sleep 300 & ps        Initiate two background processes
12560
  PID TT STAT   TIME COMMAND
12560 j  S     0:00 sleep 300
12561 j  R     0:02 ps
12562 j  S     0:00 sleep 200
$ kill 12560
12560 Terminated                    Terminate 2nd background process
$ ps                                And check that both are dead
  PID TT STAT   TIME COMMAND
12564 j  R     0:02 ps
$ 
```

By specifying the process identifier of the last component of the pipe as the
argument to **kill**, you effectively remove both processes. However, if you use the
process identifier of the first component, it is the only one removed and the
second one remains in existence:

```
$ sleep 200 | sleep 300  & ps       Initiate two background processes
12573
  PID TT STAT   TIME COMMAND
12573 j  S     0:00 sleep 300
12574 j  R     0:02 ps
12575 j  S     0:00 sleep 200
$ kill 12575                         Terminate 1st background process
$ ps                                And check that 2nd one still exists
  PID TT STAT   TIME COMMAND
12575 j  Z     0:00 <exiting>
12573 j  I     0:00 sleep 300
12578 j  R     0:02 ps
$ 
```

The status **Z** indicates that this process has terminated. You would now either
have to wait until **sleep 300** finishes or kill it by specifying its process identifier.

What happens if you try to kill the shell? First, remind yourself of the shell
PID using **fgrep** to extract the entry for the shell from the output of **ps**:

```
$ echo sh > str                     Write sh to str
$ ps -g | fgrep -f str              Output shell PID
11340 j  S      0:07 -sh (sh)
$ 
```

Now, execute a kill and check the result:

```
$ kill 11340                        Try terminating your shell
$ ps -g | fgrep -f str              And check what has happened
11340 j  S      0:07 -sh (sh)
$ 
```

Clearly you didn't succeed. Ah, but what if it's not the login shell:

```
$ sh                           Invoke a sub-shell
$ ps -g | fgrep -f str         And find its process identifier
11340 j  I     0:07 -sh (sh)
12598 j  S     0:00 sh
$ kill 12598                   Terminate the sub-shell
$ ps -g | fgrep -f str         And check that you failed
11340 j  I     0:07 -sh (sh)
12598 j  S     0:00 sh
$
```

Still no luck! Looks as though the shell is impervious to attack. But not so! There is a way. The synopsis of **kill** is:

> **kill** [*-signo* ] *PID* ...

where *signo* is the signal number sent to the process. The default value is **15** which instructs the process to terminate. However, some processes such as the shell catch signals and ignore them if they wish. But there is one signal that can't be ignored, **9** which is a sure kill. So let's try it:

```
$ kill -9 12598                Annihilate the shell
Killed
$ ps -g | fgrep -f str         And check its demise
11340 j  S     0:07 -sh (sh)
$
```

Goodbye, shell! Suppose now you try killing the login shell. Yes, that will work also but, of course, the net result will be to log you out. But before doing so, let's see what effect logout has on a background process. First of all start one up, then logout and login again:

```
$ sleep 500 &                  Initiate background process
12610
$ kill -9 11340                Logout
login:yew                      And login again
Password:
$ ps -g | fgrep -f str         Check that the process has gone
12614 j  S     0:01 -sh (sh)
$
```

Process 12610 is no longer there. Hence, the result of logging out is to cause all of your processes to terminate. This is not always convenient. What you would like to be able to do is start up a long running job in the background, logout and come back to inspect the output at some later time.

> **nohup** - no hang ups

In C-shell, you can do just that but, in the Bourne shell, you have to take some special action, in particular, execute the **nohup** command to indicate that the subsequent command is to be run immune from hangups and quit signals such as those generated at logout:

```
$ nohup sleep 500 &        Initiate process immune from hangups
12632
Sending output to 'nohup.out'
$
```

If output has not been redirected by the user, it will be sent to **nohup.out** as indicated by the above message. If this file cannot be written in the current directory, output will be sent to **nohup.out** in your home directory. Now logout and login again:

```
$ ^D                             Logout
login:yew                        And login again
Password:
$ ps -g                          Check that process is still alive
  PID TT STAT   TIME COMMAND
12632 j  I N    0:00 sleep 500
12637 j  S      0:01 -sh (sh)
12639 j  R      0:04 ps -g
$
```

The process you left behind is still there, undisturbed and sleeping peacefully. On our system, all that has happened is that its status has changed from *sleeping* to *idle*. Further, since **nohup** automatically calls **nice**, it is running at a low priority.

### 5.3.5  Scheduling Jobs

With **nice**, **nohup** and **sleep**, you have all the commands you need to run low-priority background jobs which do not interfere with other users, which do not require you to remain logged in and which could be started up some time in the future. There are, however, some slight problems with **sleep**. The time supplied as an argument must be less than 65536 seconds, the only record of the process is in the process table and, if the system goes down or is re-initialized for any reason, the process will be lost.

> **at** - execute commands at a later time

We need a more convenient way of informing the system that we want to initiate a job at a certain time in the future and know that it will be run irrespective of what happens to the system in the mean time. Such a facility is provided by the **at** command which in V.2 has the following synopsis:

> **at** *time* [ *date* ] [ + *increment* ]

It reads commands from standard input to be executed at some later time. To be able to use this facility, your username must either exist in a file */usr/lib/cron/at.allow* or not exist in a file */usr/lib/cron/at.deny*. If the facility is available to you, then try it:

```
$ at 1515                    Schedule job to run at 3.15pm
echo hi > atout
^D
job 476603400.a at Thu Feb 7 15:15:00 1985
at: this job may not be executed at the proper time
$
```

The file will be placed in a spool area **/usr/spool/cron/atjobs** together with details of your environment and current directory so that when the commands are executed, the behaviour will be the same as if you had executed them now. A job number *job* and the scheduled execution time are written on standard error output. Having submitted a job, you can change your mind and remove it before it is run by issuing the command **at −r***job*. You can also inspect the job queue with **at −l** or remind yourself of the scheduled execution time with **at −l***job*:

```
$ at -1476603400.a          Inspect at queue
476603400.a at Thu Feb 7 15:15:00 1985
$
```

The argument *time* is mandatory. If no suffix **am** or **pm** is appended, time is assumed to be on a 24-hour clock. The desired execution time may also be specified as **noon, midnight, now** and **next**. The optional *date* can be specified in most reasonable forms. The optional *increment* is an integer followed by a unit of time, e.g. **minute, hour, day, week, month** or **year**.

Sometimes it is convenient to be able to schedule a series of runs automatically. To do this so that the job reschedules itself, you must first set the job up as a shell script in an executable file. Suppose the name of this file is *earlybird* and you want to run it at 3 am every morning. Then, you must include in the file the command line:

```
echo earlybird | at 3am
```

The command will be run at 3 am each day until you remove it from the queue.

**batch** - execute commands at a later time

This command in System V.2 is very similar to **at** in that it reads commands from standard input and places the job in a queue for execution at a later time. However, it uses a different queue and the job will only be run when the load on the system permits. You can still use **at −r** to remove a job from the batch queue.

===

```
┌─────────────────────────────────────────┐
│  at - execute commands at a later time   │
└─────────────────────────────────────────┘
```

In the Berkeley system, the synopsis of **at** is:

**at** *time* [*day*] [*file*]

The contents of the file (standard input is the default) are copied into a system directory */usr/spool/at* and run as a shell script at the time and date specified. Let's try it. First of all, create a directory *atex* and change to it. Choose a time, say 15 minutes ahead of the current time, and execute **at** as follows:

```
% at 1515                    Schedule job to run at 3.15 pm.
echo hi > atout
^D
%
```

Now look in the system directory where **at** files are stored:

```
% ls -l /usr/spool/at           Inspect the at queue
-rw-r--r--  1 yew        202 Jun 30 14:57 84.181.1515.51
-rw-r-----  1 kerry      707 Jun 30 04:00 84.182.0400.87
-r--r--r--  1 root         5 Jun 30 15:00 lasttimedone
drwxr-xr-x  2 root       512 Jun 30 04:06 past
%
```

There's the file owned by **yew** with a filename composed of the year, the day number from the beginning of the year, the time and a two-digit suffix. The latter enables a user to submit more than one job to be run at the same time on the same date. Let's see what the file contains:

```
% cat /usr/spool/at/*1515*              List your at job
cd /usr/staff/yew/atex
umask 022
HOME='/usr/staff/yew'
export HOME
PATH=':/usr/ucb:/bin:/usr/bin'
export PATH
SHELL='/bin/sh'
export SHELL
TERM='esprit'
export TERM
USER='yew'
export USER
echo hi > atout
%
```

The command line you typed is preceded by commands which will enable the shell to create the correct environment in which to run the command. The first line makes *atex* the current working directory again, the second supplies the file creation mask while the remainder assign values to the shell variables and indicate that they are to be exported. Notice that we had to redirect output since the job will be run in the background and will not be connected to a terminal. If you forget to do this, your output will be lost.

Now use **ls** to check for the appearance of **atout** in your directory. The time that you specified as an argument to **at** is not necessarily the time at which the job will be run. The "granularity" of the execution of **at** jobs is an installation dependent parameter. In some systems, the **at** queue may be inspected every 5 minutes, in others, every 15. In an environment which is heavily loaded during the day, the queue may only be inspected between 8 pm and 8 am. Hence, the time at which your job is actually run will be the first time at which the queue is examined after the time you specified. Even then, it might depend on the length of the queue. You can get some idea of how frequently **at** jobs are initiated by looking at **/usr/spool/at/lasttimedone**. This will contain the last time on a 24-hour clock when the **at** queue was inspected and any jobs run.

You have a great deal of flexibility in the way in which you can specify the time at which a job is to be run. The time is from 1 to 4 digits with an optional trailing letter — **A** for **am**, **P** for **pm**, **N** for **noon** or **M** for **midnight**. If the number contains one or two digits, it is interpreted as hours. On the other hand, three or four digits means hours and minutes. If there is no trailing letter, the time is interpreted as being on a 24-hour clock.

In addition to a time argument which is mandatory, you can also specify an optional day or date. If this is followed by the word **week**, the execution of the command is delayed for 7 days. If today is Tuesday and you wanted to know who will be using the system at 2 am on Wednesday next week, then:

```
% at 2am Wed week     Schedule job to run at 2 am Wednesday week
who | lpr
^D
%
```

would accomplish this for you. You can also specify a date next year:

```
% at 2 april 1 futurejob          Schedule job to run next year
% ls /usr/spool/at
84.183.0400.69 85.91.0200.48 lasttimedone past
%
```

The second file will now be executed on 1st April, 1985. However, you cannot submit a job to be run more than 12 months ahead.

Suppose now that, after having submitted an **at** job, you change your mind and wish to remove or alter it. Providing the system administrator has not turned off the permissions on **/usr/spool/at**, you can do so. So remove the last job you submitted:

```
% rm /usr/spool/at/85*              Remove job from at queue
% ls /usr/spool/at
84.183.0400.69 lasttimedone past
%
```

Finally, it is often convenient to schedule a series of runs. Suppose you want to run a job in a file *earlybird* at 3 am every day until further notice. You could simply schedule it each day for the following morning or you could submit 7 runs at the beginning of each week. However, a more convenient way is to arrange for the job to re-schedule itself by including, as the last line in the file, the command:

**at 3am earlybird**

Now, the job is self-perpetuating and will be run each morning at 3 am until you remove it from the **at** queue.

------------------------------------------------------------------------

## 5.4 Managing Communications

Computing is not just about solving problems. Modern computer systems are concerned with communications so that a community of users can easily share and exchange programs, data and information. With the increasing availability of national and international networks, this sharing is not restricted to one computer system itself or to a group of closely coupled machines in physical proximity to each other. Information may be sent over the switched telephone network, over dedicated communications lines or over a packet-switched network provided by a public carrier. The boundaries between computers and communications systems have become increasingly blurred in recent years. More and more, computers have become an integral part of communication systems; conversely, communications have become more and more important in computer systems. Even if you are a user of a personal computer at home, your horizons will expand enormously if, over your telephone, you can communicate with other users to exchange mail, access databases and be part of a much wider community of users.

The information which flows from one person to another in a computer system or over a communications network is usually referred to as *electronic mail*. It may be a memorandum, a copy of a file, a listing or even an executable program. There is really no restriction on what can be sent. Of course, you may have to exercise some common sense since, if you are using an external network for which there is a charge, someone will have to pay the bill. It's still cheaper to send large amounts of information on magnetic tape, air freight if necessary. The electronic mail originates with a *sender* and is sent to one or more *addressees*. You may have to state the address of the receiver very explicitly. Alternatively, the computer may be able to do some of this work for you.

In some circumstances, you may want to send mail to anyone who is interested in reading it. You don't know, a priori, the address of everyone who has such an interest, nor are you likely to be able to find out anyway. Instead, you publish your information with a suitable title and leave it up to interested parties to select and read those items that take their fancy. We refer to such published material as *electronic news*. Usually, it is divided into a number of subject categories so that you can select the areas in which you are interested. By subscribing to just these areas, you can reduce the amount of material you have to scan to find those items of interest.

Although electronic mail and electronic news will function quite satisfactorily in a single time shared system, their usefulness can be greatly enhanced if the local machine is connected, in some way, to other machines supporting their own community of users, also using UNIX. We will therefore consider first what facilities are available under UNIX for exchanging information between computers.

## 5.4.1 Machine-to-Machine

For one machine to communicate with another, it is necessary that there be some physical connection between them. This may be a permanent one in the form of a dedicated communications link or a temporary one which makes use of the telephone network. Once a link has been established, there need to be programs at each end of the connection which can "talk" to each other and pass messages backwards and forwards according to some pre-arranged protocol. High level software such as an electronic mail system can then make use of these lower level facilities.

| **uucp** - UNIX-to-UNIX copy |
| --- |

In UNIX, the command which handles the transfer of data between one machine and another is **uucp** (**u**nix to **u**nix **c**opy). Its synopsis is:

   **uucp** [*option*] *source-files destination-file*

It will copy one or more files as specified by the *source-files* arguments to the *destination-file* argument. The filename may be the name of a file on your machine or one on another machine whose *system-name* is known to **uucp**. In the latter case, the filename is constructed by prepending the *system-name* to the local filename on the remote machine with an exclamation mark as a separator. Hence, if you wanted to copy a file *src* to a file *dest* on a machine called *alpha*, the command required would be:

   **$ uucp src alpha!dest**

providing the pathnames of the directories in which *src* and *dest* reside were the same on both machines.

Since it is unlikely that you will have access to another machine if you are just a beginner with UNIX, let us experiment with **uucp** on your local machine to discover some of its vagaries and idiosyncrasies. Create a directory *uuex* in your home directory and change to it. Then create a file *src*:

```
$ mkdir uuex; cd uuex          Make directory and transfer to it
$ echo line 1 > src            Create src
$ ░
```

Now, use **uucp** to copy *src* to *dest* in the same directory:

```
$ uucp src dest                Copy source to destination
permission denied
uucp failed. code 1
$ ░
```

While **cp** would have been successful and created *dest*, **uucp** has failed. The problem is that, since normally the copying would be taking place to another machine on which you are not logged in (or might not even be an authorized user), **uucp** must have write access to the file. So create *dest*, make it public write (write permission by others turned on) and try again:

```
$ echo > dest                  Create dest
$ chmod 666 dest               Make it public
$ uucp src dest                And copy src to it
$ cat dest                     Inspect result
line 1
$ ░
```

This time the copying has been carried out successfully. In a like manner, the source file must be public read as well:

```
$ chmod 640 src                Remove public read permission
$ uucp src dest                And try copying again
can't read file (usr/staff/yew/uuex/src) mode 100640
$ chmod 644 src                Restore public read
$ ░
```

If *destination-file* is a directory, a file will be created in that directory with the same name as the last part of the source file, providing **uucp** has the appropriate permissions. Create a directory *uud,* make it public write and, this time, copy both *src* and *dest* to that directory:

```
$ mkdir uud                    Create directory
$ chmod 777 uud                And set all permissions on
$ uucp src dest uud            Copy src and dest to directory
$ ls -l uud                    And check its contents
total 1
-rw-r--r--  1 uucp             7 Jul 12 07:39 dest
-rw-r--r--  1 uucp             7 Jul 12 07:39 src
$ ░
```

Both files have been copied into *uud* with the same filenames. Note, however, from the above output of **ls**, that these files are owned by **uucp** and not by **yew** since it had to create the files to effect the copy. The permissions are determined by the setting of **umask** for the user **uucp** on your machine. In our example, the permissions are **644**. If, on the other hand, the transfer had taken place to another machine, the execute permissions of the original files would be preserved but all read and write permissions would be turned on. If you now wanted to change these to, say, private read, you can't since **uucp** owns the files:

```
$ cd uud                       Change directory
$ chmod 640 src                Try changing permissions
chmod: can't change src
$
```

All you can do is copy the files and remove the original ones, which is possible since the files may be created or removed by anyone:

```
$ cp src mysrc; cp dest mydest   Preserve files by copying them
$ rm src dest                    Then remove them
src: 644 mode ?  y
dest: 644 mode ?  y
$ ls -l                          And inspect current state
total 1
-rw-r--r--  1 yew           7 Jul 12 07:49 mydest
-rw-r--r--  1 yew           7 Jul 12 07:49 mysrc
$ cd ..                          Change to parent directory
$
```

Since **yew** now owns the files, the permissions could be changed as required.

As well as creating files, **uucp** will also create directories:

```
$ uucp src uud/uue/dest    Copy src to newly created directory
$ ls -l uud                And inspect current state
total 2
-rw-r--r--  1 yew           7 Jul 12 07:49 mydest
-rw-r--r--  1 yew           7 Jul 12 07:49 mysrc
drwxrwxrwx  2 yew         512 Jul 12 07:56 uue
$ ls -l uud/uue            List contents of new directory
total 1
-rw-r--r--  1 uucp          7 Jul 12 07:56 dest
$
```

The directory **uue** that was created is owned by **yew** and all permissions are turned on. On the other hand, **dest** is owned by **uucp**. If you want to allow **uucp** to create files but not directories, use the **-f** flag:

```
$ uucp -f src uud/uuf/dest     Will fail to create uuf!
permission denied
uucp failed.   code 1
$
```

The name of a source or destination file may be a full pathname or a relative pathname prefixed by the name of the current directory or the home directory of another user. The shorthand notation for the latter prefix is ˜*user* where *user* is the username. So let's try copying *src* to **dest** again, this time supplying a full pathname for the destination:

```
$ uucp src ˜yew/uuex/dest      Copy to full pathname
$ ls -l dest                   And check modification time
-rw-rw-rw-  1 yew          7 Jul 12 08:08 dest
$
```

The copy has been completed successfully.

We have observed that, if a copy is requested to a file for which **uucp** does not have the appropriate permissions, it will fail. What would happen if you initiated a transfer to a file belonging to a non-existent user **yw:**

```
$ uucp src ˜yw/uuex/dest       Copy to non-existent destination
$
```

Believe it or not, it works! No failure message has appeared. So, what's going on? Well, a copy of *src* occurred but since **uucp** could not find the designated user, it placed the copy in the directory *usr/spool/uucppublic*:

```
$ ls -l /usr/spool/uucppublic   Inspect public directory of uucp
total 1
drwxrwxrwx  2 yew          512 Jul 12 08:18 uuex
$ ls -l /usr/spool/uucppublic/uuex   And contents of uuex
total 1
-rw-r--r--  1 uucp          7 Jul 12 08:18 dest
$
```

Remember that **uucp** was designed to copy files to a remote machine. If you know enough about the file system structure on that machine to be able to specify username and pathname, you should be informed if you have made a mistake. However, sometimes you may wish to send a file to another machine for which you simply do not have these details. Hence, **uucp** copies the file into a public directory by default if the username is invalid. In fact, you do not even have to specify one at all:

```
$ uucp src ˜/uuex/dest    Copy to public directory of uucp
$
```

would produce exactly the same effect as that of the previous **uucp** command.

---

| **uuname** - list system names |
| --- |

---

As mentioned previously, the pathname may be preceded by the system name of the machine on which the file resides. To discover the name of your machine (assuming it has been set up for **uucp** transfers), use the command **uuname** with the **-l** flag indicating that you want the local system name:

```
$ uuname -1              Output uucp name of local machine
mulga
$ 
```

So the name of our machine is **mulga**. Try the previous transfer once again, this time prefixing the pathname with the system name (substitute the name of your machine for **mulga** in the following examples):

```
$ uucp src mulga!~yew/uuex/dest Use machine name as destination prefix
$ ls -l dest                    And check modification time
-rw-rw-rw-  1 yew         7 Jul 12 08:23 dest
$ 
```

This has the same effect as the previous copy, as does:

```
$ uucp mulga!src mulga!dest   Use machine name as both source
$ ls -l dest                  and destination prefix
-rw-rw-rw-  1 yew         7 Jul 12 08:24 dest
$ 
```

=================================================

But be careful if you are using **csh**:

```
% uucp src mulga!dest     C-shell won't like it!
dest: Event not found
% 
```

The exclamation mark has been interpreted by **csh** as denoting a previous event in the history list. To avoid this interpretation, you would need to escape the exclamation mark with a backslash.

------------------------------------------------------------

Now, let us expand our horizons a little and send off a file to another machine if possible. To find out if there are any available, use **uuname** again:

```
$ uuname              Output list of uucp names
munnari
decvax
vax135
musette
ironman
$ 
```

This gives the list of machines to which **mulga** is connected for the purpose of **uucp** transactions. For our examples, we will choose **munnari** as the machine to which files will be transferred. Let us assume that **yew** has an account on this machine and that in the home directory there is a sub-directory **uuex** in which there is a file **dest** with public write access. Since it might be convenient to know when the copy was completed, you can use the **-m** flag to indicate that you want to be notified by mail of this event:

```
$ uucp -m src munnari!~yew/uuex/dest    Copy file to munnari
$
```

After some period of time has elapsed, the length of which will depend on how your system is organized and what type of connection it has to the remote machine, you will receive mail which will look something like:

```
file /usr/staff/yew/uuex/src, system munnari
copy succeeded
```

Even if you don't specify the −m flag, you will be notified by mail if the copy fails:

```
$ uucp src munnari!~yew/dest                Initiate illegal copy
$
```

The component */uuex* was omitted from the pathname and, since the home directory of **yew** on *munnari* is not public write, a file *dest* cannot be created. After some time, you will be notified of this fact:

```
file /usr/staff/yew/uuex/src, system munnari
remote access to path/file denied
```

It would also be nice to be able to notify the recipient of a machine-to-machine transfer, when the file has arrived, particularly if you are not sending the file to yourself. The −n flag allows you to do this since you can append a username to it. The command:

```
$ uucp -nyew src munnari!~yew/uuex/dest    Copy and
$                                          mail recipient
```

will cause mail to be sent to **yew** on *munnari* as soon as the copy has been completed successfully. If **yew** is logged into *munnari* and reads his mail, then the output observed would be something like:

```
/usr/staff/yew/uuex/dest from mulga!yew arrived
```

As you saw earlier, if no username is specified or if the one supplied does not exist on the remote machine, the file will be copied (and directories created if necessary) into the public directory */usr/spool/uucppublic*:

```
$ uucp src munnari!~/uuex/dest             Copy to public directory
$                                          on munnari
```

will copy *src* to *munnari* into a file whose full pathname is */usr/spool/uucppublic/uuex/dest*.

In System V, the system name prefix to the pathname is not restricted to just the name of one machine. It can also be a list of names such as :

```
system-name!system-name!....!system-name!path-name
```

For example, if there is a machine called *murdu* connected to *munnari*, you could send a file to that machine as follows:

```
$ uucp src munnari!murdu!~/uuex/dest          Copy to murdu
$ ▒                                           via munnari
```

Of course, if you construct such a path through a number of machines, you have
to know that intermediate nodes in the route are willing to forward the
information on to the next one. You should be aware that, for security reasons,
there are often severe restrictions imposed by system administrators on what files
may be accessed remotely. You may find, for example, that you cannot access
remote files by pathname but, instead, are limited to files in the public directory
*/usr/spool/uucppublic*. If you send a file to a remote machine, that is where it
is likely to finish up; conversely, if you want to fetch a file to your system from a
remote one, you may have to contact someone there and get that person to send
it to you.

One point not mentioned so far, which is worth noting, is what happens to
shell metacharacters in the command line of a **uucp** request involving a remote
machine. Obviously, it would not make much sense to expand everyone of these
on the home machine if some occur in pathnames for remote machines. Indeed,
metacharacters are expanded on the appropriate machine. Hence, in the
command:

```
$ uucp uud/my* munnari!~yew/uuex/uud          Copy 2 files
$ ▒                                           to munnari
```

the metacharacter **\*** is expanded on *mulga* as you would expect and the two files
*mysrc* and *mydest* are copied to the directory *uud* on *munnari*. Now copy
them back again (after first removing the files from *mulga* because their
permissions **644** will prevent them being overwritten by **uucp**):

```
$ rm uud/my*                                  Remove mulga files
$ uucp munnari!~yew/uuex/uud/my* uud          Copy back
$ ▒                                           from munnari
```

This time, **\*** will be expanded on *munnari* to generate *mysrc* and *mydest*.
"Why?", you might ask. In actual fact, the *mulga* shell will attempt an
expansion but will not succeed because there is no such pathname which starts
with *munnari!~yew*. Hence, **\*** will be left unchanged and transmitted to
*munnari* whereupon it will be expanded. If there is any possibility that a
metacharacter could be replaced on the local machine, you must escape it. After
some interval, the files will appear on *mulga*:

```
$ ls -l uud                          Check that files have returned
total 2
-rw-rw-rw-  1 uucp          7 Jul 12 09:02 mydest
-rw-rw-rw-  1 uucp          7 Jul 12 09:03 mysrc
drwxrwxrwx  2 yew        512 Jul 12 07:56 uue
$ ▒
```

Notice that all read and write permissions have been turned on and that the files
are owned by **uucp**.

$$\boxed{\textbf{uulog} \text{ - output } \textbf{uucp} \text{ log}}$$

To keep a record of its activities, **uucp** places entries in a file
*/usr/spool/uucp/LOGFILE*. You may inspect this file using **uulog** which
outputs the whole file by default or various sections of it if the −**u** and/or the −**s**
flags are specified. The former is followed by a username, the latter by a system
name. You could examine the work done by **uucp** for **yew** transferring files to
*munnari* by using the command:

> $ uulog -u yew -s munnari        *Inspect log of* **uucp** *transactions*

Each transaction is first queued and a link established with the remote machine.
Then, the transfer is initiated and any failure recorded. Finally, the conversation
is terminated.

There are other commands available under various versions of UNIX which
establish connections to a remote machine. For example, **tip** and **cu** set up a link
which enables you to login to the remote machine (assuming you have an account
there). The local machine becomes transparent to your input and you can
operate as though you were directly connected to the remote machine. If you
want to run a command locally, then ˜ is used as the escape character to indicate
your intention. The characters ˜. break the connection and cause control to be
returned to the local machine. Even more powerful facilities are available in the
Berkeley system. The command **rlogin** can enable you to login to a remote
machine on which you have an account without having to supply your username
and password; **rsh** connects to a specified host temporarily and executes a
command for you on that machine, returning any output to the local machine;
**rcp** copies files between machines and handles third party copies where neither
source nor destination files are on the local machine. Such facilities make it
almost as easy to use any machine in a network as it is to use your local one.

## 5.4.2  Person-to-Person

In Chapter 2, we introduced the **write** command which enables you to send
a message to another user who is currently logged into the same system as you
are. Another useful command for communicating with other users is **mail**.
Unlike **write**, the recipient of your message does not have to be logged in at the
time you send the mail. Instead, the message is stored in the system and, the next
time he logs in, he will be informed that there is mail waiting for him. He can
choose to read it, there and then, or at whatever time is convenient. If he is
actually logged in at the time you send your message, he can arrange to be
informed of that fact if he so desires. **mail** provides many facilities including
sending mail, reading mail, replying to mail and saving mail.

There are, in fact, two versions of a mail command in common use,
**/bin/mail** and **/usr/ucb/Mail**. The former is the standard command while the
latter is part of the Berkeley system. In System V 2, it is also known as **mailx**

Often, the pathname */usr/ucb/mail* is simply a link to */usr/ucb/Mail*. Hence, if */usr/ucb* precedes */bin* in your search path, then, when you issue the **mail** command, you will activate the Berkeley version rather than the standard one. If this is the situation on your system and you wish to use the standard **mail** command, you will have to specify the full pathname or change your search path. The version we will treat first in this book is the standard **mail** command. In the examples that follow, you may have to type **/bin/mail** instead of **mail** to produce the behaviour illustrated.

> **mail** - send and receive mail

First of all, send some mail to yourself:

```
$ mail yew            Send mail to yourself
test mail 1
^D
$
```

This is not as daft as it looks since you can use **mail** in this way to send yourself reminders. You can also send mail to more than one person at the same time:

```
$ mail pcp yew         Send mail to yourself and someone else
test mail 2
^D
$
```

This item of mail will be sent to **pcp** as well as to **yew**. Since **mail** reads from standard input, you can also use input redirection:

```
$ echo test mail 3 > letter    Create a letter
$ mail yew < letter            And mail it to yourself
$
```

This feature is particularly useful if you want to send a long letter. You can, first of all, set it up in a file and then edit any errors before actually sending it.

What happens if you make a mistake in the name of the addressee? The actual behaviour will depend on the version of **mail** you are using. In some versions, no check is made on the validity of the username until an attempt is made to deliver the mail. If the name does not exist, your message is saved in a file called *dead.letter* in your current directory:

```
$ mail yw              Send mail to non-existent user
test mail 4
^D
mail: cannot send to yw
Mail saved in dead.letter
$
```

You can now forward it to the correct username by input redirection without having to type the whole message over again:

```
$ mail yew < dead.letter        Recover dead letter
$ 
```

You could now remove *dead.letter* if you wish.

Other versions of **mail** make an immediate check for the existence of the addressee and inform you at once if no-one of that name exists. However, they will still accept your message in the normal manner since there may be other addressees:

```
$ mail yw                       Send mail to non-existent user
yw... user unknown
test mail 4
^D
$ 
```

The transcript of your session and your message will now be mailed back to you so that you could re-address it to the correct recipient.

By now, **yew** should have received 4 pieces of mail; so let's start reading them. In our example, we will use the simplest form of **mail** output in which the header merely indicates who sent the mail and at what time. If your machine is part of a network, you will see a more complicated header which shows when the mail was received by the system, what message identification it has and so on. We will have more to say about this later. So if what you see differs from what we show, do not be concerned — all will become clearer later.

To read mail, simply issue the **mail** command without any usernames as arguments. If the **−p** flag is specified, all items of mail saved for you are written to standard output:

```
$ mail -p                       Output all current mail items
From yew Mon Jul 16 13:18:29 1984
test mail 4
From yew Mon Jul 16 13:17:19 1984
test mail 3
From yew Mon Jul 16 13:16:06 1984
test mail 2
From yew Mon Jul 16 13:15:49 1984
test mail 1
$ 
```

The four items of mail have been displayed in reverse order i.e. **mail** works on a first in, last out basis. If you want to examine your mail in a more leisurely fashion to decide how to dispose of it, just issue **mail** on its own:

```
$ mail                          Read your mail interactively
From yew Mon Jul 16 13:18:29 1984
test mail 4
? 
```

The command prompts with a **?** and waits for you to respond. If you do so with **∗** or **?** (or any character not recognized by **mail**), you will see a summary of the internal commands available in **mail**. Try it now and you will see that you have a number of options available.    + (or **RETURN**) will take you to the next message:

```
? +                              Read next message
From yew Mon Jul 16 13:17:19 1984
test mail 3
?
```

On the other hand, − will take you back to the previous one:

```
? −                              Read previous message
From yew Mon Jul 16 13:18:29 1984
test mail 4
?
```

Another − just causes the above output to be repeated since it is the first item of mail anyway.   **p** causes the current message to be printed again while **d** deletes it and displays the next message:

```
? d                 Delete current message and display next one
From yew Mon Jul 16 13:17:19 1984
test mail 3
?
```

Actually, **d** merely marks the message as one to be deleted when exit finally occurs from **mail**. **s** causes the message to be appended to the file **mbox** which is the default *mail box* and the next message is displayed:

```
? s                              Save message in mbox
From yew Mon Jul 16 13:16:06 1984
test mail 2
?
```

If **s** is followed by a filename, the message is saved in that file rather than in **mbox**.

If you respond to **?** with **!** followed by a command, a sub-shell is created and everything following **!** is passed to it. When it terminates, control returns to **mail**. You could use this feature to examine the contents of **mbox**:

```
? !cat mbox                      Inspect mbox
From yew Mon Jul 16 13:17:19 1984
test mail 3
!
?
```

By being able to exit temporarily from **mail**, you can execute such commands as **ls**, **chmod** and so on to organize the files in which you may be disposing your messages. You can also use this facility to send mail to another user or reply to mail:

```
? !mail pcp                      Escape to shell and send mail
message for pcp
^D
!
?
```

This mail will be forwarded to **pcp** and you are still in **mail** with the third item, the current one. If you use **w** to save this instead of **s**, the contents will be preserved without the header in a specified file (*mbox* is the default):

```
? w mwh                          Save message without header in mwh
From yew Mon Jul 16 13:15:49 1984
test mail 1
? !cat mwh                       Escape from mail and inspect mwh
test mail 2
!
?
```

The body of the message has been preserved without the initial line `From.......`

You have now reached the last item of mail. If you delete or save this, **mail** will exit and the mail file will be empty (unless any mail has arrived in the mean time). If, on the other hand, you use **+**, **RETURN** or **q** (for **q**uit), then any undeleted, unsaved or unread mail will be put back in the mail file:

```
? +                              Exit from mail
$
```

There should now be at least one item of mail still in the mail file. Before inspecting it again, let us send another item:

```
$ mail yew                       Send some more mail to yourself
test mail 5
^D
$ mail                           Read your mail again
From yew Mon Jul 16 13:27:55 1984
test mail 5
?
```

The command **q** (or control–D) can be issued at any time in response to **?** to exit from mail. If you issued it now, the contents of the mail file will remain unchanged. Instead, let us try some of the remaining commands.

The **m** command allows you to mail the current message to one or more users. In the absence of any usernames, it will be mailed back to you:

```
? m                              Mail current message to yourself
From yew Mon Jul 16 13:15:49 1984
test mail 1
?
```

If now you save the last message, there will be no more left and **mail** will exit:

```
? s                              Save message in mbox and exit
$
```

There should now be two messages in **mbox** and one in the mail file. Let's add another one to the latter and read mail again:

```
$ mail yew                       Send mail again
test mail 6
^D
$ mail                           And read it
From yew Mon Jul 16 13:31:34 1984
test mail 6
?
```

The latest message is displayed. Let's delete it and proceed to the next one:

```
? d                        Delete current message and display next one
From yew Mon Jul 16 13:27:55 1984
test mail 5
?
```

Suppose now you suddenly realize that you did not mean to delete the previous message. What you must do is exit from mail with the **x** request. All mail will be put back in the mail file, irrespective of how you disposed of it:

```
? x                              Exit leaving mail in mail file
$ mail
From yew Mon Jul 16 13:31:34 1984
test mail 6
?
```

As you see, the message you deleted is still there! But, what if you had saved it:

```
? s                              Append current message to mbox
From yew Mon Jul 16 13:27:55 1984
test mail 5
? x                              Exit leaving mail in mail file
$ mail                           Read your mail
From yew Mon Jul 16 13:31:34 1984
test mail 6
?
```

It still remains in your mail file but, as we will see shortly, a copy has also been appended to **mbox**. Now, empty the mail file:

```
? d                        Delete current message and display next one
From yew Mon Jul 16 13:27:55 1984
test mail 5
? d                              Delete last message and exit
$ mail                           Is there any mail?
No mail.
$
```

We have referred frequently in the above examples to *mail file*. In our system, its name is */usr/spool/mail/yew*. On your system, the name may be different, for example, */usr/mail/yew*. However, **mail** will also process other mail files if the filename is specified following the –**f** flag:

```
$ mail -f mbox                        Read mail from mbox
From yew Mon Jul 16 13:31:34 1984
test mail 6
?
```

If *mbox* is your repository for saved messages, you can also use **mail** to manage it:

```
? d                                   Delete current item from mbox
From yew Mon Jul 16 13:15:49 1984
test mail 1
? d                                   And the next one
From yew Mon Jul 16 13:17:19 1984
test mail 3
? q                                   Then quit
$
```

There is only one message left in *mbox* and it will remain in this state until further messages are saved there.

Let's now send some mail to a user on another machine. As we saw earlier, the machine we are using is called *mulga* and it is connected to *munnari* for **uucp** transactions. You can also send mail over this link by prepending the username with the system name just as you did for **uucp**. For example, you could send mail to **pcp** on *munnari* as follows:

```
$ mail munnari!pcp        Send mail to user on another machine
Lunch at noon?
^D
$
```

Eventually **pcp** would read his mail and see something like:

```
$ mail                                pcp reads mail on munnari
From mulga!yew Tue Jul 17 10:26:32 1984
Received: by munnari.OZ (4.3)
        id AA05336; Tue, 17 Jul 84 10:26:25 EST
Received: by mulga.OZ (4.3)
        id AA04296; Tue, 17 Jul 84 10:25:44 EST
Date: Tue, 17 Jul 84 10:25:44 EST
To: munnari!pcp
Lunch at noon?
? d                                   Delete and exit
$
```

whereupon he might respond:

```
$ mail mulga!yew                    pcp replies to yew
OK
^D
$
```

Finally, **yew** will receive the reply:

```
$ mail                              yew reads mail on mulga
From munnari!pcp Tue Jul 17 10:30:44 1984
Received: by mulga.OZ (4.3)
        id AA04342; Tue, 17 Jul 84 10:30:36 EST
Received: by munnari.OZ (4.3)
        id AA05390; Tue, 17 Jul 84 10:29:28 EST
Date: Tue, 17 Jul 84 10:29:28 EST
To: mulga!yew
OK
? d                                 Delete and exit
$
```

and the conversation is complete.

As you observe from the above, the headers are somewhat more complicated since they include a time stamp indicating when the message was received by each machine. In the mail sent to **pcp** by **yew**, you see that the message was first received by *mulga* at **10:25:44**, then by *munnari* at **10:26:25** and finally by the mail system at **10:26:32**. You know therefore when the message was posted and when it was received. Depending on how many machines are in the route and how frequently they talk to each other, there could be substantial differences between various times.

Let's try a longer route by sending some mail to **yew** via *munnari*:

```
$ mail munnari!mulga!yew  Mail to munnari and back to mulga
test remote mail 1
^D
$
```

The message will first be sent to *munnari* and then this machine will forward it on to *mulga* whereupon it will be delivered to **yew** who will see something like:

```
$ mail                              Read your mail
From mulga!munnari!yew Tue Jul 17 10:58:44 1984
Received: by mulga.OZ (4.3)
        id AA04758; Tue, 17 Jul 84 10:58:38 EST
Received: by munnari.OZ (4.3)
        id AA06357; Tue, 17 Jul 84 10:56:48 EST
Received: by mulga.OZ (4.3)
        id AA04691; Tue, 17 Jul 84 10:55:48 EST
Date: Tue, 17 Jul 84 10:55:48 EST
To: munnari!mulga!yew
test remote mail 1
$
```

By reading upwards through the headers, you can follow the passage of the message through the various machines from source to destination.

If you are working in a multi-machine environment with accounts on a number of machines, it would be a good idea to collect all of your mail on the machine you use most frequently. This can be arranged by leaving a forwarding message in the mail files of the other machines. If, for instance, **yew** uses *mulga* most of the time, he could place the message:

    Forward to mulga!yew

in the file */usr/spool/mail/yew* on *munnari* and cause all mail sent to him on that machine to be redirected.

> **mailx** - interactive message processing system

The **mailx** command which is based on the Berkeley version of **mail** is a much more powerful command than the standard one for sending and receiving mail. It is an "intelligent" mail processing system with a command syntax similar to that of **ed** with lines replaced by messages. It has many facilities, some of which we will describe below. For the remainder, we refer you to the System V.2 documentation or the "Mail Reference Manual" published by the University of California (Berkeley).

To send some mail, just use the **mailx** command as you did before with one or more usernames as arguments. Then, supply the text of the message terminated by end-of-file:

```
$ mailx yew                  Send mail to yourself
test mail 1
^D
$
```

Now it may be that the command on your system will behave differently by perhaps prompting for a one-line subject or even the names of users to whom copies of the letter are to be sent. The default behaviour of **mailx** can be set by the system administrator and may vary from one system to another. However, as you will see shortly, you can specify what default operations you want so we will ignore these differences for the moment.

You can specify the subject of your message in the command line by using the –s flag. The next argument is then taken to be the text of the subject:

```
$ mailx -s 'test 2' yew      Send mail with subject
test mail 2
^D
$
```

Notice that you had to quote the subject since it contains a space. If, the previous time you used **mailx**, it prompted for a subject, this time, it won't have done so. You can cause prompting for a subject to be the default behaviour by setting the option **ask** in the file *.mailrc* in your home directory:

```
$ echo set ask > .mailrc          Set flag for subject prompt
$ mailx yew                       And send mail to yourself
Subject: test 3
test mail 3
^D
$
```

A particular option may be turned off by using the **unset** command. When **mailx** is initiated, it reads *.mailrc*, if it exists, to determine what behaviour is required. So if you want **mailx** to prompt at the end of the message for the names of users who are to receive carbon copies, set the option **askcc** on:

```
$ echo set askcc >> .mailrc       Set flag for carbon copy prompt
$ mailx yew                       Send mail to yourself
Subject:test 4                    On this subject
test mail 4
^D
Cc:pcp sharon                     And carbon copies to these users
$
```

A copy of the message will now be sent to the two users named in the response to the prompt Cc:.

If you are in the habit of regularly sending messages to the same group of people, it could be rather inconvenient having to type the list of usernames each time. There is therefore a facility in **mailx** that enables you to define **aliases** so that you can create personal distribution lists. This is done by setting up the correspondence between an alias and its expansion in *.mailrc*:

```
$ echo alias ppy pcp pru yew >> .mailrc     Define alias ppy
$
```

Now, if you send mail to the alias **ppy**, it will be forwarded to **pcp** and **pru** but not to **yew**, that is, the name of the sender of the mail is removed from the expansion of the alias. However, if you want a copy as well, you must set the option **metoo** on so that your name remains in the list:

```
$ echo set metoo >> .mailrc       Set flag for your own copy
$ mailx ppy                       Send mail to alias ppy
Subject:test 5
test mail 5
^D
Cc:
$
```

There is also a facility whereby system-wide aliases can be defined in a file */usr/lib/aliases*. You should be able to look at the contents of this file and we suggest you do so but, since it is usually owned by **root**, you will not be able to add new aliases to it (but **root** could, of course).

If you send mail to a non-existent user on the local machine, then you will be notified of this fact after the message has been completed. In any case, the undelivered message will be returned to you:

```
$ mailx yw                          Send mail to non-existent user
Subject:test 6
test mail 6
^D
Cc:yew
$ yw... User unknown
```

Now that you have sent and received some mail, let's have a look at it:

```
$ mailx                                   Read your mail
Mail version 2.18 5/19/83.  Type ? for help.
"/usr/spool/mail/yew": 7 messages 7 new
>N  1 yew        Tue Jul 31 17:18  9/169
 N  2 yew        Tue Jul 31 17:19  10/185 "test 2"
 N  3 yew        Tue Jul 31 17:21  10/185 "test 3"
 N  4 yew        Tue Jul 31 17:23  11/201 "test 4"
 N  5 yew        Tue Jul 31 17:26  10/195 "test 5"
 N  6 yew        Tue Jul 31 17:28  11/192 "test 6"
 N  7 MAILER     Tue Jul 31 17:28  24/533 "Returned mail"
&
```

The first line contains the version number of the **mailx** command you are using and a reminder that, if you have forgotten the internal commands for the system, then **?** will produce a list. If you don't want to see this line every time you use **mailx**, set the quiet option on in *.mailrc*. Next follow the name of the mail file, the number of messages it contains and how many are new or unread. The remainder of the output is a list of message headers, one for each message, containing, from left to right, the status (**N** = new, **U** = unread), a message number, the name of the sender, the date and time at which the message was received, the number of lines and characters in the message and, finally, the subject. You should have received 7 items of mail, all with status **N** with the first of these marked with an **>** in the left hand margin indicating it is the current message. The first 6 items have come from **yew** while the 7th is from the system process which handles the mail, in this case, **MAILER** (it may be called **MAILER-DAEMON** on your system and there will also be a reason such as user unknown at the end of the entry). The first message has nothing in the subject field because, as you will remember, you did not supply one. All the others have a subject as specified.

Have a look now at what actions you can perform by replying **?** to the **&** prompt. You should see a list of commands and the arguments each takes together with the functions they perform.

The command **t** will print the current message (as will its synonym **p**).

```
& t                                    Print next message
Message   1:
From yew Tue Jul 31 17:18:58 1984
Date: Tue, 31 Jul 84 17:18:42 EST
To: yew
Status: R
test mail 1
&
```

(The output you see may be somewhat different from what we illustrate above as
we have removed the time stamp showing when the message was received by the
local machine to reduce the amount of output.) The first line shows the date and
time at which the message was placed in your mail box; the line starting with
**Date** shows the date and time at which the message was posted. The status of
the message is **R** indicating that it has been read. At any time, you can examine
the current status of the mail box by using the **h** command to print out the
message headers:

```
& h                                    Print message headers
>   1 yew       Tue Jul 31 17:18  9/169
N   2 yew       Tue Jul 31 17:19  10/185 "test 2"
N   3 yew       Tue Jul 31 17:21  10/185 "test 3"
N   4 yew       Tue Jul 31 17:23  11/201 "test 4"
N   5 yew       Tue Jul 31 17:26  10/195 "test 5"
N   6 yew       Tue Jul 31 17:28  11/192 "test 6"
N   7 MAILER    Tue Jul 31 17:28  24/533 "Returned mail"
&
```

We note that the first message is still the current one but is no longer marked as
new. Let's now print the third message. This can be achieved by **t 3** or **p 3** or
just **3**:

```
& 3                                    Print 3rd message
Message   3:
From yew Tue Jul 31 17:21:34 1984
Date: Tue, 31 Jul 84 17:21:22 EST
To: yew
Subject: test 3
Status: R
test mail 3
&
```

This time, a subject line is displayed since you supplied one with the original
message. Let us delete this message using **d** and then print the headers again
followed by message 4 as shown below:

```
& d                                    Delete 3rd message
& h                                    And print headers again
     1 yew          Tue Jul 31 17:18   9/169
 N   2 yew          Tue Jul 31 17:19   10/185  "test 2"
>N   4 yew          Tue Jul 31 17:23   11/201  "test 4"
 N   5 yew          Tue Jul 31 17:26   10/195  "test 5"
 N   6 yew          Tue Jul 31 17:28   11/192  "test 6"
 N   7 MAILER       Tue Jul 31 17:28   24/533  "Returned mail"
& p
Message  4:                            Print 4th message
From yew Tue Jul 31 17:23:03 1984
Date: Tue, 31 Jul 84 17:22:47 EST
To: yew
Subject: test 4
Cc: pcp, sharon
Status: R
test mail 4
&
```

Message 4 is now the current message since message 3 was deleted. It contains an
additional line showing that carbon copies have been sent to **pcp** and **sharon**.
You can now delete this message and print the next one as follows:

```
& dp                                   Delete 4th message and print 5th one
Message  5:
From yew Tue Jul 31 17:26:49 1984
Date: Tue, 31 Jul 84 17:26:34 EST
To: pcp, pru, yew
Subject: test 5
Status: R
test mail 5
&
```

This is the message sent to the alias **ppy** and the `To:` line shows that the
appropriate expansion has taken place with the inclusion of **yew** since the `metoo`
option was set. You can check at any time which aliases are current by using the
**alias** command (**a** for short) without arguments:

```
& a                                    What aliases are set?
ppy     yew pru pcp
&
```

You can define new aliases temporarily by using **alias** with more than one
argument:

```
& a admin pru sharon pcp yew           Define admin as an alias
& a                                    And check current aliases
admin   yew pcp sharon pru
ppy     yew pru pcp
&
```

If the alias already exists, the remaining arguments will be added to the list:

```
& a admin pgt                           Add new name to existing alias
&
```

If there is only one argument and that group exists, it will be output:

```
& a admin                          Output usernames for specific alias
admin pgt yew pcp sharon pru
&
```

otherwise a failure message not a group will be produced.

The commands **n**, **t** or **RETURN** can be used to print the next message:

```
& n                                     Print 6th message
Message  6:
From yew Tue Jul 31 17:28:28 1984
Date: Tue, 31 Jul 84 17:28:17 EST
To: yw
Subject: test 6
Cc: yew
Status: R
test mail 6
&
```

This is the copy sent to **yew** of the message that could not be delivered to the non-existent user **yw**. So you see that messages are sent to any valid username specified even if one of them is invalid. You could now delete it and print the next one with **dp**. However, if you set the autoprint option, **d** will behave just like **dp** as shown below:

```
& set autoprint           Set autoprint flag on
& d                       Delete 6th message and print 7th one
Message  7:
From yew Tue Jul 31 17:28:35 1984
Date: Tue, 31 Jul 84 17:28:17 EST
Subject: Returned mail: User unknown
To: yew
Status: R

    ----- Transcript of session follows -----
yw... User unknown
yew... Connecting to .local...
yew... Sent

    ----- Unsent message follows -----
Date: Tue, 31 Jul 84 17:28:17 EST
To: yw
Subject: test 6
Cc: yew
test mail 6
&
```

This is the undelivered message returned to **yew** by the mail delivery sub-system which is a very convenient facility since it means that, if you send a lengthy message and make a mistake in the username of the addressee (and forget to send a copy to yourself), it will eventually be returned to sender.

Now, you can send the message again, this time, to the correct addressee from within **mailx** itself. However, once you commence inputting the message body, you will need to be able to insert the old message. To do this, you use an *escape* mechanism available in **mailx**.

When lines of text are being input to **mailx**, any line which commences with a tilde (˜) is treated as a command, which can be used in composing the message. We will have a look at this facility in more detail later. For the moment, you need to know that ˜f causes the current message to be inserted into the new message and that ˜e calls up the editor to work on the message body as shown below:

```
& m yew                        Send mail to yourself from within mail
Subject:test 6
˜f                             Insert current message
Interpolating: 7
(continue)
˜e                             Initiate ed
543
1,/^test/-1dp                  Remove unwanted lines
test mail 6
w                              Save message
13
q                              Quit from ed
(continue)
^D
Cc:
&
```

This message will now be mailed to **yew** where it should have gone in the first place. However, it will not affect the processing of the current contents of the mail box as we see by printing the headers again:

```
& h                                              Print headers
    1 yew       Tue Jul 31 17:18  9/169
N   2 yew       Tue Jul 31 17:19  10/185 "test 2"
   .5 yew       Tue Jul 31 17:26  10/195 "test 5"
>   7 MAILER    Tue Jul 31 17:28  24/533 "Returned mail"
&
```

From the above output, you see that message 2 has not been read yet. Let us first of all delete the last two messages. **d** along with many of the other commands in **mailx** can take, as an argument, a list of message numbers. The list may include ranges, for example, **2-4** means **2 3 4**. **\*** means **all** and **$** means **last message**:

```
& d 5 7                              Delete messages 5 and 7
Message  2:
From yew Tue Jul 31 17:19:30 1984
Date: Tue, 31 Jul 84 17:19:19 EST
To: yew
Subject: test 2
Status: R
test mail 2
&
```

Message 2 becomes the current message and is printed since autoprint is on.

Suppose now you decide to reply to this message. You could do so using **m** but, if you use **r** instead, **mailx** does some of the work for you by constructing the beginning of the reply:

```
& r                                  Reply to current message
To: yew
Subject: Re: test2
reply to test mail 2
^D
Cc:
&
```

Message 2 remains the current message, as you can show using **f** which prints the current header (or the headers specified in a message list):

```
& f                                  Print current header
>   2 yew       Tue Jul 31 17:19  10/185 "test 2"
&
```

Finally, before exiting, suppose you save message 1 in a file *test1* :

```
& s 1 test1                          Save message 1 in test1
"test1" [New file] 9/169
&
```

**save** appends messages from a message list to the nominated file (*mbox* is the default and the file is created if it does not exist already). The header is marked with **\*** indicating that the file has been saved:

```
& h                                  Print message headers
 *  1 yew       Tue Jul 31 17:18  9/169
 >  2 yew       Tue Jul 31 17:19  10/185 "test 2"
&
```

You can also check on the file *test1* by using **!** to invoke a new shell:

```
& !ls -l test1                       Escape to shell and inspect file
-rw-r--r--  1 yew           179 Jul 31 21:48 test1
!
&
```

Everything on the line following **!** is passed to the sub-shell for execution.

If you were now to exit using **x**, you would leave **mailx** immediately
without modifying the mail box, i.e. all deletes and saves would be ignored. If, on
the other hand, you quit using **q**, any unread mail is preserved in your system
mail box and any undeleted mail is appended to the *mbox* file in your home
directory. Suppose, however, before doing this, you decide that you did not mean
to delete message 4 and that you actually want to preserve message 2 in your
system mail box. You can achieve this by using the **u**ndelete and **h**old
commands:

```
& u 4                              Cancel deletion of message 4
Message  4:
From yew Tue Jul 31 17:23:03 1984
Date: Tue, 31 Jul 84 17:22:47 EST
To: yew
Subject: test 4
Cc: pcp, sharon
Status: R
test mail 4
& ho 2                             Hold message 2
& h                                Print message headers
 *  1 yew        Tue Jul 31 17:18  9/169
>P  2 yew        Tue Jul 31 17:19  10/185 "test 2"
    4 yew        Tue Jul 31 17:23  11/201 "test 4"
&
```

Message 2 now has the status **P** indicating that it is to be preserved. Now let's
exit:

```
& q                                Exit from mail
New mail has arrived.
Saved 1 message in mbox.
Held 1 message in /usr/spool/mail/yew
$
```

Since you sent some mail to **yew** during the time in **mailx**, there is new mail and
you are informed of this fact.

Before reading mail again, let us explore some of the facilities available to
help you compose mail. We saw above that ˜ is an escape character which
introduces a command in the message body rather than a line of text. In fact, ˜
is the default escape and you may choose your own by giving the mail variable
**escape** a single character value via **set**. If you executed:

```
$ echo set ´escape="´ >> .mailrc      Define " as escape
$
```

double quote would become the escape character. However, let us stick with
tilde. If the escape character is used as the first character in a line, it causes an
escape from text input mode to command mode, for example, ˜**p** causes the
message collected so far to be printed:

```
$ mailx yew                    Send mail to yourself
Subject:test 8
test mal 7
~p                             Print message collected so far
----------
Message contains
To: yew
Subject: test 8
test mal 7
(continue)
```

At this point, you realize that the mail should also go to **pcp**, that the subject should be **test 7** and that you have spelt **mail** incorrectly. We can use ~t to add names to the list of direct recipients, ~s to correct the subject and ~e to invoke the text editor:

```
~t pcp                         Add pcp to list of addressees
~s test 7                      Replace subject
~e                             Invoke the editor
11
1
test mal 7                     Locate incorrect line
s/a/ai/p                       Correct error
test mail 7
w                              Preserve message
12
q                              Return to mailx
(continue)
```

You could now go on adding to the message as required. Before sending it off, let's look at it again:

```
~p                             Print message collected so far
--------------
Message contains:
To: yew pcp
Subject: test 7
test mail 7
(continue)
^D
Cc:
$
```

The required corrections have been made and the message could therefore be sent.

If at any time you wish to abort input to **mailx**, you can do so with ~q or by interrupting twice. If the **save** option has been set, then the message collected so far will be saved in *dead.letter* in your home directory:

```
$ echo set save >> .mailrc          Set the save flag on
$ mailx yew                          Send mail to yourself
Subject:aborted mail
this line should be saved
(I)                                  Abort mailx command
(Interrupt -- one more to kill letter)
(I)
$
```

Check *dead.letter* to see that the body of the message was indeed saved.

Now, let's read mail again. We won't give another example of its output but you should issue the command and check what it does. You should see 4 messages — 3 new ones with message 2, the current one. Message 3 should be the reply to **test mail 2** and message 4 is the one you corrected:

```
& f 3 4                    Print headers for message 3 and 4
 N  3 yew      Tue Jul 31 21:39  11/209 "Re:  test 2"
 N  4 yew      Wed Aug  1 15:54  11/198 "test 7"
&
```

If you want to see more than just the header but not the whole message, you can use **to**p which prints the first 5 lines of each message in a message list (5 is the default and can be altered by giving the variable **toplines** a different value via the **set** command). Next read the messages, then quit:

```
& q                        Exit from mailx
Saved 4 messages in mbox
$
```

*mbox* should now contain 5 messages. You can manage the contents of this file by using **mailx** itself with the −**f** option just as you did with the standard mail program:

```
$ mailx -f mbox            Read mail from mbox
"mbox":5 messages
& h                        Print headers
>    1 yew      Tue Jul 31 17:23  12/212 "test 4"
     2 yew      Tue Jul 31 17:19  11/196 "test 2"
     3 yew      Tue Jul 31 18:38  11/196 "test 6"
     4 yew      Tue Jul 31 21:39  11/210 "Re:  test 2"
     5 yew      Wed Aug  1 15:54  11/199 "test 7"
&
```

Suppose now, you delete messages 2–5 and then quit:

```
& d 2-5                    Delete message 2,3,4 and 5
& q                        Exit from mailx
"mbox" complete
$
```

Only 1 message remains now in *mbox* which you can check by inspection.

As you see from the previous examples, **mailx** is a very powerful system for managing your mail. It contains many more facilities than we have described here and you should consult the documentation for further details. However, what we have illustrated should give you a good understanding of how to use it conveniently and effectively.

Well, so much for the mail. Now let us see if there is any news to read.

| **news** - print news items |
|---|

In System V, the **news** command is used to keep you informed of current events. These are usually stored in files in */usr/news*. If you use the **−n** option, you will obtain a list of the names of current news items. If you supply one or more such names to **news** as arguments, it will print out the contents of those items. Alternatively, **news** without any arguments prints the contents of any current files, most recent first and each preceded by an appropriate header. So that you don't have to read news items more than once, **news** uses a file *.news_time* in your home directory to define a "currency" time. Only files more recent than this currency time are output when you give the **news** command.

The facilities available for handling news in the Berkeley system are much more powerful than those in System V. However, you will often find them implemented in "standard" UNIX systems.

| **checknews** - check to see if user has news |
|---|

The first command to try is **checknews** which will tell you whether there is any news available for you or not:

```
% checknews                    See if there is any news
There is news
%
```

If no output occurs, there is no news for you although you can arrange for the output of a message **No news** or something similar by issuing the command with a **−n** argument.

| **readnews** - read news articles |
|---|

This command enables you to read and dispose of current news items which have arrived since the last time you read the news. If issued without an argument, it simply prints unread articles:

```
$ readnews                              Read the news


------------------
Newsgroup general
------------------


Article 82 of 82, Nov  1 04:42.
Subject: some news
From: yew@mulga.OZ (Yorick Whiffle @ Comp Sci, Melb Uni)
(1 lines) More? [ynq]
```

News items are divided into a number of newsgroups so that you can select those areas in which you are interested. In the above example, the newsgroup **general** is usually read by everyone on the local machine. In the news item header, you are told the number of the item and the number in the newsgroup, when it was posted, what it is about, who sent it and how many lines it contains. You are then asked whether you want to see the complete item. If you reply **y** or **RETURN**, it will be output on your screen followed by the header of the next item or a message indicating that there are no more news items:

```
(1 lines) More? [ynq] y             Print actual news items
No news is good news!
```

```
Last article.  [qfr]
```

A reply of **n** will cause the current item to be skipped and the next header displayed. If you've seen enough for the moment, just type **q** to exit back to the shell.

When the last article message appears, you can type **q** or **RETURN** to exit. Before doing so, **readnews** will update a file *.newsrc* in your home directory indicating which news items you have read. Each entry in this file is the name of a newsgroup followed by a list of numbers of the items read separated by commas with sequential numbers collapsed by hyphens. For example, the entry for **general** before the last item was read would have been:

```
general: 1-81
```

If you want to re-read news items which you haven't saved, then, providing the items are still available, you can do so by editing the appropriate entry in *.newsrc*. If you use **x** instead of **q** to quit, the file *.newsrc* will not be updated.

There are a number of other commands which you can issue in response to the **readnews** query. There are also a number of arguments which you can use with **readnews** to modify its default behaviour. We refer you to the glossary for a description of these facilities.

> **postnews** - submit news articles

The simplest way for casual users to submit a news item is to use **postnews**. It will prompt for a subject, a newsgroup and distribution list. The default newsgroup is `general`. The distribution list is a set of valid newsgroup names and defaults to the same as that for the newsgroup. After entering this header information, you will be placed in an editor defined by the environment variable `EDITOR` with **vi** being the default editor.

So there you have it — you can send and receive mail, you can post and read items of news. These are very powerful facilities which can be of great value to you. But remember, don't abuse the system by sending lots of junk mail or posting useless news items. Such activities will not endear you to the other members of your user community.


## SUMMARY


- Use **find** to locate files which match certain criteria such as filename, permissions, number of links, username, group, size and time of last access, change or modification.

- To remove unwanted files which have not been accessed for some time, first locate each such file using **find** and then execute **rm** supplied as an argument.

□ To locate directory entries for the source, binary and manual entries for system commands in 4.2, use **whereis**.

- Some idea about what kind of information is stored in a file may be obtained by using **file** (but be careful — it sometimes makes mistakes).

- Use **ln** to establish additional links to a file, the number of which is stored in the i-node and displayed whenever a directory entry is listed.

- A large file may be broken into a number of smaller pieces using **split**.

- Use **cat** to reverse the effect of **split** and recombine sections into the original file.

- Use **df** to determine how much disk space is available in a particular file system or all file systems.

- To reduce the amount of space occupied by your files, use **ar** to combine a number of files into an archive file and then delete those files.

- **ar** can also be used to output a table of contents for an archive file and recover or delete files from the archive.

- More disk space can be freed if files are archived to some other medium such as magnetic tape or floppy disk.

- Use **tar** to copy files and/or directories (including their contents) to some other storage medium and to recover them when needed at some later time.

- **tar** can also be used to move file hierarchies from one position in the filing system to another since it can write to standard output and read from standard input.

- Files can be compressed using **pack** which reduces the space occupied by character files to about 60—75% of their original size.

- Use **unpack** or **pcat** to restore compressed files to their original form.

- To compare the contents of two files use **comp** or **diff**.

- If the contents of one file differs from that of another, **diff** can be used to generate an **ed** script which will convert the first file into the second one.

- If two files have been ordered in the same way, **comm** will output a list of those lines which are common to both files and those which are unique to each file.

- For a single file containing lines sorted into order, **uniq** will output the lines without any replications, those lines which are not replicated or one copy of each replicated line.

- To sort lines in a file means to order them according to some criteria.

- A field is a non-empty non-blank string separated by blanks.

- The machine collating sequence is an ordering based on the value of each character on a particular machine.

- **sort** may be used to sort one or more files into lexicographic order on the basis of whole lines, particular fields or sequences of fields taking into account or ignoring leading blanks in a field.

- Other orderings that can be produced by **sort** are reverse, lexicographic with case ignored, dictionary and arithmetic.

- The –**u** option of **sort** enables it to suppress the output of all but one in each set of lines having equal fields used for sorting.

- Merging produces an output file which has the same order as two or more ordered input files and is carried out by **sort** –**m**.

- **join** produces an ordered output file containing lines consisting of a common field from lines in two ordered input files followed by the rest of the line from the first file, then the rest of the line from the second file.

- **join** provides options for redefining the default separator (blank or tab), outputting unpairable lines, constructing the output line from specified fields and marking missing fields.

- To search one or more files for lines containing a particular string of characters, use a member of the "grep" family.

- **fgrep** outputs lines that match or do not match fixed strings supplied as an argument or read from a file and optionally will attach a line number, ignore case, match only whole lines, suppress output of the filename and produce only a line count.

- **grep** is similar to **fgrep** except that it uses a limited regular expression supplied as an argument.

- **egrep** is more powerful than **grep** in that it handles full regular expressions supplied as an argument or read from a file.

- To determine the number of lines, words and characters in one or more files, use **wc**.

- Use **tr** to substitute or delete selected characters from a file.

- Use **od** to dump a file with or without an offset in a variety of different formats including bytes in octal, hexadecimal and as ASCII characters, words in octal, hexadecimal and decimal.

- To copy files from or for a foreign system, use **dd** specifying such conversions as one character set to another, a change of case or the interchange of each pair of bytes.

- To encrypt or decrypt a file, use **crypt** supplying a secret password which will be used to control the transformation.

- A process is an executing program and is the child of the parent process that created it.

- The state of a process may be running, ready-to-run, waiting, sleeping, stopped or terminated.

- To initiate a background job, terminate the command line with an ampersand (**&**).

- To suspend a foreground job, type ^**Z** (N.B. this facility will only work for the standard shell if the shell layer facility has been activated via **shl**).

□ To suspend a background job in the C-shell, use **stop** supplying the jobname as an argument.

- To restart a foreground job, use **fg** in C-shell or **resume** in the shell layer manager.

□ To restart a job in the background, use **bg**.

- To examine the status of your job, use **jobs** in the C-shell, **ps** or **layers** in the shell layer manager.

- Use **ps** to produce a long or a short listing showing what processes you have initiated and what state they are in.

- To run a program at low priority, **nice** it so that its "niceness" number is increased and it gets less of the CPU.

- To send a terminate signal to a process telling it to die, use **kill**.

- Some processes can ignore terminate signals but the kill signal issued by using **kill –9** cannot be ignored and is a sure kill even for a login shell.

- To ensure that a background job will continue to execute after you have logged out, use **nohup** to start the command line.

- To run a job at some time in the future, use **at** to place it in a queue which will be inspected from time to time by the system and any jobs initiated at the appropriate time.

- To make a job self-perpetuating, place an **at** command line at the end of the command file.

- To transfer a file between one machine and another, use **uucp** specifying the system name of the remote machine as a prefix separated by a ! for any pathname on that machine.

- To find out the names of machines known to your system, use **uuname** (the –l option produces the name of the local machine).

- To inspect a log of **uucp** transfers, use **uulog** which can select entries from the log for specified users and systems.

- Electronic mail consists of messages sent by a user to one or more specified users.

- **mail** is an early version of a command to send or receive electronic mail which is still widely available.

- To send mail, supply the usernames of the recipients as arguments to **mail** and terminate the messages with ^**D**.

- To read mail if any, issue **mail** without any arguments and dispose of each message by responding to the **?** prompt with a single character command (**\*** or **?** will produce a list of the commands available).

- To send mail to a user on another machine, prefix the username with one or more system names separated from each other by !.

- **Mail** and **mailx** are interactive message processing systems in 4.2BSD and System V.2 respectively.

□ In the Berkeley system, **mail** is often a link to **Mail** and the earlier version can only be activated by using **/bin/mail**.

- The behaviour of these mail commands is controlled by options and variables which may be set or given values initially by commands in the file *.mailrc* in your home directory read at start-up time.

- To send mail, issue the command with arguments which may be usernames or aliases (both system and private).

- In input mode, the mail command prompts for a subject, a carbon copy list and then accepts the message terminated by ^D.

- During the input of a message, an escape character (default is tilde) at the beginning of a line causes entry to command mode which enables you to review, edit or abort partially formed messages.

- To read mail (if any), issue the mail command without arguments to produce a list of message headers and enter command mode which prompts with ? or &.

- Commands which may take a list of message numbers as arguments are available to facilitate saving, deleting and replying to messages (a ? in response to the prompt will produce a list of the available commands and their actions).

- Electronic news consists of messages sent by a user which may be read by anyone who subscribes to the particular newsgroup in which the item is placed.

- In System V.2, **news** is used to read current news items.

- In another electronic news system which is widely available, **readnews** is used to peruse news items, **checknews** to see if any news items exist and **postnews** to submit new articles.

*Chapter 6*

# CONCLUDING

And so we come to the end. By this time, hopefully, you will no longer be a beginner with UNIX, but, instead, have some degree of familiarity with the system and some confidence that you can make it do your bidding to accomplish your goals. It really wasn't all that hard, although initially it might have looked a little forbidding. You have met and mastered many of the UNIX commands, you know where to look in case you've forgotten something about one of them, you understand the structure of the file system and how to organize, manage and change the data you store in it. You have seen how to interface programs written in Pascal, FORTRAN 77 and C to UNIX and how to write shell scripts to tailor your interface to the system to one of your own choosing. All in all, it should have been an interesting experience and we certainly hope that it was.

Before closing, there are a few remaining topics that we would like to consider briefly — first, a little history about the development of UNIX so that you have some appreciation about where it came from and how it fits into the scheme of things, then some last words of advice and finally some thoughts about the future.

## 6.1 A Little History

Unlike many operating systems, UNIX was not designed by a committee and implemented by vast teams of programmers. Instead, it started life back in 1969 on a cast-off PDP 7 computer at Bell Laboratories in the USA. Two of the researchers there, who were dissatisfied with the poor response and long turn-around time of the big mainframe systems in use at the laboratory, were given permission to bring the machine back into service to support a space travel game which required an interactive graphics terminal for its input-output. A rudimentary file system was added and UNIX was born. The name is a pun on

MULTICS (Multiplexed Information and Computing System), a large scale time-sharing system designed to support many hundreds of simultaneously active users.

The original version of UNIX was written in assembly language for the PDP 7 which was manufactured by Digital Equipment Corporation (DEC). When a new DEC machine, the PDP 11/20, became available, UNIX was transferred to it in 1971, still in assembly code. This became known as the First Edition and contained all the important concepts found in modern UNIX with the exception of pipes. These were added in the Second Edition which appeared in 1972.

A major change took place in 1973 when the system was rewritten, largely by the two original designers, in C which was also developed at Bell. In 1975, Sixth Edition UNIX was made available to other institutions, mainly universities, at a nominal fee. This became known as Version 6 and is still used on some PDP 11 machines today.

Although UNIX was never designed to be portable, the fact that over 90% of the system was written in a high level language suggested to a number of people that it could be ported to other computers whose architecture was different from that of the PDP 11 series. At Bell Labs, the system was transferred to an Interdata 8/32, a 32-bit minicomputer with an architecture similar to the IBM 370. In the process, machine dependencies were brought to light and corrected, some improvements and additions were made to the system and it was released for general use on PDP 11 machines as Version 7 in 1979. This system is still widely used throughout the world on these machines today. Another project carried out at the same time by the University of Wollongong in Australia also moved UNIX from a PDP 11/45 to an Interdata 7/32. This has become the basis of the UNIX system available today on Perkin-Elmer 3200 machines.

Since the early ports, UNIX has been moved to many other computers, from mainframes to micros. The first port to the 32-bit DEC VAX 11/780 called 32V was carried out at Bell Labs and this has subsequently been developed into System III and later System V which is currently available from AT&T under licence. Extensions to 32V were also carried out by the University of California at Berkeley whose latest release is 4.2BSD. The advent of the 16-bit microprocessor such as the Motorola M68000 led to the development of many new computer systems designed around these chips and to many new ports of UNIX. The most well known of these is Xenix developed by Microsoft who have added a number of enhancements to improve the suitability of UNIX in the commercial environment.

## 6.2 Last Words of Advice

Before we part, some final words of advice:

- Remember that much of the UNIX documentation exists online and there are tools that enable you to consult it conveniently — when in doubt, do so!

- Before writing a new command of your own, look to see what is already available. It may be that one near enough to your requirements already exists, perhaps written by another user, perhaps a system command itself.

- To create your own commands, try gluing together existing components using pipes and shell programming rather than starting right at the beginning each time.

- Don't be afraid to create directories so that you can exploit the hierarchical structure of the file system; lots of sub-directories containing small files are much easier to manage than one directory with many large files.

- Make sure you get plenty of practice with the editors, particularly **vi**. They will be your most frequently used tools and, if you are proficient with them, you will save yourself a great deal of time.

- Be prepared to exploit the electronic mail and news facilities of UNIX. You can keep others informed of what you are doing, find out what they are doing and so come to be part of the world of UNIX.

## 6.3  The Future

It is always hazardous to try to predict the future, particularly in the computer field where new developments take place at a very rapid rate. Nevertheless, all indicators at the moment suggest that UNIX will become the standard operating system (if it has not already done so). It is now almost mandatory for a manufacturer to offer UNIX on its range of hardware if it wishes to compete successfully in the market place. Even IBM has joined the ever increasing number of machine manufacturers who offer UNIX because of the demand from customers.

What this explosive growth in the use of UNIX means to you starting down the UNIX pathway is that what you have learnt from this book will stand you in good stead for a long time to come. Of course, there is much more to learn as we have only covered a fraction of the facilities available in UNIX; there will be improved versions with enhancements and additions, new facilities to try out and new commands to explore. But, you have a good foundation on which to build and should have little trouble in coping with the future.

# Glossary

This section defines the terms, files, commands and shell variables encountered in this book. All words in **bold italic** type are terms or files in the glossary; commands are shown in **bold** and arguments in *italics*; variables are indicated by a `constant width` font. Where a command exists in both the Berkeley and AT&T versions of UNIX, the synopsis included in the glossary is that for System V. Any significant differences are noted in the accompanying description.

*.c* : A *suffix* added to a *filename* which indicates that the *file* contains a *C program*.

*.cshrc* : An *optional file* in a *home directory* containing *commands* which are *executed* each time the *C-shell* is invoked.

*.f* : A *suffix* added to a *filename* which indicates that the *file* contains a *FORTRAN program*.

*.h* : A *suffix* added to a *filename* which indicates that the *file* contains header information for a *C program*.

*.login* : An *optional file* in a *home directory* containing *commands* which are *executed* each time the *user* activates *C-shell* as the *login shell*.

*.logout* : An *optional file* in a *home directory* containing *commands* which are *executed* each time the *user logs out* from the *C-shell* as the *login shell*.

*.newsrc* : A *file* in a *home directory* used to record which news articles have already been *read* by **readnews**.

*.o* : A *suffix* added to a *filename* which indicates that the *file* contains an *object module*.

*.p* : A *suffix* added to a *filename* which indicates that the *file* contains a *Pascal program*.

*.profile* : An *optional file* in a *home directory* containing *commands* which are *executed* each time the *user* activates the *standard shell* as the *login* shell.

*/* : The *root directory* which is the base of the *directory hierarchy*.

*/bin* : A *directory* of frequently used *system commands*.

*/bin/mail* : An *executable file* in the *directory /bin* containing the standard **mail** *command*. In the Berkeley *system*, **mail** may simply be a *link* to **Mail** and the *full pathname* must be supplied to cause the command to be executed.

*/dev* : A *directory* of **peripheral devices**.

*/dev/mt* : A *directory* of **magnetic tape** units connected to the **system** in V.2.

*/dev/null* : A non-existent **device** which is a sink used to discard unwanted *output* or a *source* of **end-of-files**.

*/dev/rmt?* : A **magnetic tape** unit connected to the **system** in 4.2.

*/etc* : A *directory* of **files** containing miscellaneous **system** information.

*/etc/motd* : A **file** containing the **message of the day** which is *output* after **login** has been completed successfully.

*/etc/passwd* : A **file** containing details including **usernames** and **passwords** of the authorized **users** of a UNIX **system**.

*/lib* : A *directory* of the subroutine libraries.

*/tmp* : A *directory* which is **accessible** by all **users** for the **creation** of **files** for temporary **storage**.

*/usr* : A *directory* which is the root of the **user file system**.

*/usr/bin* : A *directory* of the less frequently used **system commands**.

*/usr/games* : A *directory* of the games available to **users**.

*/usr/include* : A *directory* of header **files** for **C programs**.

*/usr/include/math.h* : A **file** containing headers for the mathematical subroutine **library**.

*/usr/include/stdio.h* : A **file** containing headers for the standard **input-output** subroutine **library**.

*/usr/lib* : A *directory* of the subroutine libraries for **high level languages**.

*/usr/lib/aliases* : A **file** containing details of system-wide distribution lists for **Mail** in 4.2.

*/usr/lib/libm.a* : A **file** containing the mathematical subroutines in **archived object module** format.

*/usr/mail* : A *directory* of the **mailboxes** of authorized **users** of a V.2 **system**.

*/usr/man* : A *directory* of the **online manual**.

*/usr/news* : A *directory* of news items in System V.

*/usr/pub* : A *directory* of **files** of public interest.

*/usr/pub/ascii* : A **file** containing tables showing the values of **characters** in the **ASCII** character set expressed in both **octal** and **hexadecimal**.

*/usr/spool* : A *directory* of **spooled files**.

*/usr/spool/at* : A *directory* of **jobs** submitted through **at** to be **executed** at a later time in 4.2.

*/usr/spool/cron/atjobs* : A *directory* of *jobs* submitted through **at** to be *executed* at a later time in V.2.

*/usr/spool/mail* : A *directory* of the *mailboxes* of authorized *users* of a 4.2 *system*.

*/usr/spool/uucp* : A *directory* of *files* that could not be delivered by **uucp** in 4.2.

*/usr/spool/uucppublic* : A *directory* of *files* that could not be delivered by **uucp** in V.2.

*/usr/ucb* : A *directory* of *commands* only available in the Berkeley *system*.

*a.out* : The *default filename* of the *object file* produced by most of the UNIX *compilers*. (cf. **cc**, **f77**, **pc**)

*abort* : Causes the *execution* of a *command* to terminate prematurely. (cf. *interrupt*)

*access* : A *file* may be accessed for *reading*, *writing* or *appending*. The time of last access is *stored* in the *i-node* of the file.

*access mode* : Each *file* in UNIX has associated with it an access mode. This enables the *owner* of the file to restrict access by allowing or disallowing *read*, *write*, or *execute permission* for the file or *directory*. These permissions can be granted to the owner, to members of the owner's *group* or to all *users*. (cf. *file creation mask*, **ls**, **chmod**, **umask**)

*access time* : The time required to access an item of *data* on a *storage device*.

*account* : Before accessing a UNIX *system*, a *user* must first establish an account so that usage of system resources can be recorded and perhaps charged for. An account is established by the *system administrator* or *superuser*. The name of the account is the *username* used to *login* to the system.

*address* : The *memory* of a *computer* is divided into a number of *words*, each of which can be referenced by its address so that the contents can be used in a computation.
The term is also used to describe part of an *editor command* which specifies a particular *line* in a *file*.

*administrator* : see *system administrator*.

*algorithm* : A set of rules or steps describing how a computation may be carried out to solve a problem.

*alias* : A *C-shell* facility which enables a *user* to define new *commands* in terms of existing ones.
In **mailx**, an alias is a name associated with a list of *usernames* to which *mail* will be sent if it is used as an *argument* to the command.

**alias** [ *name* ] [ *list* ]

A *C-shell command* to define or print command *aliases*. If no *arguments* are supplied, the current list of alias name-value pairs is printed; if only *name* is specified, the alias list for that name is printed. Otherwise, the elements of *list* are assigned as the alias of *name*.

**append** : To append information to a *file* means to add it to the end of the file without altering the information already there. The *shell metacharacter* >> causes *standard output* to be *redirected* and appended to a file.

*Editors* such as **ed** and **vi** have an append mode in which *text* entered from the *keyboard* is added to the *buffer* after the current position. The opposite of append is *prepend*.

**applications software** : *Programs* developed to solve specific problems of interest to *users* of *computer systems*. It is to be contrasted with *systems software*.

**ar** *key* [ *posname* ] *afile* [ *file* ... ]

Maintains groups of *files* combined into a single *archive* file *afile*. *key* selects one of the many *options* and is an optional − followed by one *character* from the set **dprtx** optionally *concatenated* with one or more of **abuv**. The meanings of the characters are:

|   |   |
|---|---|
| a | Used with **r** to cause new files to be placed after an existing file *posname* already in *afile*. |
| b | As for **a** except new files are placed before *posname*. |
| d | *Delete* named files from the archive file. |
| p | Print named files from the archive file. |
| r | Replace named files in *afile*, creating a new archive file if necessary. |
| t | Print a table of contents of the archive file. |
| u | Used with **r** to cause only those files with *modification* times later than those in the archive file to be used in the replacement. |
| v | Produce verbose *output* when used with **r**, **t** and **x**. |
| x | Extract the named files or all files if no names are given. |

**archive** : Archiving a *file* usually means *copying* the file from *disk* to some cheaper form of *storage* medium such as *magnetic tape* so that the space it occupies can be used for other purposes. The term is also used to refer to the process of combining a number of files into a single file, again with the objective of reducing the space they occupy. The process of recovering a file from an archive is called *restoring*. (cf. **ar, tar**)

**argument** : An argument or *parameter* provides a *command* with information about when, how or on what to perform its functions. (cf. *default*, *option*, *shell*, **sh**)

*Articles* : The *default file* used by **readnews** for saving news items.

*ASCII* : An acronym for **A**merican **S**tandard **C**ode for **I**nformation **I**nterchange and pronounced "asskey". It is used widely throughout the *computer* industry as a *standard 7-bit code* for representing *characters*. (cf. *EBCDIC*)

*assemble* : The process of translating a *program* written in *assembly language* into *machine code*.

*assembler* : A *program* like a *compiler* which translates *assembly language* into actual *machine code*. It is said to *assemble* the program.

*assembly code* : see *assembly language*.

*assembly language* : A *programming language* in which there is a one-to-one correspondence between the *instructions* in the language and the basic operations of the *machine*. Writing in assembly language is a convenient way to construct a *program* directly in machine instructions. Rather than having to use numeric *operation codes*, *addresses* etc., *symbolic opcode* mnemonics and symbolic addresses are used instead.

*asynchronous* : The *shell* makes it possible for a *user* to initiate the *execution* of a *command* and then issue further commands without waiting for the previous command to terminate. An ampersand in the *command line* is the *metacharacter* which tells the shell to *execute* the preceding command(s) asynchronously in the *background*. (cf. *process*, **sh**, **csh**, **ps**)

**at** *time* [ *date* ] [ + *increment* ]
*Reads commands* from *standard input* and *spools* them for *execution* at a later time which may be specified as 1, 2 or 4 digits, the first two being interpreted as hours and the last as hours and minutes. Alternatively, *time* may be specified as *hour: minute* for a 24-hour clock, otherwise an *optional* **am** or **pm** may be appended for a 12-hour clock. The names **noon**, **midnight**, **now** and **next** are also recognized. An optional *date* may be supplied in most reasonable forms to specify a day of the week or a month followed by a day and possibly a year. The days **today** and **tomorrow** are also recognized. The optional *increment* is simply an integer suffixed by the name of a unit of time.
**at** −**r***number* ... removes previously scheduled *jobs* with the specified job numbers.
The 4.2 version of **at** does not permit an optional increment but does enable commands to be read from a *file* specified as the final *argument* as well as from standard input. (cf. *batch processing*, **batch**)

*background* : An environment in which one or more *jobs* can be *executed* at a lower *priority* than and *asynchronously* with a *foreground job*.

*background job* : A *job executing* in the *background*. Normally, such jobs do not *read* from or *write* to the *terminal*. (cf. **bg**, **stop**) *backup* : To ensure against loss of information when a *machine* breaks down, *computer* installations regularly make backup copies of all *files* on *magnetic tapes*. Then, if files are destroyed on the *disk*, they may be recovered from the backup tapes. However, any *changes* made to files since the last backup copies were made will be lost. (cf. *crash*)

*basename* : The last component of a *pathname*.

**basename** *string* [ *suffix* ]
> *Delete* any prefix ending in / and *suffix* (if any) from *string*; *write results* on *standard output*.

**batch**
> *Reads commands* from *standard input* and places them on a queue to be *executed* as soon as possible. (cf. **at**)

*batch processing* : A way of *operating* a *computer* in which *jobs* are collected together in batches and submitted to the *machine* for processing. It suffers from the disadvantage that it is not *interactive* and *users* may experience long *turn-around times*.

*baud* : The speed of a *communication* line is measured by the number of *bits* of information that can be transmitted each second. A baud is defined as 1 bit/sec. Typical transmission rates for lines connecting *terminals* to *computers* are 110, 300, 1200, 2400, 4800, 9600 and 19200 bauds. To convert bauds into *characters*/sec., an approximate rule is to divide by 10 i.e. 300 baud is equivalent to 30 characters/sec.

**bfs** [ − ] *file*
> Used for scanning large *files* with an ed-like *command syntax*. It cannot be used as an *editor* but is useful for locating positions within the file and extracting portions of it. The − suppresses printing of sizes.

**bg** [ *jobname* ... ]
> A *C-shell command* to restart a *suspended job* jobname in the *background*. If no *argument* is supplied, the *current job* is restarted. A background job is suspended by using the **stop** command.

*binary file* : A term often used to describe *computer output* which has no printable representation e.g. an *executable program* produced by a *compiler*.

*binary system* : A *number system* using only the digits 0 and 1 in contrast with the decimal system which uses ten digits from 0 to 9. Modern *computers* operate on binary information since it is possible to construct electronic circuits which can manipulate such information very rapidly.

*bit* : A contraction of the words "binary dig**it**". A bit has a value of 0 or 1.

*blank* : A *space* or *tab character*.

*block* : A unit of *storage* on *disk* or *tape*. A disk block contains 1024 *bytes* in V.2 and 4.2 but only 512 bytes in earlier versions of UNIX.

*boolean* : Boolean algebra is one in which *variables* only have the values true or false. (cf. *logical operator*)

*Bourne shell* : The *standard shell* in UNIX written by S. Bourne of Bell Laboratories. It is activated by the **sh** *command*. (cf. *C-shell*)

**break**

Exits from the current loop in **sh** and **csh**.

*buffer* : A *storage* area used to hold information temporarily, perhaps as part of an *input-output* transfer. Both **ed** and **vi** *copy* the *file* to be edited into a buffer and any *changes* are only made to the contents of that buffer. To preserve such changes permanently, it is necessary to issue specific *commands* to cause the buffer to be *written* back to the file.

*bug* : A colloquial term for an *error* in a *program*.

*byte* : A unit of *memory* of size 8 *bits* which is sufficient to *store* one *character*. A *kilobyte* (kbyte, Kb) is 1024 bytes. A *megabyte* (mbyte, Mb) is 1,048,576 bytes. Note that a byte can also be used to store a small number and a sequence of bytes can represent larger values.

*C* : A *high level language* used for writing much of the UNIX *system*.

*CAI* : see *computer aided instruction*.

**cal** [ [ *month* ] *year* ]

Prints a calendar on *standard output* for a specified *year* (1—9999) or a specified *month* (1—12) in a given year. In the absence of any *arguments*, it outputs a calendar for the current month in V.2 or a synopsis in 4.2.

*calendar* : A *file* used to *store* reminder information which is consulted by the **calendar** *command*.

**calendar** [ – ]

Provides a reminder service by consulting the *file calendar* in the *current directory* and printing any *line* that contains today's or tomorrow's date. Most reasonable month-day dates are recognized.

The *system administrator* can use the *command* with an *argument* to scan every *user's home directory* for *calendar* and send them any *results* by *mail*.

**cancel** [ *options* ]

Cancel *line printer* requests made with **lp**. *options* enable *job identifiers* and line printers to be specified.

*cast* : An *operator* in the *C programming language* used to convert information from one type to another e.g. from integer to floating point.

**cat** [ *options* ] *file ...*

> *Reads* each named *file* in sequence and *writes* it on *standard output*. If more than one *file* is mentioned, the effect is to concatenate the files, hence the name of the *command*. If no *file* is mentioned or if − is encountered as an *argument*, the command reads from *standard input*. The *options* available are:

> −e    Used with −v to print a **$** at the end of each *line*.

> −n    Precede each output line by a line number, numbered sequentially from 1. (4.2)

> −s    Make command silent for non-existent files (V.2); reduce multiple adjacent empty lines to a single line (4.2).

> −t    Used with −v to cause a tab to be printed as ^**I**.

> −u    Make output completely unbuffered.

> −v    Print non-printing *characters* visibly, except for *tabs*, *newlines* and *linefeeds*.

**cc** [ *options* ] *file ...*

> The UNIX *C compiler*. It *reads* named *files* with a *.c suffix* and compiles them to produce files of the same name with the *.c* changed to *.o*. All *.o* files whether named in the *argument* list or created are then passed on to the *loader* which produces an *executable* file *a.out*. If a single C *program* is compiled, the *.o* file is *deleted.*

> There are many *options* available with **cc**, a few of which are described below:

> −c    Suppress the *loading* phase and force production of an *object file* even if only one program is compiled.

> −g    Generate additional *symbol table* information for a *symbolic debugger*.

> −O    Invoke an object code *optimizer*.

> −o *file*    Name the object file *file* instead of *a.out*.

**ccat** [ *file ...* ]

> A 4.2 *command* similar to **uncompact** except that the specified *file* is not expanded. *Results* are *written* to *standard output*.

**cd** [ *directory* ]

> Change *working directory* to the one specified or to the *home directory* if no *argument* is supplied. If *directory* is not a *full pathname* or a *sub-directory* of the *current directory*, the *command* tries to find the required directory relative to one of the *search paths* defined in the *shell variable* CDPATH.

**CDPATH** : A *shell variable* which holds the *search path* for the **cd** *command.*

*central processing unit* : The component of a *computer* which *executes* the *instructions* in a *program* to control the behaviour of the *machine*. The speed of a *CPU* is measured in millions of instructions per second (*Mips*).

*change* : A *file* is changed when existing information is overwritten or new information is *appended* to the end of the file. The time of last change is *stored* in the *i-node* of the file. Since the i-node contains the size of the file as well, changing a file also causes the time of last *modification* to be updated. A *variable* is changed when a new value is assigned to it.

*character* : Characters are used to represent the *symbols* people use for written communication. This is done by assigning to each symbol a unique numerical value e.g. in *ASCII*. Many of the *devices* that go to make up a *computer system* are used for translating these values to and from a form that people can understand. For example, pressing a key on a *terminal* causes a character to be sent to the computer. Similarly, the computer may send a character to a *line printer* so that it can be printed on paper. (cf. *byte*)

**checknews** [ *options* ]

Reports to the *user* whether there is news to be *read* or not. Some of the *options* available are as follows:

e        *Executes* **readnews** if there is news.

n        *Outputs* "No news" if there is no news to be read.

q        Suppresses output of any messages.

y        Outputs "There is news" if there is news to be read (*default* option).

The *exit code* is 0 if there is no news and 1 otherwise.

*child process* : When a *process* is *created* in UNIX, it is called the child of the process that created it which is also known as the *parent*.

**chmod** *mode file* ...

Enables the *owner* to alter the *access mode* for the named *files*. *mode* may be absolute or *symbolic*. The former is a 3-digit *octal* number, the digits of which from the left represent the *permissions* of the owner, the *group* and *others* respectively. The *binary* digits in each octal digit represent the *read*, *write* and *execute permissions* with 1 for on and 0 for off.

A symbolic *mode* has the form:

[ *who* ] *op permission* [ *op permission* ]

where *who* is **a** (all) or some combination of the letters **u** (*user*), **g** (group) and **o** (others). *op* may be + to add a permission, − to take a permission away or = to set a permission and reset all others. *permission* is any combination of the letters **r** (read), **w** (write) and **x** (execute). Multiple symbolic modes may be specified separated by commas.

**cmp** [ –l ] [ –s ] *file1 file2*

*Compares* the named **files**. If *file1* is –, **standard input** is used. If the files differ, the first **byte** and **line** number at which a difference occurs is **written** on **standard output**, otherwise no output occurs. The meanings of the **options** are:

–l  Print decimal byte number and differing bytes in **octal** for each difference.

–s  Print nothing for differing files.

The **exit codes** returned by the **command** are 0 for identical files, 1 for different files and 2 for inaccessible or missing **arguments**.

**code** : A term colloquially used to describe a **program** or the writing of a program. It is also used to mean the numerical value of a **character** or **symbol** inside a **computer**. (cf. *ASCII, EBCDIC, machine code*)

**comm** [ – [ **123** ] ] *file1 file2*

*Reads* the ordered **files**, *file1* and *file2*, and **writes** to **standard output** in 3 columns: **lines** only in *file1*, lines only in *file2* and lines in both files. If the **filename** is –, **standard input** is read. The **flags 1, 2** or **3** suppress output of the corresponding column. (cf. *lexicographic*, **sort**)

**command** : A **user** instructs a **computer** to perform **tasks** by issuing a series of commands, usually by typing the requests at a **terminal**. Typically, there are commands that print the contents of a **file**, alter the **password**, **execute** the **program**, and a host of other functions. These commands are simply special programs provided for the convenience of all users. Users can also **create** their own commands by writing programs themselves or combining some of the **system** commands. (cf. *argument, option, shell*, **sh**)

**command file** : see **shell procedure**.

**command language** : The set of **commands** available in a **system** and the **syntax** for specifying a command and its **arguments** define the command language.

**command language interpreter** : A **program** which accepts **commands** from a **user** expressed in the **command language** and causes them to be **executed**. In UNIX, the command language interpreter is called the **shell**. The two most widely available shells are **sh** (the *Bourne shell* ) and **csh** (the *C-shell*).

**command line** : A **line** containing one or more **commands** with their **arguments**. If **input** from a **terminal**, the command line must be terminated by **RETURN** before the commands will be **executed**.

**command mode** : When UNIX is in this mode, a **user** is communicating with the **shell**; once a **command** starts to **execute**, the **system** will switch to **data mode** if it requires **input**. Some commands themselves have a command mode and a data mode e.g. **ed, vi, Mail, mailx**.

*command substitution* : A *shell* facility whereby one or more *commands* and their *arguments* enclosed between graves (`) in a *command line* are replaced by the *output* of the commands after they have been *executed*. *Newlines* in the output are replaced by *spaces*. (cf. **csh**, **sh**)

*comment* : A construct in a *programming language* which is ignored by the *compiler* and which therefore does not generate any *object code*. It is used to convey information to a human reader.

*communication* : There are many *commands* in UNIX which enable *users* to send and receive messages to and from one another e.g. **write**, **mail**, **news**. For the basic communication between *machines*, the UNIX-to-UNIX *copy* command **uucp** is available.

*compact* : To save space on the *disk*, it is possible to compact a *character file* using the **pack** *command* (**compact** in 4.2). The original file may be recovered using **unpack** or **pcat** (**uncompact** or **ccat** in 4.2).

**compact** [ *name* ... ]
The 4.2 equivalent of **pack**. It will also *read* from *standard input* and *write* to *standard output* if no *name* is supplied. The packed *file* is called *name.C*.

*comparison* : Often, one wants to know whether two *files* are the same and, if they are not, where they differ. The *commands* to carry out such functions are **cmp**, **comm** and **diff**. On the other hand, **uniq** compares adjacent *lines* in a single file.

*compilation* : The process of translating a *program* in a *high level language* into the primitive instructions of the *computer*.

*compiler* : A *computer* is only able to *execute* a very primitive set of *instructions*. Writing computer *programs* using these instructions is both tedious and error-prone. It is much easier to write programs in *high level languages* which are akin to natural languages and mathematics. It is the function of a program called a compiler to translate (compile) these high level language programs into the corresponding primitive instructions. The resulting sequence of instructions can then be executed. (cf. *interpreter*, **pc**, **f77**, **cc**)

*computer* : A computer is a *machine* composed of electronic and electro-mechanical *devices*, designed to *store*, *retrieve* and *transform data* at high speed. What this data represents, and how it is transformed, is determined by a sequence of *instructions* called a *program*. A computer can perform primitive calculations very quickly (typically one million per second), is very accurate (computer errors, as distinct from *errors* made by programmers, are extremely rare), and its ability to be programmed allows one computer to perform a diverse range of *tasks*. (cf. *CPU*, *memory*)

*computer-aided instruction* : A *computer* can be *programmed* to ask questions of a *user* and assess the response. The subsequent behaviour of the program then depends on whether the answer was right or wrong. The *CAI* facility in UNIX is provided by the **learn** *command*. The lessons available vary from *system* to system but many of them provide a useful introduction to the facilities available in UNIX.

*concatenation* : The joining together of entities such as *strings*. The concatenation of the strings abc and XYX is the string abcXYZ.

*connect mode* : see *online*.

*context search* : A technique for locating in a *file* a *string* of *characters* which match a *pattern*. It is used by the *editors* ed and vi, also by **fgrep**, **grep** and **egrep**.

**continue**
Commences execution of the next iteration of a loop in **sh** and **csh**.

*control character* : Some *characters* have a printable representation, others do not but can be used to send signals to the *computer*. These are called control characters. Some such as **RETURN** and **ESCAPE** have a special key associated with the character; others are generated by holding down the **CONTROL** key while pressing some other key e.g. **control—D** is generated by simultaneously depressing **CONTROL** and **D**.

*control—D* : A *control character* usually used to signal *end-of-file*.

*control—H* : A *control character* used as the *default erase character* on many *terminals*.

*control—Q* : A *control character* used to restart *output* to a *terminal*.

*control—S* : A *control character* used to stop *output* to a *terminal*.

*control—X* : A *control character* often used as the *kill character*.

*control—Z* : The *default control character* used to *suspend* a *job* initiated by the *C-shell* or shl.

*copy* : The **cp** *command* can be used to make a copy of a *file* providing the *user* issuing the request has the appropriate *permission* to *access* the file. A copy of a file can also be made using **cat** with *output redirection*.

**cp** [ *options* ] *file1* [ *file2* ... ] *target*
**Copies** *file1* to *target* which may be a *file* or a *directory*. In the former case, only one file is copied, the *filenames* must be different and *target* is overwritten; in the latter case, one or more files are copied to the specified directory. Any file with the same *basename* is overwritten, otherwise a new file is *created*.
Only the 4.2 version of **cp** provides *options*. These are:

    −i    *Prompt* the *user* with the name of any file about to be overwritten.

    −r    If the *source* file is a directory, copy the *subtree* rooted at that directory to the target directory.

*CPU* : A shortened form of **central processing unit**.

*crash* : Although modern **computers** are very reliable, they are still prone to the occasional breakdown, usually referred to as a crash. These may be caused by the failure of some component in the computer **hardware**, or more commonly because of a **logical error** in an important **program**, such as the **operating system**. The severity of a crash may vary greatly, with the worst cases resulting in loss of information. (cf. **backup**)

*create* : To bring into existence some entity such as a **file**, a **directory** or a **process**. (cf. **delete**, **mkdir**, **cp**)

**crypt** [ *key* ]
> **Reads** from **standard input**, **transforms** the **file** according to *key* and **writes encrypted** file on **standard output**. If no *key* is given, **crypt prompts** for one from the **terminal** and turns off printing while the key is being typed. The encryption process is reversible using the same **command** with an identical key.

**csh** [ *options* ] [ *args* ]
> The **command language interpreter** known as the **C-shell** that **reads command lines** from a **terminal** or from a **file**. *options* are those described for **set**. The first **argument** is assumed to be the name of the file containing the commands to be **executed**; the remainder then become the **positional parameters** passed to that command. For a description of how to use the C-shell **interactively**, see Section 2.5.

*C-shell* : The **shell** **csh** developed at the University of California (Berkeley) by W. Joy and others.

*current directory* : At any time, a **user** has a current directory. All **filenames** not beginning with **/** referred to by the user will be **created**, or **searched** for, in the current directory. For convenience, the current directory is given the special name **.** called "dot". Also, the **directory** which contains the current directory is called **..** (the "**parent directory**"). (cf. **home directory**, **pathname**, **cd**, **ls**, **pwd**)

*current job* : The **job** most recently initiated by the **C-shell**. It can be referenced by the **jobname** **%+**. (cf. **previous job**)

*current line* : The **editors** **ed** and **ex** maintain a **pointer** to the current line. Many of the editing **commands** operate on this **line** by **default**. It is only changed when the **user** selects a new one. Initially, the current line is set to the last line of the **file**.

*cursor* : An indicator on the screen of a **VDU** which shows where the next **character** will be displayed. It is usually a rectangle or a line which sometimes blinks.

*daemon* : A special *program* which is continually *running* on a *computer*. It is usually responsible for *managing* some public resource, for example, controlling access to the *line printers*. The line printer daemon is always *waiting* for items to be printed; it queues requests as they are made and prints each one in turn (cf. *spooling*, **lp**, **lpr**)

*data* : *Computers transform data*. *Programs* operate on *input* data (sometimes called *parameters* or *arguments*) and produce *output* data (sometimes called *results*).

*data mode* : see *command mode*.

*database* : A collection of interrelated *data stored* together and *accessible* to many *users*. (cf. *relational database*)

**date** [ +*format* ]
  *Writes* the current date and time on *standard output*. If in V.2 an *argument* is given starting with a +, the layout of the output is determined by *format*.

**dd** [ *option=value ...* ]
  *Copies* the specified input *file* to the specified output file with possible conversions. *Standard input* and *output* are used by *default*. Some of the more commonly used *options* are:

|  |  |
|---|---|
| **if**=*file* | Define input *filename file*. |
| **of**=*file* | Define output filename *file*. |
| **skip**=*n* | Skip *n* input *blocks* before starting to copy. |
| **seek**=*n* | Skip *n* output blocks before starting to copy. |
| **count**=*n* | Copy *n* input blocks. |
| **conv=ascii** | Convert *EBCDIC* to *ASCII*. |
| **ebcdic** | Convert ASCII to EBCDIC. |
| **ucase** | Translate lower case alphabetics to upper case. |
| **lcase** | Translate upper case alphabetics to lower case. |
| **swab** | Swap every pair of *bytes*. |
| **noerror** | Do not stop processing if an error is detected. |

More than one value may be assigned to **conv** in which case they are separated by commas.
After completion, **dd** outputs a count of the number of whole and partial input and output blocks it has processed.

*debug* : *Programs* often contain *logical errors* which are commonly referred to as *bugs*. To debug a program means to locate and correct the error which is causing it to behave incorrectly.

*debugger* : A *software tool* to assist in the process of locating *errors*.

*decrypt* : see *encrypt*.

*default* : A value or condition which is assigned or exists automatically unless some specific action is taken to change it e.g. the default *address* in many **ed** *commands* is the *current line*.

*default argument* : Many *commands* allow the *user* to modify their action by supplying *optional arguments*. If these *options* are not specified, the command is said to *default* to some particular action, thereby saving unnecessary typing.

*delete* : To delete a *file* means to remove the *filename* from its *directory*. The file will only be physically removed from the *disk*, thereby freeing the space it occupies, when the number of *links* to the file becomes 0. The file may still exist, however, on an *archive* or *backup tape*. Hence, a file deleted in error may not be lost forever.
*Characters* and *lines* may be deleted from a character file using an *editor* such as **ed** or **vi**. Again they are not completely lost since both editors provide an *undo* facility. (cf. **rm**, **rmdir**)

*delimiter* : A *character* or *symbol* in a *programming language* that terminates some *syntactic* construct and separates it from the next one.

*device* : see *peripheral device*.

**df** [ –i ] [ *filesystem* ... ] [ *file* ... ]
*Outputs* the amount of used and free *disk* space available on the specified *filesystem* or on the *file system* in which the specified *file* exists. If no *argument* is supplied, it prints the free disk space on all normally mounted file systems. The –i *option* causes it to report on the number of *i-nodes* which are used and free.

*diagnostic output* : A message produced by a *program* indicating that an error has been encountered. It usually appears on *standard error output*.

**diff** [ –beh ] *file1 file2*
*Compares* two *files* and tells what *lines* must be *changed* to bring them into agreement. If – is used to designate one of the files, *standard input* is *read*. If *file1* is a *directory*, then a file of name *file2* in that directory is compared with a file of the same name in the *current directory* (and vice-versa). The normal *output* consists of lines that resemble **ed** *commands* to convert *file1* into *file2*. The most useful *options* are:

    **b**    Causes trailing *spaces* and *tabs* to be ignored and other *strings* of spaces and/or tabs to compare equal.

    **e**    Produces a script of **a**, **c** and **d** commands which can be input to **ed** to *create* *file2* from *file1*.

    **h**    Does a fast but half-hearted job for very large files.

The meaning of the *exit codes* are 0 for no differences, 1 for some differences and 2 for problems such as a non-existent file.

*directory* : A type of *file* used to group together a collection of files. This is done by placing the *filenames* and *i-node numbers* of all these files in the directory. A directory may contain other directories which are called *sub-directories*. The *directory hierarchy* in UNIX is in the shape of a *tree* with each directory representing a node. (cf. *current directory*, *home directory*, *link*, *pathname*, **ln**, **ls**, **mkdir**)

*directory hierarchy* : see *full pathname*.

*disk* : see *hard disk*, *floppy disk*.

*display* : see *visual display unit*.

*documentation* : **Programs** must be written in such a way that they are understandable by people as well as by *computers*. Documentation is textual material for human readers which describes such things as how the program works, what *input data* it requires, what *results* it will produce and how to use it. Some parts of the documentation may be included in the *source code* in the form of *comments*. (cf. *manual*, **man**)

**du** [ −**as** ] [ *file* ... ]
Summarize *disk* usage by printing the number of *blocks* contained in all *files* and (*recursively*) *directories* within each directory and file specified by *file* (the *default* is the *current directory*). The meanings of the *options* are:

    **a**    Generate an entry for each *file*.

    **s**    Generate only a grand total for each specified *file*.

*EBCDIC* : An acronym for **E**xtended **B**inary **C**oded **D**ecimal **I**nformation **C**ode. It is used widely throughout the *computer* industry as a *standard* 8-*bit* *code* for representing *characters*. (cf. *ASCII*)

**echo** [ *arg* ... ]
*Writes* its *arguments* separated by *spaces* and terminated by *newline* on *standard output*. In 4.2, if the −**n** *flag* is used, no newline is added to the output.

**ed** [ − ] [ −**p** *string* ] [ *file* ]
The standard *text editor* in UNIX. When **ed** is invoked on *file*, it copies it into a temporary *file* called the *buffer*. Thereafter, it *interactively* accepts *commands* from *standard input* to locate positions in the buffer and make *changes* to the text. These changes are only preserved if the buffer is *written* back to the file using the **w** command. The *optional* − suppresses the printing of various messages and should be used when commands are being *read* from a file. The −**p** *flag* allows a *user* to specify a *prompt string* which will be *output* whenever **ed** is waiting for a command (V.2 only). For a summary of the facilities in **ed**, see Appendix 4.

*ed.hup* : A *file* used to preserve the **ed** *buffer* in the event of *terminal hangup*.

*editor* : A *program* that allows a *user* to *create* and *change* arbitrary *files* of *text*. (cf. *line editor*, *screen editor*, **ed**, **ex**, **vi**)

**egrep** [ *options* ] [ *expression* ] [ *file ...* ]
An extended version of **grep** which *searches file* for a *pattern* defined by *expression*. (cf. *regular expression*)

*electronic mail* : Messages sent by a *user* of a *computer* to one or more users on the same *machine* or a *remote machine*. (cf. **mail**, **Mail**, **mailx**)

*ellipsis* : A short *string* of periods (full stops) which implies repetition of the preceding term.

*emulator* : see *interpreter*.

*encode* : see *encrypt*.

*encrypt* : If the set of *characters* in a *file* are *transformed* according to some rule into another set such that the information they contain is not readily discernible, then the file is said to have been encrypted. The reverse process which enables the original information to be recovered is called *decryption*.
In UNIX, *passwords* are encrypted using a one-way *algorithm* so that, even if one knows the encrypted form, it is virtually impossible to reconstruct the original password providing it contains sufficient characters. (cf. **crypt**)

*end-of-file* : An indicator at the end of a *file* which signals that there is no more information to be *read* from the file. It can be detected by *commands* and *programs* and hence can be used to terminate processing. It is often referred to as *EOF*.
Since many UNIX commands allow information required by the command to be entered directly from the *terminal* rather than from a file, there must be some way to indicate the end of such *input*. This is done by typing, at the beginning of a new *line*, an end-of-file *character*, usually **control–D**. (cf. *control character*)

*environment* : A list of *variables* and associated values that is passed to a *program* to be *executed* in much the same way as a normal *argument* list. When the *shell* is invoked, it scans the environment and *creates* a *parameter* for each name found giving it the corresponding value. A *user* may *modify* the value of any of these parameters or create new ones. However, such changes do not affect the environment unless the **export** *command* in **sh** is used to bind the parameters to the environment. In **csh**, environment variables are defined and their values altered using **setenv**.

*EOF* : see *end-of-file*.

*erase character* : A *character* used to *delete* preceding characters from the current *input line*. The *default* value is usually BACKSPACE (control–H) or #. It may be redefined using **stty** (also by **tset** in 4.2).

*error* : see *logical error, semantic error, syntactic error*.

*escape* : A temporary exit from a *command* into the *shell* or from one mode of operation to another. The *character* ! is interpreted by many commands as the signal to escape to the shell. The subsequent characters are then treated as a *command line* and obeyed by the shell. After it has terminated, control returns to the command. (cf. **ed**, **vi**, **mail**, **mailx**, **Mail**)

*escape character* : A *character* which precedes another character to give the latter a different meaning in the given context. The most frequently used escape character in UNIX is backslash (\). It can be used in a *command line* to prevent *shell metacharacters* from being interpreted as such or in *regular expressions* to convert special characters into ordinary ones. In **Mail** and **mailx** during message *input*, the escape character (usually tilde ~) is used to indicate that the next character is a command rather than just more *text*.

**eval** [ *arg ...* ]
Takes the *arguments* as *input* to the *shell* and *executes* the resulting *commands*.

**ex** [ *options* ] *file ...*
A *line editor* which is a superset of **ed**. It is the basis of the *screen editor* **vi**.

*executable* : For a *program* to be executable, it must be in a form either directly understood by the *computer* or able to be *interpreted* by another program such as the *shell* or **px**. (cf. *a.out, compiler, object file, process*)

*executable file* : A *file* containing an *executable program* for which *execute permission* has been turned on.

*execute* : For a *computer* to execute a *program*, it must first load the program into *memory* and then obey the *instructions* constituting the program to perform the desired *task*.

*execute permission* : If this permission is set on, the *file* can be *executed* providing it contains a *program* in the correct form. For a *directory*, execute permission on allows its contents to be *searched* when the *system* is looking for a file.

**EXINIT** : The *shell variable* containing *commands* to initialize **ex** and **vi**.

**exit** [ *expr* ]
Exits from a *shell* with the value of *expr* as the *exit code*.

*exit code* : An integer value returned by a *command* to indicate its *exit status*.

*exit status* : One of the facilities offered by UNIX is that *programs* can provide an exit status when they have completed *execution*. Typically, this value will be used by a *command* to indicate that it has successfully performed the requested operation (the so-called "true exit status", with a value of zero). A program, such as the *shell*, may inspect this value and perform some appropriate action such as reporting an *error* or *running* another program.

**export** [ *name* ... ]

Marks the given names for automatic *export* to the *environment* of subsequently *executed commands*. In the absence of any *arguments*, a list of exported *variables* is printed.

**expr** *arg* ...

Evaluate *arguments* as an *expression* and *write results* on *standard output*. Each token of the expression is a separate argument and hence must be separated from others by a *blank*. *Characters* which have special significance to the *shell* must be *escaped*. The *operators* available include integer arithmetic (+ − * / %), relational (< <= = != >= >) and matching (:) which compares a *string* with a *regular expression* and returns the number of characters matched or a portion of the string. The operator | returns its left-hand value if it is neither null nor 0, otherwise, its right-hand value; & returns its left-hand value if both left and right are neither null nor 0, otherwise it returns 0.

The *exit codes* are 0 for a null or zero valued expression, 1 otherwise or 2 for an invalid expression.

*expression* : A *symbolic* representation of a mathematical or *logical* statement. It is composed of *operators* and *operands*.

**f77** [ *options* ] *file* ...

The *FORTRAN* 77 *compiler* in UNIX. *Files* with a *suffix* .f containing FORTRAN *source* and those with a suffix .c containing *C* source are compiled to produce corresponding .o files. Unless the *loading* phase has been suppressed, these are combined to produce an *executable program* in a file *a.out*.

Some of the *options* available in **f77** are as follows:

| | |
|---|---|
| −1 | Same as −**onetrip**. |
| −C | Generate code for *run time* checking of *subscript* ranges. |
| −c | Suppress the loading phase and force production of an *object file* even if only one *program* is compiled. |
| −g | Generate additional *symbol table* information for a *symbolic debugger*. |
| −O | Invoke an *object code optimizer*. |

    –o *file*      Name the object file *file* instead of **a.out**.

    **–onetrip**    Compile code for **do** loops to cause them to be executed at least once.

    **–U**      Treat upper and lower cases as distinct.

    **–u**      Make the **default** type of a **variable** undefined rather than using the default rules of FORTRAN.

**false**
Does nothing except return a non-zero **exit code**.

**fg** [ *jobname ...* ]
A **C-shell command** to restart specified **suspended jobs** in the **foreground**. If no **argument** is supplied, the **current job** is restarted. A foreground job is suspended by issuing ^**Z** from the **terminal**.

**fgrep** [ *options* ] [ *string ...* ] [ *file ...* ]
A fast version of **grep** which **searches** *file* for *string*.

*field* : A sequence of **characters** either of fixed length or separated from another field by a **delimiter**.

*file* : A mechanism for the long-term **storage** of information in a **computer system**. A file is referred to by a **symbolic** name called a **filename**. To make it possible to look for a particular file, these filenames are collected together in other files called **directories**. A directory contains an **i-node number** for each filename. Each file has only one i-node but may have many names. The storage of the information in the file requires the allocation of **secondary memory** to contain it. (cf. **backup**, **byte**, **disk**, **link**, **ls**)

**file** [ *options* ] *file ...*
Attempts to classify the type of each *file* whose name is supplied as an **argument**. If the file appears to contain **ASCII characters**, the **command** attempts to guess the **language** used. However, it is not always accurate. In V.2, the **option** –**f** followed by a **filename** enables the names of files to be **stored** in that file.

*file creation mask* : A 3-digit **octal** number which determines which **permissions** will be turned off when a new *file* is created. (cf. **access mode**, **mkdir**, **umask**).

*file descriptor* : A small positive integer returned to a **program** by the **operating system** when a *file* is opened. It can then be used in subsequent **read** and **write** operations.

*file system* : A collection of **files** organized in some particular manner. In UNIX, the structure of the file system is that of a **tree**, the base of which is a **directory** called **root**. The components of the system are **ordinary files**, directories and **special files**.

*filename* : A *symbolic* name used to reference a **file**. There is virtually no limit on its length or the **characters** it may contain. However, since filenames often appear in **command lines**, it is best to restrict oneself to alphanumeric characters, underscores and periods to avoid any possibility of confusion due to the inclusion of **shell metacharacters**. Non-printable characters should be avoided at all costs.

*filter* : A **program** that produces **output** which is usually a subset of its **input**, possibly **transformed** in some way. The input is **read** from **standard input** and **written** to **standard output**. By joining filters together end-to-end using the **pipe** mechanism, it is possible to construct powerful tools from simple building blocks or to expand the functions of a **command**.

Many of the commands in UNIX are designed to be used as filters. Also, the output format of many commands allows that output to be filtered. The UNIX philosophy is that it is better to provide a set of simple commands which can be joined together to perform more complex **tasks** than a smaller set of complex inflexible commands.

**find** *pathname ... expression*

Locates **files** that match a **boolean expression** while descending the **directory hierarchy** for each *pathname*. The **expression** is constructed using the following primaries:

| | |
|---|---|
| **−name** *file* | True if *file* matches the current **filename**. |
| **−perm** *onum* | True if the **file permission flags** exactly match the **octal** number *onum*. |
| **−links** *n* | True if the file has *n* **links**. |
| **−user** *uname* | True if the file belongs to the **user** *uname*. |
| **−group** *gname* | True if the file belongs to the **group** *gname*. |
| **−size** *n*[c] | True if the size is *n* **blocks** or *nc* **characters**. |
| **−atime** *n* | True if the file has been **accessed** in *n* days. |
| **−mtime** *n* | True if the file has been **modified** in *n* days. |
| **−ctime** *n* | True if the file has been **changed** in *n* days. |
| **−exec** *cmd* | True if the **executed command** returns 0 **exit status**. The end of *cmd* must be terminated by an **escaped** semi-colon. The **argument** {} is replaced by the current **pathname**. |
| **−ok** *cmd* | Like **−exec** except **interactive**. |
| **−print** | Always true and causes current pathname to be printed. |
| **−newer** *file* | True if current file has been modified more recently than *file*. |

In the above descriptions, *n* is a decimal integer which means exactly *n*. If +*n* is used instead, it is interpreted as more than *n* while −*n* means less than *n*. The primaries may be combined using the **logical operators** and, or and not represented by juxtaposition, −o and ! respectively.

*flag* : An **argument** which selects a particular **optional** mode of behaviour of a **command**. It is also used to refer to the individual **bits** specifying the **permissions** in the **access mode** of a **file**.

*floppy disk* : A flexible **magnetic disk** used for **storing data** in a **computer system**. When the disk rotates inside its cardboard jacket at say 300 r.p.m., it becomes rigid. Data may then be **written** on or **read** from concentric tracks, each of which is divided into sectors. Disks come in various sizes (3.5", 5.25" and 8" diameters) and may be single or double sided, single or double density and soft or hard sectored. Typical capacities range from 256 **kilobytes** to 1 **megabyte**.

*foreground* : When a **command line** is terminated by **RETURN**, an attempt is made by UNIX to **execute** the command immediately. This is in contrast with **background** execution where commands are executed **asynchronously** with subsequent foreground commands.

*foreground job* : A **job executing** in the foreground and communicating with the **user's terminal**.

*FORTRAN* : The first of the **high level programming languages**. It has been widely used for scientific calculations. The most recent version of the language is called FORTRAN 77. (cf. **f77**)

*full duplex* : Transmission circuits which are capable of transmitting messages in both directions at the same time. UNIX expects **terminals** connected to it to operate in a full duplex mode. **Characters** are echoed by the **computer** rather than by the terminal and **read-ahead** is made possible. (cf. **half duplex**)

*full pathname* : The **file system** supports a hierarchical naming structure. Each **directory** commencing with the **root** directory contains the names of **files** and further directories lower down the **directory hierarchy**. The complete **filename** or full pathname is a sequence of component names separated by /. It commences with a / which stands for the **root** directory and each component except the last one is the name of a directory that must be **searched** to locate the file. The last component is simply the name of the file. (cf. **relative pathname, basename**)

*general purpose* : A general purpose **computer system** is one that can be **programmed** to carry out a wide variety of different **tasks**. UNIX is one such general purpose system. (cf. **special purpose**)

**grep** [ *options* ] *expression* [ *file...* ]
　　**Search file** for **lines** matching a **pattern** defined by *expression* and **write** these to **standard output**. **grep** patterns are limited **regular expressions**, **egrep**

handles full regular expressions while **fgrep** is restricted to fixed *strings*. The following *options* are available:

| | |
|---|---|
| −c | Only a count of matching lines is printed. |
| −e | Precedes an expression which begins with a − (**egrep** and **fgrep**). |
| −f *file* | *Read* from *file* the regular expression for **egrep** or a list of *strings* for **fgrep**. |
| −i | Ignore distinction between upper and lower case during *comparisons*. |
| −l | Only the names of *files* containing matching lines are listed. |
| −n | Each line is preceded by its relative line number in the file. |
| −s | Makes **grep** silent about *errors*. |
| −v | All lines except those matching are printed. |
| −x | Only lines matched in their entirety are printed (**fgrep**). |

**grep** and **egrep** both accept the limited regular expressions used in **ed**. In addition, **egrep** recognizes two more closure *operators*, + and ?, permits the specification of alternatives with | and provides a grouping facility using parentheses. For a full discussion of regular expressions, see Section 5.2.4 and the examples in Table 5.1.

*group* : UNIX provides a facility whereby several *users* working on a project may be made members of the same group with a *groupname*. This allows each member *access* to the group's *files* without necessarily making them available to the public. (cf. *access mode*)

*group identifier* : A unique integer associated with each *groupname*.

*groupname* : A unique *identifier* assigned to each *group*. (cf. *username*)

*half duplex* : Transmission circuits which are capable of transmitting messages in both directions but not simultaneously. (cf. *full duplex*)

*hangup* : A special *signal* generated whenever a *user logs off* UNIX. This signal causes any *commands* or *programs* the user was *executing* to be terminated. (cf. **nice, nohup, sh**)

*hard copy* : *Computer output* that has been printed on paper or photographic film rather than being displayed on a *visual display unit*. Its advantage is that it is a permanent and portable record. (cf. *soft copy, line printer*)

*hard disk* : A *memory device* used for *storing files*. It consists of a set of rotating platters or disks which are coated with a magnetic recording compound. A set of moving heads allow *characters* to be *read* from or *written* onto selected portions of the disks. Typical storage capabilities range from 10 *megabytes* to over 500 megabytes. (cf. *backup, crash*, **df**) *hardware* : The collective name given to the electronic and electro-mechanical *devices* that go together to make a *computer* as opposed to the collection of *programs* that make the computer perform various *tasks*. (cf. *software*)

*hardware configuration* : For a particular *computer*, the configuration describes what *hardware* components are included in the the the *machine* e.g. which *CPU* and how many, how much high speed *memory* and how much *disk storage*, how many *magnetic tape* units and the number and type of other *peripheral devices*.

**head** [ −n ] [ *file* ... ]
    A 4.2 *command* which *writes* the first *n lines* of the specified *file* on *standard output*. The *default* value of *n* is 10.

*here document* : The *shell metacharacter* << followed by a *character string* causes subsequent *lines* in a *shell procedure* up to but not including a line consisting only of the specified string to be *read* as *standard input*.

*hexadecimal system* : A number system using the 16 digits, 0−9 and A−F in contrast with the decimal system which uses 10 digits from 0 to 9. The hexadecimal *characters* A to F represent the decimal numbers 10 to 15 respectively. Each hexadecimal digit is normally represented by 4 *binary* digits.

*high level language* : *Programming* languages which are much more akin to natural languages and mathematics than are the languages understood directly by *computers*. Consequently, they are easier for people to use and the resulting *programs* are less likely to contain residual *errors*. The high level languages referred to in this book are *Pascal*, *FORTRAN* and *C*. The *command language* processed by the *shell* also provides a form of high level language. (cf. *assembler*, *compiler*)

*high level object* : The *editor* **vi** provides facilities for *searching* through a *file* for a *character*, a *word*, a *line* and various high level objects such as sentences and paragraphs.

**history** : A *C-shell variable* which can be set to an integer value to determine the number of previous *commands* to be remembered in the *history event list*.

**history** [ −r ] [ *n* ]
    A *C-shell command* which displays the *history event list*. If *n* is supplied, only the most recent *n* events are displayed. The −r *flag* reverses the order of the printout.

*history event list* : A list of previously *executed command lines* which is remembered by *C-shell*. The length of the list is determined by the value of the *variable* history.

**HOME** : The *shell variable* which contains the *full pathname* of a *user's home directory*. It is the *default argument* for the **cd** *command*.

*home directory* : A *user's* initial *current directory*, that is, the directory in which the user is placed immediately after *login* (cf. **cd**, **pwd**)

**id**

A V.2 *command* which *writes user* and *group identifier* on *standard output* together with the corresponding names of the invoking *process*.

*identifier* : A name or number used to reference an item of *data*. (cf. *group identifier*, *process identifier*, *user identifier*)

*idle* : After a *process* in 4.2 has been *sleeping* for more than about 20 secs., its *status* is changed to idle.

IFS : The *shell variable* containing the *internal field separators*, normally *space*, *tab* and *newline*.

**ignoreeof** : A *C-shell variable* which, if set, causes the shell to ignore an *end-of-file signal* from a *terminal*, thereby preventing it from being *killed* accidentally.

*index node* : A record kept by the UNIX *file system* about a *file*. Each file has exactly one index node which specifies its size, location on *disk*, *owner*, *access mode* and other attributes. (cf. *directory*, *link*, **ls**)

*i-node* : A shortened form of *index node*.

*i-node number* : An integer that enables the *system* to locate a particular *i-node*.

*input* : see *input-output*

*input-output* : *Data* supplied to a *program* for processing is called *input* data; *results* produced by a program are referred to as *output* data. (cf. *peripheral device*)

*insert* : To insert *lines* into a *file* means to place them before the *current line*; similarly, *characters* are inserted into a line by placing them before the current position of the *cursor*. (cf. *append*)

*instruction* : A *machine* instruction usually consists of an *operation code* specifying what function the machine is to carry out and a number of *addresses* which specify the addresses or values of the *operands*.

*interactive system* : A system designed to carry out a dialogue with a *user* is said to be interactive. UNIX is such a system since it *reads commands* from a *terminal* and then *executes* them immediately in the *foreground*. **ed** and **vi** are interactive *text editors* since they obey commands and report the *results* to the user immediately. (cf. *batch processing*)

*internal field separator* : After *parameter* and *command substitution* have been carried out for a *command line*, the *shell* scans the line and breaks it into a number of distinct *arguments* according to the internal field separator *characters* defined in the *variable* IFS. The *default* separators are *space*, *tab* and *newline*.

*interpreter* : A *program* that directly *executes* another program or a set of *commands*. This is in contrast to a *compiler* which translates the program into a form that can then be executed either by the *computer* itself or by an interpreter. (cf. *assembler*, **px**, **sh**)

*interrupt* : A special *signal* that can be sent to an *executing program* or *command* to cause it to *abort*. For example, a command that is producing voluminous quantities of unwanted *output* can be interrupted and hence terminated. This is usually done by pressing the **RUBOUT** or **DELETE** key on a *terminal*. (cf. *hangup*)

*I/O* : A shortened form of *input-output*

*job* : A unit of work on a *computer* consisting of one or more *commands* which may be *executed* in either the *foreground* or the *background*. (cf. *process*, **bg**, **fg**, **jobs**, **kill**, **ps**, **shl**)

*jobname* : An *argument* in *C-shell* to **bg**, **fg**, **kill** and **stop**. It consists of **%** followed by + (*current job*), − (*previous job*), an integer job number or the prefix *string* of the *command* used to start the job.

**jobs** [ −l ]

A *C-shell command* to print details of *suspended jobs* and those *executing* in the *background*. The −l *option* produces *process identifiers* in addition to the normal information.

**join** [ *options* ] *file1 file2*

A *relational database operator* which forms the join of the two relations specified by the *lines* in *file1* and *file2* which must be *sorted* on the *fields* on which they are to be joined. If *file1* is −, *standard input* is *read*. The combined *file*, in which each line consists of the common field followed by the rest of the line from *file1* and the rest of the line from *file2*, is *written* to *standard output*. The *default* input field *separators* are *space*, *tab* or *newline*. Multiple separators count as 1 and leading separators are ignored; the default output field separator is a space.

For full details about how the *command* works and the various *options* available, see Section 5.2. A summary of the options is as follows:

−**a** *n*     Produce a line for each unpairable line in the specified file, *n*, which may have a value of 1 or 2.

−**e** *str*    Replace empty output fields by specified *string str*.

−**j** *n*     Specify the field *n* as the one on which the join is to take place.

−**o** *list*   Select specified fields from *list* to form output line. Each element in the list has the form *n.m* where *n* is the file number and *m* is the field number.

−**t***c*      Define input field separator as the *character c*.

*keyboard* : An *input device* which generates a signal representing a *character* corresponding to the key that has been depressed.

**kill** [ *−signo* ] *PID* ...

Sends a terminate *signal* to a *process* whose *PID* is specified as an *argument*. This will normally kill processes that do not catch or ignore the signal. A specific signal may be sent by supplying a signal number *signo* preceded by a minus sign as an argument. **kill −9** is a sure kill and if sent to a *login shell* is equivalent to *logout*.

In 4.2, a *jobname* may also be specified as an argument instead of a *PID*. Also, **kill −1** will list the names of the signals which may be used instead of numbers.

*kill character* : A *character* which causes the current *input line* to be discarded. It usually has the *default* value of **@** or **^X**. It may be redefined using **stty** or **tset** (4.2 only).

*kilobyte* : 1024 *bytes* which is $2^{10}$ bytes but is frequently used to mean approximately 1000 bytes.

*language* : see *command language*, *programming language*.

**learn** [ *subject* [ *lesson* ] ]

Gives *computer aided instruction* on the use of UNIX, the *shell* and the *text editors*. Without any *arguments*, **learn** will ask questions to find out what the *user* wants to do. Some of these may be avoided by supplying a *subject* and a *lesson* as arguments. A reply of **bye** to any query terminates the *session* and **where** reports on the user's progress. **again** causes the text of a lesson to be redisplayed.

*lexicographic* : Dictionary order based on all *characters* in the underlying character set. (cf. *ASCII*)

*library* : A collection of public *files* containing subroutines already in *object module* form. These files are *searched* by the *loader* to resolve external references and routines extracted to be combined with modules generated from the *program* supplied by the *user* to produce an *executable* file.

*line* : A sequence of *characters* terminated by a *newline* which is generated by the **RETURN** key.

*line editor* : A type of *editor* that allows a *user* to locate *lines* in a *file* so that the *text* in the file may be *changed*. (cf. *screen editor*, **ed**, **ex**.)

*line printer* : An *output device* for printing *characters* on paper. The main differences between a line printer and other types of printers are its speed (60 to 1000 *lines* per minute) and its page size (132 columns by 66 lines per page). (cf. *terminal*, *VDU*) *linefeed* : A *control character* which causes the *cursor* to move to the next *line*. (cf. *newline*)

*link* : The connection between a *filename* and a *file* (in fact, its *i-node*). Any file may have multiple links to it from one or more filenames, possibly in different *directories*. A file will only be physically removed from the *file system* when the count of the number of links reaches 0. (cf. **ln**, **rm**)

**lint** [ *options* ] *file* ...

Checks *C programs* in *file* attempting to detect features which are likely to be *errors*, non-*portable* or wasteful of resources. It also checks type usage much more strictly than does the C *compiler*. *options* are used to suppress certain complaints and to alter the behaviour of the *command*.

**ln** *file1* [ *file2* ... ] *target*

Creates *links*. If *target* is a *file*, a link with that name is *created* in the *current directory* to *file1*. If *target* is a directory, one or more links are created in that directory to the specified files.

*loader* : A *program* which combines one or more *object modules* produced by *compilers* or *assemblers*, resolves external references and possibly *creates* an *executable* program.

*local machine* : The *computer* on which the *user logs on* initially.

*local mode* : see *online*, *offline*.

*log off* : see *logout*.

*log on* : see *login*.

*logical error* : These occur when a *program* contains incorrect *instructions* which perform some function other than what the programmer intended. The *computer* will do exactly as instructed and will produce incorrect *results*.

*logical operator* : One of the *operators* and, or and not which take the *boolean* values true and false as *operands*.

*logical product* : A synonym for the *logical operator* and.

*login* : The act of starting a UNIX *session*. Logging in (on) requires the *user* to give the *computer* a *username* and a *password* for identification purposes.

**login** [ *username* ]

Used to start a *terminal session* and to check that a *user* is authorized to access the UNIX *system*. It may also be invoked as a *command* during a session. The command *prompts* for *username* if one has not been supplied as an *argument* and for a *password* if one is required. During *input* of the password, echoing is turned off so that it is not displayed on the screen or printed on paper. After a successful login, various messages including *message of the day* may appear on the terminal.

*login identifier* : see **user identifier**.

*login name* : see **username**.

*login shell* : The shell with which a **user** is communicating immediately after login.

*logout* : Logging out (off) indicates to the **computer** that the **user** is finished and is done by typing an **end-of-file** (**control–D**) to the *login shell*.

**logout**
A **C-shell command** which terminates a *login shell*. It must be used instead of ˆ**D** if ignoreeof is set.

**lp** [ *options* ] [ *file ...* ]
**Spools** named **files** for printing by a **line printer**. If *file* is not specified or if – is supplied as an **argument**, **reading** takes place from **standard input**. *options* can be used to select a particular printer, specify the number of copies to be printed, whether to send a message to the **user** after the printing has taken place etc. For full details, see **lp(1)**.
A printing request may be removed from the queue and printing terminated by using the **cancel** *command*.

**lpr** [ *options* ] [ *file ...* ]
The 4.2 version of **lp**. For full details, see **lpr(1)**.
**lprm** may be used to remove requests from the **line printer spooling** queue and **lpq** to inspect it.

**ls** [ *options* ] [ *name ...* ]
Lists the contents of **directory arguments** and the names of **file** arguments. The **default** argument is the **current directory**. Output is **written** on **standard output** and, by default, is **sorted** alphabetically. In V.2, names are listed one per **line** unless a formatting **option** has been selected. The default behaviour in 4.2 is to produce output in columns to maximize the amount of information displayed on a screen.
There are a large number of options, some of which vary in behaviour between the two **systems**. Some of the more frequently used ones are shown below:

| | |
|---|---|
| –**a** | List all entries including names beginning with a period. |
| –**c** | Use time of last **modification** for **sorting** or printing. |
| –**C** | Produce multi-column output. |
| –**d** | List name of a directory rather than its contents. |
| –**F** | Put **/** after a directory name and **\*** after the name of an **executable file**. |
| –**g** | Include **group** of a file in a long listing (4.2). Same as –**l** except that the **owner** is not included (V.2). |
| –**i** | Output the **i-node number** for each file in a long listing. |

    −l      List in long format showing *mode*, *link* count, owner, group, size and time of last modification. (No group in 4.2).

    −r      Reverse the order of any sort.

    **−R**     *Recursively* list any *sub-directories*.

    −s      Give size of each file in *blocks* (V.2) or *kilobytes* (4.2).

    −t      Sort by time modified instead of by name.

    −u      Use time of last *access* for sorting or printing.

The first *character* of the 10-character mode printed by the −l option is **d** for a directory, **b** for a *block special file*, **c** for a character special file and − for an *ordinary file*. The remaining 3 groups of 3 characters each are the *permissions* for the owner of the file, for the group and for all *others* respectively. A permission not set is indicated by a −, otherwise, it is **r** for *read*, **w** for *write* and **x** for *execute* in that order.

*machine* : A *computer* is a *general purpose* machine which can perform a wide variety of complex *tasks* depending on the *program* of *instructions* supplied to it.

*machine code* : The basic *instructions* which can be *executed* directly by a *computer*.

*machine collating sequence* : Each *character* in the underlying character set is represented in the *machine* by a small positive integer, e.g. in *ASCII*, these lie in the range 0−127. The numeric ordering of these characters defines the machine collating sequence.

*magnetic disk* : see *hard disk*, *floppy disk*.

*magnetic tape* : see *tape*.

**MAIL** : The *shell variable* which, if set to the name of the *mailbox*, causes the shell to inform the *user* when new *mail* arrives.

**mail** : The *C-shell variable* which, if set to the name of the *mailbox*, causes the shell to inform the *user* when new *mail* arrives.

**Mail** [ *options* ] [ *username* ... ]

Provides a powerful, *interactive* facility for sending and receiving *mail* electronically in 4.2. **mail** is often a *link* to this *command* and /bin/mail must be used to activate the earlier version. For a description of how to use this command, see Section 5.4 "Managing Communications" and Appendix 6 "Mail and mailx Summary".

**mail** [ *options* ] [ *username* ... ]

If *username* is supplied as an *argument*, *standard input* is *read* up to *end-of-file* and the message is added to the *user's mailbox* preceded by the name of the sender and a postmark. If the −t *option* is used, the message is preceded by the names of all persons to whom the *mail* has been sent.

Mail may be sent to a user on a *remote machine* by preceding *username* by a *system name* and an exclamation mark. This procedure may be extended to allow mail to pass through a number of machines before it reaches its final destination.

If no *usernames* are mentioned, messages are read (if there are any) from the user's mailbox and presented to the user in a last-in first-out sequence. The user is *prompted* with a **?** after each message and responds with a *command* to tell the system what it is to do with the message. For a description of these commands, see Section 5.4 or simply respond to the query with **?** or **\*** which will cause a command summary to be printed. *options* which alter the way mail is printed are as follows:

| | |
|---|---|
| **−e** | Do not print mail. |
| **−f** *file* | Use *file* instead of the *default* mail file. |
| **−p** | Print all mail without prompting. |
| **−r** | Print mail on a first-in first-out basis. |

*Exit codes* are 0 if the user has mail and 1 if there is none.

*mailbox* : Incoming *mail* is *stored* in a standard *file* for each *user*. In 4.2, the name of a user's mailbox is */usr/spool/mail/username* while in System V.2 it is called */usr/mail/username*.

**mailx** [ *options* ] [ *username* ... ]

The System V.2 version of the Berkeley **Mail** *command*. For a description of how to use this command, see Section 5.4 "Managing Communications" and Appendix 6 "Mail and mailx Summary".

*mainframe* : Large *general purpose computers* capable of processing *instructions* at rates in excess of several *Mips*. Usually such *machines* incorporate a few *megabytes* of high speed *memory*, have access to some hundreds of megabytes of *disk* and are capable of supporting in excess of 100 simultaneously active *users*.

**man** [ *section* ] *title* ...

Print *manual* entries for specified *commands* on *standard output*. If an integer *section* is specified, only that section is examined; otherwise, all sections are *searched*.

*manage* : *Computers store* and process large amounts of data. *Software tools* are required to assist *users* in managing these operations. In UNIX, *commands* are available for the management of *files*, *data*, *jobs* and *communications*.

*manual* : The "UNIX User's Manual".

*megabyte* : 1,048,576 *bytes* which is $2^{20}$ bytes but is frequently used to mean approximately 1 million *bytes*.

*memory* : The general name given to all types of *hardware* that can be used for the *storage* and *retrieval* of information. Memory *devices* are divided into two main classes based on their usage. *Primary memory* is used for the storage of *programs* while they are being *executed*; it is relatively expensive but very fast with *access times* measured in *microseconds*. *Secondary memory*, on the other hand, which is used for the long-term storage of information in *files*, is relatively slower and less expensive than primary memory. Typically, it is *magnetic disk* or *tape*. Access times are measured in *milliseconds* for the former and seconds or even minutes for the latter.

*merge* : Combine two or more *input files* ordered in the same way such that the resultant *output* file is similarly ordered. In UNIX, merging is performed with **sort** using the –m *option*.

**mesg** [ **n** ] [ **y** ]

With an *argument* **n**, prevents messages being sent to the *user's terminal* via **write**. If used with **y**, *permission* is set to accept such messages. If used without arguments, the current status is reported on *standard output*.

*message of the day* : This message is *output* after a *user* has *logged in* successfully. It is *stored* in */etc/motd* and is changed from time to time by the *system administrator*.

*metacharacter* : A *character* used to represent something other than itself. For example, metacharacters are used in *patterns* to represent such things as the beginning or the end of a *line* of *text*. The UNIX User's Manual uses the metacharacters [ and ] to denote *optional arguments* when describing *commands*. The meaning of a metacharacter may change depending on its context. Thus, an asterisk matches zero or more occurrences of the preceding character when used in a *regular expression* in **ed**, **vi** or **grep**. However, in a *command line*, it is interpreted by the *shell* as matching zero or more characters in a *filename*.

*microcomputer* : A small *computer system* which incorporates a *microprocessor* as the *CPU*. Typically, a microcomputer will support only one *user* at a time although some can service a few users simultaneously. Providing there is sufficient high speed *memory* and a *hard disk*, UNIX will *run* on a 16-*bit* or 32-bit microcomputer.

*microprocessor* : A *central processing unit* built on a single chip of silicon. Typical processing speeds are of the order of .5 *Mips*. 8-*bit* and 16-bit microprocessors are commonplace today and 32-bit microprocessors are now becoming available.

*microsecond* : 1 millionth of a second, $10^{-6}$ sec.

*millisecond* : 1 thousandth of a second, $10^{-3}$ sec.

*minicomputer* : A small-to-medium sized *computer system*. They are usually 16-*bit* or 32-bit *machines* with a few *megabytes* of high speed *memory* and some tens of megabytes of *hard disk*. Typically, they will support 10–50 simultaneously active *users*. UNIX is available on a wide variety of minicomputers from many different manufacturers.

*Mips* : An acronym for millions of *instructions* per second. It is a measure of the rate at which a *computer* can *execute* instructions.

mkdir *file*

>*Creates directories* with a *default mode* which is the *logical product* of 777 and the *file creation mask*. The latter may be set or inspected using **umask**.

*modification* : A *file* is said to have been modified if some alteration has been made to information *stored* in its *i-node* e.g. the setting of new *permissions*. (cf. *change*)

MORE : The *C-shell environment variable* in which *flags* may be preset to control the operation of the **more** *command*.

more [ *options* ] [ +*n* ] [ +/*re* ] [ *file* ... ]

>A 4.2 *file* perusal *filter* which prints *text* files one screenful at a time on *standard output*. If *file* is not specified, *standard input* is *read*. Output is paused at the end of each screenful and will only be resumed when the *user* issues a *command*. A *space* causes the next screenful to be displayed while a *newline* adds the next *line* to the current screen. **q** may be used to exit and **h** to print a description of all the commands available. The most useful of these are **d** to *scroll* down half a screen, *n***s** to skip *n* lines, *n***f** to skip *n* screenfuls and *n*/*re* to *search* for the *n*th occurrence of the *regular expression re*. In each case, a screenful of information is displayed at the new position.
>
>If +*n* is supplied as an *argument*, the first screen displayed commences at line *n*; in the case of +/*re*, the first display commences 2 lines before the line containing the regular expression *re*.
>
>Some of the *options* which may be specified on the command line are:
>
>>−c    Draw each new *page* from the top of the screen rather than by scrolling.
>>
>>−d    *Prompt* the user with the message "Hit space to continue, Rubout to abort" at the end of each screenful.
>>
>>−s    Squeeze multiple *blank* lines into a single blank line.
>
>The *environment variable* MORE may be used to hold any *flags* that the user desires to preset. (cf. **pg**)

*multiprogramming* : A mechanism which allows a *computer* to *execute* several *programs* apparently concurrently. This is done by switching the *CPU* between the programs. This is possible because of the rapid speed at which a computer can operate and the fact that programs often have to wait for some information to become available before they can proceed with a computation.

When a program is held up waiting for an *I/O* transfer to terminate, another program can be allocated the CPU.

*multiuser* : A property of an *operating system* that enables it to process requests from more than one *user* apparently simultaneously.

**mv** *file1* [ *file2* ... ] *target*

Moves or renames *files*. If *target* is a file, *file1* is renamed as *target*. If *target* is a *directory*, one or more files are moved from their existing directory to the new one retaining their current *filenames*. In V.2, the first *argument* may be a directory name in which case it is given the name supplied as the second argument.

*nanosecond* : 1 thousand-millionth of a second, $10^{-9}$ sec.

*newline* : A *control character* used by UNIX to mark the end of a *line* of *text*. It is usually generated by striking the **RETURN** key.

**news** [ *options* ] [ *items* ]

Prints news items in V.2 on *standard output*. If no *items* are specified, all items in */usr/news* with a *modification* date later than that of *news_time* in the *user's home directory* are listed with the most recent first. *news_time* is then modified to record the current date. If *items* are supplied as *arguments*, those news items are printed.

The available *options* are:

-**a**   Print all news items whether current or not.

-**n**   Print names of current news items.

-**s**   Print number of current items.

In each of the above cases, the current date is not changed. (cf. **readnews**)

*newsgroup* : A collection of news articles relating to the same area of interest. (cf. **postnews**, **readnews**)

*news_time* : A *file* used to remember the last time news was *read* with the **news** *command*.

**nice** [ *-number* ] *command* [ *arguments* ]

Runs *command* at low *priority* under **sh**. *number* in the range 1—19 is used to increment the "niceness" number, otherwise 10 is assumed as the *default*. The higher the "niceness", the lower the priority of the *command*.

The command also exists in the *C-shell* but takes an *argument* of the form +*number* as an increment.

**nohup** *command* [ *arguments* ]

*Execute command* under **sh** ignoring *hangup* and *quit signals*. Both *standard output* and *standard error output* are sent to the *file nohup.out* if not already *redirected* by the *user*. To *run* a *pipeline* or sequence of *commands* immune from hangups, it is necessary to place them in a file and then execute the file as a *shell script* under **nohup**.

Note that it is necessary to use this command to ensure that *background jobs* will continue to execute after a user has *logged out* from **sh**. It is not required for background jobs in **csh**.

*nohup.out* : A *file created* by the *system* to receive *standard output* and *standard error output* from a *command run* in the *background* under the control of **nohup** if output was not *redirected* by the *user*.

*non-volatile* : A *memory* that retains information even when the power has been turned off. Examples include *magnetic disk* and *tape* as well as some forms of *primary memory*.

*number system* : see *binary system, hexadecimal system, octal system*.

*obj* : The *default filename* for the *file* produced by **pi**. It is also the default *argument* to **px**.

*object* : Some *commands* in **vi** are composed of an *operator* and an object on which it operates. For example, **dw**, which *deletes* the next *word*, consists of an operator **d** and an object **w**. (cf. *high level object*)

*object code* : The *executable instructions* produced by a *compiler* or *assembler*.

*object file* : A *file* containing an *object module*.

*object module* : *Machine code instructions* and other *data* in *binary* generated by a *compiler* or *assembler*. Before it can be *executed*, it needs to be processed by the *loader*.

*octal system* : A number system using the eight digits, 0—7 in contrast with the decimal system which uses ten digits from 0 to 9. Each octal digit represents 3 *binary* digits.

**od** [ *options* ] [ *file* ] [ *offset* ]
Dumps *file* or *standard input* in a format selected by *options* which have the following meanings:

   **−b**    *Bytes* as unsigned *octal*.

   **−c**    Bytes as *ASCII characters* with some non-printable characters appearing as *C escapes* and the remainder as 3-digit octal numbers.

   **−d**    *Words* as unsigned decimal.

   **−i**    Short words in signed decimal (4.2).

   **−o**    Words as unsigned octal.

   **−s**    Short words in signed decimal (V.2).

   **−x**    Words in *hexadecimal*.

The *default* format is **−o**. The offset is an *optional* + (mandatory if standard input is being *read*) followed by an octal integer which specifies the byte at which dumping is to start. A decimal integer may be specified by terminating it with a period. If **b** is *appended*, the offset is taken as a number of 512 byte *blocks* (**B** for 1024 byte blocks in 4.2).

*offline* : An *input-output device* is said to be in this state if it is not currently capable of *communicating* with a *computer*. (cf. *online*)

*online* : An *input-output device* is said to be in this state if it is currently capable of *communicating* with a *computer*. One can usually see the *online/offline* switch on many input-output devices. For *terminals*, online is often referred to as *connect mode* and offline as *local mode*. *Executing* a *program* online means *running* it *interactively* from a terminal which is connected to a computer. (cf. *timesharing*)

*opcode* : Shorthand for *operation code*.

*operand* : A value acted on by an *operator*.

*operating system* : A *systems program* responsible for controlling the utilization of the resources of a *computer*. It does this primarily by dividing up and sharing the limited amounts of *memory* and computational power of the *machine* amongst a number of *users* in an equitable fashion. It may also provide such facilities as *timesharing* and the protection of each user's programs and *files* from accidental or malicious tampering by others.

*operation code* : The portion of a *machine instruction* which specifies what action the *computer* is to perform.

*operator* : A *symbol* defining the action to be performed on one or more *operands* to obtain a *result*.

*optimizer* : A *compiler* or *assembler* phase which attempts to improve the efficiency of the generated *code* with respect to both *execution* efficiency and *memory* occupancy.

*option* : A mode of operation of a *command* which differs from its *default* behaviour. Options are selected by including *flags* (usually preceded by a minus sign) as the first *argument*.

*optional argument* : An *argument* that does not have to be specified for a particular *command*. If not given, the command usually assumes some *default* value.

*ordinary file* : A UNIX *file* which contains *character* or *binary* information. (cf. *directory*, *special file*)

*others* : The authorized *users* of a particular *system* other than the *owner* of a *file* and those users who have *group access* to a file.

*output* : see *input-output*.

*owner* : The authorized *user* who *created* and hence owns a *file*.

**pack** [ −f ] *file* ...

Attempts to compress specified *files* in V.2 to save *disk* space. The compressed file is given the name *file.z* and replaces the original one. Typical savings are 25–40% for *character* files but only perhaps 10% for *binary* files. The −f *option* forces the packing to take place even if the savings are small and is useful for packing all the files in a *directory*. Packed files can be *restored* with their original contents using **unpack** or **pcat**.

The 4.2 equivalents of these *commands* are **compact**, **uncompact** and **ccat**.

*page* : To page through a *file* means to display a screenful of *characters* at a time. When a new page is selected, the screen is rewritten. (cf. **more**, **pg**)

In *virtual memory* systems, a page is a unit of *memory* allocation and paging refers to the transfer of pages between *primary* and *secondary memory*.

*paper tape* : Punched paper tape has been used as an *input–output* medium since *computers* were first invented. The holes in the tape are detected photoelectrically and *reading* speeds of 1000 *characters*/sec. are achievable.

*parameter* : see *argument*.

*parameter substitution* : The *character string* $ followed by a digit is replaced in a *command line* by the value of the corresponding *positional parameter*. (cf. *quote*, *command substitution*)

*parent directory* : A directory is the parent of any *sub-directories* it contains.

*parent process* : A *process* is *created* by another process which is called its parent. (cf. *child process*)

*Pascal* : A *high level language* which is well suited to the writing of *structured programs*. It is widely used as an introductory programming language. (cf. **pc**, **pi**, **px**, **pix**).

**passwd**

*Changes password* for the *user*. The *command prompts* for the old password if one exists and then for the new one twice. If the former is invalid or the two instances of the latter do not agree, the new password is rejected. It will also not be accepted if it does not conform to certain construction rules.

*password* : Each authorized *user* of a UNIX *system* has a private password which must be supplied before any use of the *computer* can be made under a given *username*. It must be longer than 6 *characters* and contain at least 2 alphabetic characters and at least 1 numeric or special character. It should be changed from time to time just in case someone else has "accidentally" discovered it. A new password must differ from the old one by at least 3 characters. (cf. **passwd**)

PATH : The *shell variable* containing the *search path* for *commands*.

*pathname* : The UNIX *file system* is organized as a *tree* of *directories*. Therefore, to name a particular *file* to be *accessed*, it is necessary to specify the sequence of directories that must be passed through to reach the file. This list of names separated by slashes is called a pathname since it gives the path to be followed to find some file. As with any path, there must be a starting point. The simplest instance is when the path begins in the *user's current directory*. In this case, it is called a *relative pathname*.

In all cases, to be able to access the specified file, it is necessary to have *execute permission* to the directories along the path. (cf. *access mode*, *full pathname*, **chmod**, **ls**, **pwd**)

*pattern* : There are several UNIX *commands* that can *search* through *text* for the occurrence of certain sequences of *characters* within the text. Patterns may include *metacharacters* to construct more complicated patterns than just a simple *string*. (cf. *regular expression*, **ed**, **vi**, **grep**)

**pc** [ *options* ] *file ...*

The Berkeley *Pascal compiler* which *reads argument files* with *suffix* .c and .p, compiles them and *creates* an *executable file* with the *default* name *a.out*.

There are many *options* available with **pc**, some of which are described below:

| | |
|---|---|
| −C | Compile code to perform *run time* checks and initialize all *variables* to 0. |
| −c | Suppress the *loading* phase and force production of an *object file* even if only one *program* is compiled. |
| −g | Generate additional *symbol table* information for a *symbolic debugger*. |
| −i | Produce a listing for the specified procedure, function or include file whose name follows. |
| −l | Produce a program listing. |
| −O | Invoke an *object code optimizer*. |
| −o *file* | Name the object file *file* instead of *a.out*. |
| −s | Produce warning messages for non-standard Pascal constructs. |

**pcat** *name ...*

Unpacks specified *files* and *writes* them to *standard output*.

*peripheral device* : An *input-output* device which operates under the control of a *computer*. (cf. *disk*, *line printer*, *tape*, *terminal*)

*permanent file* : One that remains in the *file system* after a *user* has *logged out*. It can only be *deleted* by using **rm**.

*permission* : see *access mode*.

*personal computer* : A *microcomputer* which will only support one *user* at a time is often called a personal computer.

**pg** [ *options* ] [ *+n* ] [ *+/re/* ] [ *file* ... ]

A V.2 *file* perusal *filter* which prints *text* files one screenful at a time on *standard output*. If no *file* is specified, *standard input* is *read*. Output is paused at the end of each screenful and will only be resumed when the *user* issues a *command* in response to a *prompt*. A *space* or *newline* causes the next screenful to be displayed while **l** adds the next *line* to the current screen. **q** may be used to exit and **h** to print a description of all the commands available. The most useful of these are **d** or **–d** to *scroll* down or up half a screen, *n***l** to skip to the *n*th line, *±n***l** to scroll forwards or backwards the number of lines specified, *n***f** to skip *n* screenfuls and *n/re* to *search* forwards for the *n*th occurrence of the *regular expression re*. If **?** is used in the last command instead of **/**, the search is carried out backwards. In each case, a screenful of information is displayed at the new position.

If *+n* is supplied as an *argument*, the first screen displayed commences at line *n*; in the case of *+/re/*, the first display commences at the line containing the regular expression *re*.

Some of the *options* which may be specified on the *command line* are:

|  |  |
|---|---|
| **–c** | Draw each new *page* from the top of the screen rather than by scrolling. |
| **–p** *str* | Prompt the user with the *string* *str* at the end of each screenful instead of the *default* :. |
| **–s** | Print all messages and prompts in high-lighted mode |

(cf. **more**)

**pi** [ *options* ] *name*.**p**

The Berkeley *Pascal interpreter* code translator which translates a *program* in a *file* with a *suffix* .*p* and produces a file *obj* in the *current directory*. The *interpretive code* may then be *executed* with **px**.

Some of the *options* available are as follows:

|  |  |
|---|---|
| **–i** | Produce a listing for the specified procedure, function or include file whose name follows. |
| **–l** | Produce a program listing. |
| **–n** | Begin each listed include file on a new page. |
| **–p** | Suppress *output* by **px** of number of *statements* executed and total execution time. |
| **–s** | Produce warning messages for non-standard Pascal constructs. |

For a basic explanation of **pi**, execute the *command* without any *arguments*. *Syntactic errors* are flagged in the listing indicating the point at which the error was detected. Diagnostics for *semantic errors* specify a *source text line* near the point of the error. The first *character* of each error message has the following significance:

|   |   |
|---|---|
| **E** | Error is fatal and no *code* will be generated. |
| **e** | A non-fatal error. |
| **s** | A warning that non-standard Pascal has been used. |
| **w** | A warning about a possible problem. |

*PID* : An acronym for *process identifier*.

*pipe* : One of the novel features of UNIX is the pipe. This is a mechanism which enables the *output* of one *command* to be used as the *input* of another concurrently *executing* command. The *shell* provides a notation for piping the output from one to the other.

*pipeline* : A *command* sequence which contains two or more commands connected by *pipes* is called a *pipeline*. (cf. *filter*)

**pix** [ *options* ] *name*.**p** [ *args* ]
Combines the functions of the *Pascal* translator **pi** and the executor **px** into a load-and-go *system*. The *file* with .*p suffix* is translated and, if there are no fatal *errors*, the resulting *interpretive code* in a temporary file is *executed* with the specified *arguments*. The *options* available are the same as those for **pi**.

*pointer* : A pointer to a *variable* is simply the *address* of the *memory* location that has been allocated to that variable. The *C* language supports pointers and pointer arithmetic.

*portable* : This is a property of *software* that enables it to be moved from one *computer* environment to another at a cost far less than would be required to create it anew in the different environment. UNIX is an example of a portable *operating system* since about 95% of it is written in *C*. For this reason, it is available on a wide variety of *machines* from many different manufacturers.

*positional parameters* : *Variables* which hold the *arguments* supplied to a *shell procedure*. They can be referenced in a *command line* by $n where n is 0-9. $0 is set to the name of the *file* containing the shell procedure.

**postnews**
Enables a *user* to submit news articles. It will *prompt* for a title of the article, for a *newsgroup* (*default* is "general") and for the distribution (default is the newsgroup). After this information has been supplied, the user is placed in an *editor* (default is **vi**). Various headers are *created* automatically and the article can then be *appended* to the *buffer*. When *exit* occurs from the editor, the news article will be posted.

**pr** [ *options* ] [ *files* ]
Produces a printed listing of the specified *files* on *standard output*. If *files* are not specified or if *file* is −, standard output is *read*. The listing is separated into *pages*, each of which has a header consisting of a page number, a date and

time, and the name of the file.

Some of the *options* available are as follows:

+*n*     Begin printing at page *n* rather than the *default* 1.

−*n*     Produce *n*-column output rather than the default single column.

−**d**     Double space the output (V.2).

−**h**     Use the next *argument* as a page header rather than the name of the file.

−l*n*     Use the integer *n* as the number of *lines* in the page rather than the default 66.

−**m**     Print all *argument* files simultaneously, one per column.

−**s**     Use *tab* instead of the appropriate number of *spaces* to separate columns.

−**t**     Suppress the printing of headers or trailers.

−**w***n*     Use the integer *n* as the number of *characters* in a line rather than the default 72.

While **pr** is *writing* on a *terminal*, it is impossible for other *users* to send messages to that terminal.

*prepend* : Add *characters* before the first character of a *string* or *lines* before the first line in a *file*. (cf. *append*)

*previous job* : The last but one *job* initiated by the *C-shell*. It can be referenced by the *jobname* **%−**.

*primary memory* : see *memory*

**printenv** [ *name* ... ]

A 4.2 *command* which prints the value of an *environment variable name*. In the absence of any *arguments*, it *outputs* the names and values of all environment variables.

*printer* : An *output peripheral device* which *writes characters* on *hard copy*. *Line printers* print one line at a time and reach speeds as high as 1000 lines/min.; other printers which only print one character at a time can operate at speeds up to 200 characters/sec.; laser printers produce a whole page of information at a time and vary in speed from 8 pages/min. to 100 pages/min.

*priority* : The priority of a *process* determines how the *CPU* will be allocated to it. Thus, a low priority process might only be given the CPU when higher priority processes are held up *waiting* for *I/O* transfers to terminate. In this way, the *operating system* attempts to maintain an acceptable *response time* for *interactive jobs* and ensure that short jobs not requiring large amounts of *machine* resources are completed before longer ones.

*procedure* : A named sequence of *statements* in a *high level language program* which can be activated simply by stating its name and supplying *arguments* if required.

*process* : An *executing program*. In UNIX, every currently active *command* has an associated process. After a *user logs on*, a process is *created* to execute the *shell* so that the user may enter commands. A command process is the *child* of its *parent process*, the shell. Most UNIX *systems* impose a limit on the number of processes that a user can have at any one time. (cf. *asynchronous*, **ps**, **kill**)

*process identifier* : When a *process* is *created*, it is assigned a unique integer called the process identifier (*PID*). This can be used to reference the process in various *commands*. (cf. **ps**, **kill**)

*program* : To make a *computer* solve a problem, it is necessary to give it a series of *instructions* called a program. These programs are written in *programming languages*, of which there are several hundred. However, before a program can be *executed* by the computer, it must be translated into *machine code* that the *hardware* can obey.

Designing and writing a program is called "programming". (cf. *compile*, *assemble*, *process*)

*programming language* : An artificial language used for writing *computer programs*. (cf. *assembly language*, *high level language*)

*prompt* : A sequence of one or more *characters* printed by a *program* to indicate that the *user* should enter some information. For example, the *Bourne shell* normally prints a $ to indicate that it is ready to *execute* a *command*. The *C-shell* usually uses a % for this purpose.

**prompt** : The *C-shell variable* containing the *prompt string*, by *default* %.

**ps** [ *options* ]

Prints information about active *processes* on *standard output*. There are many *options*, some of which control the format of the output which is different in certain respects between the two *systems*, V.2 and 4.2. The items common to all formats are the *process identifier* (*PID*), the controlling *terminal* number (TTY in V.2 or TT in 4.2), the cumulative *CPU* time used by the process (TIME), the state of the process (S in V.2 or STAT in 4.2) and the *command* which is *running* (CMD in V.2 or COMMAND in 4.2). This information is printed about processes associated with the current *terminal* if the command is used without *arguments*. Some of the *options* available are as follows:

　　**−a**　　Print information about processes with terminals (excludes process group leaders in V.2).

　　**−d**　　Print information about all processes except process group leaders (V.2).

-e     Print information about all processes (V.2); print the *environment* (4.2).

-g     Print information about all processes (4.2); only print information about processes whose group leaders are given in the *file* whose name follows the option (V.2).

-l     Generate a long listing.

For a complete description of this command, see **ps(1)**.

**PS1** : The *shell variable* containing the primary *prompt string*, by *default* $.

**PS2** : The *shell variable* containing the secondary *prompt string*, by *default* >.

*punched card* : A rectangular card containing holes to represent information which was used extensively for the *input* of *programs* and *data* prior to the development of *interactive timesharing systems*.

**pwd**
Prints the *pathname* of the *working directory*. (cf. **cd**)

**px** [ *object* [ *args* ] ]
Execute the *interpretive code* generated by **pi**. The first *argument* is the name of the *file* containing that code and *defaults* to *obj*. The arguments can be accessed by the *Pascal program* using argv and argc.

The −p *option* of **pi** suppresses the *output* of the number of *statements executed* and the total execution time which are printed after normal termination. If the program terminates abnormally, an *error* message and an indication of where the error occurred are printed.

*quit* : Transfer control from the currently *executing process* to its *parent process*.

**quota**
Prints *user's disk* usage and limits (4.2).

*quote* : A sequence of *characters* enclosed in single quotes ( '' ) in a *command line* is not processed in any way by the *shell*. Instead, it is simply passed as an *argument* to the command. If double quotes (" ") are used instead of single quotes, *parameter* and *command substitution* are performed but no expansion of *metacharacters* takes place. (cf. *escape*)

*random access* : A type of *storage device* that provides a constant or almost constant *access time* to any item of *data* stored on the device. (cf. *disk*, *sequential access*)

*read* : The *input* of *data* to a *program* from an external *peripheral device*.

**read** [ *name* ... ]
*Read* one *line* from *standard input* and assign the first *word* to the first *name*, the second word to the second *name* etc. All the remaining words are assigned to the last name.

*read only* : A *file* or *variable* which cannot be *changed.* (cf. **readonly**)

*read permission* : For a *file*, read permission on means that the file may be *read.* This implies that it can be copied or its contents used as *input data* to a *program.*
If read permission is set on for a *directory*, the contents of the directory may be listed. (cf. **ls**)

*read-ahead* : UNIX allows a *user* to type in *characters* at a *terminal* at any time, even when not explicitly requested to do so. This facility is called read-ahead. These characters will be saved and used for any later requests for *input.* This means, for example, that it is not necessary to wait for a *program* like the *shell* or an *editor* to *prompt* for a *command* before typing it in. (cf. *full duplex*)

**readnews** [ *options* ]
Enables a *user* to read news articles. A record of the articles **read** is kept in .*newsrc* in the user's *home directory.* If no *arguments* are supplied, the *command* prints headers of unread articles and *prompts* the user for the subsequent course of action. Some of the possible responses and their effects are as follows:

| | |
|---|---|
| c | Cancel the article (author or *superuser* only). |
| d | Break up a digest into separate articles. |
| D | *Decrypt* an *encrypted* article. |
| e | Forget that the article was read. |
| f | Submit a follow up article. |
| n | Go to next article without printing current one. |
| N [*newsgroup*] | Go to specified *newsgroup* (*default* is the next one). |
| q | Quit after updating record of articles read. |
| r | Reply to the article's author by *mail.* |
| s | Save article by *appending* it to specified *file* (default is *Articles*). |
| U | Unsubscribe from this newsgroup and go to the next one. |
| x | *Exit* without updating record of articles read. |
| y | Print current article and go to the next one. |
| +[*n*] | Skip *n* articles leaving them marked as unread (default is 1). |
| − | Return to last article. |
| # | Report the name and size of the newsgroup. |
| ! | Escape to *shell.* |
| *number* | Go to *number.* |

Some of the *options* available in the command are as follows:

| | |
|---|---|
| **−a** [*date*] | Select all articles posted later than the given date. |
| **−l** | List the titles only. |
| **−n** *newsgroups* | Select all articles belonging to specified newsgroups. |
| **−p** | **Write** all selected articles on **standard output** without prompting the user. |
| **−r** | Print the selected articles in reverse order. |
| **−s** | Print the newsgroup subscription list. |
| **−t** *titles* | Select only articles with titles containing a **string** specified in *titles*. |
| **−x** | Ignore *.newsrc* and select previously read articles as well as new ones. |

A user can choose to specify options in the first *line* of *.newsrc* following the left justified keyword **options**. These are overridden by any options supplied as part of the command line.

**readonly** [ *name* ... ]
Marks *name* so that the value of the **shell variable** cannot be changed by assignment.

**ready-to-run status** : This status means that a **process** is **runnable**, that is, could be allocated to the **CPU**.

**real time** : A type of **computer system** in which the processing of **input data** and the generation of **output** occur virtually simultaneously with the event that generated the input. Examples of real time systems are airline reservation and process control systems. **Timesharing** systems also exhibit some real time behaviour since the **response time** to **users** must not be allowed to increase to an unacceptable level.

**recursive** : Recursion is a technique for describing something partly in terms of itself. A recursive **procedure** or **command** is one that contains within itself a call on itself. Thus, if **ls** is used recursively, it will list the contents of any **sub-directories** in the **directory** being listed and the contents of any sub-sub-directories in a sub-directory and so on.

**redirection** : A facility provided by the **shell** which enables **standard input** to be **read** from a **file** or **standard output** and **standard error output** to be **written** to a file.

**regular expression** : A rule for generating a set of **character strings**. In **ed**, **ex** and **grep**, a regular expression is used to locate **lines** containing any member of the set.

**rehash**
A **C-shell command** which determines the whereabouts of **files** in **directories** in the **search path** so that they may be **accessed** rapidly. **Users** need to issue

this command if they add a new command to a directory in the search path while *logged in*.

*relational database* : A database in which *data* can be viewed as being organized into two-dimensional tables.

*relative pathname* : see *pathname*

*remote machine* : A *computer system* other than the *local machine*. (cf. **mail**, **uucp**, **uuname**).

*response time* : In a *timesharing system*, a measure of how rapidly the *computer* can respond to simple requests from *users*. Acceptable response times are of the order of a few seconds; if much longer, it means that the system is overloaded and that there are too many users making heavier demands on *machine* resources than the computer can satisfy.

*restore* : The inverse process to *archiving*. It implies recovering *files* from some other *storage* medium or format and returning them to the *file system*. (cf. **ar**, **tar**)

*result* : Commonly used to describe the *output* of a *program*. It may be information displayed on a *VDU*, printed on a *line printer* or *stored* in a *file*. It is also the value obtained by applying an *operator* to one or more *operands*.

*retrieve* : *Computer systems* are often used for information retrieval, that is, the location in a large *database* of an item of information which satisfies some particular criterion. In UNIX, the **grep** family of *commands* provides an elementary facility for the retrieval of information.

**rm** [ –fir ] *file* ...

Removes *directory* entry for the specified *file*. If the *link* count becomes 0, the *file* is destroyed and the space it occupies is returned to the *system*. To remove a file requires the *user* to have *write permission* in its directory. A directory will only be removed if –r has been specified.

The meanings of the *options* are as follows:

-f    Force the removal even if the file is write protected i.e. *read* only.

-i    Ask about each file and only remove it if the user responds **y**.

-r    Removes files and directories *recursively*.

**rmdir** *name* ...

Removes entry for the named *directory* which must be empty.

*root* : The base *directory* of the *file system* which is designated by a slash (/). It is also the *username* of the *superuser*.

*run* : see *execute*.

*run time* : The period of time during which a *program* is being *executed*.

*run time errors* : Errors which occur when a *program* is *executing*. They may be *logical errors* or *semantic errors*. (cf. *syntactic error*)

*running status* : When a *process* is allocated the *CPU*, its status changes from *ready-to-run* to running.

*screen editor* : A type of *editor* which displays a screenful of *text* at a time and provides the *user* with *commands* for moving the *cursor* around in the *page* and selecting new pages. (cf. *line editor*, **vi**)

*scroll* : The movement of *lines* of *text* on the screen of a *VDU*. Once the screen is full, the addition of further lines causes those at the top of the screen to be scrolled up and off the screen. A *screen editor* will include facilities for scrolling up or down through a *file*. (cf. *page*, **vi**)

*search* : Many *commands* in UNIX perform searches through *files* and *directories*. The *shell* searches through a sequence of directories looking for a *command* to *execute*; **login** searches the *password* file to check that the *username* and *password* are valid; the *editors* provide facilities for searching through a file looking for *lines* that match *patterns*; a member of the **grep** family of commands can be used to search through a number of files in sequence. (cf. *retrieve*)

*search path* : The sequence of *directories* searched by the *shell* to locate a *command* to *execute*. It is *stored* in the *shell variable* PATH.

*secondary memory* : see *memory*.

*secondary prompt* : If the *command* typed in response to the *primary prompt* of the *shell* is incomplete, a second prompt is printed to tell the *user* that more information is required. The *default* in **sh** is >. There is no secondary prompt in *C-shell*.

*semantic error* : Misuse of a construct in a *high level language* such that a *program* although *syntactically* correct is not valid i.e. is meaningless.

*semantics* : The meaning of *symbols* and groups of symbols used in a *programming language*. (cf. *syntax*)

*separator* : A *character* which *delimits* the previous *string* and separates it from the next one.

*sequential access* : A form of *access* to information on a *storage device* such as a *magnetic tape* where, after one *block* of information has been accessed, the only block which may then be accessed immediately is the next one in sequence. The time to access a given block varies widely depending on the distance of the block from the read-write head. (cf. *random access*)

*session* : The period between *login* and *logout*.

set [ *args* ]

In the absence of any *arguments*, the action of this *command* in both *shells* is to *output* a list of the *shell variables* and their values. In the *C-shell*, it is also used to assign a value to a variable with an argument of the form *name=string*. If only the variable name is specified, *name* is set to the null *string*.

In the *standard shell*, set can be used to assign values to the *positional parameters* and to turn on or off various *flags* which control the behaviour of the shell. Its arguments take the form [ *flags* ] *values*. The significance of the flags is as follows:

**−a**   Mark for *export* all variables which have been *created* or have had their values modified.

**−e**   Exit immediately if a command fails (non-zero *exit code*).

**−f**   Disable *filename* generation.

**−n**   *Read* commands but do not *execute* them.

**−u**   Treat undefined variables as an *error*.

**−v**   Print *lines* read by the shell.

**−x**   Print commands with their arguments as they are executed.

**−−**   Make − the value of the first positional parameter.

If + is used instead of −, the corresponding flag is turned off. The remaining arguments are assigned in order to **$1, $2** ... etc.

**setenv** *name value*

A *C-shell command* which assigns a single *string value* to an *environment variable name*.

**sh** [ *options* ] [ *args* ]

The *command language interpreter* known as the *shell* that *reads command lines* from a *terminal* or from a *file*. *options* are those described for **set**. The first *argument* is assumed to be the name of the file containing the commands to be *executed*; the remainder then become the *positional parameters* passed to that command. For a description of how to use the shell *interactively*, see Section 2.5; shell *programming* and the use of *command files* is discussed in Section 4.4. See also Appendix 3 for a summary of frequently used *metacharacter* sequences.

*shell* : The shell, otherwise known as **sh**, is a *program* that accepts *commands* from a *user* and arranges for the commands to be *executed*. It is a *command language interpreter* as well as providing many other useful facilities. These include *input-output redirection*, the construction of *pipelines*, the *running* of *asynchronous* commands, the preparation of *argument* lists, and even a *programming* language. An extended shell called *C-shell* or **csh** is also available in the Berkeley version of UNIX. Its features include advanced asynchronous *job* control and a *history* mechanism for convenient re-execution of recent commands.

*shell procedure* : An *executable file* which contains *shell commands* rather than the *output* of a *compiler* or *assembler*.

*shell script* : see *shell procedure*.

shift [ *n* ]
Shift the *positional parameters* n places to the left (*default*=1).

shl
The *shell layer manager* in System V.2 which enables the *user* to interact with more than one *shell* (known as layers) from a single *terminal*. *Input* from the terminal goes to the current layer; others attempting to *read* are blocked. *Outputs* from multiple layers are *merged* onto the terminal unless output from particular layers has been blocked.
The **shl** *prompt* is >>>. It recognizes a number of *commands*, a list of which may be obtained by issuing the **help** or **?** command. These enable a user to **create** and **delete** named layers up to a maximum of 7, **block** or **unblock** output from named layers, **resume** a named layer, **toggle** to restart the previous layer, list details of named layers with **layers** and **quit** from the shell layer manager. The name of a layer may be defined by the user and it replaces the standard shell prompt. Alternatively, **shl** generates *default* names **(1)** – **(7)**.
The default *control character* to switch control from a layer to **shl** is ˆZ.

*signal* : A message sent to a *process* usually instructing it to terminate. (cf. **kill**)

sleep *time*
Suspends *execution* for *time* seconds. It can be used to execute a *command* after a certain period of time.

*sleeping status* : The status assigned to a *process* which is *waiting* for some event to occur to wake it up.

*soft copy* : *Output* of a *program* displayed on a *visual display unit* where it is of a transient nature. (cf. *hard copy*)

*software* : The general name given to all forms of *computer programs* as opposed to computer *hardware*.

*software tools* : A class of *systems software* which can be used to assist in the construction of other software.

sort [ *–flags* ] [ *+pos1* [ *–pos2* ] ] [ *files* ]
*Reads lines* from the named *files*, sorts them into a specified order and *writes* the sorted *file* onto *standard output*. If no files are specified, *standard input* is read as it is for − supplied as a *filename argument*.
Sorting is carried out by *comparing fields* where a field is a non-empty sequence of *characters* followed by a *field separator* or a *newline*. If the field separator character is repeated, the subsequent characters after the first one are considered to be part of the next field. The *default* field separator is a

*blank*, the default sort key is an entire line, the default ordering is *lexicographic* by *bytes* in the *machine collating sequence*. The first and last characters of a key may be defined by supplying as arguments the position specifiers +*pos1* and −*pos2* *optionally* followed by the *flags* **bdfinr**. A position specifier has the form *m.n* where *m* defines the number of fields to skip from the beginning of the line and the optional  .*n*, the number of further characters to skip (including the separator character). If  −*pos2* is missing, end of line is assumed.

If multiple sort keys are specified, each key is used in turn to order lines which compare as equal for the preceding keys. When all keys have been used, equal lines are ordered with all bytes significant.

Various options may be selected by specifying flags after an initial − for a global effect or a subset of these *appended* to a position specifier which will only affect that particular field. The meanings of the various options are as follows:

| | |
|---|---|
| **b** | Ignore leading blanks when determining first and last character positions of a sort key. |
| **c** | Check that the input files are sorted according to the specified ordering rules and only produce a warning message if they are not. |
| **d** | Use only letters, digits and blanks in comparisons (dictionary order). |
| **f** | Fold upper case letters into lower case so that they compare equal. |
| **i** | Ignore *ASCII* characters which do not have a *symbolic* representation in non-numeric comparisons i.e. those outside the range 040–176. |
| **m** | *Merge* the sorted input files. |
| **n** | Sort on the arithmetic value of an initial numeric *string* of the form [*blanks*] [−]*digits*[. *digits*]. |
| **o** *file* | Use *file* as the name of the output file which may have the same name as one of the input files. |
| **r** | Reverse the sense of the comparisons. |
| **t***c* | Use the character *c* as the field separator. |
| **u** | Only lines which are unique with regard to the specified sort keys are output. |

*sort* : The process of ordering the *lines* (or records) in a *file* according to some criterion e.g. *lexicographic*. (cf. *merge*)

**source** *file*

A *C-shell command* which **reads** and **executes** commands from *file*.

*source code* : The version of the **program** that exists in a *high level language* or *assembly language*.

*space* : A *character* which causes the **cursor** to move one position to the right without producing any visible representation.

*special file* : Used in UNIX to refer to the *input-output devices* connected to the *computer*. Details of these files can be found in the **directory** */dev*.

*special purpose* : A special purpose *computer system* is one **programmed** to carry out a set of specific *tasks*. (cf. *general purpose, real time*)

**split** [ −*n* ] [ *file* [ *name* ] ]

**Reads** *file* and splits it up, **writing** *n-line* pieces (*default* 1000) onto a set of **output files** called *nameaa, nameab* etc., as many as are needed up to *namezz*. The default value of *name* is *x*. **Standard input** is read if *file* is not specified or is given as −.

*spool* : Sometimes the transfer of **files** within a *computer* has to be delayed while some **device** is busy e.g. a *line printer* can only print one file at a time. If a *user* wants a listing printed when the printer is busy, the file must be placed on a queue for printing when the line printer becomes available. This technique is called **spooling**. (cf. *daemon*)

*standard* : Internationally accepted standards exist for many programming languages and character sets.

Features available in System V UNIX are often referred as "standard" to differentiate them from those found in other UNIX *systems*.

*standard error output* : see *standard output*

*standard input* : After *login*, the **terminal** used for this purpose becomes the standard input **device** with a *file descriptor* of 0. **Commands** then **read** their **input** from this device. The input *redirection* facilities of the **shell** enable a command to read such input from a **file**.

*standard output* : The **terminal** used for *logging in* is connected initially to UNIX as both the standard output and *standard error output devices*. These have *file descriptors* of 1 and 2 respectively. The former is used by **commands** for the output of **results** and the latter for the output of failure messages. Such output may be **written** to a **file** using the **redirection** facilities of the **shell**.

*standard shell* : The *command language interpreter* **sh** in System V.

*statement* : A **program** contains a sequence of statements, each of which instructs the **computer** to carry out a particular action.

**stop** [ *jobname ...* ]

A *C-shell command* to *suspend* specified *background jobs*. If no *argument* is supplied, the *current job* is suspended. A suspended background job is restarted using **bg** or **fg**.

*storage device* : *Hardware* capable of preserving *data* so that it can be *retrieved* at some later time. (cf. *memory*)

*store* : To place information on a *storage device*.

*string* : A sequence of *characters* usually terminated by a *delimiter*.

*structured programming* : The writing of *programs* whose form and organization makes them readily comprehensible to people. Such programs are less likely than unstructured ones to contain residual *errors*.

**stty** [ *options* ]

Set operating characteristics for the current *terminal*. In the absence of any *arguments*, it reports the values of certain *options*. If **all** is supplied as an argument in 4.2, it reports all normally used option settings. A complete list of option settings is obtained by specifying **everything** as an argument in 4.2 or **−a** in V.2.

The way the *command* functions varies between V.2 and 4.2 (and even from one installation to another). For an exact specification of the command, consult **stty(1)** in the local *documentation*.

*sub-directory* : A *directory created* in another directory.

*subscript* : An index to a set of items of *data*.

*substitute* : To replace one *character string* by another.

*substitution* : see *command substitution, parameter substitution*.

*subtree* : Part of a *tree* commencing at a branching point other than the *root*.

*suffix* : Additional *characters* added to the end of a *filename* to give some information about the contents of the *file*, e.g. **.c** indicates that the file contains a *C program*. Some *compilers* will refuse to compile the contents of a file unless the appropriate suffix exists.

*superuser* : A *system administrator* who has privileges over and above those available to ordinary *users*. A superuser can *access* any *file* in the system whether owned by **root** or not, irrespective of the settings of the *permissions*.

*suspend* : A facility available in the *C-shell* which enables a *user* to halt a *job* so that it can be restarted at a later time. (cf. **stop**)

*symbol* : A *character* or sequence of characters representing an object, relationship or operation.

*symbol table* : A table produced by a *compiler* which shows the layout of the *program* in *memory*.

*symbolic debugger* : A *debugger* which allows a *user* to make debugging requests in terms of the *high level language symbols* used to write the original *program*.

*syntactic error* : A grammatical error in the use of a *programming language*.

*syntax* : The set of rules defining the grammar of a *programming language*. (cf. *semantics*)

*system* : see *operating system, the system*.

*system administrator* : Someone who manages the operation of a UNIX system and is responsible for creating and deleting *accounts*. The system administrator is usually a *superuser*.

*system name* : The name of a UNIX system which may be used to construct a path for sending *electronic mail* to a *user* on a *remote machine*.

*systems software* : *Software* which is part of the *computer system* and which is designed to enable *users* to develop *applications software* more rapidly and more conveniently than they could on a bare *machine*.

*tab* : A *control character* which causes the *cursor* to advance to the next tabstop position.

**tail** [ *options* ] [ *file* ]
   *Copy* the named *file* from a specified position to *standard output*. If *file* is not specified, *standard input* is used instead. The starting position is specified as +*n lines* from the start of the *file* or −*n* lines from the end of the file. If **b** or **c** is *appended* to *n*, *blocks* of *characters* are used instead of lines. The *default* value of *n* is 10.

*tape* : A *magnetic tape* is a medium for the *storage* of information. A *computer* tape is similar to audio or video tapes except that it stores computer information in a digital form. (cf. *backup, disk*)

**tar** [ *key* ] [ *files* ]
   *Archives* and *restores* multiple *files* on a single *file* (usually *magnetic tape* or *floppy disk*). *key* is one of the letters **crtux** specifying a function *optionally* followed by one or more function modifiers. *files* are the names of files and *directories* to be archived and restored. If a directory name is specified, then all the files and *recursively* the *sub-directories* it contains are processed. The meanings of the function *characters* are as follows:

    c    *Create* a new archive and *write* named files at the beginning instead of at the end.

    r    *Append* named files to the archive.

    t    List the names of the named files if they occur in the archive; if no files are specified, the names of all files in the archive are listed.

    **w**    Append named files to the archive if not already there or if they have been **modified** since being placed in the archive.

    **x**    Restore named files from the archive; if no files are specified, all files in the archive are restored.

To modify the selected function, **append** one or more of the following characters to the function letter:

    *nd*    Use tape drive *n* (**0–7**) to mount a magnetic tape of density *d* (**1** — 800 bpi, **m** — 1600 bpi, **h** — 6250 bpi). The **default** is **0m**. (In 4.2, only *n* is specified and not *d*.)

    **f**    Use the next **argument** as the name of the archive instead of the default (*/dev/mt/nd* in V.2 or */dev/rmtn* in 4.2). If − is specified as the name, **tar reads** from **standard input** or writes to **standard output** as appropriate.

    **m**    Make the time of last **modification** equal to the extraction time rather than restoring it from the archive.

    **v**    Activate verbose mode.

    **w**    Proceed **interactively** and only apply function to a specified file if the **user** responds **y** to a query.

*task* : see *job*.

**tee** [ −a ] [ *file* ... ]
    *Copies standard input* to *standard output* as well as to *file*. −a causes output to be **appended** to *file*.

**TERM** : The *shell variable* used to hold the type of a *user's terminal*. (cf. **vi**)

*terminal* : A *device* for the exchange of information between the **user** and the **computer**. Terminals consist of two main parts — a **keyboard** for the entry of **commands** and other **text**, and a display device for the presentation of the computer's responses. These fall into two main categories — **hard copy**, which prints on paper rather like a typewriter and **soft copy**. (cf. **visual display unit**)

**test** *expression*
    Evaluate *expression* and return zero **exit code** if true, otherwise non-zero for false. *expression* is composed of primitives which may be combined using the **logical operators** and (−a), or (−o), not (!). Parentheses may be used for grouping.
    A **file** primitive has the form −*flag file* which is true if *file* exists and is **readable** (**r**), **writable** (**w**), **executable** (**x**), an **ordinary file** (**f**), a **directory** (**d**), a **character special file** (**c**), a **block** special file (**b**) or has a size greater than 0 (**s**). The **flags** are the single letters shown in **bold**.
    **String** primitives exist which are true if string *s1* is not null (*s1*), has zero length (−**z***s1*), has non-zero length (−**n***s1*), is identical to *s2* (*s1* = *s2*), is not

identical to *s2* (*s1* != *s2*).

Integers may be compared algebraically in relations with primitives of the form *n1 op n2* where *op* can be **−eq**, **−ne**, **−gt**, **−ge**, **−lt** or **−le**. Note that all operators, flags and parentheses are separate **arguments** to **test** and must be **escaped** where necessary.

**text** : One or more **lines** composed of printable **characters**.

**text editor** : see **editor**.

**text input mode** : A mode of operation in **ed** and **vi** which allows the entry of **text** from the **keyboard** to supplement or replace existing text. (cf. **command mode**)

**the system** : A shorthand way of referring to the **computer** and its **operating system**.

**time** *command*

After *command* has been completed, **writes** on **standard error output** in seconds the elapsed time, the time spent in **the system** and the time spent in **executing** the **command**.

**timesharing** : A mode of operating a **computer** in which a number of **users** appear to be simultaneously active. The computer switches its attention rapidly from one user to another to service each request. UNIX is a timesharing **system**. (cf. **batch processing**, **response time**)

**tr** [ **−cds** ] [ *string1* [ *string2* ] ]

**Substitute** or **delete** selected **characters read** from **standard input** and **write** the **results** to **standard output**. The characters in *string1* specify the input characters which are to be mapped into the corresponding output characters in *string2*. If *string2* is shorter than *string1*, it is extended to the required length by replicating the last character. Ranges of the form **[a–z]** in V.2 or just **a–z** in 4.2 may be included in either **string**. In V.2 only, the construct **[a\*n]** stands for *n* repetitions of the character **a**. A backslash (\\) followed by one, two or three **octal** digits stands for the character with the **ASCII code** given by the digits.

The meaning of each of the **flags** is as follows:

**−c**  Define the input characters to be those **ASCII** characters which are not in *string1*.

**−d**  Delete all input characters in *string1*. (*string2* is not required.)

**−s**  Squeeze all strings of repeated output characters defined in *string2* into single characters.

**transform** : To convert information from one form to another. (cf. **tr**)

**tree** : A particular way of organising items of information into a structure analogous to that of a family tree, that is, one starts at some point and descends down the hierarchy until reaching the required destination. The *directories* in UNIX are organised as a tree, with the starting point called (appropriately) the "root", or "/" for short. Any *file* in the *system* can be reached by following down a chain of directories. (cf. *pathname*)

**true**

Does nothing except return a zero *exit code*.

**tset** [ *options* ]

A 4.2 *command* which sets up after *login* the characteristics of a *terminal* dependent on what type of terminal it is. Commonly used *options* are:

    **−e***c*    Define *c* as the *erase character* which, if a *control character*, may be entered as such or as two characters, e.g. **^H**. The *default* is **BACKSPACE** for the terminal.

    **−k***c*    As for **−e** but defining the *line kill character*. The default is **^X**.

    **−Q**    Suppress printing of confirmatory messages.

*tty* : An acronym for a "teletype" *terminal*, now generally used to denote any *user* terminal.

**tty** [ **−s** ]

Prints *pathname* of *user's terminal* on *standard output*. If **−s** is specified, no output occurs. *Exit codes* are 0 if *standard input* is a terminal, 1 otherwise, 2 for invalid *options*.

*ttyname* : The name of a *user terminal*.

*turn-around time* : The time between when a *job* is submitted to a *batch processing system* and the *results* of the run are returned to the *user*.

*UID* : An acronym for *user identifier*.

**umask** [ *mask* ]

Sets the *file creation mask* to *mask*, a 3-digit *octal* number. If no *argument* is supplied, the current value of *mask* is printed on *standard output*. The mode of a newly *created file* is formed by the *logical product* of *mask* and **777**. Thus a *bit* set to 0 in *mask* causes the corresponding *permission* to be removed.

**unalias** *pattern*

A *C-shell command* to remove any *alias* which matches *pattern*.

**uncompact** [ *name* ... ]

The 4.2 equivalent of **unpack**. If *name* is not specified, *standard input* is uncompacted to *standard output*.

*undo* : A facility in **ed** and **vi** which enables a *user* to reverse *changes* made to the *buffer*.

**uniq** [ –cdu ] [ *file* [ *output* ] ]

Reads *sorted lines* from *file*, removes all but one **copy** of adjacent replicated lines and **writes** lines to *output* if specified, otherwise to **standard output**. If *file* is not specified, **standard input** is **read**.

The *options* available are:

–c    Precede each of the output lines by a count.

–d    Only output is one copy of any repeated line.

–u    Output only those lines which are not repeated i.e. are really unique.

**unpack** *name* ...

Expands **files** created by **pack** with **filenames** of the form *name.z*. An expanded file is given the filename *name*.

**unset** *name* ...

Removes **shell variable** *name*.

**unsetenv** *pattern*

A **C-shell command** which removes **environment variables** whose names match *pattern*.

**user** : Anyone with a **username** and **password** who is authorized to use a UNIX **system**.

**user identifier** : A unique integer associated with each **username**. (cf. **login identifier**)

**username** : A **character string** assigned by the **system administrator** to each authorized **user** of a UNIX system to identify that individual uniquely. (cf. **login name**)

**utility** : **Software** used to perform routine functions and **tasks**.

**uucp** [ *option* ] *source* ... *destination*

**Copies** *source* **files** to *destination* which may be a file for one **source** file or a **directory** for one or more source files. A **filename** may be a **pathname** on the **local machine** or one on a **remote machine** in which case, *system-name*! is **prepended** to the pathname. Expansion of **shell metacharacters** will take place on the appropriate **system**. A pathname may be a **full pathname** or a pathname preceded by ~*user* which is replaced by the **home directory** for *user* on the specified system.

The following *options* are available:

–c    Use the source files when copying rather than **storing** them temporarily in the **spool** directory.

–d    Make all directories necessary to copy the file (*default* in V.2 but not in 4.2).

–f    Do not make intermediate directories (V.2).

> −m   Send *mail* to the user who issued the copy request when it is completed.
>
> −n   Notify *user* specified by the next *argument* that a file has been sent.

All files delivered by **uucp** are owned by **uucp**. If a file cannot be delivered on a remote system, it is stored as */usr/spool/uucp/file* in 4.2 or as */usr/spool/uucppublic/file* in V.2.

**uulog** [ *options* ]

Used to query a summary *file* of **uucp** transactions. *Options* are:

> −s   Print information only about a specified *system* whose name appears as the next *argument*.
>
> −u   Print information only about a specified *user* whose name appears as the next argument.

**uuname** [ −l ] [ −v ]

Prints the **uucp** names of known systems. −v will produce additional information about each system. If the −l *option* is used, the name of the local system is printed.

*variable* : An item of *data* in a *program* which has a name and a value which can change. (cf. *environment*)

*VDT* : An acronym for *visual display terminal*.

*VDU* : An acronym for *visual display unit*.

**vedit** [ *options* ] *file* ...

A version of **vi** intended for beginners which makes it easier to learn how to use the *editor* (V.2 only).

**vi** [ *options* ] *file* ...

A *screen-oriented text editor* based on the *line editor* **ex**. In fact, **ex** and **vi** are the same *program* and it is possible to switch from one to the other as required.

Some of the *options* available are as follows:

> −r   If *file* is specified after this *flag*, recover that *file* after a *system crash* for further editing; in the absence of *file*, a list of the preserved files is printed.
>
> −R   Set *read only mode* to prevent accidental overwriting.

In addition, an *argument* of the form +*command* causes the **ex** *command* to be *executed* before editing begins.

For examples of the use of **vi**, see Section 3.2; for a summary of **vi** commands, see Appendix 5.

**view** [ *options* ] *file* ...

Equivalent to **vi** −R i.e. read only mode is set.

*virtual memory* : A management strategy that enables a **program** to **address** a **storage** space that is much larger than that actually available in **primary memory**.

*visual display terminal* : see *visual display unit*

*visual display unit* : A **soft copy terminal** on which information is displayed on a television-like screen rather then being printed on paper. (cf. **hard copy**)

*waiting status* : The **status** assigned to a **process** which is halted until some particular event occurs which will enable it to continue.

**wc** [ –lwc ] [ *file ...* ]
    **Reads** *file* (or **standard input** if no *file* is specified) and counts the number of **lines**, **words** and **characters** for each *file* determined by the **flags**:

      –c    Output a character count.

      –l    Output a line count.

      –w    Output a word count.

    The *default* is equivalent to –lwc. A grand total for all **files** is also **output** if more than one **input** file is specified .

**whereis** [ *–flags* ] *name ...*
    A 4.2 *command* which **searches** for **source**, **binary** and **manual** entries for specified commands. The **flags** s, **b** and **m** select the particular type of entries to be located. The *default* is equivalent to –sbm.

*white space* : A collective name for a sequence of **spaces**, **tabs** and/or **newlines**.

**who** [ *options* ]
    Prints on **standard output** the **username**, **terminal** name and **login** time for each **user** active on a UNIX **system**. In V.2, the –u *option* will also produce output of the elapsed time since the last activity on the line, and the **process identifier** of the **user's shell**. If the –q option is used, only the names and number of users **logged in** are displayed.
    If the **arguments** **am I** or **am i** are specified, the *command* tells the user what username was used to login.

**whoami**
    A 4.2 *command* which prints the current **username** on **standard output**.

*window* : A rectangular area on a **VDU** screen in which **text** may be displayed by a **screen editor**.

*word* : An **addressable** unit of **storage** in a **computer memory**, usually 1, 2 or 4 **bytes** but may be larger. It may also be a sequence of **characters** in a **line** of **text delimited** in some way.

*working directory* : see **current directory**.

*write* : The *output* of *data* from a *program* to an external *peripheral device*.

**write** *user* [ *ttyname* ]

*Copies lines* from *standard input* to another *terminal* at which *user* is *logged in*. The input is terminated by *end-of-file* or *interrupt*. If *user* is logged in more than once, the *argument ttyname* may be used to specify which terminal is to receive the message.

*Permission* for *others* to *write* to a terminal may be denied or granted by a *user* via **mesg**.

*write permission* : For a *file*, permission to *change* it; for a *directory*, permission to *create* and *delete* files within it.

# *Appendix 1*

# Getting to know your terminal

Terminals come in all shapes and sizes. They are devices connected to a computer, either directly or over a communications network, which enable users to input information to the computer from a typewriter-like keyboard and see output returned by the computer. Some produce hard copy, that is, characters printed on paper, either by impact or by heat. Most of these operate at 300 baud which is equivalent to about 30 characters per second (cps). If it is a very old terminal, it may only support a line speed of 10 cps (110 baud). Other terminals produce characters on a cathode ray tube (CRT) and are called *visual display units* (VDU) or *visual display terminals* (VDT). Typically, VDUs can display up to 24 lines of alphanumeric information on the screen, each line containing up to 80 characters. They operate at much higher line speeds than the hard copy devices (1200, 2400 and 9600 baud). Another type of terminal is one which can draw pictures and diagrams as well as display characters. These are often called *graphical displays* and operate at even higher speeds than do the VDUs.

A personal computer can be thought of as a CRT screen and a keyboard which incorporates the other components of a computer – processor, memory etc. They are usually stand-alone devices but some may be connected to another computer in much the same way as a terminal. You will have received a set of operating instructions with your PC and you will need to follow these closely, once you have set up the machine and wish to power it up. You will then have to familiarize yourself with its keyboard, just as you would if you were using a terminal. Much of what follows applies to PCs as well as to terminals.

Since there are so many different types of terminals, it is impossible to describe all of them in this book. However, UNIX supports a wide variety of devices, all the way from hard copy printers to graphical displays. If you are not familiar with the terminal you are using, it will be sensible to spend a little time getting to know some of its characteristics. In order to do this, first of all, put it into *local* mode. How you do this will depend on the terminal; often, it is simply a matter of depressing a key marked **LOCAL**. In this mode, whenever a key is struck, the corresponding character is printed on the paper or displayed on the screen. This is to be contrasted with *remote* mode where the character is also sent to the computer. Obviously, when you are actually talking to UNIX, you will need to be in *remote* mode. (Sometimes, *local* and *remote* are called respectively *offline* and *online*.)

Once the terminal is in local mode, you can begin experimenting with the keys. Whenever a key associated with a printable character is depressed, that character will be printed or will appear on the screen. In the case of a hard copy device, the position at which the character is printed is determined by the current position of the print head; for a VDU, the position is determined by the current position of the *cursor*, a blob of light on the screen, usually rectangular and sometimes blinking. The character replaces the cursor which moves one position to the right. If you press the key marked **A**, then, if the terminal supports both upper and lower case letters, **a** will be printed on the paper and the print head will move one position to the right or **a** will appear on the screen and the cursor will move to the next position. If your terminal supports only upper case characters, then **A** will appear instead of **a**. (Don't worry if this occurs — UNIX can handle upper case only terminals as well as those which generate both cases.) If **a** was generated, then to produce **A**, it will be necessary to hold down the **SHIFT** key while the key marked **A** is depressed. If you want to produce a whole sequence of capital letters, then you can often do so by depressing the **CAPS** or **CAPS-LOCK** key. Pressing this key a second time will return the terminal to the lower case state. (Note that some terminals which handle both cases will automatically be placed in upper case mode when first powered on. In such situations, it will be necessary to depress the **CAPS** or **CAPS-LOCK** key before lower case characters can be generated.)

Now let us produce some digits. Normally these are generated when the corresponding key is depressed. Punctuation marks and special symbols, on the other hand, are usually a mixture of normal and shifted mode. Those which occur on the upper part of the key face are generated in the same manner as for upper case characters. Try a few punctuation marks and digits to get a feel for things.

Another important character is **SPACE**. Because this is used so frequently, a whole bar is provided rather than just a single key. Try depressing this a few times and observe the result. Another key which will generate spaces is **TAB**. It is not, however, equivalent to a fixed number of spaces but instead moves the print head or cursor to a predetermined position each time it is struck. Try typing:

```
How are you
```

using the tab key instead of the space bar and observe the result. The tab key is very convenient for tabulating columns of information or for laying out programs.

By this time, you will have generated a number of characters, all on the same line, and may be wondering what will happen when the line is full. On virtually all terminals, there is a key marked **RETURN** (sometimes, it is called **ENTER**). If this is struck, the print head or cursor will return to the beginning of the current line. The key marked **LINE FEED** will then move the current printing position to the start of the next line. Thus, **RETURN/LINE FEED** enables you to continue typing on a new line whilst still preserving information generated on the previous line. Having to hit two keys to start a new line looks like being a bit of a nuisance. Fortunately, as you will see when you are actually talking to UNIX, you will only have to press **RETURN** in order to get to the beginning of the next line.

As you go on typing line after line, in the case of a hard copy device, the continuous roll of paper is fed past the print head and you could go on typing until the paper is exhausted. But what happens in the case of a VDU? As each new line is initiated, the cursor moves one position lower on the screen until finally it reaches the last line. Thereafter, each time you execute **RETURN/LINE FEED**, all lines currently displayed move up one position and the top-most line disappears. This is called *scrolling*. You can go on typing, line after line, but only the most recent 24 lines will be displayed at any one time (assuming that is the capacity of your VDU). Since you are still in local mode, lines scrolled off the top of the screen will be lost, but if you had been talking to UNIX, they would, of course, have been received and used by the system. One of the big disadvantages of a VDU is that you cannot look back very far to see what you typed earlier.

There may be other keys on your keyboard which we will not discuss in this appendix e.g. **DELETE**, **RUBOUT**, **BREAK**, **ESCAPE** and so on. What effects these have on UNIX will be described in the appropriate place in the book. You should have a good look around the keyboard whilst you are in local mode so that you have some idea where particular keys are located and can find them quickly when they are referenced in the text. One key that is very important is the one marked **CONTROL** or **CTRL**. This acts like another shift key i.e. you hold it down whilst you depress some other key. If you hold down **CONTROL** and then press **A**, nothing will be printed or appear on the screen but a special character would be transmitted to UNIX if you had been connected to it. In this book, we will refer to this character as **control–A** or **^A**.

One final thing to check is whether the terminal is operating in *full* or *half duplex* mode. The difference between these modes of communication is as follows:

In half duplex, whenever a key is struck, a character is transmitted to the computer and simultaneously printed or displayed; in full duplex, no printing or display occurs automatically. If **A** is struck, then only the code for **a** is sent to the computer. In order to cause **a** to be printed or displayed, the computer sends back the appropriate code to produce the desired effect. The advantage of this mode of operation is that sometimes the computer may send back nothing (in order, say, to preserve the secrecy of what you typed), sometimes it may send back more than one character so that non-printable characters can be displayed intelligibly.

UNIX expects all terminals to operate in full duplex mode. There may be a key marked **FULL** which needs to be depressed or a switch somewhere that needs to be set to the appropriate position. If you can't find it, don't worry! Terminals connected to a UNIX system are usually left in the full duplex mode and you probably won't have any problems.

# Appendix 2
# Command summary

The following table provides a quick reference to the commands discussed in this book. The last column gives the page on which the command is mentioned or described in detail. The letters **A** and **B** indicate whether a command is available in the AT&T or Berkeley version of UNIX respectively. Some commands are executed directly by the shell and their availability and format depend on whether you are using the standard shell or the C-shell. These are denoted by **S** and **C** respectively.

The abbreviations used in the table and their meanings are as follows:

| | | | |
|---|---|---|---|
| *afile* | archive file | *incr* | increment |
| *arg* | argument | *nm* | name |
| *cl* | command list | *posn* | position |
| *dest* | destination | *pts* | patterns |
| *expr* | expression | *str* | string |
| *file* | filename | *user* | username |
| *filesys* | file system | *wd* | word |

<table>
<tr><td colspan="4" align="center">Table A2.1</td></tr>
<tr><td colspan="4" align="center">UNIX Commands</td></tr>
<tr><td>Command</td><td>Arguments</td><td>Description</td><td>Page</td></tr>
<tr><td>.</td><td>file</td><td>read commands from file</td><td>193S</td></tr>
<tr><td>:</td><td></td><td>null command</td><td>192S</td></tr>
<tr><td>alias</td><td>[name] [list]</td><td>define command aliases</td><td>212C</td></tr>
<tr><td>ar</td><td>key [posn] afile [files]</td><td>archive maintainer</td><td>230AB</td></tr>
<tr><td>at</td><td>time [date] [+incr]</td><td>execute commands later</td><td>276A</td></tr>
<tr><td>at</td><td>time [day] [file]</td><td>execute commands later</td><td>278B</td></tr>
<tr><td>basename</td><td>string [suffix]</td><td>output base of pathname</td><td>202AB</td></tr>
<tr><td>batch</td><td></td><td>submit batch job</td><td>277A</td></tr>
<tr><td>bfs</td><td>[–] file</td><td>big file scanner</td><td>228A</td></tr>
<tr><td>bg</td><td>[jobnames]</td><td>resume job in background</td><td>267C</td></tr>
<tr><td>break</td><td></td><td>exit from loop</td><td>206S</td></tr>
</table>

| Table A2.1 |||| |
| :---: |
| **UNIX Commands** |||| |
| **Command** | **Arguments** | **Description** | **Page** |
| --- | --- | --- | --- |
| cal | [[*month*] *year*] | print calendar | 16AB |
| case | *wd* **in** [*pts*) *cl* **;;**] ... **esac** | select commands | 207S |
| cat | [*options*] [*files*] | concatenate files | 38AB |
| cc | [*options*] [*files*] | C compiler | 179AB |
| cd | [*directory*] | change working directory | 30AB |
| checknews | [*options*] | check if user has news | 307B |
| chmod | *mode files* | change mode | 44AB |
| cmp | [*options*] *file1 file2* | compare 2 files | 235AB |
| comm | [–[**123**]] *file1 file2* | output common lines | 237AB |
| continue | | start next iteration | 206S |
| cp | *files target* | copy files | 43AB |
| crypt | [*password*] | encode or decode a file | 262AB |
| csh | [*options*] [*args*] | command interpreter | 194B |
| date | [*options*] | print date | 15AB |
| dd | [*option*=*value*] ... | convert and copy a file | 261AB |
| df | [–i] [*filesys*] [*files*] | print free disk space | 228AB |
| diff | [*options*] *file1 file2* | find file differences | 236AB |
| du | [–**as**] [*files*] | summarize disk usage | 53AB |
| echo | [*args*] | echo arguments | 63AB |
| ed | [–] [*options*] [*file*] | text editor | 80AB |
| egrep | [*options*] [*expr*] [*files*] | search file for pattern | 254AB |
| exit | [*n*] | exit from shell | 208S |
| export | [*names*] | mark export variables | 71S |
| expr | *args* | evaluate expression | 206AB |
| f77 | [*options*] *files* | FORTRAN 77 compiler | 165AB |
| fg | [*jobnames*] | resume job in foreground | 266C |
| fgrep | [*options*] [*string*] [*file*] | search file for string | 250AB |
| file | [*options*] *files* | determine file type | 225AB |
| find | *pathnames expr* | find files | 223AB |
| for | *nm* [**in** *wd* ...] **do** *cl* **done** | repeated execution | 201S |
| grep | [*options*] *expr* [*files*] | search file for pattern | 251AB |
| head | [–*n*] [*files*] | print first lines of a file | 41B |

| Table A2.1 | | | |
|---|---|---|---|
| **UNIX Commands** | | | |
| **Command** | **Arguments** | **Description** | **Page** |
| **help** | [*args*] | ask for help | 17A |
| **history** | [−**r**] [*n*] | print history list | 73C |
| **id** | | print user and group IDs | 18A |
| **if** | *cl1* **then** *cl2* [**else** *cl3*] **fi** | conditional execution | 208S |
| **jobs** | [−**l**] | print list of jobs | 265C |
| **join** | [*options*] *file1 file2* | relational database oper. | 247AB |
| **kill** | [−*signno*] *PIDs* | terminate a process | 273AB |
| **learn** | [*subject*] [*lesson*] | computer instruction | 24AB |
| **lint** | [*options*] *files* | check C programs | 182AB |
| **ln** | *files target* | make link | 225AB |
| **login** | [*username*] | sign on to system | 12AB |
| **logout** | | terminate session | 24C |
| **lp** | [*options*] [*files*] | line printer spooler | 60A |
| **lpr** | [*options*] [*files*] | off line printer | 60B |
| **ls** | [*options*] [*files*] | list contents of directory | 28AB |
| **Mail** | [*options*] [*users*] | interactive message sys. | 288B |
| **mail** | [*options*] [*users*] | send and receive mail | 289AB |
| **mailx** | [*options*] [*users*] | interactive message sys. | 296A |
| **man** | [*options*] [*section*] *titles* | print manual entries | 21AB |
| **mesg** | [n] [**y**] | permit or deny messages | 23AB |
| **mkdir** | [*files*] | make a directory | 49AB |
| **more** | [*options*] [*files*] | file perusal filter | 38B |
| **mv** | *files target* | move or rename files | 48AB |
| **news** | [*options*] [*items*] | print news items | 307A |
| **nice** | [−*incr*] *command* | low priority command | 271AB |
| **nl** | [*options*] *file* | line number filter | 167A |
| **nohup** | *command* | no hang up command | 275AB |
| **od** | [*options*] [*file*] [*offset*] | octal dump | 259AB |
| **pack** | [−] [−**f**] *files* | pack files | 233A |
| **passwd** | | change login password | 14AB |
| **pc** | [*options*] *files* | Pascal compiler | 148B |
| **pcat** | *files* | output packed files | 234A |

| | *Table A2.1* | | |
|---|---|---|---|
| | **UNIX Commands** | | |
| **Command** | **Arguments** | **Description** | **Page** |
| pg | [*options*] [*files*] | file perusal filter | 38A |
| pi | [*options*] *file* | Pascal translator | 145B |
| pix | [*options*] *file* [*args*] | **pi** and **px** combined | 147B |
| postnews | | submit news articles | 309B |
| pr | [*options*] [*files*] | print file | 60AB |
| printenv | [*name*] | print environment | 72B |
| ps | [*options*] | report process status | 270AB |
| pwd | | print working directory | 29AB |
| px | [*object* [*args*]] | Pascal interpreter | 146B |
| quota | | display quota limits | 229B |
| read | [*names*] | read standard input | 198S |
| readnews | [*options*] | read news articles | 307B |
| rehash | | recompute hash table | 185C |
| rm | [–fri] *files* | remove files | 47AB |
| rmdir | *files* | remove directories | 54AB |
| set | [*flags* [*args*]] | set flags and parameters | 67S |
| set | [*name*[=*word*]] | set value of variables | 68C |
| setenv | *name value* | set environment variable | 72C |
| sh | [*options*] [*args*] | command interpreter | 193AB |
| shift | [*n*] | rename parameters | 238CS |
| shl | | shell layer manager | 268A |
| sleep | *seconds* | suspend execution | 272AB |
| sort | [*options*] [*files*] | sort and/or merge files | 240AB |
| source | *file* | read commands from file | 193C |
| split | [–*n*] [*file*] [*name*] | split a file into pieces | 227AB |
| stop | [*jobnames*] | suspend background job | 267C |
| stty | [*options*] | set terminal options | 19AB |
| tail | [*options*] [*files*] | print last part of a file | 41AB |
| tar | [*key*] [*files*] | tape file archiver | 231AB |
| tee | [*options*] [*files*] | pipe fitting | 61AB |
| test | *expression* | condition evaluation | 209AB |
| time | *command* | time a command | 162AB |

<table>
<tr><td colspan="4" align="center">*Table A2.1*</td></tr>
<tr><td colspan="4" align="center">**UNIX Commands**</td></tr>
<tr><td>**Command**</td><td align="center">**Arguments**</td><td align="center">**Description**</td><td>**Page**</td></tr>
<tr><td>**tr**</td><td>[−**cds**] [*str1*] [*str2*]</td><td>translate characters</td><td>256AB</td></tr>
<tr><td>**tset**</td><td>[*options*]</td><td>set terminal modes</td><td>20B</td></tr>
<tr><td>**tty**</td><td>[*options*]</td><td>get name of terminal</td><td>42AB</td></tr>
<tr><td>**umask**</td><td>[*octal number*]</td><td>set file creation mask</td><td>46CS</td></tr>
<tr><td>**unalias**</td><td>*pattern*</td><td>remove command aliases</td><td>214C</td></tr>
<tr><td>**uniq**</td><td>[*options*] [*file* [*output*]]</td><td>report repeated lines</td><td>239AB</td></tr>
<tr><td>**unpack**</td><td>*names*</td><td>unpack a packed file</td><td>234A</td></tr>
<tr><td>**unset**</td><td>[*pattern*]</td><td>remove shell variables</td><td>67CS</td></tr>
<tr><td>**unsetenv**</td><td>[*pattern*]</td><td>remove env. variables</td><td>72C</td></tr>
<tr><td>**until**</td><td>*cl1* **do** *cl2* **done**</td><td>repeated execution</td><td>204S</td></tr>
<tr><td>**uucp**</td><td>[*options*] *sources dest*</td><td>UNIX to UNIX copy</td><td>281AB</td></tr>
<tr><td>**uulog**</td><td>[*options*]</td><td>print logging information</td><td>288AB</td></tr>
<tr><td>**uuname**</td><td>[−**l**] [−**v**]</td><td>list names of systems</td><td>284AB</td></tr>
<tr><td>**vedit**</td><td>[*options*] *files*</td><td>**vi** for novices</td><td>109A</td></tr>
<tr><td>**vi**</td><td>[*options*] *files*</td><td>screen-oriented editor</td><td>107AB</td></tr>
<tr><td>**view**</td><td>[*options*] *files*</td><td>readonly version of **vi**</td><td>110AB</td></tr>
<tr><td>**wc**</td><td>[−**lwc**] [*files*]</td><td>word count</td><td>255AB</td></tr>
<tr><td>**whereis**</td><td>[−*flags*] *names*</td><td>locate program</td><td>224B</td></tr>
<tr><td>**while**</td><td>*cl1* **do** *cl2* **done**</td><td>repeated execution</td><td>204S</td></tr>
<tr><td>**who**</td><td>[*options*]</td><td>who is on the system</td><td>17AB</td></tr>
<tr><td>**whoami**</td><td></td><td>print current username</td><td>18B</td></tr>
<tr><td>**write**</td><td>*user* [*line*]</td><td>write to another user</td><td>21AB</td></tr>
</table>

# Appendix 3

# Shell summary

Both shells, **sh** and **csh** detect various metacharacters in a command line. These are characters such as   `<  >  *  ?  [ ]  |  &  $  ;  ( )  { }  \ `` ´  ■`  which cause the shell to perform such functions as input-output redirection, filename substitution, creating a pipe, initiating a background job, variable substitution, command substitution, sequencing commands, executing commands in a sub-shell and quoting.

In Table A3.1, the interpretation of commonly used metacharacter sequences is given for **sh** and **csh**. In most instances, the interpretation is the same for both shells; where the interpretation applies to one shell only, the corresponding position in the far left or far right column  has been left blank.

| | Table A3.1 | |
|---|---|---|
| | **Shell Metacharacter  Sequences** | |
| **sh** | **Interpretation** | **csh** |
| $>f$ | Write standard output to file $f$ | $>f$ |
| $<f$ | Read standard input from file $f$ | $<f$ |
| $>>f$ | Append standard output to file $f$ | $>>f$ |
| $<<s$ | Read standard input from here document up to $s$ | $<<s$ |
| $2>f$ | Write standard error output to file $f$ | |
| $2>>f$ | Append standard error output to file $f$ | |
| $2>\&1$ | Merge standard error output with standard output | |
| $>f\ 2>\&1$ | Write standard output and error output to file $f$ | $>\&f$ |
| $>>f\ 2>\&1$ | Append standard output and error output to file $f$ | $>>\&f$ |
| $c1\,|\,c2$ | Pipe standard output from $c1$ as input to $c2$ | $c1\,|\,c2$ |
| $c1\ 2>\&1\,|\,c2$ | Pipe standard outputs from $c1$ as input to $c2$ | $c1\,|\&c2$ |
| * | Match any string of characters including null string | * |
| ? | Match any single character | ? |
| $[s]$ | Match any of the characters in string $s$ | $[s]$ |
| $c1;c2$ | Execute commands $c1$ and $c2$ sequentially | $c1;c2$ |

| | *Table A3.1* | |
|---|---|---|
| **Shell Metacharacter Sequences** | | |
| **sh** | **Interpretation** | **csh** |
| *c&* | Execute command *c* asynchronously in background | *c&* |
| (*c*) | Group commands *c* to execute in a sub-shell | (*c*) |
| {*c*;} | Group commands *c* to execute in current shell | |
| | Specify common strings *s1*,... for filename expansion | {*s1*,...} |
| \\*c* | Escape the next character *c* | \\*c* |
| ´*s*´ | Quote the characters in *s* except for ´ | ´*s*´ |
| "*s*" | Quote the characters in *s* except for $ ` \\ " | "*s*" |
| `*c*` | Substitute the output of the enclosed command | `*c*` |
| $*v* | Substitute value of shell variable *v* | $*v* |
| ${*v*} | Substitute value of shell variable *v* | ${*v*} |
| $0 | Substitute name of command | $0 |
| $*n* | Substitute *n*th positional parameter | $*n* |
| $* | Substitute all positional parameters except $0 | $* |
| $# | Substitute number of positional parameters | $# |
| $? | Substitute exit status of last command executed | $? |
| $$ | Substitute process number of the current shell | $$ |
| | Substitute a line read from standard input | $< |
| Ⓢ | Internal field separator | Ⓢ |
| Ⓣ | Internal field separator | Ⓣ |
| Ⓡ | Terminate command line unless escaped | Ⓡ |

**csh** performs history substitutions when it detects the special characters ⌃ at the beginning of a command line or **!** in any position provided it is not preceded by **\** or followed by space, tab, newline, equals or left parenthesis. In certain circumstances, **~** is treated as a special character. If it stands alone, it is replaced by the pathname of the user's home directory; if it is followed by a username, the combination is replaced by the pathname of the home directory of that user. The character **%** is used to introduce a jobname.

Table A3.2 summarizes the commonly used special character sequences in C-shell.

<table>
<tr><td colspan="2" align="center">Table A3.2</td></tr>
<tr><td colspan="2" align="center">C-shell Special Character  Sequences</td></tr>
<tr><td align="center">Sequence</td><td align="center">Interpretation</td></tr>
<tr><td align="center">$\tilde{\phantom{u}} u$</td><td>Substitute home directory for user $u$</td></tr>
<tr><td align="center">! ⌃</td><td>Substitute first argument from previous command line</td></tr>
<tr><td align="center">! $</td><td>Substitute last argument from previous command line</td></tr>
<tr><td align="center">! *</td><td>Substitute all arguments from previous command line</td></tr>
<tr><td align="center">! !</td><td>Select the previous command line and re-run</td></tr>
<tr><td align="center">⌃$t$⌃$r$</td><td>Select the previous command line and re-run with $t$ for $r$</td></tr>
<tr><td align="center">! $n$</td><td>Select command line $n$ and re-run</td></tr>
<tr><td align="center">! −$n$</td><td>Select command line $n$ lines before current one  and re-run</td></tr>
<tr><td align="center">! $p$</td><td>Select command line with prefix $p$ and re-run</td></tr>
<tr><td align="center">! ?$s$?</td><td>Select command line containing string $s$ and re-run</td></tr>
<tr><td align="center">$h$ : p</td><td>Print selected command line $h$ but do not execute</td></tr>
<tr><td align="center">$h$ : s/$t$/$r$/</td><td>Substitute $t$ for $r$ in selected command line $h$ and re-run.</td></tr>
<tr><td align="center">%+</td><td>Name of current job</td></tr>
<tr><td align="center">%−</td><td>Name of previous job</td></tr>
<tr><td align="center">%$n$</td><td>Name of job $n$</td></tr>
<tr><td align="center">%$p$</td><td>Name of job with prefix $p$ in command line</td></tr>
<tr><td align="center">%?$s$?</td><td>Name of job containing string $s$ in command line</td></tr>
</table>

# *Appendix 4*

# ed summary

When **ed** is invoked to edit a file, it first copies the file into a temporary buffer and then enters command mode with the last line of the file as the *current line*. It reads commands from standard input and writes its results on standard output. Any changes are made to the contents of the buffer and these will only be preserved if the user causes the buffer to be written back to a file.

The syntax of an **ed** command is:

[ *addr1* [ ,*addr2* ] ] *command* [ *parameters* ]

where *command* is a single character specifying the function to be performed and *parameters* are its arguments. The addresses *addr1* and *addr2* specify a range of lines to which the command will be applied. If ,*addr2* is omitted, the command operates on the single line addressed by *addr1*. If no addresses are supplied, the command assumes default addresses. Often, this is just the current line.

Certain commands cause entry to text input mode in which lines of text are read from standard input and added to the buffer. This process continues until a line consisting of a single period only is read. This line is not added to the buffer but causes a return to command mode.

At any time, the editor has available the address of the current line which, in most cases, is the last line affected by the previous command. The syntax of an address is:

[ *line* ] [ ± [ *disp* ] ]

where *line* is the address of a line in the buffer and *disp* is an integer displacement added or subtracted to the integer value of *line* to obtain the required line number. *disp* has a default value of 1. Allowable formats for *line* are:

- .       the current line in the buffer;
- \$       the last line in the buffer;
- *n*       the *n*th line in the buffer where *n* is a positive integer in the range 0 to N, the number of lines in the buffer;
- '*x*       the line marked by the command k*x* where *x* is a lower case letter;
- /*re*/       the next line which contains a string matching the regular expression *re*. If necessary, the search wraps around and continues from the beginning of the buffer up to and including the current line:

*?re?*    the previous line which contains a string matching the regular expression *re*. If necessary, the search wraps around and continues from the end of the buffer up to and including the current line.

If *line* is omitted, the default is the current line.

A regular expression is a rule for generating a set of character strings and is said to match any member of the set that it generates. It is constructed by concatenating one-character regular expressions *ocre*, each of which matches a single character. An *ocre* is defined as one of the following:

*o*    matches an ordinary character *o* which is any character *c* except . *
       [ ˆ $ \ ;

\\*c*    matches any character *c* except ( ) or a digit *d* in the range 1−9;

.    matches any character *c* except a newline;

[*s*]    matches any character *c* in the set of characters *s*. If *s* contains ], it must be the first character. *s* may contain one or more constructs of the form *x−y* which specifies a range of consecutive characters *x* through to *y* where *x* must precede *y* in the ASCII character set. If − is to be member of *s*, it must be positioned so that it cannot be interpreted as a range specifier, e.g. at the beginning or end of the set;

[ˆ*s*]    as for [*s*] except that it matches any character *c* not in *s*.

If an *ocre* is followed by *, the regular expression *ocre** matches zero or more occurrences of the characters which match *ocre*. If the regular expression starts with ˆ, it is constrained to match the beginning of a line; if it ends with $, it is constrained to match the end of a line.

A regular expression enclosed between \( and \) is called a tagged regular expression and matches whatever the regular expression itself matches. The matched string may subsequently be referenced in the regular expression by \\*d* where *d* in the range 1−9 is the number of the tagged regular expression counting from the left.

As well as denoting line addresses, regular expressions are also used in the substitute command **s** to specify the string to be replaced. The metacharacters used to form regular expressions have no special significance in the replacement string with the exception of \ which must be escaped by preceding it with another \. However, **&** in the replacement string stands for the string that was matched by the regular expression while \\*d* references the string matched by the *d*th tagged regular expression.

The following table contains a summary of **ed** commands. The first column headed **D. A.** shows the default addresses for the command if none is supplied by the user. The second column contains the command characters which, for the alphabetic commands, are shown in ***bold italics*** if the command exists in both the AT&T and Berkeley versions of **ed**. Those commands which only exist in the Berkeley system or System V are shown in **bold** or *italics* respectively. The non-alphabetic commands are the same in both systems. The third column contains the parameters associated with the command. Optional parameters are enclosed between [ and ]. The abbreviations used are:

| | |
|---|---|
| *addr* | legal address |
| *cmds* | list of **ed** commands |
| *command* | shell command line |
| *fn* | valid filename |
| *l* | lower case letter |
| *re* | regular expression |
| *s* | string |

The last column gives a brief description of the function performed by each command. If an optional parameter is supplied, text enclosed between [ and ] is to be included in the description, otherwise, it is omitted. The default value of *fn* is the current file, the initial value of which is the filename supplied to **ed** as an argument.

| | | | Table A4.1 |
|---|---|---|---|
| | | | **ed Commands** |
| **D. A.** | **C** | **Params** | **Function** |
| • | *a* | | Append subsequent input lines after addressed line |
| •,• | *c* | | Replace addressed lines with subsequent input lines |
| •,• | *d* | | Delete addressed lines |
| | *e* | [ *fn* ] | Read file [ *fn* ] into buffer |
| | *E* | [ *fn* ] | Same as **e** except no check is made for changes |
| | *f* | [ *fn* ] | [ Make file *fn* the current file and ] print filename |
| 1,$ | *g* | /*re*/*cmds* | Execute *cmds* for lines matching *re* |
| 1,$ | *G* | /*re*/ | Execute standard input for lines matching *re* |
| | *h* | | Explain reason for most recent **?** diagnostic |
| | *H* | | Enter or exit help mode for error messages |
| • | *i* | | Insert subsequent input lines before addressed line |
| •,•+1 | *j* | | Join addressed contiguous lines |
| • | *k* | *l* | Mark addressed line with single lower case letter *l* |
| •,• | *l* | | Print addressed lines in an unambiguous way |
| •,• | *m* | *addr* | Move addressed lines after line *addr* |
| •,• | *n* | | Print addressed lines with line numbers |
| •,• | *p* | | Print addressed lines |
| | *P* | | Turn **\*** prompt on or off |
| | *q* | | Exit from **ed** if buffer unchanged |
| | *Q* | | Exit from **ed**, no questions asked |
| $ | *r* | *fn* | Append file *fn* after addressed line |
| •,• | *s* | /*re*/*s*/[g] | Substitute *s* for [every] *re* in addressed lines |
| •,• | *t* | *addr* | Copy addressed lines after line *addr* |
| | *u* | | Undo last change to buffer |
| 1,$ | *v* | /*re*/*cmds* | Execute *cmds* for lines not matching *re* |
| 1,$ | *V* | /*re*/ | Execute standard input for lines not matching *re* |
| 1,$ | *w* | [ *fn* ] | Write the addressed lines to file [ *fn* ] |
| 1,$ | *W* | [ *fn* ] | Append the addressed lines to file [ *fn* ] |
| $ | = | | Output line number of addressed line |
| | ! | *command* | Execute *command* in a sub-shell |
| •+1 | ⓡ | | Print addressed line |

# *Appendix 5*

# vi summary

When **vi** is invoked of a file to be edited, it displays a screenful of information showing the start of the file and enters *command mode*. It is now ready to accept single character commands which control what function it is to perform. These commands do not require a **RETURN** to cause them to be executed. Some operate immediately and then return to command mode; others cause entry to *text input mode*, in that arbitrary text may then be entered; a few place the user in *last line* mode to read further input from the last line of the screen.

The following tables summarize the actions of commands in **vi**. The first table shows the operation of alphabetic commands in each of the 3 possible modes – lower case, upper case and control. The second table performs a similar function for the remaining characters which are meaningful to **vi**. Different fonts and cases are used to indicate the action of each command as follows:

**bold**　　　　　These commands cause **vi** to switch from *command mode* to *text input mode* and read in arbitrary text. This mode is terminated normally by **ESCAPE** or abnormally by an interrupt. In both cases, a return to command mode takes place.

*italics*　　　　　These commands are operators and precede an object (see lower roman below). If the command character is repeated, the object is a line. An incomplete command is cancelled by **ESCAPE** and **vi** stays in command mode.

***bold italics***　　There is only one operator which takes an object and causes a change to text input mode. This is the **c** operator which changes objects e.g. **cc** changes lines.

lower roman　　These are commands in their own right but may also serve as objects, that is, be preceded by an operator (see *italics* above). Again **ESCAPE** is used to cancel an incomplete command.

UPPER ROMAN　These commands may not be used as objects and are primarily associated with window control, command repetition and execution of commands in other systems.

In the description of many commands in the table, reference is made to an integer **n**, which is usually a repetition count. This implies that the command may be preceded by an integer. Thus **2w** moves the cursor over 2 words; **3dw** or **d3w** deletes 3 words. Note that the command **3d2w** is legal and will delete 6 words, i.e. **d2w** is repeated three times.

The meanings of symbols, terms and abbreviations used in the tables are as follows:

|  |  |
|---|---|
| ▓ | the cursor |
| ← | cursor movement to the left |
| → | cursor movement to the right |
| ↑ | cursor movement up |
| ↓ | cursor movement down |
| *char* | a single character |
| *line* | a sequence of characters delimited by newline |
| *line tail* | a sequence of characters from the current position of the cursor up to but not including the terminating newline |
| *non-white* | a character other than space, tab or newline |
| *nw-word* | a string of non-white characters |
| *paragraph* | a sequence of lines terminated by a blank line or end-of-file |
| *pattern* | a regular expression similar to that available in **ed** |
| *sentence* | a sequence of characters delimited by  .  ! or  ?  which is followed by newline or two spaces with any number of intervening  )  ]  ▪ or  ´ characters |
| *string* | a sequence of characters |
| *word* | a string of letters, digits and underlines OR a string of non-white non-alphanumeric characters (excluding underlines) |

| | | | |
|---|---|---|---|
| | *Table A5.1* | | |
| | **Alphabetic Commands** | | |
| **C** | **ACTION** | | |
| | lower case | UPPER CASE | **control** |
| **a** | **append after** | **append after line tail** | |
| **b** | ←↑ n words | ←↑ n nw-words | ↑ n WINDOWS |
| **c** | *change* n *objects* | **change line tail** | |
| **d** | *delete* n *objects* | DELETE LINE TAIL | SCROLL ↓ n LINES |
| **e** | →↓ n end words | →↓ n end nw-words | EXPOSE BELOW |
| **f** | → to nth char | ← to nth char | ↓ n WINDOWS |
| **g** | | to line n | FILE DETAILS |
| **h** | ← n positions | to nth home line | ← n positions |
| **i** | **insert before** | **insert at start of line** | |
| **j** | ↓ n positions | JOIN n LINES | ↓ n positions |
| **k** | ↑ n positions | | |
| **l** | → n positions | to nth last line | REDRAW SCREEN |
| **m** | MARK POSITION | to middle line | ↓ n lines |
| **n** | →↓ to next pattern | ←↑ to next pattern | ↓ n lines |
| **o** | **open new line below** | **open new line above** | |
| **p** | PUT AFTER/BELOW | PUT BEFORE/ABOVE | ↑ n LINES |
| **q** | | QUIT TO **ex** | |
| **r** | REPLACE n CHARS | **replace n strings** | REFORM SCREEN |
| **s** | **change n chars** | **change n lines** | |
| **t** | → before nth char | ← after nth char | |
| **u** | UNDO LAST CHANGE | UNDO LINE CHANGES | SCROLL ↑ n LINES |
| **v** | | | |
| **w** | →↓ n words | →↓ n nw-words | |
| **x** | DELETE n CHARS → | DELETE n CHARS ← | |
| **y** | *yank* n *objects* | YANK n LINES | EXPOSE ABOVE |
| **z** | REDRAW WINDOW | ZZ – exit | STOP (if supported) |

| | |
|---|---|
| *Table A5.2* | |
| **Non-Alphabetic Commands** | |
| **C** | **ACTION** |
| Ⓡ | ↓ n lines |
| + | ↓ n lines |
| − | ↑ n lines |
| ) | →↓ n sentences |
| ( | ←↑ n sentences |
| } | →↓ n paragraphs |
| { | ←↑ n paragraphs |
| / | →↓ to next *pattern* read from last line |
| ? | ←↑ to previous *pattern* read from last line |
| ` | to context marked by following *letter* |
| ` ` | to previous context |
| ' | to start of context marked by following *letter* |
| ' ' | to start of previous context |
| 0 | ← to first position in line |
| ^ | to first non-white character in line |
| $ | →↓ to last position in nth line |
| \| | to nth position in line |
| Ⓢ | → n positions |
| Ⓑ | ← n positions |
| . | REPEAT LAST BUFFER CHANGE COMMAND n TIMES |
| ; | REPEAT LAST **f**, **F**, **t** OR **T** COMMAND n TIMES |
| , | REVERSE LAST **f**, **F**, **t** or **T** COMMAND AND REPEAT n TIMES |
| : | EXECUTE AN **ex** COMMAND READ FROM LAST LINE |
| & | REPEAT THE PREVIOUS **:s** COMMAND |
| ~ | CHANGE CASE OF A LETTER |
| ! | *filter* n *objects to* UNIX *command and replace by output* |
| > | *right shift* n *line objects* |
| < | *left shift* n *line objects* |
| Ⓔ | TERMINATE INSERT OR ABORT COMMAND |
| " | precedes a buffer name **1–9** or **a–z** |

The next table shows some of the **ex** commands which may be executed from **vi** in last line mode after the **:** command or by switching into **ex** using **Q**. Most of the commands available in **ed** may also be used in **ex**. Operations such as repetitive changes over a range of lines are more conveniently carried out in **ex** than in **vi**.

<table>
<tr><td colspan="2" align="center">*Table A5.3*</td></tr>
<tr><td colspan="2" align="center">**ex Commands**</td></tr>
<tr><td align="center">**COMMAND**</td><td align="center">**ACTION**</td></tr>
<tr><td>**ab** *word rhs*</td><td>Add abbreviation to replace *word* by *rhs* during input</td></tr>
<tr><td>**e** [*file*]</td><td>Edit current or new file if buffer saved</td></tr>
<tr><td>**e!** [*file*]</td><td>Edit current or new file ignoring changes to buffer</td></tr>
<tr><td>**e +***n* [file]</td><td>As for **e** but starting at line *n*</td></tr>
<tr><td>**e #**</td><td>Edit alternate file</td></tr>
<tr><td>**map** *lhs rhs*</td><td>Define macro *lhs* to be command sequence *rhs*</td></tr>
<tr><td>**n** [*args*]</td><td>Replace current argument list, otherwise edit next file</td></tr>
<tr><td>**p** *n*</td><td>Print *n* lines</td></tr>
<tr><td>**q**</td><td>Quit if buffer saved</td></tr>
<tr><td>**q!**</td><td>Quit, discarding changes</td></tr>
<tr><td>**rew**</td><td>Rewind argument list to edit first file</td></tr>
<tr><td>**set**</td><td>Print or set options</td></tr>
<tr><td>**una** *word*</td><td>Remove *word* from list of abbreviations</td></tr>
<tr><td>**unmap** *lhs*</td><td>Remove macro *lhs*</td></tr>
<tr><td>**vi**</td><td>Enter visual mode</td></tr>
<tr><td>**w** [*file*]</td><td>Write buffer to *file*, default is current file</td></tr>
<tr><td>**w>>** [file]</td><td>Append buffer to *file*</td></tr>
<tr><td>**w!** [file]</td><td>Like **w** but checks are ignored</td></tr>
<tr><td>**wq** [*file*]</td><td>Like **w**, then quit</td></tr>
<tr><td>**wq!** [file]</td><td>Like **wq** but checks are ignored</td></tr>
</table>

The final table shows some of the options which may be set in **ex** to affect the operation of **vi**. The first column gives the name of the option. Some of these are boolean options which may be turned on by **set** *option* or off by **set no** *option*; others have values which may be assigned by **set** *option=value*. The second column shows the effect of setting the option on or the interpretation of the value. The last column shows the default settings of the options.

<table>
<tr><td colspan="3" align="center">*Table A5.4*</td></tr>
<tr><td colspan="3" align="center">**ex Options**</td></tr>
<tr><td align="center">**Name**</td><td align="center">**Effect**</td><td align="center">**Default**</td></tr>
<tr><td>autoindent</td><td>Supply program indentation automatically</td><td>**noai**</td></tr>
<tr><td>autowrite</td><td>Automatic write when :**n** or **!** issued</td><td>**noaw**</td></tr>
<tr><td>hardtabs</td><td>Define tab settings</td><td>**ht=8**</td></tr>
<tr><td>ignorecase</td><td>Ignore case when searching</td><td>**noic**</td></tr>
<tr><td>list</td><td>Display lines unambiguously</td><td>**nolist**</td></tr>
<tr><td>number</td><td>Display lines prefixed by numbers</td><td>**nonu**</td></tr>
<tr><td>redraw</td><td>Simulate intelligent terminal</td><td>**noredraw**</td></tr>
<tr><td>showmatch</td><td>Show matching ( or {</td><td>**nosm**</td></tr>
<tr><td>shiftwidth</td><td>Shift distance for << and >></td><td>**sw=8**</td></tr>
<tr><td>term</td><td>Define terminal type</td><td>**term=**type</td></tr>
<tr><td>terse</td><td>Produce shorter error diagnostics</td><td>**noterse**</td></tr>
<tr><td>wrapmargin</td><td>Set automatic right margin</td><td>**wm=0**</td></tr>
<tr><td>writeany</td><td>Inhibit checks made before **w**</td><td>**nowa**</td></tr>
</table>

# Appendix 6

# Mail and mailx Summary

In the following table A6.1, a summary of the effect of single character commands is given for both **Mail** in 4.2 BSD and **mailx** in System V.2. The summary includes actions for both command mode and tilde escape mode, that is, where the command is preceded by an escape character (usually ˜) to perform special functions when composing a message. Actions which are available in both **Mail** and **mailx** are shown in *bold italics*; those only found in one system or the other are shown in **bold** for 4.2 BSD or *italics* for System V.2 respectively.

Table A6.2 summarizes the more important variables and options that may be set in **Mail** and **mailx**. The first column contains the variable name. Those that may receive a value are terminated with an = sign; the remainder are options which may be turned on or off. The font conventions are the same as those used in Table A6.1. The second column describes the effect of the variable while the third column shows the default value or setting. The **set** command is used to assign a new value to a variable or alter the setting of an option.

When **mailx** is invoked, it reads commands from a public file */usr/lib/mailx/mailx.rc*; similarly, **Mail** accesses the file */usr/lib/mail.rc*. These files may contain commands set by the system administrator which alter the default settings and values given in Table A6.2. If the user's home directory contains the file *.mailrc*, both commands will read and obey commands from it so that the user can also change default values and settings.

| | *Table A6.1* | |
|---|---|---|
| | **Mail and mailx Commands** | |
| **C** | **NORMAL ACTION** | **TILDE ESCAPE ACTION** |
| a | *define or print aliases* | *insert autograph string* |
| b | | *add to blind carbon copy list* |
| c | *copy to file* | *add to carbon copy list* |
| d | *delete messages* | *read dead letter file* |
| e | *edit messages* | *edit partial message* |
| f | *print message headers* | *forward messages* |
| g | *define or print aliases* | |
| h | *list headers* | *edit header fields* |
| i | **ignore headers** | *insert variable value* |
| l | *list commands available* | |
| m | *send mail* | *insert messages* |
| n | *print next message* | |
| p | *print messages* | *print partial message* |
| q | *quit* | *abort message input* |
| r | *reply to messages* | *read in named file* |
| s | *save messages* | *set subject line* |
| t | *type messages* | *add names to* To *list* |
| u | *undelete messages* | |
| v | *visual edit messages* | *visual edit partial message* |
| w | *save messages* | *write partial message to file* |
| x | *exit from mail* | *abort immediately* |
| z | *scroll message headers* | |
| + | *print next message* | |
| − | *print previous message* | |
| Ⓡ | *print next message* | |
| ? | *print command summary* | *print tilde escape summary* |
| ! | *escape to shell* | *escape to shell* |
| = | *print message number* | |
| \| | | *pipe message to command* |

| VARIABLE | EFFECT | DEFAULT |
|---|---|---|
| *Table A6.2* | | |
| **Mail and mailx Options and Variables** | | |
| *append* | append messages to *mbox* | off |
| *askcc* | prompt for Cc list | off |
| *asksub* | prompt for subject | on |
| **ask** | prompt for subject | on |
| *autoprint* | print message automatically after **d** or **u** | off |
| *DEAD=* | define name of dead letter file | *dead.letter* |
| *EDITOR=* | define editor to be used after **e** or **˜e** | **ed (ex** in 4.2) |
| *escape=* | define escape character | ˜ |
| *folder=* | define directory for saving standard mail files | null |
| *header* | print header summary | on |
| *hold* | preserve message in *mailbox* | off |
| *keep* | do not remove *mailbox* when empty | off |
| *MBOX=* | define file for saving messages when read | *mbox* |
| *metoo* | do not delete your username from alias list | off |
| **nosave** | do not save in *dead.letter* on interrupt | off |
| *PAGER=* | define command for paginating output | **pg** |
| *PROMPT=* | define command mode prompt string | **?** |
| *quiet* | do not print initial message and version | off |
| *save* | save messages in *dead.letter* on interrupt | on |
| *SHELL=* | define name of preferred shell | **sh** |
| *sign=* | define string to be used by **˜a** | null |
| *toplines=* | define number of lines used by **top** | 5 |
| *VISUAL=* | name of preferred screen editor | **vi** |

# Bibliography

Bourne, S.R., (1982), *The UNIX System*, Addison-Wesley: Reading, MA.

Deitel, H.M., (1984), *An Introduction to Operating Systems*, Addison-Wesley: Reading, MA.

Findlay, W. and Watt, D.A., (1982), *Pascal - An Introduction to Methodical Programming*, Pitman: London.

Harbison, S.P. and Steele Jr., G.L., (1984), *C - A Reference Manual*, Prentice-Hall: Englewood Cliffs, NJ.

Joy, W., *An Introduction to Display Editing with Vi*, Department of Electrical Engineering and Computer Science, University of California, Berkeley, Ca. 94720, 1980.

Joy, W., *Ex Reference Manual*, Department of Electrical Engineering and Computer Science, University of California, Berkeley, Ca. 94720, 1980.

Kernighan, B.W. and Pike, R., (1984), *The UNIX Programming Environment*, Prentice-Hall: Englewood Cliffs, NJ.

Kernighan, B.W. and Ritchie, D.M., (1978), *The C Programming Language*, Prentice-Hall: Englewood Cliffs, NJ.

Koffman, E.B., (1981), *Problem Solving and Structured Programming in Pascal*, Addison-Wesley: Reading, MA.

Meissner, L.P. and Organick, E.I., (1980), *FORTRAN 77 featuring Structured Programming*, Addison-Wesley: Reading, MA.

*UNIX System V - Release 2.0 User Reference Manual*, AT&T Technologies, 1984.

*UNIX User's Manual - Reference Guide*, Department of Electrical Engineering and Computer Science, University of California, Berkeley, Ca. 94720, 1984.

# Index